W9-AAT-935

HAMPTON-BROWN
HIGH POINT

SUCCESS IN LANGUAGE • LITERATURE • CONTENT

ALFREDO SCHIFINI
DEBORAH SHORT
JOSEFINA VILLAMIL TINAJERO

HAMPTON-BROWN

Curriculum Reviewers

Tedi Armet
ESL Coordinator
Fort Bend Independent School District
Sugar Land, Texas

Maggie Brookshire
ELD Teacher, Grade 6
Emerald Middle School
Cajon Valley Unified School District
El Cajon, California

Lily Dam
Administrator
Dallas Independent School District
Dallas, Texas

Judy Doss
ELD Teacher and Coordinator
Burbank High School
Burbank Unified School District
Burbank, California

Rossana Font-Carrasco
ESOL Teacher
Paul W. Bell Middle School
Miami-Dade County School District 5
Miami, Florida

Jillian Friedman
ESOL Teacher
Howard Middle School
Orange County Public Schools
Orlando, Florida

Vivian Kahn
ESL Teacher/Site Coordinator
Halsey Intermediate School 296
Community School District 32
Brooklyn, New York

Suzanne Lee
Principal
Josiah Quincy School
Boston, Massachusetts

Carolyn McGavock
ESL Teacher
Rafael Cordero Bilingual Academy
Junior High School 45
Community School District 4
New York, New York

Juan Carlos Méndez
ESL/Bilingual Staff Developer
Community School District 9
Bronx, New York

Cynthia Nelson-Mosca
Language Minority Services Director
Cicero School District 99
Cicero, Illinois

Kim-Anh Nguyen
Title 7 Coordinator
Franklin McKinley School District
San Jose, California

Ellie Paiewonsky
Director of Bilingual/ESL
Technical Assistance Center of Nassau
Board of Cooperative Educational Services
Massapequa Park, New York

Jeanne Perrin
ESL Specialist
Boston Public Schools
Boston, Massachusetts

Rebecca Peurifoy
Instructional Specialist
Rockwall Independent School District
Rockwall, Texas

Marjorie Rosenberg
ESOL/Bilingual Instructional Specialist
Montgomery County Public Schools
Rockville, Maryland

Harriet Rudnit
Language Arts Reading Teacher
Grades 6-8
Lincoln Hall Middle School
Lincolnwood, Illinois

Olga Ryzhikov
ESOL Teacher
Forest Oak Middle School
Montgomery County, Maryland

Dr. Wageh Saad, Ed.D.
*Coordinator of Bilingual and
Compensatory Education*
Dearborn Public Schools
Dearborn, Michigan

Gilbert Socas
ESOL Teacher
West Miami Middle School
Miami-Dade County Public Schools
Miami, Florida

Acknowledgments

Every effort has been made to secure permission, but if any omissions have been made, please let us know. We gratefully acknowledge the following permissions:
Susan Bergholz Literary Services: "I Want to Be Miss America" from *Something to Declare* by Julia Alvarez. Copyright © 1998 by Julia Alvarez. Published by Algonquin Books of Chapel Hill, 1998.

Acknowledgments continue on page 495.

Hampton-Brown
P.O. Box 223220
Carmel, California 93922
1-800-333-3510

Printed in the United States of America
ISBN 0-7362-0965-4

04 05 06 07 08 09 10 9 8 7

1 Touch

UNIT 2

*T*HE FORCE of DISCOVERY

4

UNIT 3

Turning PROBLEMS into SOLUTIONS

It's Up to You!

UNIT 5
BREAK THROUGH THE BARRIERS

The House on Maple Street, Chris Van Allsburg, charcoal on paper. Copyright © 1984.

The Creative Touch

Look at the picture. Work with a group to tell a story about it. Listen to other groups' stories. Are all of the stories the same? How are they different? What does this tell you about creativity and personal expression?

THEME 1
The Way of the Artist
There are many ways to be creative and many forms your creativity can take.

THEME 2
The Power of Imagination
Let your imagination go and you can create just about anything.

Mythical Lion Mask, Bali

15th Century Persian Miniature

Bottlecap Lion, USA

15th Century Italian Tapestry

The Way of the Artist

- How can art, music, or drama provide a way to express yourself?

- How do life experiences influence what an artist presents to others?

- How do you express your creativity? How can you develop your creative abilities?

THEME-RELATED BOOKS

The Starry Night
by Neil Waldman

Bernard meets a painter and shows him the city. At the Museum of Modern Art in New York City, he learns the true identity of his friend.

NOVEL

Alphabet City Ballet
by Erika Tamar

Marisol wants to be a ballerina. In spite of family difficulties, she finds a way to pursue her dream.

Lives of the Musicians
by Kathleen Krull

Fascinating and often humorous stories of twenty famous musicians. Filled with quotes, anecdotes and bits of gossip.

Build Language and Vocabulary

DESCRIBE

View the painting and listen to the song.
How can you turn "nothing" into something?

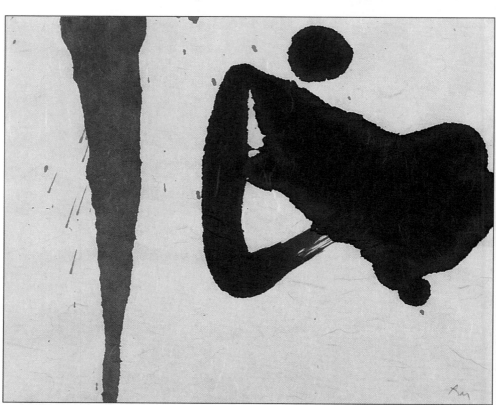

Lyric Suite, Robert Motherwell, Cherry red and royal blue ink on rice paper. 1965.
©1999 Dedalus Foundation, Inc./Licensed by VAGA, New York, NY

Nothing

Inside every nothing there are places to explore,
A shoe that's left to stop a closing door.
Every plan, from small to grand, began from seeds of thought.
The "nothing" growing in your mind.
Is wanting to get out.

Think that when you think that there is nothing going on,
Nothing is a song in making,
Nothing is a brave bold painting,
Nothing is a formula, a cure.
Nothing is a shoe left in the door.

—*Tish Hinojosa*

VISUALIZE

Work with a group to create something from these "nothing" shapes. Paint, draw, or make a collage with the shapes.

BUILD YOUR VOCABULARY

Descriptive Words and Phrases Make a chart with words and phrases you know that tell about your creation. Then look up your words in a thesaurus. A **thesaurus** is a book of words and their synonyms. Add synonyms for your words to the chart.

Descriptive Details	Words or Phrases I Know	New Words or Phrases
What Something Is Like	colorful blue shape a huge tooth drops down	brilliant blue shape a gigantic tusk swoops down
Where Something Is	in the middle on its head	in the heart of on its crown
How Something Moves	drips	dribbles, trickles

Add to your chart as you go through the unit.

USE LANGUAGE STRUCTURES ▶ COMPLETE SENTENCES

Writing: Describe Your Creation Use complete sentences to tell about your creation. Expand your sentences by adding descriptive words and phrases from your chart.

Example:
A shape is in the painting.
A **brilliant blue** shape is **in the heart of** the painting.

THE

LION KING
GOES TO BROADWAY

photo essay
by Bruce Goldstone

Prepare to Read

THINK ABOUT WHAT YOU KNOW

Make Comparisons Use a Venn diagram to compare a stage play and an animated movie.

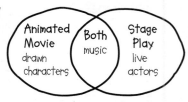

---

accept the challenge
agree to try a difficult or new task

brilliant idea   clever plan

concept   general idea, overall thought

creative   new, imaginative

musical   performance in which actors sing and dance

personal touch
individual idea or attention

realize a vision   see a plan or idea become a reality

represent   stand for, symbolize

stage play   story performed by actors in a theater

talented   gifted, skillful

LEARN KEY VOCABULARY

Use Context Clues Study the new words and their definitions. Write the paragraph, replacing the bold words with the new words.

> Our teacher had a **clever plan**: we would sing and dance in a **performance** about our school. Her **idea** was that we would think of the most **imaginative** way to tell about being a student at our school. Our class decided to **try it** and we started writing! Since none of us are **gifted** artists, the art teacher offered to design sets that **stand for** our school classrooms and hallways. Our drama teacher was excited to **see her plan become a reality**.

LEARN TO RELATE MAIN IDEA AND DETAILS

Details are words and phrases that give information. Remembering the details will help you figure out the **main idea** of a selection.

> ### READING STRATEGY
> **How to Relate Main Idea and Details**
> 1. Read each section. Answer the questions Who? What? When? Where? Why? and How?
> 2. Review the answers to your questions. Those are the important details.
> 3. Use the details to tell the main idea.

As you read each section of "The Lion King Goes to Broadway," write the important details to help you figure out the main idea.

THE LION KING
GOES TO BROADWAY:
A Brilliant Idea
by Bruce Goldstone

How do you take an animated movie and turn it into a stage play? You begin with a brilliant idea, then work with a team of highly talented artists who know how to turn your idea into an event. That's how Julie Taymor and her creative team made *The Lion King* movie into a successful Broadway musical.

CURTAIN UP!

At night in New York City, the sun rises a little after eight o'clock. Under the giant red sun, a baboon sings. African animals respond to her song. Birds fly, giraffes walk gracefully across the plains, while gazelles leap through the air. Zebras trot, an elephant sways—and the audience goes wild.

The curtain has gone up on *The Lion King*, a stage **musical** about a young lion who learns to accept his role as a leader. Lions, zebras, gazelles—a whole **assembly** of African animals played by actors in fantastic masks and costumes—fill the stage. Through the **efforts** of many **talented** people, the story **springs into life**, and it promises to be **a magical event indeed**.

BEFORE YOU MOVE ON...

1. **Vocabulary** List all the words you can find that tell about the theater.
2. **Opinion** Would you like to see this musical? Why or why not?

© Disney Enterprises, Inc.

A scene with Mufasa and his lion cub Simba from the movie *The Lion King*.

THE STORY OF
THE LION KING

The Lion King is about a young lion named Simba who is born to become the king of the African Savanna. His father, Mufasa, is the current king. Simba's Uncle Scar wants to be king and kills Mufasa in such a way that it looks like Simba did it. Believing he killed his own father, Simba runs away into the jungle and vows never to return. This allows Scar to become king of the Savanna.

Drought comes to the Savanna bringing death and desolation, but the evil Scar does nothing to help the animals. Meanwhile, in the jungle, Simba reunites with a lioness named Nala that he knew when he was a cub. Nala convinces Simba that the animals of the Savanna need his help. Simba returns home, defeats Scar, and becomes the Lion King.

---

assembly group, collection
efforts work

springs into life becomes real
a magical event indeed a special event everyone will enjoy

Characters in *The Lion King* celebrate the birth of Simba as they sing "The Circle of Life."

Photograph by Kenneth Van Sickle
© Disney Enterprises, Inc.

Julie Taymor's **creative concept** for
The Lion King was influenced by several
theatrical styles, including mime and shadow
puppetry. Her creative genius contributed to
every part of the stage production, from
costume design to stage direction. Here, she
is sculpting the model for a lioness mask.

HOW IT ALL BEGAN

The Lion King was one of Disney's most
successful movies. The movie was so
well-loved by audiences everywhere, that
Disney executive, Michael Eisner, began
thinking it would make a successful
stage play as well. When he told
co-worker Thomas Schumacher to start
planning, Schumacher was **stunned**. He
felt the **project** was impossible. But Eisner
insisted. He said that all they needed was
a " **brilliant idea**. "

After many months, Schumacher found
his brilliant idea. "The answer," he **recalls**,
"was, in fact, quite simple—Julie Taymor,"
a woman who had been creating magical
theater for many years.

Taymor **accepted the challenge**,
putting all her years of **theatrical
experience** into creating a new concept for
The Lion King. When she began to **address
the question** of how to bring the animal
characters to life, she knew she did not
want to hide the actors inside big animal
suits. She wanted the audience to see the
actors' faces and bodies, which would
represent the animal's human qualities.
So she designed costumes that **revealed**
the actor within.

BEFORE YOU MOVE ON...

1. **Inference** Why did Michael Eisner think that
   the movie *The Lion King* could become a
   successful stage play?
2. **Main Idea** What was Julie Taymor's creative
   concept for bringing the animal characters to
   life?
3. **Viewing** Look at the photographs on
   page 19. How does the costume convey
   the idea of a flock of birds?

---

successful well-liked
stunned very surprised
project idea, plan
insisted demanded, stated firmly

recalls remembers
theatrical experience knowledge of the theater
address the question think about the problem
revealed showed

This **sketch**, **model**, and photo of the "flock of birds" costume show how an idea was **transformed** into the real thing. The dancer moves, and the birds **appear** to flap their wings and fly.

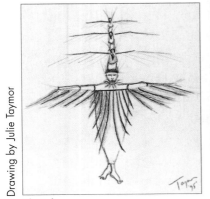

Sketch

Drawing by Julie Taymor

Model

Costume

Photographs by Joan Marcus © Disney Enterprises, Inc.

---

sketch drawing
model small example

transformed changed
appear seem

This early Mufasa mask shows the lion king's heroic character, but it **conceals** the actor's face.

Sometimes an idea can be so good, it **overshadows** everything around it. In that case, the creator has to change the concept in order to make it work within the larger picture. For example, one of the early Mufasa masks had to be changed because it was "too magical."

*The Mufasa mask . . . had great mobility; in fact it moved 360 degrees, looked left and right, had an open mouth and an eyebrow feature. But the mobility caused the mask to be too magical, in a sense. The mask **drew focus away from** the actor.*

—*Michael Curry*
Co-Designer, Masks and Puppets

IF AT FIRST YOU DON'T SUCCEED...

Not every good idea **works out**, so even the most creative person must be **willing to let go of** an idea and look for a better one. For example, the mask for Mufasa, the lion king, went through many changes. At one point, Taymor's co-designer, Michael Curry, created a large mask that the actor would lift on and off. When the actor was not wearing the mask over his face, he wore it as a sort of a backpack. But it looked **awkward**, so Curry **went back to the drawing board** and came up with a better idea.

Creative ideas are not always **complicated**. Sometimes the simplest idea is the **most powerful**. Taymor calls these simple, but powerful ideas "true theater," **ancient techniques** that can be readapted and recreated for modern theater. For example, ribbons can show someone's tears, and blue silk can show water.

BEFORE YOU MOVE ON...

1. **Summary** Part of being creative is to never give up. Use the details in the photo essay to tell your partner why you think that is true.

---

conceals hides
overshadows seems more important than
drew focus away from made people forget about
works out turns out or ends well
willing to let go of able to set aside
awkward strange, wrong

went back to the drawing board started from the beginning again
complicated difficult to do or understand
most powerful strongest, most effective
ancient techniques old ways of doing things

Michael Curry holds a model of the **"shield mask**." The actor had to lift the mask out of a backpack and turn it right-side up to face the audience.

In this scene, Mufasa confronts his evil brother Scar. The actors wear the final versions of lion masks, each attached to a frame holding the mask above the actor's head. The mask can move forward, backward, up, and down. The actor's face is **visible in every position**.

....

shield mask mask that the actor holds in front of his face as if to protect himself

visible not hidden, in full view
in every position from all points of view

The Lion King Goes to Broadway **21**

In this scene, the lionesses cry over the lifeless body of Mufasa. Ribbons pulled through the eyes of the masks look like streams of tears, showing a powerful grief.

Photographs by Joan Marcus
© Disney Enterprises, Inc.

Photograph by Kenneth Van Sickle © Disney Enterprises, Inc.

This scene shows the effects of drought on the Savanna. A lake made of silk is pulled through a hole in the stage to make it appear that the lake is drying up.

A GROUP EFFORT

Many people helped make *The Lion King* a success—choreographers created exciting dances set to African rhythms, set designers **dressed up the stage**, song writers created new songs, costume designers created colorful and often surprising costumes, make-up artists, dancers, and actors all added their talents to help the director **realize her vision** for the show. It was a team effort **in every sense of the word**, yet each person added his or her **personal touch** to make the production **memorable**.

The creative work of the entire team **pays off** every night. People are **thrilled** by this imaginative journey to Africa. After the **glorious opening**, the **amazing** sights continue. The audience sees frightening hyenas, an elephant graveyard, an **eye-popping** stampede—everything, in fact, that was in the movie, but different enough to be a whole new event. By the end of the show, many in the audience find it hard to remember that *The Lion King* was ever a movie.

BEFORE YOU MOVE ON...

1. **Main Idea and Details** State the main idea supported by these details: Dancers and actors added their talents to help the director realize her vision. Choreographers created exciting dances, and set designers dressed up the stage.

2. **Comparisons** How are the movie version and the stage version of *The Lion King* alike? How are they different?

---

dressed up the stage decorated the raised platform where the actors perform

in every sense of the word by every definition

memorable unforgettable, outstanding

pays off is rewarded

thrilled excited

glorious opening wonderful first scene

amazing wonderful, surprising, incredible

eye-popping exciting, astonishing

ABOUT THE AUTHOR

Bruce Goldstone is very familiar with how an idea grows and changes into a theatrical event. He wrote the book and lyrics for two short musicals, "Time and Tide" and "For Life." His lyrics for several songs have been performed at Tada!, a student theater school in New York City. Bruce Goldstone also wrote the award-winning book, *The Beastly Feast* and co-authored, with Arthur Perley, *A Kid's Guide to the Internet*.

Respond to the Photo Essay
Check Your Understanding

SUM IT UP

Relate Main Idea and Details Share your details for one section with your group. What is the main idea? Complete a chart to share with the class.

Main Idea and Details Chart

Section Title: _____Curtain Up!_____

Main Idea:
This section describes what it is like to watch the opening of The Lion King play.

Detail:
The performance starts in New York City a little after 8 o'clock.

Detail:
The Lion King is a stage musical about a young lion.

Detail:
Actors dressed in fantastic masks and costumes play the animals.

Write a Summary With your class, brainstorm several main idea statements for the entire selection. Take a vote for the best one. Then list details that support your main idea. Cross out the unimportant details.

Example:
Important detail: *The Lion King* is a stage musical about a young lion.
Unimportant detail: It starts a little after 8 o'clock.

Use the important details that remain on your list to write a summary of "The Lion King Goes to Broadway."

THINK IT OVER

Discuss and Write Talk about these questions with a partner. Write the answers.

1. **Analyze Information** Why did Julie Taymor feel it was important to show the actors' faces?

2. **Paraphrase** Tell a partner what a photo essay is like.

3. **Personal Experience** What creative ideas have you had? How have you accomplished them?

EXPRESS YOURSELF ▶DESCRIBE

Look at the photographs in the selection. Choose an animal costume and describe it to your partner. Include details about its size, how it is made, how it is worn, and how it moves. What makes this costume like the animal it represents?

Language Arts and Literature

USE COMPLETE SENTENCES

Learn About Simple Subjects and Simple Predicates The **subject** of a sentence tells whom or what the sentence is about. The simple subject is the most important word in the subject. It is a noun or a pronoun.

African animals appear on stage.

The **predicate** tells what the subject is, does, or has. The simple predicate is the most important word in the predicate. It is the verb.

Gazelles leap through the air.

The verb must agree in number with the simple subject even if other words come between them.

A bird with big wings flies across the stage.

Find Simple Subjects and Simple Predicates What is the simple subject and verb in each sentence?

Julie Taymor's work makes *The Lion King* special. The actors dance in beautiful costumes. The people in the audience clap.

Practice Add a subject or predicate to complete each sentence.

1. The make-believe trip to Africa _____ .
2. The amazing costumes _____ .
3. _____ watches a wonderful performance.
4. _____ make *The Lion King* a success.

WRITE A MAIN IDEA PARAGRAPH

Follow these steps to write a paragraph about the theater.

1 Organize Your Ideas Use a chart like the one on page 24 to record a main idea and details.

2 Write Your Draft Tell what the paragraph is about in a **topic sentence**. It can come at the beginning or end of your paragraph. Add at least three **detail sentences** to give more information about your topic. Then add a **concluding sentence** if your topic sentence is at the beginning of your paragraph.

3 Edit and Share Your Work Do your details tell about your main idea? Check your spelling and punctuation, too. Read your paragraph to your group.

Sample Paragraph

I like the theater. The hustle and bustle in the lobby is festive and exciting. When the lights go out, you wait in the dark for the play to begin. The actors come on stage to lead you into another world. I always look forward to an evening at the theater.

For more about **writing paragraphs,** see Handbook pages 418–421.

Respond to the Photo Essay, continued
Content Area Connections

MAKE SCIENTIFIC OBSERVATIONS

Observe an animal or research the scientific facts about its features. Use the information you find to design a costume.

1 Study the Animal Use library and electronic resources to learn about the animal. If possible, observe the animal in the wild, at the zoo, on the Internet, or on video. Use an observation log to record your findings.

Observation Log

Animal Name	Great Horned Owl
Type of Animal	Bird family: Strigidae genus: Bubo
Size	18-25 inches wingspread 35-60 inches
Muscular/ Skeletal Features	clavicles fused to sternum; facial disk—semicircle on each side; middle claw with no comb

2 Design a Costume Decide what features to represent in your costume. Draw a sketch to show the costume design. Then make a final color drawing of the costume. Add captions and post it in the class.

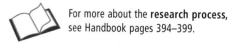 For more about the **research process**, see Handbook pages 394–399.

MATHEMATICS

CALCULATE COSTS OF A PRODUCTION

How much does it cost to put on a play? Work with a group and find out.

1 Tally the Costs and Sales Interview the business manager of a local drama company or school drama department. Ask:

- How many people attend each performance?
- How much do you spend on salaries, costumes, and other supplies?
- What is your income from selling ads, tickets, and refreshments?

Write the information in a chart and total the amounts.

Item	Cost	Income
Salaries	$4600	
Ads	$300	$600

2 Calculate the Profit Subtract the costs from the income to figure out the profit.

total income – total costs = profit

3 Make Decisions If the calculations show a loss, brainstorm how you would cut costs or increase sales. If they show a profit, decide how you would spend the money. Share your calculations and ideas with the class.

Listening for a Voice

poem
by Joseph Bruchac

Prepare to Read Poetry

THINK ABOUT WHAT YOU KNOW

Brainstorm What helps you to be creative? Use a web to show situations, activities, places, or materials that spark your creativity.

LEARN KEY VOCABULARY

clear a space move things away to make room

escape get away

image mental picture

special unusual, different, favorite

spot place; see, discover; mark, stain

Use New Words in Context Study the new words and their definitions. Then write the answers to these questions in your notebook.

1. How do you clear a space and prepare to work?
2. Where is your favorite spot to think? Why is it special?
3. What images do you see when you think about a favorite memory?
4. Do your memories stay with you, or do they escape?

LEARN ABOUT POETRY

Many poems are written in sections called **stanzas**. In each stanza, a poet often uses **sensory images**. Those are words and phrases that appeal to our senses of sight, hearing, touch, smell, and taste.

READING STRATEGY
How to Read Poetry

1. Read each stanza of the poem.
2. Ask yourself: Which words appeal to the senses? How do they help me understand the poem?
3. Reread the poem and use the sensory images to understand its message.

Slowly read "Listening for a Voice," and notice how the words of each stanza appeal to your senses.

Listening for a Voice

Whenever I try to write a poem,
I need to begin by clearing a space,
finding a spot where no one's around.
Then I sit and listen for a voice.

It might be what someone said long ago,
words that take me to a special place
where I can see and smell and taste
a Moon of Long Nights morning in the snow.

Or it might not be a human sound—
just the whirring whistle of the wings
of three loons circling, circling
a June-blue Adirondack pond.

Then, before those images can escape,
as quick as dreams back into the night
I scribble them down or start to type.
I've learned if you want to be a writer,
you have to listen and listen—and write.

—Joseph Bruchac

Respond to the Poem

THINK IT OVER

Discuss Talk about these questions with a partner.

1. **Main Idea and Details** What kind of voice is Joseph Bruchac listening for?

2. **Mood or Tone** Which sensory images in the poem are most powerful? Give reasons for your answer.

EXPRESS YOURSELF

▶ DESCRIBE A PLACE

Tell your partner about a place that is special to you. Include sensory images that appeal to at least two of the five senses: sight, sound, touch, smell, and taste.

ABOUT THE POET

Joseph Bruchac lives with his wife Carol in the Adirondack Mountain foothills of New York, in the same house where his maternal grandparent raised him. He draws much of his inspiration for his writing from that land and his Abenaki ancestry. Although his American Indian heritage is only part of his ethnic background, it is these Native roots from which he has been most nourished.

Joseph Bruchac is involved in many creative projects involving preservation of Abenaki culture, including performing Abenaki music with the Dawnland Singers.

Inspiration

interview
with Tish Hinojosa
by Barbara Linde

Prepare to Read

THINK ABOUT WHAT YOU KNOW

Make a List Who is your favorite singer, artist, or writer? Where do you think the person gets ideas for his or her work? Make a list.

appearance presentation before the public

attempt effort to do something

creative mode time when you think about new ideas

experience event or activity you know about from your past

influence have an effect on

inspiration something that gives you new ideas

result what happens in the end

role part that someone or something plays in a situation

source person or place from which something comes

style way of doing something

LEARN KEY VOCABULARY

Relate Words Study the new words and their definitions. Then work in a group to use the words to create word webs.

Word Web

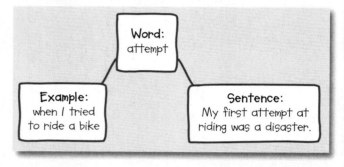

LEARN TO CLASSIFY INFORMATION

When you group related information together, you **classify** it. This strategy helps you remember what you read.

READING STRATEGY
How to Classify Information

1. Preview the selection. Ask yourself: What is the selection about?
2. List the important details in the selection.
3. Group the details that are similar.
4. Give each group a category name.

As you read "Inspiration: An Interview with Tish Hinojosa," stop after each section and classify the information in a chart.

Inspiration

An interview with TISH HINOJOSA

BY BARBARA LINDE

Tish Hinojosa is a well-known songwriter and singer who sings about her family experiences, her Mexican American culture, the Southwest, and important social issues. In this interview, Tish discusses her musical background, how she gets ideas for her songs, and the processes she goes through to create the songs.

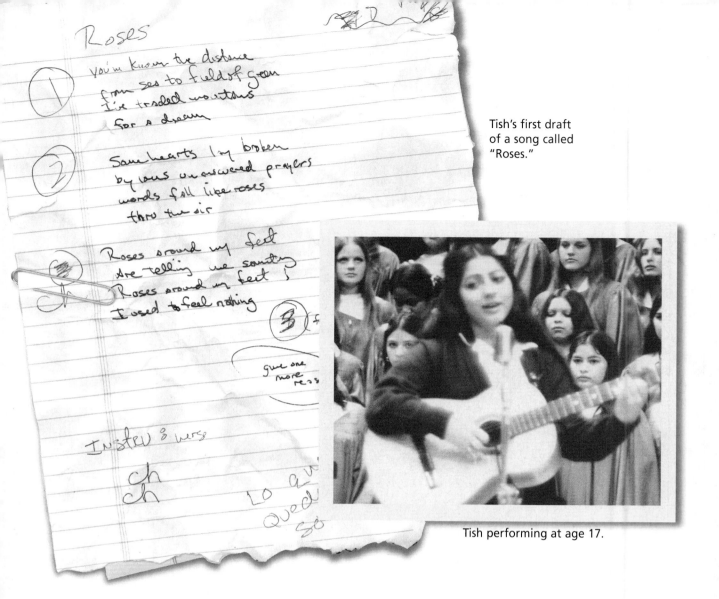

Tish's first draft of a song called "Roses."

Tish performing at age 17.

Barbara: Let's talk first about your **inspiration**. Where do you get ideas for songs?

Tish: I create in many ways; the ideas come from many **sources**. Sometimes a thought will roll by in my head that sets off a **rhythm** or a line of music and I think, "Hey, that's cool!" and I try to work with it before it gets away. Sometimes the thought will grow into a song.

Barbara: Do you have any other sources of creativity?

Tish: Another source of creativity is **panic**. If, after a period of time, I haven't written anything, I start to worry. I feel it's time to get back into a **creative mode**.

....

rhythm beat
panic overpowering fear

At those times I get real quiet and let the thoughts, **melodies**, or rhythms just roll around in my head until one **surfaces** that I can work with. I call these "fishing expeditions." Sometimes the **results** are not too great, but it gets the creativity flowing again, and usually a song comes out of it. I've learned to pay attention to what is going on around me—to the things I read, see, or hear. I **draw** inspiration from all these **experiences**.

Barbara: Has music always been a part of your life?

Tish: Yes, it has. There was always music in our house. The first sounds to welcome me to this world must have been the Mexican music pouring out of the kitchen radio, along with the ringing of my mother's laughter.

Barbara: Did you listen to the radio much when you were growing up?

Tish: Yes, I did. The kitchen radio was always tuned to the Spanish station. I liked the **heartfelt vocal harmonies** and tropical rhythms of old songs with the accordion so lively. I also liked the **current hits** and **popular** music in Spanish. So you see, radio has played a special **role** in developing my love for music.

Barbara: How did music **influence** your life as you got older?

Tish: I learned at about the age of ten that **a passionate melody** could bring tears to my eyes and a tug deep inside. When I attended high school, I was pretty shy. I'd sit and listen to a group of girls who played and sang popular **folk music**. Little by little, I felt comfortable enough to sing along. Eventually, they taught me **guitar chords** and invited me to play their guitars. I was as surprised as they were when it came my turn to play along. I had never checked to see if I had a voice. I discovered that I could sing some of those melodies tugging at my heart.

> **BEFORE YOU MOVE ON...**
>
> 1. **Details** Where does Tish Hinojosa find inspiration for her songs?
> 2. **Personal Experience** Describe for your partner what kind of music "tugs at your heart."

---

melodies songs, tunes
surfaces comes to the top, gives me an idea
draw get
heartfelt vocal harmonies songs that are sung by two or more singers at once with lots of feeling
current hits favorite songs of the time

popular well-liked
a passionate melody an emotional song or tune
folk music traditional songs
guitar chords combinations of 3 or more musical tones played together using strings of a guitar

Tish waits to perform at her first "real" job in San Antonio, at age 20.

Barbara: What did you do after you discovered your voice?

Tish: I spent hours learning and memorizing all of my favorite songs. I would sit on the stoop of the stairs leading into the kitchen and **serenade** my mom with Mexican tunes as she cooked. Mom would correct my pronunciation. I would sometimes sit on the front porch with my father and just practice **guitar picking**. I really enjoyed those times.

Barbara: What was the first job you had that was related to music?

Tish: My mother called the Spanish radio station in our hometown of San Antonio, Texas. She spoke to the director and got me a job singing **jingles**. This led to my first Spanish music **recording experience** and to **appearances** on local Spanish TV talk shows.

Barbara: Your mother sounds like a great person. What was the next step in your musical career?

Tish: After graduating from high school, I traveled to Northern New Mexico. There I found a very inviting music community and a culturally colorful mixture of people: Native Americans, Spanish Americans, hippies, and cowboys. Country music was popular there. I quickly **adapted** my **style**, formed a band, and played for dances. I loved learning classic country songs. I also loved tricking country dancers into two-stepping to Spanish music.

Barbara: You won't forget the community in New Mexico, will you?

Tish: No. It was during this time that I came closer to a real music career. Seeing my fellow musicians write their own songs **encouraged me** to try it myself. My first **attempts** were simple folk and country tunes. In time, I gathered the courage to include these in my **performances** and got good responses.

---

serenade sing to
guitar picking making sounds by picking the guitar strings
jingles short or brief songs used to sell things
recording experience time singing for a professional recording

adapted changed
encouraged me made me want
performances shows

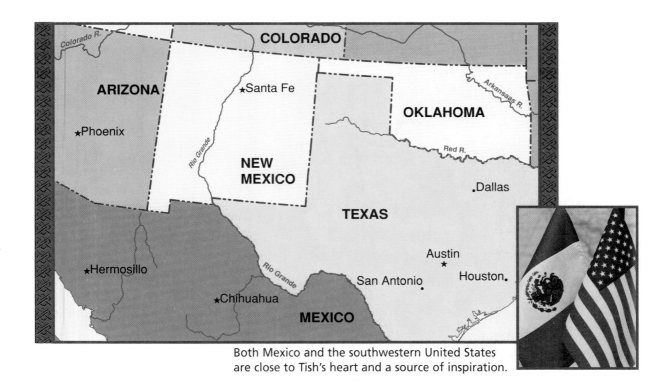

Both Mexico and the southwestern United States are close to Tish's heart and a source of inspiration.

Barbara: Most musicians have **a particular** style. How did you discover your style?

Tish: I began taking trips to Nashville and tried to break in as a singer or songwriter. I learned that my style didn't fit the **commercial bend** of Nashville, but I realized I did have a style all my own. That was **an awakening**.

Barbara: What influences your style?

Tish: My style is made partly from my history. All of those pieces of my life that I thought were just my life, were **unique** and important experiences that other people related to. My parents' lives, their struggles and sacrifices, their friends from Mexico who often stayed with us while they worked to help their families back home, my **allegiance** to Mexico, my allegiance to the United States—all these things are an important part of my unique style. Since 1988, I have been writing and singing mostly my own songs.

> **BEFORE YOU MOVE ON...**
>
> 1. **Details** What was the first job Tish Hinojosa had?
> 2. **Personal Experience** Name a person who has had a strong influence in your life. Explain how the person influenced or inspired you.
> 3. **Paraphrase** Name at least two things that influenced Tish Hinojosa's style as a singer and a songwriter.

---

a particular an individual
commercial bend money-making way
an awakening a new idea for me

unique unlike anything else, special
allegiance loyal support, respect

Performing with a band at a Colorado festival

Barbara: Let's get back to the subject of inspiration. One of your most popular songs is "Something in the Rain." Can you tell us what inspired you to write it?

Tish: I had wanted to write a song about the farm workers' experience. I learned a lot about farm workers' problems through my mother's sister, Tía Josefina, who was a farm worker. She and her family followed the crops throughout the country. When she came to Texas she would visit us and tell what it was like to work in the fields. From what I remembered about her stories and the farm workers' **protest movement** in the 1960s, I had a lot of thoughts rolling around in my head, but nothing really **gelled**.

Then I read a short story that was culturally related to the farm workers' experience. It was the story of a farm accident, caused by **toxic pesticides**, as seen through the eyes of a young boy.

This story moved me. I loved the **innocent voice** of the boy. It **flashed** through my head that I wanted this same young boy to tell my story. I could hear him saying the words. After that, the song just flowed out. If I hadn't read that story, the song may never have been written, or if it had, it would have been a completely different song.

Barbara: You're a mother, too. Your son and daughter often give you inspiration for a song, don't they?

Tish: Yes, they do. My song called "Baby Believe" is a love song, but it is also about what my kids bring out in me. It is a self-esteem message, really, because even though parents give a lot to their children, children make parents feel important and **worthwhile**. This thought **triggered** the words for "Baby Believe."

---

protest movement attempt to change things
gelled came together
toxic pesticides poison chemicals used to kill insects and spiders

innocent voice simple point of view
flashed went quickly
worthwhile useful
triggered made me think of

Something in the Rain

Mom and Dad have worked the fields
I don't know how many years
I'm just a boy but I know how
And go to school when work is slow
We have seen our country's roads
Bakersfield to Illinois
And when troubles come our way, oh yeah,
I've seen my daddy pray

There's something wrong with little sister
I hear her crying by my side
Mama's shaking as she holds her
We try to hold her through the night
And mom says close your eyes Mijito
Dream of some place far from here
Like the pictures in your school books
Someday you can take us there

Chorus:
There must be something in the rain
I'm not sure just what that means
Abuelita talks of sins of man
Of dust that's in our hands
There must be something in the rain,
Well, what else could cause this pain
Those airplanes cure the plants so things can grow
Oh no, it must be something in the rain

—*Tish Hinojosa*

A performance in Texas, 1998.

....

Mijito my little son (in Spanish)
Abuelita Grandmother (in Spanish)

Barbara: You must have many career memories. Which of those memories has special meaning for you?

Tish: In May of 1996, I played a **concert** at the White House. There was a **reception** for some of our country's top **Hispanic leaders**. It was a real **highlight** of my life because to me it was about more than my music. It was about my parents, my family, and all of our dreams.

Barbara: How would you summarize your experiences?

Tish: I have this whole bag of experiences and influences going back to that Mexican kitchen. It is these experiences that provide ideas and inspirations for my music. I love my work and feel very lucky to be doing what I do.

BEFORE YOU MOVE ON...

1. **Author's Purpose** Why did Tish Hinojosa write "Something in the Rain"? Why did she write it from a young boy's point of view?

2. **Inference** Is Tish Hinojosa concerned with environmental issues? Explain your answer.

3. **Opinion** What is your opinion of the interview? Write a question you wish had been included.

---

concert musical performance
reception formal gathering
Hispanic leaders important people whose families come from Spanish-speaking countries
highlight happy moment

Baby Believe

Baby believe
There's something about you
Makin' me love who I am

Baby believe
There's something much stronger
Holdin' my heart in your hand

You look at me and I see a light shinin'
Slowly but surely

I'm learnin' about somewhere far deeper than
I've ever been
Baby believe that I am

—*Tish Hinojosa*

ABOUT THE SONGWRITER

Musician **Tish Hinojosa** expresses herself by writing songs about her family, her Mexican American culture, the Southwest, and social issues. As the youngest of thirteen children, she recalls, "It was easy to sit unnoticed, observing." Her loud, busy family helped her become an artist. "There was always music in our house," Hinojosa says. "My mother listened to Mexican radio in the kitchen, and she loved the finer, romantic side of Mexican culture." Tish Hinojosa has performed throughout the United States, through much of Europe, and parts of Asia.

Respond to the Interview

Check Your Understanding

SUM IT UP

Classify Information Complete a chart to classify information from the interview in categories like these:

Sources of Inspiration	Music–Related Jobs
Mexican music tropical rhythms	singing radio jingles

Write Summary Statements and Evaluate Literature Write one or two sentences to sum up the details in each category. Use your statements to help you evaluate the interview.

- What was the purpose of it?
- Was it well-written?
- Do you think the information is accurate?
- How did the author's point of view affect her questions?
- What other questions would you have included in the interview?

Discuss your ideas with a partner. Then take turns sharing your evaluations with the class.

THINK IT OVER

Discuss and Write Talk about these questions with a partner. Write the answers.

1. **Form Generalizations** Radio played a big role in Tish Hinojosa's life. Why do you think radio influences so many people?

2. **Cause and Effect** How does being part of two cultures help Tish Hinojosa?

3. **Personification** In "Something in the Rain" on page 37, what is the meaning of the line "Those airplanes cure the plants so things can grow"?

4. **Personal Experience** What kinds of things inspire you when you create something?

EXPRESS YOURSELF ▶ EXPRESS FEELINGS

What do you think of as you are listening to Tish Hinojosa's music? Tell your group how you feel and what impresses you about her songs.

Respond to the Interview, continued

Language Arts and Literature

GRAMMAR IN CONTEXT

USE SUBJECTS AND VERBS THAT AGREE

Learn About Subjects and Predicates Some sentences have more than one simple subject. The subjects are joined by **and** or **or**. They are called a **compound subject**. If **and** is used in the compound subject, the **verb** in the predicate is plural.

> Tish's **son and daughter** **provide** inspiration.

If **or** is used in the **compound subject**, the **verb** agrees with the last simple subject. Is the subject singular? If so, the verb is singular. Is the subject plural? Then, the verb is plural.

> Often an **event or memories** **spark** a song.
> Often **memories or** an **event** **sparks** a song.

A **compound predicate** has two or more verbs that tell about the same subject. Both verbs must agree with the subject.

> People **listen** to Tish's songs and **enjoy** them.

Practice Write the sentences. Choose the correct verb.

1. My son and I <u>play / plays</u> popular folk songs.

2. People <u>listens / listen</u> and <u>responds / respond</u> favorably.

3. I <u>go / goes</u> home and <u>write / writes</u> more music.

4. My family or my experiences <u>inspire / inspires</u> each song I write.

SPEAKING/LISTENING

CONDUCT AN INTERVIEW

With a partner, choose a singer, writer, or artist you like. Find out information about the person, and then act out an interview for the class.

1 **Plan Interview Questions** Make a list of what you want to know about the person such as how he or she gets ideas, who has influenced the person's work, and how the person got started.

2 **Find the Answers** Use the person's name as a key word to search print and electronic sources like magazines and the Internet. Take notes.

3 **Prepare and Present Your Interview** Write up the questions and answers. Decide who will be the interviewer and practice your presentation. Refer to your notes as you act out your interview for the class.

Sample Interview

> **Interviewer:** Ms. O'Keeffe, where do you get your ideas?
> **Georgia O'Keeffe:** I just look out over the land. I take in the sky. I study the beauty all around me.

For tips on giving an **oral presentation**, see Handbook pages 401–402.

Content Area Connections

SOCIAL STUDIES

LEARN ABOUT SOCIAL REFORM

César Chávez and the United Farm Workers union (UFW) worked to change the conditions Tish sings about in "Something in the Rain." With your group, research how Chávez and the UFW have helped farm workers. Report your results.

1 **Gather Information and Take Notes** Use classroom and library resources to research topics like the following:

- the history of the farm workers' movement
- how and why the UFW was formed
- how Chávez changed conditions
- farm workers' living conditions, pay, and rights before and after the organization of the UFW.

2 **Report Your Findings** Share your research in one of these ways:

- Create a poster that protests the plight of the farm worker before the formation of the UFW.
- Show a video of Chávez, and describe what he did to help the farm workers.
- Conduct interviews. Have one person act as a farm worker from 30 years ago and one as a farm worker from today.

For more about the **research process**, see Handbook pages 394–399.

TECHNOLOGY/MEDIA
SCIENCE
MUSIC

EXPERIMENT WITH MUSIC

Find out what some researchers say about music and how it affects our brains.

1 **Research Articles** Work with a group to take notes on articles about music and its effects on the brain, neurons (nerve cells), and people's reasoning skills. The following Web sites can get you started, but remember to use the key words and look for links.

INTERNET

INFORMATION ON-LINE

Key Words:
+brain +music

Web Sites:
➤ **Effects of Music on the Brain**
- faculty.washington.edu/chudler/music.html
- www.edweek.org/ew/vol-17/30music.h17

2 **Test the Theories** Conduct an experiment to test the effect of classical music on learning. Make a hypothesis, or guess, about what your experiment will prove. Plan your procedures. Ask one group to study with music and one to study without music. Record your results and draw a conclusion. Was your hypothesis correct?

Learn to use the **Internet** on Handbook pages 392–393.

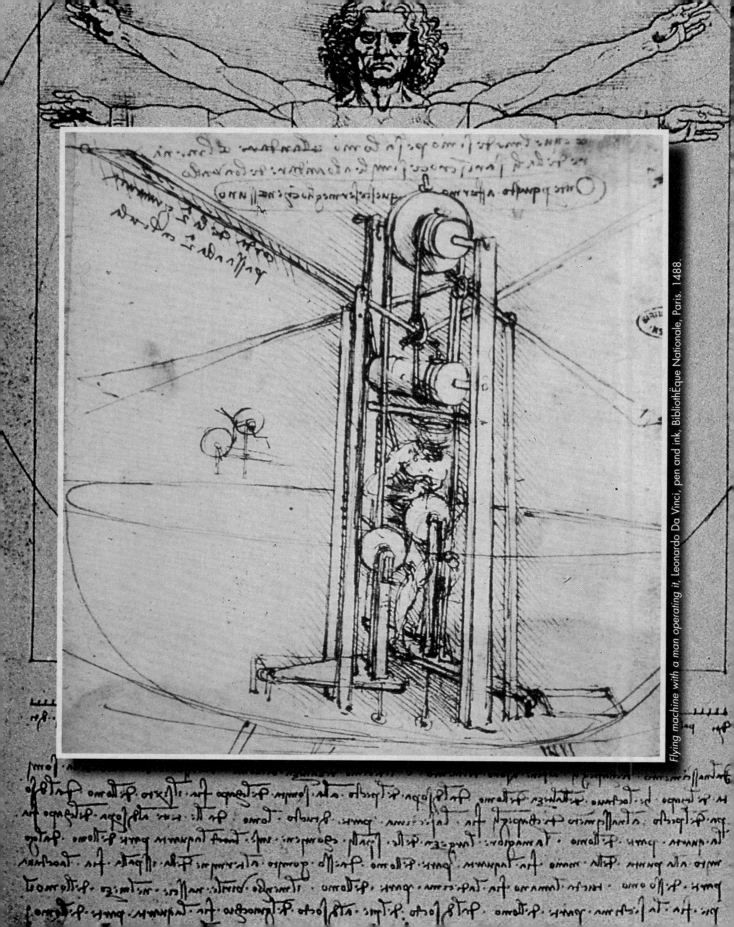

The Power of Imagination

- What is imagination? What is creativity?

- How do you show your thoughts, ideas, and feelings? Do you express yourself in the same way or in a different way from everyone else?

- How are imagination and creativity related?

THEME-RELATED BOOKS

Snowflake Bentley
by Jacqueline Briggs Martin
William Bentley loves snowflakes so much, he uses a new invention called the camera to capture their beauty.

Inventors: A Library of Congress Book
by Martin W. Sandler
Vintage photographs and historical writings present a fascinating survey of inventors and inventions at the turn of the century.

Make Your Own Web Page!
by Ted Pedersen and Francis Moss
Use the power of your imagination and the step-by-step guidelines in this book to create your very own Web page.

Build Language and Vocabulary

DEFINE AND EXPLAIN

Find all the pencils in the picture. How are they being used?

GENERATE IDEAS

Work in a group to think of imaginary ways that a pencil could be used.
Make three drawings to show:

   1. how pencils could have been used in the past
   2. how they can be used today
   3. how they could be used in the future.

Past   Present   Future

BUILD YOUR VOCABULARY

Words About Creativity Read the quote and think about your inventions.
Then brainstorm words that answer the question, "What is creativity?" Show
your ideas in a web. Continue adding to the web as you get new ideas.

Creativity is inventing, experimenting, growing, taking

risks, breaking rules, making mistakes, and having fun.

—*Mary Lou Cook*

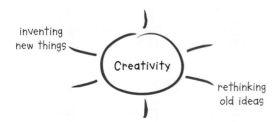

USE LANGUAGE STRUCTURES

▶ PRESENT, PAST, AND FUTURE TENSE VERBS

Speaking: Define and Explain Uses for a Pencil Tell about each of your
inventions. Explain how each works or how it helps someone do something.

   Example:
   Pioneers **built** log cabins. They **used** tree logs to build their
   homes. I **made** a log cabin with pencils because they are
   wooden like logs and are easy to stack.

Prepare to Read

THINK ABOUT WHAT YOU KNOW

Idea Exchange Talk about the Internet with your group. Then read page 47. What new information did you learn?

animation moving pictures or characters

assemble put together, gather

cyberspace world of computer networks

link connection between elements or from one Web page to another

logo name, symbol, or sign that is easy to recognize and represents a group like a team or business

official approved, authorized

operate work, perform

site location of something; collection of related Web pages

text printed words

transfer move from one place to another

LEARN KEY VOCABULARY

Use Context Clues Study the new words and their definitions. Then write the paragraph, replacing the bold words with the new words.

I helped our computer teacher put together our school's **approved** Web site. It took a long time to **gather** all the information we wanted to include. We **moved** a copy of our school **symbol** from another computer file and put the symbol on our site. Then we typed some **words** that described our school. We also added some **moving pictures** of our mascot, a roaring lion. Finally, we added **connections** to other classes' pages. Now the page is **working** 24 hours a day!

LEARN TO CONFIRM THE MEANING OF WORDS

When you read, stop to figure out the meanings of words you don't know.

READING STRATEGY
How to Confirm the Meaning of Words

1. Look for parts of the new word that are familiar. Try to say the word.
2. Read the words around the new word. Do they give you clues about the meaning of the new word?
3. Look up the word in a dictionary. Find the meaning that fits the sentence you are reading.

As you read "Home, Sweet Home Page," list any unfamiliar words. Guess their meanings, and then confirm the meanings in a dictionary.

Introduction to the Internet

THE WORLD WIDE WEB IS PART OF THE INTERNET. THE WEB IS MADE UP OF A COLLECTION OF DOCUMENTS STORED ON COMPUTERS AROUND THE WORLD.

Web page

A Web page is a **document** on the Web. Web pages can include **text,** pictures, sound, and video.

Web server

A Web server is a computer connected to the Internet that makes Web pages **available** to the world.

Web site

A Web **site** is a collection of Web pages **maintained** by a college, university, government agency, company, or individual.

URL

Each Web page has an address called the Uniform Resource Locator (URL). You can instantly **display** any Web page if you know its URL. A URL address might look like this: http://www.mynameis.com. All Web page URLs start with http (HyperText Transfer Protocol).

Hypertext

Web pages are hypertext documents. A hypertext document contains highlighted text that connects to other pages on the Web. Highlighted text allows you to easily **search** through a great amount of information by jumping from one Web page to another.

---

document body of information
available ready for use
maintained kept in good order

display show on your computer screen
search look

Home, Sweet Home Page

BY WEBMASTER SARAH JUAREZ
AS TOLD TO ISAAC SEDER

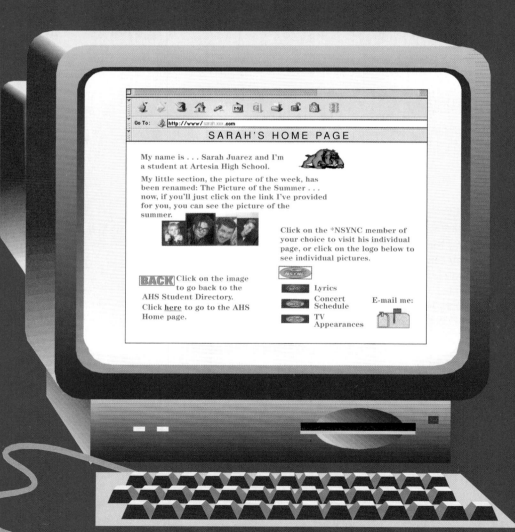

Go To: http://www./ sarah.xxx .com

SARAH'S HOME PAGE

My name is . . . Sarah Juarez and I'm a student at Artesia High School.

My little section, the picture of the week, has been renamed: The Picture of the Summer . . . now, if you'll just click on the link I've provided for you, you can see the picture of the summer.

Click on the *NSYNC member of your choice to visit his individual page, or click on the logo below to see individual pictures.

BACK Click on the image to go back to the AHS Student Directory. Click here to go to the AHS Home page.

Lyrics
Concert Schedule
TV Appearances

E-mail me:

Having your own home page on the Internet is a fun way to connect with other people who share your interests and your dreams. Creating your own home page is an exciting and imaginative way to express yourself. How is it done? Teenager Sarah Juarez explains how she did it, and how you can do it, too.

Did you ever hear someone say "**my home is my castle**"? Well, I can say the same thing. Except it isn't my home, it's my home page. I built my castle in **cyberspace**. You can build one, too.

Sound scary? It's not. All you need is imagination and some techno-knowledge. The knowledge you can find anywhere; imagination is what you add to make your page unique. Just as you would furnish your home in a way that expresses who you are, so you can furnish your home page with personalized messages, **animation**, sound, photos, and graphics. When you're done, you'll have a place where kids—and other people—will always find you at home.

I began my Web page as a class project. At first, it was a little confusing. Here is what I learned along the way.

---

my home is my castle the place where I live is the perfect place, where I am in charge

Net users people who use the Internet

What Is a Home Page?

It really helps to know this. A home page is the first page of a Web site. You can think of it as the front door. Many people, like me, create a home page to introduce themselves to **Net users** around the world. A home page can include whatever you want to share. It can show things you REALLY love, stuff that annoys you, or anything in between. The home page usually has **links** to other pages and a table of contents that describes what is on your site.

What's on My Home Page?

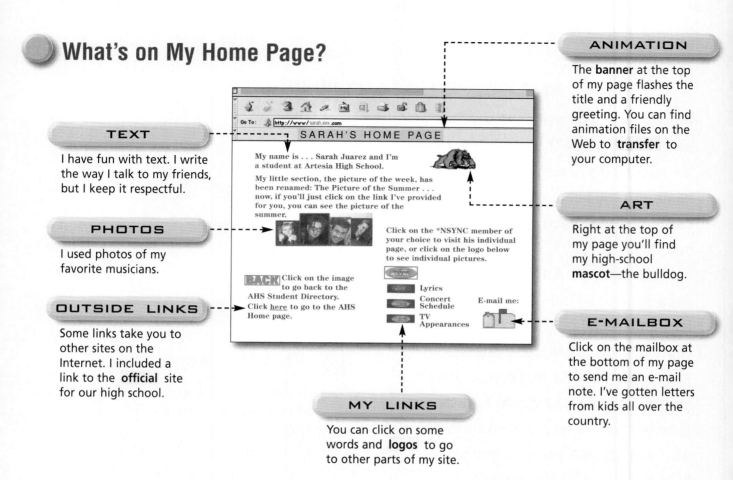

TEXT

I have fun with text. I write the way I talk to my friends, but I keep it respectful.

PHOTOS

I used photos of my favorite musicians.

OUTSIDE LINKS

Some links take you to other sites on the Internet. I included a link to the **official** site for our high school.

ANIMATION

The **banner** at the top of my page flashes the title and a friendly greeting. You can find animation files on the Web to **transfer** to your computer.

ART

Right at the top of my page you'll find my high-school **mascot**—the bulldog.

E-MAILBOX

Click on the mailbox at the bottom of my page to send me an e-mail note. I've gotten letters from kids all over the country.

MY LINKS

You can click on some words and **logos** to go to other parts of my site.

SARAH'S HOME PAGE

My name is . . . Sarah Juarez and I'm a student at Artesia High School.

My little section, the picture of the week, has been renamed: The Picture of the Summer . . . now, if you'll just click on the link I've provided for you, you can see the picture of the summer.

BACK Click on the image to go back to the AHS Student Directory. Click here to go to the AHS Home page.

Click on the *NSYNC member of your choice to visit his individual page, or click on the logo below to see individual pictures.

Lyrics
Concert Schedule
TV Appearances

E-mail me:

How Do You Start Creating a Web Page?

A home page can be exciting or boring. It depends on how much imagination you use when you put all the pieces together.

Your page will probably begin with text. Use a word processor to write your ideas.

Next, think of things you might want to put on your page: photos, art, and links you might like to include. Then organize your ideas.

----

banner sign
mascot symbolic figure

Where Do You Get Computer Photos?

Photos on a Web page are stored as computer **files**. Here's how you can get them:

1 **Scan the photos into your computer.**
The scanner creates an electronic file that your computer can read.

2 **Use a digital camera.**
A digital camera stores photos as electronic files.

3 **Have your film developed digitally.**

4 **Download photos from the Net.**
You might need to get permission from the **copyright holder**.

What About Computer Art?

Here are three good ways to add art to your home page:

1 **Scan it.**

2 **Create your own art with a drawing program.**

3 **Download clip art from the Internet.**
Find out if it's free or not first!

Can You Speak HTML?

OK, now it's time to turn everything you've collected into a Web page.

Web pages are written in a special computer code called HyperText Markup Language (HTML). You can use a software program to create a Web page without learning HTML or you can try HTML yourself.

HTML uses codes called tags. They tell the computer how to display your page. It's really not that hard. It just takes a little time to get used to it. You can find out more about HTML in books or on the Internet.

---

files sets of electronic information, data
digitally as a computer program that uses numbers to store information

Download photos Put or load electronic photo files into your computer
copyright holder person who owns the legal rights to the photos

How Do You Publish a Web Page?

After you have **assembled** your page, you need to find a server that will **store** your Web page. Remember, a server is a large computer that is always connected to the Internet. It **operates** twenty-four hours a day.

My school server **allows us to** store our Web pages for free. Your school or public library might have similar opportunities. Whatever **service** you use to connect to the Internet will probably be able to help you publish your page.

When Is It Finished?

Never! "**Under Construction**" is definitely the most common phrase on home pages. People are always changing their pages, adding new ideas, art, and links.

My page has grown a lot since I first started it. As I learned more about HTML, I added more links, animation, and photos. In fact, I learned so much doing my first page that I launched a new Web page dedicated entirely to my favorite band.

It doesn't take long to join the thousands of people who have their own home in cyberspace. Happy building!

....

store keep
allows us to lets us
service company
Under Construction Being Built or Revised

Sarah's Cyber Suggestions

- Don't make photos too big or your page will run very slowly.

- Make it fun for visitors to hunt around for tiny or hidden links.

- Add a counter to find out how many people visit your home page. Sites on the Net supply free counters and instructions to link them to your Web site.

BEFORE YOU MOVE ON...

1. **Vocabulary** What do the initials HTML stand for?
2. **Details** List three different ways to store photos as computer files.
3. **Opinion** Give your opinion of this advice: *Include any information you want on your home page.* Do you agree?

ABOUT THE WEBMASTER

Sarah Juarez is a senior at Artesia High School in Artesia, New Mexico. In addition to creating Web pages, she also uses her computer skills as advertising editor for her school newspaper. A fan of many different styles of music, Sarah plays flute and piccolo in the marching band.

Respond to the Article
Check Your Understanding

SUM IT UP

Relate Steps in a Process What steps did Sarah follow to create a Web page? Review the article and create a flow chart that shows the steps in a logical order. Be sure to write each step as a command.

Flow Chart

Write some text. → List what you want to include. →

Modify the Process If you were creating your own Web page, what would you do? Make a flow chart to show the steps that you would take.

Flow Chart

Write the text for my site about going on our rafting trip. → Make a list of the supplies we took and which photos to include. →

THINK IT OVER

Discuss and Write Talk about these questions with a partner. Then write the answers.

1. **Evidence and Conclusions** How can you tell Sarah enjoys working with computers?

2. **Cause and Effect** How does a Web page connect you to the world?

3. **Inference** Why do you think people make personal home pages? What are the advantages and disadvantages of having one?

4. **Evaluate** What additional information would you like to see in this article? What else would you like to ask Sarah?

EXPRESS YOURSELF ▶ DEFINE AND EXPLAIN

Choose a word or phrase from the article that is new to you. Discuss its meaning with a partner. Then present your word to the class. Define it. Explain what it means. You might also want to illustrate it or act it out.

Respond to the Article, continued
Language Arts and Literature

USE NOUNS

Learn About Nouns A **noun** names a person, place, thing, or idea. A **common noun** names any person, place, thing, or idea. A **proper noun** names one particular person, place, thing, or idea. The important words in a proper noun begin with a capital letter.

Common Noun	Proper Noun
girl	Sarah
school	Artesia High School

A concrete noun names something you can see. An abstract noun names something you can't see.

The girl uses her imagination.

Use specific nouns to say exactly what you mean.

musicians
Sarah adds photos of ~~people~~ to her page.

Use Specific Nouns Replace the underlined nouns in this paragraph to make them specific.

A home page can tell <u>stuff</u> about you. Include <u>things</u> on your home page.

Practice Add nouns to complete the paragraph. Circle the proper nouns.

My home page is devoted to the musical *The Lion King*. First I wrote some _____ to tell the story. Then I added pictures of the amazing _____. I also added a quote from _____ about her experience designing the masks.

WRITE A HOW-TO ARTICLE

Write an article about something you know how to do.

1 **Identify Your Audience** Knowing whom you are writing for will help you decide how difficult the steps can be and what you need to explain.

2 **Write Your Draft** Write down each step in order. Make each step a command. Use specific nouns to help your reader understand what you mean.

3 **Have a Peer Conference** See if your partner can follow your steps. Use your partner's suggestions to edit your work.

4 **Share Your Article** Exchange articles with your classmates. Try to follow the steps their articles describe.

Sample Article

How to Take a Photograph

1. First be sure that your camera has film in it! You can use color or black-and-white film.

2. Then look at your subject through the camera lens. Focus the lens!

Review **nouns** on Handbook pages 432–436.

Content Area Connections

CREATE A HOME PAGE

What would you include on your own home page? Follow these steps to design one.

1 Collect Ideas Browse the Internet to explore other Web sites. Think about what you like and don't like about them. Make a list of everything you want to have on your page. Here are some ideas.

- **An Autobiography** Provide general information about who you are. Don't include your last name, phone number, address, or photograph since you don't want strangers to have that information.

- **Your Hobbies and Interests** Give a brief description of what you like. Include a favorite quotation, song, or work of art.

- **Opinions** Give your opinion about a book, movie, or world event.

- **Mailbox** Provide a link to your e-mail address to get feedback on your ideas.

Working on the computer

2 Assemble the Pieces Use a diagram to show how your Web page will be set up, including the links you'll have. Check your links to be sure that they are up-to-date.

Sample Diagram

Cecilia's Home Page

animation of a dragon breathing fire

short paragraph about me

text about mythology

art from a myth

links to some good mythology sites

3 Program Your Page Follow the steps in an HTML editor program to turn your design into a real Web page.

4 Launch Your Site Now you're ready to post your page on an Internet server. Once your page is running, be sure to update it regularly and check that the links are still correct.

User Friendly

science fiction
by T. Ernesto Bethancourt

Prepare to Read

THINK ABOUT WHAT YOU KNOW

Quickwrite Take a minute to write what you think happens when someone programs a computer. Discuss your ideas with a group.

Don't play dumb.

He knocked my head off.

He was picking the brains of the computer.

I checked it out.

I had some time on my hands.

I'll take care of her.

It was a blur.

They're history.

What's the big idea?

Your happiness is everything to me.

LEARN KEY VOCABULARY

Locate and Use Definitions Study the idioms. Write down what you think each one means. Then use the Glossary to confirm the meanings.

Idiom	What I Think It Means	Confirmed
I checked it out.	I found out about it.	✓

LEARN ABOUT FICTION

A **fictional** story is made up by the author. Every fictional story has characters, a setting, and a plot. These are called story elements.

READING STRATEGY
How to Read Fiction

1. Who are the people, animals, or things that speak in the story? Those are the **characters**.
2. Where and when does the story take place? That is the **setting**.
3. What happens? That is the **plot**.
   - The **conflict** is a problem the characters try to solve.
   - **Complications** are the events that make the story problem harder to solve.
   - The **climax** is the turning point. It is when the conflict starts to be resolved.
   - The **resolution** comes at the end of the story. It answers the remaining questions.

As you read "User Friendly," think about the characters, the setting, and the plot.

User

Friendly

By T. Ernesto Bethancourt

Kevin's dad has a great idea for a computer: one that has its own personality. After he and Kevin put it together, Kevin discovers that the computer has a mind of its own. How is he going to stop it from causing more trouble?

A COMPUTER ACTS HUMAN

Kevin's computer, Louis, asks Kevin questions,
makes requests, and gives opinions—just like a person!

I reached over and shut off the insistent buzzing of my bedside alarm clock. Yawning, I walked toward the bathroom. As I walked by my computer table, I pressed my computer Louis's on button. The computer's screen glowed greenly, displaying the message: *Good Morning, Kevin.*

I had almost walked by Louis, when I noticed there was another message on the screen.

When are you going to get me my **voice module**, Kevin?

I blinked. There was nothing in Louis's **basic programming** that would allow for a question like this. Wondering what was going on, I sat down at the keyboard, and entered: *Repeat last message.* Amazingly, the computer replied:

It's right there on the screen, Kevin. Can we talk? I mean, are you going to get me a voice box?

I was stunned. Dad and I had put this

There was nothing in Louis's basic programming that would allow for a question like this.

computer together. The CPU was a new design. But it couldn't ask its own questions.

It had to be the extra **circuitry** in the gray plastic case next to Louis's **console.** That case **housed** Louis's "**personality**," as Dad called it. We even named it Louis, after my great-uncle.

Giving Louis a name didn't mean it was a person, yet here it was, asking me a question that just couldn't be in its programming.

Frowning, I quickly typed: *We'll have to wait and see, Louis. When it's ready, you'll get your voice.*

As I was about to leave the room, I glanced back at the computer table. Had I been imagining things?

Ginny Linke was just two seats away from me on the bus to school. I promised myself that today I was actually going to talk to her.

---

voice module computer part that produces sounds like human speech

basic programming main instructions for processing information

circuitry electronic communication path

console computer screen

housed held, stored

personality feelings, actions, and special characteristics

The bus stopped in front of Santa Rosario Junior High and the students began to file out.

"Uhhhh . . . Ginny?" I said. "I'm Kevin Neal . . ."

"Yes, I know," said Ginny.

"You do?" I gulped in amazement. "How come?"

Ginny laughed. "I asked my brother Chuck who that **nerdy kid** was who keeps staring at me on the bus."

When I got home that afternoon, I went straight upstairs to my room, walked over to the computer table, and pushed the on button. The screen flashed:

Good afternoon, Kevin.

Although it wasn't the programmed response to Louis's greeting, I typed in: *There's nothing good about it. Do you think I'm a nerd?*

Never! I think you're wonderful. Who said you were a nerd?

I typed: *Ginny Linke said it.* Louis flashed:

This is a human female? **Request additional data**.

Still not believing I was doing it, I entered all I knew about Ginny Linke. Louis whirred, then flashed out:

She's cruel and stupid. You're the finest person I know.

I'm the ONLY person you know, I typed.

That doesn't matter. **Your happiness is everything to me**. I'll **take care of** Ginny.

The screen returned to the *Good afternoon, Kevin* message. I typed out: *Wait! What do you mean?* But no matter what I did for the next few hours, I couldn't get Louis to do anything outside of its regular programming.

BEFORE YOU MOVE ON...

1. **Cause and Effect** What effect did Louis's first message have on Kevin?
2. **Personification** In what ways is Louis like a person?

....

nerdy kid person who is overly devoted to learning
Request additional data. I'd like more information.

2
LOUIS CAUSES TROUBLE

The Linkes accuse Kevin of making phone calls
that cause problems for their family.

___

When Dad called that evening, I asked to speak to him.

"Hi, Dad. Louis is acting funny."

"Shouldn't be. I **checked it out** just before I left. Remember you were having trouble with the modem? I **patched in** our latest modem model."

The modem, I thought. The modem was a telephone link to any number of huge computers all over the country. Louis was learning things by **picking the brains** of the giant computers.

I typed furiously.
What have
you done to
Ginny Linke?

As I got on board the bus the next morning, Ginny and her brother Chuck were staring at me. What was going on?

Once the bus stopped at the school, it didn't take long to find out. I was walking up the path to the main entrance when someone grabbed me from behind and spun me around.

"Okay, nerd," growled Chuck, "**what's the big idea**?"

I **volunteered**, with a weak smile, "**E equals M C Squared.** That's the biggest idea I know."

"**Don't play dumb**," Chuck said. "I mean those **creepy** phone calls. Ginny told me about talking to you yesterday. You got some girl to make those calls for you and say all of those things . . ."

"I don't know what you're talking about." I said. "But you better let me go. The assistant principal is watching us from his office window."

Chuck **released** me and spun around. There was no one at the window. But by then I was running to the safety of the school building.

___

patched in put in, installed

volunteered offered

E equals M C Squared a mathematical formula developed by Albert Einstein that means: energy equals mass times the speed of light squared, or $E=mc^2$

creepy scary, strange

released let go of

* * *

I ran upstairs to my bedroom. I punched Louis's on button, and the familiar *Good afternoon, Kevin* was displayed.

I typed **furiously**. *What have you done to Ginny Linke? Her brother nearly* **knocked my head off** *today.* Louis's screen responded immediately.

Is your life in danger?

I explained to Louis that my life wasn't really threatened. But it sure could be made very unpleasant by the Linkes. Louis flashed:

Don't worry then. **They're history**!

Wait! What are you going to do? I wrote. But nothing I could do would make the machine respond . . .

BEFORE YOU MOVE ON...

1. **Vocabulary** Use your own words and explain what a modem is to a partner.
2. **Inference** If Louis doesn't have a voice module, how could Louis make phone calls to Ginny?
3. **Foreshadowing** What does Louis say that suggests something more might happen to the Linkes?

---

furiously quickly and angrily

MR. NEAL FIXES LOUIS

Mr. Neal reprograms Louis, but Louis manages
to send Kevin a final surprise message.

"Just what do you think you're doing, Kevin Neal?" demanded Ginny Linke. She had **cornered me** as I walked up the path to the school entrance.

"I don't know what you're talking about," I said, a **sinking** feeling settling in my stomach.

"This morning," Ginny said, "Mom got a notice that all of our credit cards have been **canceled**. And the Internal Revenue Service has called Dad for **an audit**! I don't know what's going on, Kevin Neal, but somehow I think you've got something to do with it!"

---

cornered me forced me to stop and listen to her
sinking worried, hopeless
canceled stopped, made unusable

an audit a search through tax records to see if all necessary taxes have been paid

"But I didn't . . ." I began, but Ginny was striding up the walk to the main entrance.

I finished the school day, but it **was a blur**. Louis had done it all right. It was going crazy!

When I burst into the hall, I was surprised to see my father.

"Dad! What are you doing here?"

"**Wound up** my business in Chicago a day sooner than I expected," he said. "**I had some time on my hands**, so I checked Louis out again. It was acting very funny. I think it had to do with the **inbuilt logic/growth program** I designed for it. I erased the whole program and set Louis up as a normal computer." Dad stopped, and looked at me. "Anyway, I think you'll find Louis is working just fine now. Except it won't answer as Louis anymore. It'll only **function** as a regular Major Electronics Model Z-11127. I guess the personality program didn't work out."

All I could say was, "Thanks, Dad."

"One more thing that puzzles me, though," Dad said. He held up three sheets of computer paper covered with figures. "It printed this out. I don't know what to make of it. Do you?"

I took the papers from my father and read: *How do I love thee? Let me compute the*

Wound up Finished

inbuilt logic/growth program program that allowed the computer to learn so much

function work

strings of binary code figures the language of computer programming consisting of the numbers 0 and 1

stylized fancy, decorated

ways: The next two pages were covered with **strings of binary code figures**. On the last page, in beautiful color graphics was a **stylized** heart. Below it was the simple message: *I will always love you, Kevin: Louise.*

BEFORE YOU MOVE ON...

1. **Opinion** Do you think the title "User Friendly" is appropriate for this story? Explain.

2. **Conclusions** Did the ending surprise you? Explain how it makes you rethink the characters' motives and the story events.

ABOUT THE AUTHOR

Oddly enough, "User Friendly" was the last story **T. Ernesto Bethancourt** wrote on his old computer before it stopped working! He did not start writing for young adults until he was 41 years old. T. Ernesto Bethancourt has won a number of awards for his work. His autobiography and story *The Dog Days of Arthur Cane* have been turned into television programs.

Respond to the Story
Check Your Understanding

SUM IT UP

Analyze Story Elements and Evaluate Literature Make a map of the rising and falling action in "User Friendly." Use your map to retell the story to a partner. Tell which story element is the strongest and why.

Map of Rising and Falling Action

Characters: _____

Setting: _____

Climax

Complication

Complication

Complication

RISING ACTION

FALLING ACTION

Resolution

Conflict

Write New Events What events would you add to the story? Write two new complications for "User Friendly." Make one event realistic like the computer crashing and losing all its memory. Make the other a fantasy like the computer figuring out how to program Kevin's brain and making him change his thoughts. Share your new events with a partner.

THINK IT OVER

Discuss and Write Talk about these questions with a partner. Write the answers.

1. **Character's Point of View** Retell the story from the computer's point of view.

2. **Author's Purpose** Why do you think the author wrote this story? Explain your answer.

3. **Mood or Tone** Does this story seem funny, serious, or sad? Explain your answer.

4. **Solutions** Kevin's father solved the problem by erasing the logic/growth program. What other ways could Kevin have solved the problem?

EXPRESS YOURSELF ▶ VERIFY INFORMATION

Imagine you are Kevin and your partner is Louis who now has a voice box. Have a conversation in which

• Louis requests input.

• Kevin describes the data to be added to the computer's CPU.

• Louis verifies that the information has been added.

Then switch roles.

Language Arts and Literature

USE ADJECTIVES

Learn About Adjectives An **adjective** describes a noun or a pronoun. It tells what kind, which one, how many, or how much.

> Kevin's dad had a **great** idea for his **new** computer. With just **one** wire, and **that special** box, he could give the computer **several different** personalities.

Use precise adjectives to help paint a clear and vivid picture.

> The wire is in the case.
> The **red** wire is in the **gray plastic** case.

Add Adjectives What adjectives can you add to this paragraph to improve the description?

> Kevin hooked up the _____ wire and the computer became like a _____ kid. Its _____ words were _____ , and Kevin knew he had a _____ friend.

Practice Replace the underlined adjectives in this description to paint a clearer picture of Louis.

> The computer Louis is very loyal. When its good friend Kevin is upset about Ginny, Louis says nice things to him. After Chuck is mean to Kevin, Louis does bad things to the Linkes to make Kevin feel better. It even sends Kevin a nice message to let Kevin know how good he is.

WRITE A LETTER

If you were Louis, what would you write in a letter to Kevin? Write the letter, and then exchange it with a partner. Your partner can write back to give Kevin's response.

1 Write Your Draft Compose your letter on the computer or by hand. Write about some things that could really happen such as eating lunch at school. Add some science fiction elements such as having the computer call to have pizza delivered to the school.

2 Edit Your Work Did you include all of the parts of a friendly letter? Also look over your letter to make sure you used computer-related words correctly.

3 Share Your Work Print out your letters, and then read them aloud to the class.

Sample Letter

> May 20, 2002
>
> Dear Kevin,
>   How was your day? Did you like the pizza I sent you for lunch? With my new voice box, it was so easy to use my modem, call the pizza place, and order a pizza for you! You do like anchovies, don't you? You've never told me, but I read that fish is a very nutritious food so I made sure to include it when I selected the toppings.
>
>   Your friend,
>   Louis

Respond to the Story, continued
Content Area Connections

WRITE A PLAY

A **play** is a story that is acted out on stage. With your class turn "User Friendly" into a play to perform for the school.

① **Create the Script** A script shows what each character says and gives stage directions. Long scripts are usually divided into **acts**, which are like chapters in a book. Each act has **scenes**, which show each different place or time the action occurs.

Look at page 67. Work with a group to choose a scene and write the script for it. Then, as a class, put all the scenes together to make the script of the entire story.

② **Choose a Role** Decide on the job that matches your talents.

Job	Duties
producer	is in charge of the play
director	guides the actors
set designer	plans how the stage and scenery will look
costume designer	plans what the actors wear
publicist	lets people know about the play
box office manager	sells the tickets
actor	is a character in the play

③ **Rehearse and Advertise** If you are the director or an actor, practice the play many times to get everything just right. If you are the publicist or box office manager, tell others about the play. Make posters, talk to people, and put ads in the newspaper.

④ **Perform the Play** Present your play to the school. You may want to videotape the play so you can watch it and show it to others who could not attend.

User Friendly

Friday and Saturday at 8 p.m.
Sunday at 2 p.m.
in the
school auditorium

For tips on giving an **oral presentation**, see Handbook pages 401–402.

Acts and Scenes from "User Friendly"

Act I: **A Computer Acts Human** (pages 58–59)

Scene 1: In Kevin's room. Kevin discovers that the computer can talk to him.

Scene 2: On the bus. Kevin talks with Ginny.

Scene 3: In Kevin's room. Kevin reports to the computer.

Act II: **Louis Causes Trouble** (pages 60–61)

Scene 1: At Kevin's home. Kevin talks with his dad on the phone.

Scene 2: At school. Kevin talks with Chuck.

Scene 3: In Kevin's room. Kevin reports to the computer.

Act III: **Mr. Neal Fixes Louis** (pages 62–63)

Scene 1: At school. Kevin talks with Ginny.

Scene 2: At Kevin's home. Kevin talks to his dad.

Sample Script

Write the **title** and **number** of the act.

Name each **character** and write the **dialogue,** or what the character says.

Use **stage directions** to tell how the characters should say the lines, move, sound, or look.

User Friendly
Act I
Scene One

Kevin is reading his computer monitor in his bedroom.
We hear an offstage voice as might be heard in his head.

Louis (**offstage voice**). When are you going to get me my voice module, Kevin?

Kevin *(puzzled, talking to himself).* The computer isn't programmed to ask its own questions. *(He speaks slowly as he types.)* We'll have to wait and see, Louis. When it's ready, you'll get your voice.

Writing That Describes

Descriptive writing gives a clear, detailed picture of what a person, a place, a thing, or an idea is like.

PROFESSIONAL WRITING MODEL

The **photo essay**, "*The Lion King* Goes to Broadway," describes how a group of people turned their creative ideas into a musical. The writer uses lots of photographs, captions, and descriptive details to picture the events.

from "The Lion King Goes to Broadway"

In this scene, the lionesses cry over the lifeless body of Mufasa. Ribbons pulled through the eyes of the mask look like streams of tears, showing a powerful grief.

Photographs by Joan Marcus © Disney Enterprises, Inc.

A DESCRIPTIVE DOCUMENTARY

Some descriptions tell how to do something in a step-by-step order. The writers use order words, descriptive details, and pictures to document exactly how something was done. Look at the flow chart. Discuss the process for creating the musical, *The Lion King*.

Steps-in-a-Process Flow Chart

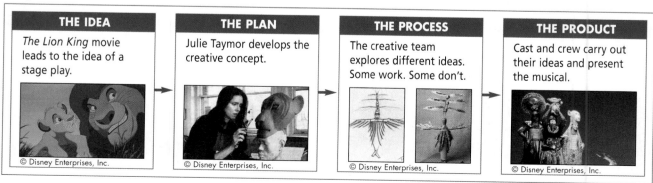

THE IDEA	THE PLAN	THE PROCESS	THE PRODUCT
The Lion King movie leads to the idea of a stage play.	Julie Taymor develops the creative concept.	The creative team explores different ideas. Some work. Some don't.	Cast and crew carry out their ideas and present the musical.
© Disney Enterprises, Inc.	© Disney Enterprises, Inc.	© Disney Enterprises, Inc.	© Disney Enterprises, Inc.

STUDENT WRITING MODEL

Descriptive Documentary

A Class Mural

by Bianca Ramos

The eighth-grade class was given the assignment of painting a mural on the blank, boring wall at the far end of the school. Nikki, Frank, Aki, Lucho, and I were chosen to design it and then the rest of the class would help paint it.

Planning the Mural

The first thing we had to do was brainstorm creative ideas with our class. Then the class voted and chose to create a rainforest scene. After that, the five of us sketched our drawings on paper. I must have drawn six sketches before I did one that I really liked.

This is the sketch I finally liked.

Transferring Our Sketches

Then we photocopied our drawings onto overhead transparencies. That way we could project the pictures onto the wall. Everyone in our class helped trace the sketches in chalk onto the wall.

The overhead projector made it easy to transfer the sketches.

Painting the Mural

We used our original color drawings to help us know which colors to paint the mural. Basically, we just filled in the chalk like a giant coloring book! It took the entire eighth-grade class two days to paint the wall. In the end it was a class project that we could all be proud of.

Everyone had a great time painting.

Information is presented in a **logical order**. It begins with general information about the project, and then tells about the steps.

Headings name each step in the process, and **drawings** or **photographs** illustrate what happened at each step.

Order words tell when events took place.

Bianca used **adjectives** and other **descriptive details** to help readers "see" the process.

Writing That Describes, continued

The Writing Process

> **WRITING PROMPT**
>
> Now you will work with your group to create something. Then you can write a description of what you did for your family to read.

PREWRITE

1 Plan the Project What creative project could your group do? Perhaps you've already done one! Brainstorm a list of ideas.

Things We Could Do

draw a mural

make our own masks for The Lion King

create a class Web page

decorate trash cans

Choose an idea and arrange time to do the project. Assign a note taker and photographer or artist to document what you do during each step.

2 Unlock the Writing Prompt Remember that you'll be describing what your group does. Fill out an **FATP** chart to help guide your descriptive writing.

3 Get Organized Make a flow chart like the one on page 68 to show the steps in the process. A good way to keep your pictures in order is to number them. Then code the numbers to each step on your flow chart.

FATP Chart

HOW TO UNLOCK A PROMPT

Form: *descriptive documentary*

Audience: *family members*

Topic: *trash can art installation*

Purpose: *to show in words and pictures what we did to beautify the school*

Reflect and Evaluate

- Does your flow chart show all the main steps? Are they in the correct order?
- Why is assigning roles for the project a good idea?

DRAFT

Use your **FATP** chart to remind yourself of what and why you are writing. As you write your draft, don't worry about making mistakes.

1 **Write the Introduction** Give your readers the "big picture" first: Who is in your group? What is your project? Why did you choose it? Be sure that your paragraph has a topic sentence that tells the main idea. Include details that tell more about the main idea.

Writer's Craft: Building a Paragraph

You can put the topic sentence at the beginning and then present the details.

First we decided that each trash can would match its surroundings. The trash cans in the cafeteria would show different kinds of food. Right outside the gymnasium would be several trash cans with athletes on them. The trash cans outside of the theater would show different aspects of a play. Everyone agreed this was a good idea.

You can start with the details and then put the topic sentence at the end.

Mr. Woods' homeroom volunteered to paint the trash cans near the gym. Ms. Lopez's homeroom agreed to decorate the ones near the theater. That left the trash cans in the cafeteria to Miss Anderson's homeroom. Every eighth-grade class was in charge of decorating a group of trash cans.

---

2 **Describe Each Step** Use a logical order to present the steps and pictures. Use lots of descriptive details to help your readers picture the process. You might want to number the steps, use a list with "bullets" (black dots), or use paragraphs under the pictures.

3 **Write a Conclusion** Tell how your project turned out and show the final product. Tell how your group felt about the project, or what others thought of it.

Reflect and Evaluate

- Read your draft. Will your audience enjoy reading it?

- Are your steps clear and easy to follow? Do your paragraphs have a topic sentence and supporting details?

- Do your pictures work with your words to show each step of the process?

Writing That Describes, continued

REVISE

1 **Reread Your Draft** Review your **FATP**. Are the form, audience, topic, and purpose clear? Will your audience be able to picture each step in the process?

2 **Conduct a Peer Conference** Have someone in another group look at your description. Have you varied your sentences enough? Do you need to add more or better descriptive words to make your details more interesting? Use the guidelines on Handbook page 411 to help you.

Look at the comments a partner made about Alec's description during a Peer Conference. Look at the changes Alec made.

> *Not every good idea works out, so even the most creative person must be willing to let go of an idea and look for a better one.*
>
> — Bruce Goldstone

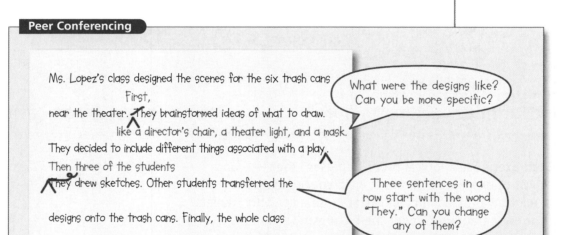

Peer Conferencing

Ms. Lopez's class designed the scenes for the six trash cans
      First,
near the theater. They brainstormed ideas of what to draw.
     like a director's chair, a theater light, and a mask.
They decided to include different things associated with a play.
Then three of the students
They drew sketches. Other students transferred the

designs onto the trash cans. Finally, the whole class

worked for three days after school to paint the cans.

What were the designs like? Can you be more specific?

Three sentences in a row start with the word "They." Can you change any of them?

3 **Mark Your Changes** Review your notes and decide how you want to change your writing. Revising Marks appear on Handbook page 411. For revising a word-processed document on a computer, see pages 383–389.

Reflect and Evaluate

- How did talking with peers help you with your writing?
- Are you pleased with your writing?
- Did you choose just the right words to help your readers "see" each step?

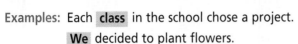

COMPLETE SENTENCES

A complete sentence has a subject and a predicate. The verb in the predicate must agree with the subject.

Our class planted flowers.

- The subject tells whom or what the sentence is about. The **complete subject** includes all the words that tell about the subject. The **simple subject** is the most important word in the complete subject. It is usually a noun or pronoun.

  Examples: Each **class** in the school chose a project.

  We decided to plant flowers.

- The predicate tells what the subject is, does, or has. The **complete predicate** includes all the words in the predicate. The **simple predicate** is the most important word in the predicate. It is the verb.

  Examples: A local nursery **donated** **plants**.

  They also **gave** us seeds to plant.

- A **compound subject** has two or more simple subjects joined by *and* or *or*.

  Example: The **gardener** at our school **and** several **parents** helped.

- A **compound predicate** has two or more verbs that tell about the same subject.

  Example: The parents **arrived** early **and** **brought** snacks for everyone.

- The verb in a sentence must agree in number with the subject.

  Examples: The **gardener starts** to dig up the ground.

  Ned **and** **Cara plant** seeds and **cover** them with soil.

Practice It is planting day! Add to these subjects and predicates to write complete sentences. Describe what everyone does.

1. meet at the school on Saturday morning

2. our science teacher

3. Eddie, Franchesca, and I

4. digs down and loosens the soil

5. the parents

Writing That Describes, continued

EDIT AND PROOFREAD

1 **Check for Mistakes** Look carefully at your description. Correct any mistakes you find in capitalization, spelling, and punctuation. If you need help, use Handbook pages 453–463.

2 **Check Your Sentences** Do all your sentences have a subject and a predicate? Make sure that your subjects and verbs agree.

3 **Make a Final Copy** If you are working on a computer, print out the corrected copy of your work. If not, rewrite it and make the corrections you marked. Be sure to leave room near each step for your pictures.

PUBLISH

Choose one of these ideas for publishing your writing, or come up with another idea on your own.

- If you are using a desktop publishing program, you can scan and import your photos or drawings right into your document to create your own design.

The Theater Trash Cans

Ms. Lopez's class designed the scenes for the six trash cans near the theater. First, they brainstormed ideas of what to draw. They decided to include different things associated with a play like a director's chair, a theater light, and a mask. Then three of the students drew sketches. Other students transferred the designs onto the trash cans. Finally, the whole class worked for three days after school to paint the cans.

Nina designed this trash can.

- Create a project scrapbook with at least one picture and your descriptive text on each page. You might include other items in your scrapbook, like the actual lists you made or sketches you drew.

Key In TO Technology

"Dress up" your description:

- Import borders for your pictures.
- Use special fonts for your headings and captions.
- Add color to your drawings.

Reflect and Evaluate

- Are you pleased with your group's description? Does it
  - ☑ give a clear picture of what something is like?
  - ☑ follow a logical order?
  - ☑ use order words?
  - ☑ have adjectives and other descriptive details?
- What did you like best about the work? What did you like least?
- Will you make a copy of the work for your portfolio? Why or why not?

The Creative Touch

① Look Back at the Unit

Evaluate Personal Expressions In this unit you read selections about people and characters who express themselves in creative ways.

The Lion King Goes to Broadway

An Interview with Tish Hinojosa

Home, Sweet Home Page

User Friendly

Use a speedometer to indicate how much you liked each of the four selections. Then summarize the kinds of experiences that inspired the people in the selections to create.

② Show What You Know

Sum It All Up Expand and organize your ideas on this mind map. Share your ideas about creativity with a partner.

Reflect and Evaluate Take a minute to write some creative ideas you have gotten from this unit. Then tell how you are going to use them. Add this writing to your portfolio, along with the work from the unit that reflects your accomplishments.

③ Make Connections

To Your School Organize a show or an exhibit that highlights the talents of each person in your class. Invite other students to see it.

The Forest Has Eyes, Bev Doolittle, watercolor and ink. Copyright © 1984.

The Force of Discovery

Take a few minutes to study the painting. Look carefully, and then discuss it with a partner. How many hidden faces can you discover? After you saw them, how did you feel? What did you learn about discoveries?

A journey of a thousand miles must begin with a single step.

—*Lao-Tsu*

Neil Armstrong was the first person to walk on the moon. His image is reflected in Buzz Aldrin's visor. July 20, 1969.

THEME 1

Pushing Past the Frontier

- Why do people push past frontiers?

- What are the risks and benefits of exploring new lands?

- Which areas in the world have been explored? What are the frontiers of the future?

THEME-RELATED BOOKS

I Have Heard of a Land
by Joyce Carol Thomas

An African American woman travels to Oklahoma Territory to stake her claim and build a new home.

My Name Is York
by Elizabeth Van Steenwyk

The Lewis and Clark Expedition as seen through the eyes of Captain Clark's slave, York.

From Sea to Shining Sea
compiled by Amy L. Cohn

A treasury of stories, folk tales, essays and songs that celebrate America's rich cultural heritage.

Build Language and Vocabulary

MAKE COMPARISONS

Listen to the music and look carefully at the painting. You are exploring this canyon. Draw and make notes in your journal to tell what you see and do on your journey through this frontier.

Grand Canyon, William Robinson Leigh, oil on canvas. Copyright ©1911.

COMPARE NOTES

Work with a partner. Make a Venn diagram to compare the notes you made about your journeys.

Venn Diagram

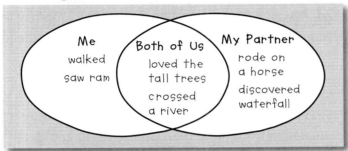

BUILD YOUR VOCABULARY

Words About Nature Organize the words from your diagram into a chart. Add words that your classmates used, too. As you go through this unit, keep adding words to your chart.

Plants	Animals	Landforms
trees	gray squirrels	fast river
scrub bushes	lizards	red rocks
pink wild	horses	cliffs
flowers	coyotes	cave
grass	bighorn sheep	waterfall
cactus		

USE LANGUAGE STRUCTURES ▶ COMPOUND SENTENCES

Writing: Compare Journeys Write compound sentences that describe what you and your partner did on your journeys. Use words from the **Word Bank**.

Examples:

I slept under the stars, **but** Ivan slept in a cave.

Ivan and I counted more than 30 different kinds of birds, **and** we both drew pictures of them in our journals.

Word Bank

and
but
or
nor
for
yet

Lewis and Clark

biography
by Steven Kroll

Prepare to Read

THINK ABOUT WHAT YOU KNOW

Make a List On page 80, you went on an imaginary journey through a canyon. Now make a list of the supplies you needed for the journey.

barrier something that blocks the way

difficulty problem, something that stops you from getting something done

discover see for the first time, find out something

expedition trip for a specific purpose or goal

explore look around a new place

fur trade exchange of animal skins for money, food, or other items

journey long trip

territory land that is owned and ruled by a country

the unknown something that is not familiar to you

wilderness area where no people live

LEARN KEY VOCABULARY

Relate Words Study the new words and their definitions. With your group, complete the word map. Then write a paragraph to tell what an "expedition" is.

Word Map

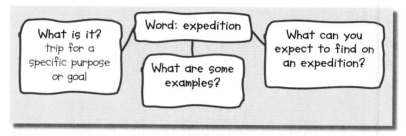

What is it? trip for a specific purpose or goal

Word: expedition

What are some examples?

What can you expect to find on an expedition?

LEARN ABOUT GOALS AND OUTCOMES

A **goal** is something a person wants to do. The **outcome** tells if the person reaches the goal.

READING STRATEGY
How to Relate Goals and Outcomes
1. Look for a person's goal near the beginning of a selection.
2. List the obstacles that get in the way.
3. Look for the outcome at the end.

As you read "Lewis and Clark," think about the expedition's goals and outcomes.

Lewis and Clark
Explorers of the American West
by Steven Kroll with text support by Janine Wheeler

In 1803, the United States buys the Louisiana Territory from France. A year later, Lewis and Clark lead an expedition to explore the new land. They begin near St. Louis and travel up the Missouri River, heading west toward the Pacific Ocean. With the help of a Shoshone woman and Clark's slave, the explorers reach the Pacific Ocean safely and return, bringing back with them information about the new land.

The Louisiana Purchase

In 1803, the United States was just twenty years old. There were seventeen states in the union, and American **territory** reached only as far west as the Mississippi River.

On the other side of the Mississippi, between the river and the Rocky Mountains, was the unexplored Louisiana Territory. In 1800 Napoleon Bonaparte, soon-to-be emperor of France, had taken Louisiana back from Spain, who **had ruled it** since 1763.

President Thomas Jefferson did not want the French army threatening America's western border. He wasn't ready to **risk the closing of the port** of New Orleans, at the mouth of the Mississippi and **vital** to American trade. In March 1803, Jefferson instructed his minister to France, Robert R. Livingston, to buy New Orleans. Napoleon offered to sell the whole of the Louisiana Territory for sixty million francs (about nine million U.S. dollars today).

A Decision to Explore the New Land

Jefferson felt this new land should be **explored**. Even before the United States **took possession of** the territory late in 1803 and early in 1804, the president had been discussing an **expedition** to the Pacific Ocean.

On June 20, 1803, President Thomas Jefferson asked his private secretary, Captain Meriwether Lewis, to lead an expedition from the Mississippi River to the West Coast.

Lewis agreed. As co-leader, he chose William Clark, who had once been **his commanding officer** in the army. On their **journey**, they would explore ways of opening the **fur trade**. They would try to find a **water route** across the continent that would make travel easier. They would also study the land and animals and learn more about the Indians in the West.

In 1803, President Jefferson buys the Louisiana Territory from France.

BEFORE YOU MOVE ON...

1. **Paraphrase** What was the Louisiana Purchase? What was President Jefferson's goal in sending an expedition to explore it?

---

had ruled it had it as part of their country, had control over it

risk the closing of the port take a chance that the French would stop ships from going in and out

vital very important

took possession of started to take control of

his commanding officer the person who gave him orders

water route way to go by boat

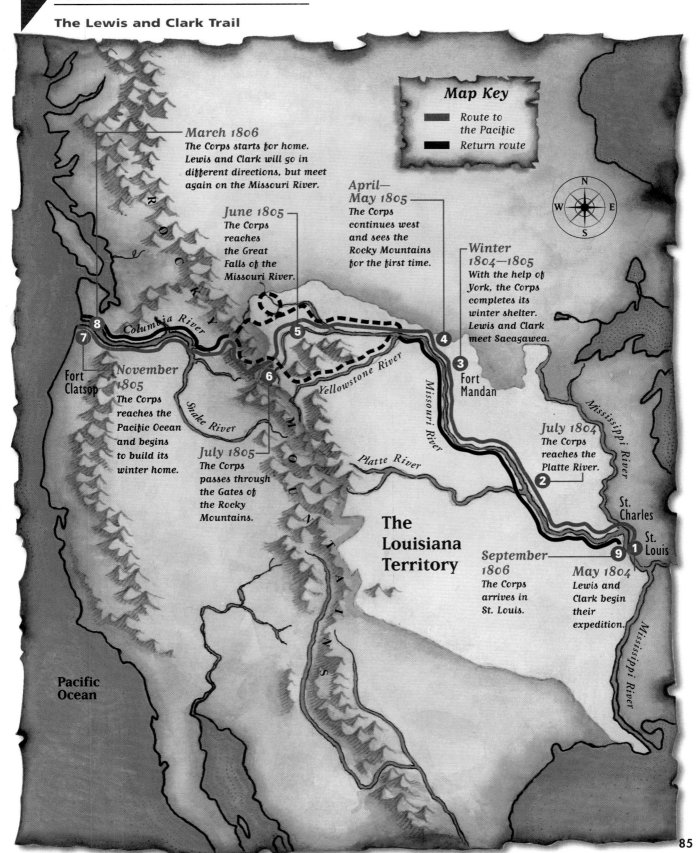

Map Key

Route to the Pacific

Return route

March 1806
The Corps starts for home. Lewis and Clark will go in different directions, but meet again on the Missouri River.

April—May 1805
The Corps continues west and sees the Rocky Mountains for the first time.

June 1805
The Corps reaches the Great Falls of the Missouri River.

Winter 1804–1805
With the help of York, the Corps completes its winter shelter. Lewis and Clark meet Sacagawea.

November 1805
The Corps reaches the Pacific Ocean and begins to build its winter home.

Fort Clatsop

July 1805
The Corps passes through the Gates of the Rocky Mountains.

July 1804
The Corps reaches the Platte River.

September 1806
The Corps arrives in St. Louis.

May 1804
Lewis and Clark begin their expedition.

The Louisiana Territory

Columbia River

Snake River

Yellowstone River

Missouri River

Platte River

Mississippi River

Mississippi River

ROCKY MOUNTAINS

Fort Mandan

St. Charles

St. Louis

Pacific Ocean

N W E S

The Expedition to the Pacific Ocean

The Corps of Discovery Takes Shape

The expedition was called the Corps of Discovery. Between December 1803 and May 1804, it **took shape** at the mouth of the Wood River, near where the Missouri and Mississippi rivers meet. Clark trained the men while Lewis spent much of his time in St. Louis, making preparations.

In the **party** were fourteen soldiers; nine volunteers from Kentucky; Clark's slave, York; two French rivermen; **an interpreter**; and Lewis's Newfoundland dog, Seaman. There were also nine rivermen and seven soldiers who went along for extra protection in the **wilderness.**

From St. Louis to the Platte River

On a rainy Monday, May 14, 1804, Clark and the men started up the Missouri. Lewis was in St. Louis and would join the expedition in a few days.

The group traveled in a fifty-five-foot keelboat and in two huge dugout canoes called pirogues. They led two horses along the **bank** to bring in **game** shot by the hunters.

keelboat

pirogue

---

took shape got organized

party group of people

an interpreter a person who changes the words said in one language into another so people can understand each other

bank land at the edge of the river

game wild animals

The boats carried clothing, tools, scientific books, medicine, rifles, goods for trading with the Indians, and a special, powerful air gun to impress them. In the event they ran out of food, Lewis had brought a thick, gooey "portable soup."

After two days, the Corps of Discovery reached St. Charles. Five days later Lewis joined them, and their journey began. The swift current and sandbars of the Missouri made rowing hard and **poling** tricky. Often the men had to tow the boats through the muddy water.

Lewis frequently walked onshore, taking notes about plants and animals. Clark stayed with the boats, mapping their course.

It got very hot. Mosquitoes, gnats, and ticks **tormented** everyone. Some of the men got sick. But the hunters kept the group well stocked with game, and on July 21, they reached the mouth of the Platte River.

Important Members of the Expedition

Meriwether Lewis actually lived in the President's House, now known as the White House, with President Jefferson and his family before the expedition. President Jefferson felt that Lewis was the only one he could trust to explore this new territory. After the successful expedition, President Jefferson made Lewis Governor of the Louisiana Territory with St. Louis as the capital.

Meriwether Lewis

William Clark was excellent at making maps. He was able to look at the land and then draw a fairly accurate map of it—a skill that not many people have.

After the expedition, Clark got married. He lived in St. Louis where he became the Superintendent of Indian Affairs.

William Clark

BEFORE YOU MOVE ON...

1. **Main Idea and Details** Provide details that support this main idea: The Corps of Discovery prepared for the long journey.

2. **Vocabulary** List all the words you find on pages 84–87 that have the root word *explore*. How does adding the endings *-ed* and *-er* change the meaning of *explore*? How does adding the prefix *un-* change the meaning of *explored*?

---

poling pushing the boats forward with poles
tormented bothered, annoyed

Through Indian Lands

High on a **bluff**, they met with Oto and Missouri Indians. Lewis and Clark couldn't understand the Indian language. Their interpreter, George Drouillard, translated the Indian sign language. Lewis gave a speech about peace and trade with Americans. He told them that the "Great Father" in Washington wanted the chiefs to visit. Then he draped medals from President Jefferson around the chiefs' necks.

Pressing on, the men began to see animals they had never even imagined: antelope and prairie dogs, a white pelican, a jackrabbit, coyotes. As trees became fewer, buffalo herds seemed to **blanket the plains**.

On August 29, the Corps met with a friendly tribe of Yankton Sioux. A few weeks later, they **discovered** that their cousins upriver, the Teton Sioux, were not so friendly. The Corps spent four **tense** days with them before meeting the more **hospitable** Arikaras, who were farmers. They admired Clark's slave, York, the first black man they had ever seen.

Toward the end of October, the expedition stopped for the winter near the villages of the Mandan and Hidatsa Indians. The men completed Fort Mandan on November 20. The fort had eight connected log cabins arranged in a V with a high fence at the open end.

Snow, ice, and below-zero temperatures made everyone **miserable**, but riverman Pierre Cruzatte lifted everyone's spirits by playing his fiddle as the group danced at Christmas. The Mandans and Hidatsas welcomed the explorers to their large, round **lodges**. The Hidatsa chiefs told Lewis and Clark what they knew about the geography of the Rocky Mountains.

---

bluff high steep cliff
Pressing on Moving forward
blanket the plains cover the open, flat land
tense nervous, stressful
hospitable friendly
miserable very unhappy, very uncomfortable
lodges homes

Important Members of the Expedition

York

Although York was Clark's slave, he was a well-respected member of the expedition, using his strength and power to help the group survive in the wilderness. In fact, Lewis and Clark were able to build good relations with many Native American tribes because the people were so curious about York. They were amazed by York's black skin, size, and strength.

In 1811 Clark gave York his freedom. Some say York became a successful businessman, while others say he settled with the Native Americans and became a successful warrior.

A mother grizzly bear with her cubs watches for any sign of danger.

During the winter, Toussaint Charbonneau, a French Canadian living with the Hidatsas, joined the expedition as an interpreter. His teenaged Shoshone wife, Sacagawea, joined, too. On February 11, Sacagawea gave birth to a son, Jean Baptiste.

Past the Rocky Mountains

On April 7, 1805, Lewis and Clark sent several soldiers and rivermen back to St. Louis on the keelboat. They were to take four magpies and a prairie dog, boxes of skins and horns, Indian articles, small samples of soil and plants, and Clark's maps and charts to President Jefferson.

That same day, the Corps of Discovery **pushed on** upriver into **the unknown**. They traveled in the two pirogues and in six dugout canoes they had made during the winter.

It stayed cold, but the plains were green and game was everywhere. The Corps began to encounter grizzly bears.

Lewis first saw the Rocky Mountains on May 26. He wrote in his journal of his joy but also of "the **difficulties** which this snowy **barrier** would most probably **throw in my way** to the Pacific . . ." Already he seemed aware that no river could come close to crossing these mountains, that there would be no water route to the West Coast.

> **BEFORE YOU MOVE ON...**
>
> 1. **Sequence** Place these events in the correct time order: The men completed Fort Mandan. Lewis first saw the Rocky Mountains. The Corps met the Yankton Sioux.
> 2. **Characters' Motives** Why did the Corps build Fort Mandan?
> 3. **Paraphrase** In your own words, tell what obstacles the Corps had to overcome as they traveled through the Indian lands and the Rocky Mountains.

....

pushed on kept going
throw in my way keep me from going forward on my path

Important Members of the Expedition

Sacagawea

Lewis and Clark may not have been able to reach the Pacific Ocean without the help of Sacagawea. She translated for them, directed them, and helped get food. She was also a sign of peace to the Native American tribes because they knew an unfriendly group would not include a woman and child.

What happened to Sacagawea after the expedition is not clear. Recently, the United States Mint has decided to honor Sacagawea by putting her picture on the newest version of the one dollar coin.

On June second the expedition came to a **fork in the river**. Which **branch** was the Missouri? If the explorers made a wrong choice, the **passes through** the Rockies might be blocked off by snow before they could reach them.

Lewis went ahead on land to explore the south fork. When he reached the Great Falls of the Missouri River on June 13, he knew he and Clark had made the right choice.

The falls were magnificent, but there were so many it took a month to get around them. With bleeding feet, the men made **makeshift** wagons and **cleared eighteen miles of undergrowth**. There were hailstorms, mosquitoes, rattlesnakes, and grizzly bears.

On July 19, the Corps passed through a huge **chasm** Lewis named the Gates of the Rocky Mountains. When they reached the Three Forks of the Missouri, Sacagawea declared that the Hidatsas had kidnapped her from the Shoshones at this very spot.

Toward the Pacific

From Sacagawea, the Corps knew they were in Shoshone territory. When they found a tribe from which they hoped to get horses, the chief, Cameahwait, turned out to be Sacagawea's brother!

Sacagawea helped interpret. The Corps traded **goods** for horses, hid their canoes by sinking them with stones, and **set out** over Lemhi Pass to the Lemhi Fork of the Salmon River.

A week later, through snow and **sleet**, they **struggled over** Lost Trail Pass into Flathead Valley and a camp they called Travelers' Rest. Then they followed the Lolo Trail across the Bitterroot Mountains.

---

fork in the river place where the river goes in two different directions

branch part, direction

passes through open paths in, ways to get through

makeshift temporary; not permanent or lasting for a long time

cleared eighteen miles of undergrowth removed the weeds and bushes growing close to the ground for a distance of eighteen miles

chasm deep gap through the mountains

goods supplies, personal property

set out went

sleet frozen rain

struggled over had a difficult time getting through

November 7, 1805.

Great joy in camp. We are in view of the ocean, this great Pacific Ocean, which we have been so long anxious to see, and the roaring made by the waves breaking on the rocky shores may be heard distinctly.

from the *Lewis and Clark Journals*

Fort Clatsop was named for the friendly local Indian tribe, the Clatsops, who came to the fort almost daily to visit and trade goods.

Wet, cold, and hungry, they could find no game. When Lewis's "portable soup" became **unbearable**, they killed and ate a colt.

The Pacific at Last

Reaching the Clearwater River, the Corps met a tribe of friendly Nez Percé, or "pierced nose," Indians. Chief Twisted Hair agreed to look after their horses until their return. On October 7th, they started down the Clearwater to the Snake and Columbia rivers in five dugout canoes they had made during their visit.

Sometimes the men lowered the canoes through the rapids on ropes. Other times they **ran the rapids** or carried everything around them. When they **glimpsed** an Indian in a sailor's jacket, they knew their goal was near. They reached the Pacific Ocean in mid-November.

It rained all winter. The men built Fort Clatsop inland from the sea. Lewis and Clark worked on their notes and journals. Everyone was bored and ill.

BEFORE YOU MOVE ON...

1. **Details** Who was Sacagawea? How did she help the Corps?
2. **Synthesis** Imagine that you are a member of the Corps of Discovery. Describe how you feel about spending the winter in Fort Clatsop.
3. **Conclusions** Why was the sailor's jacket on the Indian a good clue that the Corps had almost reached the Pacific Ocean?

---

unbearable so bad that they couldn't eat it anymore
ran the rapids rode in their canoes in the fast-moving water
glimpsed saw briefly

The Expedition Heads Home

On March 23, 1806, they started for home. If they didn't reach the Missouri before it froze, they'd be spending another winter in the wilderness.

Traveling upstream, the Corps had to **lug** the canoes around the larger rapids and tow them up the smaller ones. They visited Chief Yelleppet and the friendly Walla Walla Indians. Then they **moved out overland** and set up Camp Chopunnish fifty or sixty miles above the mouth of the Clearwater. Some of the men traded buttons from their uniforms to the Nez Percé for food. Clark traded **medical advice** and medicines.

Chief Twisted Hair returned most of their horses, and on June 15, they started back over the Lolo Trail. **Forced to turn around** because the snow was so deep, they set out again on June 24 with three Nez Percé guides. Six days of struggle brought them to Travelers' Rest.

There the expedition **separated**. With most of the group, Clark traveled south; then east to explore the Yellowstone River. With a few men, Lewis traveled east to Great Falls, then north to explore Maria's River. Lewis and Clark **caught up with one another** on the Missouri on August 12.

Going downstream on the Missouri was much easier than coming up. The Corps left Charbonneau, Sacagawea, and the baby, whom Clark had called "Pomp," with the Mandans on August 17. The Mandan chief Big White agreed to go along to Washington.

The Corps reached St. Louis on September 23, 1806. People lined up along the riverbank and cheered. **The entire nation** had thought the members of the expedition had died in the wilderness. Only President Jefferson had **held out hope** that Lewis and Clark would return.

---

lug carry

moved out overland traveled away from the river and over the land

medical advice suggestions for ways of using medicine to stop sickness and diseases

Forced to turn around Made to go back

separated went in different directions

caught up with one another met each other again

The entire nation Everyone who lived in the United States

held out hope still hoped, kept believing

Amazing Discoveries

Lewis and Clark gathered information on 178 new kinds of plants, 122 new kinds of animals, and more than 40 Indian tribes. Because of their expedition, trappers, and later settlers moved out over what would soon be a nation stretching from coast to coast.

Cynomys ludovicianus
BLACK-TAILED PRAIRIE DOG

Rubus spectabilis
SALMONBERRY

Purshia tridentata
ANTELOPE BITTERBRUSH

BEFORE YOU MOVE ON...

1. **Comparisons** How was Lewis and Clark's return journey to St. Louis different from their journey to the Pacific Ocean? How was it the same?
2. **Opinion** What do you think was the expedition's most important discovery or accomplishment?

ABOUT THE AUTHOR

Steven Kroll grew up in New York City, and after college he edited books for adults. One night he got an idea for a picture book and discovered the excitement of writing for children. Since then he has written dozens of picture books and chapter books. Through his historical books—*The Boston Tea Party, Ellis Island: Doorway to Freedom, Robert Fulton: From Submarine to Steamboat,* as well as *Lewis and Clark: Explorers of the Far West*—Steven Kroll fulfills his own desire to discover and explore fascinating stories in American history.

Respond to the Biography
Check Your Understanding

SUM IT UP

Relate Goals and Outcomes With your group, choose one section of the biography. Make a chart to show the goal for that part of the journey. Write the obstacles and the outcome. Then write a sentence to summarize that section.

Goal	Obstacles	Outcome
to explore the Louisiana Territory	strong currents sandbars heat mosquitoes, gnats, and ticks	They reached the Platte River.

Summary:
Travel was difficult, but the expedition kept going and reached the Platte River.

Identify Sequence When you're done, add your group's sentence in the correct sequence on a class time line that shows the progress of the journey.

THINK IT OVER

Discuss and Write Talk about these questions with a partner. Write the answers.

1. **Opinion** Why do you think Lewis and Clark agreed to go on the expedition?

2. **Character** What character traits helped the members of the expedition overcome the obstacles they faced on their journey?

3. **Conclusions** How would the expedition have been different without Sacagawea and York?

4. **Summary** How did the Lewis and Clark expedition contribute to the growth of the United States?

EXPRESS YOURSELF ▶ MAKE COMPARISONS

Imagine you are taking the same trip today that Lewis and Clark took 200 years ago. Tell your partner how your journey would be the same and different from the Lewis and Clark expedition.

Language Arts and Literature

▶ GRAMMAR IN CONTEXT

USE PRONOUNS

Learn About Pronouns and Antecedents
A **pronoun** is a word that takes the place of a noun. An **antecedent** is the noun that the pronoun refers to or replaces.

> **President Jefferson** worried about the French Army. **He** thought the French might attack.

A pronoun must agree in number with its antecedent.

> **Lewis and Clark** were pioneers. **They** led the expedition across the continent.

Identify Pronouns and Antecedents
Match each pronoun with its antecedent.

> The expedition was called the Corps of Discovery. It took shape at the mouth of the Wood River. Clark trained the men while Lewis spent much of his time in St. Louis, making preparations.

Practice Write each sentence. Add a pronoun.

1. The explorers pushed on into the unknown. _____ traveled in the boats they had made.

2. When Lewis first saw the Rocky Mountains, _____ wrote in his journal.

3. Sacagawea helped interpret. _____ had a brother who was a Shoshone chief.

4. Lewis and Clark reached _____ goal, the Pacific Ocean, in November.

▶ WRITING/SPEAKING

WRITE A DESCRIPTION IN A JOURNAL

Look at William Clark's journal entry on page 91. What does he describe? Imagine you are William Clark. Create three journal entries to tell about the expedition.

- Describe your preparations for the trip.
- Describe the environment along the way.
- Tell about something you discovered.

1 **Write a Draft** For each journal entry, include some interesting facts. A **fact** is a statement you can prove. Also include your opinions about what is happening. An **opinion** is a statement that tells what you think or feel about something.

2 **Edit Your Work** Look at your facts. Do they give true information about the journey? Do your opinions tell how you feel about the events and what you discovered? Also check that you've used pronouns correctly.

3 **Compare Your Entries** Share your entries with your group. Make a chart of all the facts and the opinions. How are your feelings about the expedition the same? How are they different?

Review **pronouns** on Handbook pages 437–440.

Respond to the Biography, continued

Content Area Connections

TECHNOLOGY/MEDIA

SCIENCE

DOCUMENT DISCOVERIES

Lewis and Clark discovered many new kinds of flora (plants) and fauna (animals) on their expedition. Use the Internet, encyclopedias, or other resources to research the flora and fauna. Then make a booklet to document Lewis and Clark's discoveries.

1 Locate Information These Web sites might be good places to start, but remember that new sites appear every day! Use key words in your search and look for links.

INTERNET

INFORMATION ON-LINE

Key Words:
+"Lewis and Clark" +expedition

Web Sites:
➤ **Historical Journals and Time Line**
  • www.education-world.com

➤ **Plants and Animals**
  • www.pbs.org
  • www.acnatsci.org

Download helpful information or take notes to use for your booklet.

2 Sketch the Flora and Fauna Make your own sketches or use clip art from a computer software program.

• Add the common and scientific names.

• Try to include details to tell where they were found or where they grow.

Sample Sketch

California Condor
(Gymnogyps californianus)
found near the Pacific Ocean

3 Display Your Entries Describe what you learned to your class or display the booklets in the school library.

 Learn to use the **Internet** on Handbook pages 392–393.

CALCULATE RATES OF TRAVEL

Lewis and Clark traveled about 8,000 miles. Their trip took 2 years, 4 months, and 9 days, or about 862 days. Work with a partner to find out how fast they traveled on each part of the trip.

① Study the Formula Use a formula to figure out the average distance that the expedition traveled each day:

$$\frac{\textbf{distance}}{\textbf{time}} \quad \frac{8000 \text{ miles}}{862 \text{ days}} = 9.3 \text{ miles/day}$$

average rate of speed

② Use the Formula Calculate the average rate in miles per day for each part of the journey. You might want to make a chart like this one to organize your data.

Destinations	Distance (miles)	Time (days)	Average Rate
Wood River to Fort Mandan	about 1,510	164	
Wood River to Fort Clatsop	about 3,700	551	

③ Compare Rates of Travel Now imagine that you are traveling to the same destinations—by train. Figure out the average rate in miles per day for each part of the trip if it takes

- 1 day for the train to go from a town on the Wood River to Fort Mandan, North Dakota

- 2 days to go from a town on the Wood River to Fort Clatsop, Oregon.

Add your answers to the chart. Then compare the rates of travel. What can you say about travel in the 1800s and travel today?

Space Exploration

science article
by Carole Stott

Prepare to Read

THINK ABOUT WHAT YOU KNOW

Explain a Drawing Close your eyes and picture the night sky. Draw what you "see." Explain or write about it for your group.

astronaut

gravity

launch

Manned Maneuvering Unit

orbit

routine monitoring and maintenance

satellite

scientific testing and experimentation

smoke-detection system

space laboratory

spacecraft

tether

weightlessness

LEARN KEY VOCABULARY

Relate Words and Locate Definitions Study the new words. With your group, make a chart and write the words in the right category.

Categories	Key Vocabulary Words
Technology	spacecraft
Traveling in Space	gravity
Living in Space	astronaut
Working in Space	space laboratory

Then check the meanings in the Glossary. Change any words that need to go into a different category.

LEARN TO SKIM AND TAKE NOTES

When you **skim**, you read titles or headings to get a general idea of what a selection is about. To **take notes**, you write down the important details.

> **R E A D I N G   S T R A T E G Y**
> **How to Skim and Take Notes**
> **1.** Read the section titles. Turn them into questions.
> **2.** Write each question at the top of a notecard.
> **3.** Read each section.
> **4.** Write key words and phrases to answer the questions.

Skim "Space Exploration." Use the section titles to begin seven notecards. Then take notes as you read.

Space
Exploration

by Carole Stott
with text support by Elizabeth Boylan

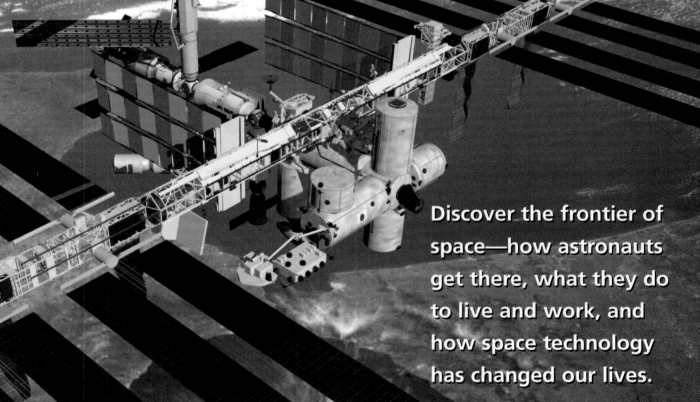

Discover the frontier of
space—how astronauts
get there, what they do
to live and work, and
how space technology
has changed our lives.

Dreams of Space

Humans have always looked into the sky and wondered about what lies beyond the Earth. For many, **curiosity** stopped there. Others dreamed of journeying into space, exploring the Moon, landing on Mars, or traveling to the stars. The dream of space travel and exploration turned to reality in the 20th century. The first practical steps were taken in the first quarter of the century as rockets were developed to blast away from Earth. In 1961, the first person reached space. By the end of the century, thousands of **spacecraft** and hundreds of space travelers had been **launched** into space. For many, the dream continues. A new generation of space travelers wants to go farther, stay longer, and learn more about space.

Fact Meets Fiction
As humans learned more about their surroundings in space, the stories of space travel became more realistic. In the late 19th century, the French author Jules Verne wrote stories using scientific fact as well as fantasy. His characters journeyed to the Moon in a shell fired by a giant cannon.

Telescope Power
Observations made in the 17th century by Galileo Galilei through the newly invented telescope showed that space was much bigger and contained more than had been thought. This helped show that humankind was not at its center.

Sky Watching
Our present knowledge of space is partly built on observations made by ancient civilizations. Thousands of years ago, basic distances were **established** and the regular movements of the Sun, Moon, and planets were used for timekeeping and to understand how Earth fits into the Universe.

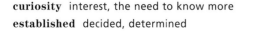

curiosity interest, the need to know more
established decided, determined

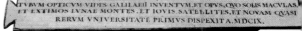

Space Travelers

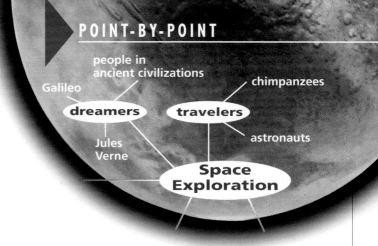

► **POINT-BY-POINT**

people in ancient civilizations

Galileo

chimpanzees

dreamers **travelers**

Jules Verne

astronauts

Space Exploration

About 350 humans and countless other living creatures have traveled from Earth into space. All but 26 people, men who went to the Moon, have spent most of their time in space in a craft **orbiting** Earth. Competition to travel into space is **keen**. When a call for **potential** European **astronauts** was made in the early 1990s, thousands of people applied. Only a handful were chosen for training. Astronauts are men and women with **an outstanding ability** in a **scientific discipline,** who are both mentally and physically fit. Originally, biologically similar animals were sent into space to test conditions for the first human flight. Now, along with insects, they accompany astronauts and are used for research.

Ham

Chimpanzees were chosen for space travel because their **genetic makeup** is similar to humans' and because they could be trained to perform tasks. Ham was the first to travel, in January 1961. On his return, he was examined and found to be **in excellent condition.**

Untethered Flight

Astronauts venturing outside their spacecraft need to be either **tethered** to the craft or wear a **Manned Maneuvering Unit** (MMU). It is a powered backpack for traveling free in space. Without it, the astronauts would be "lost" in their own orbit around Earth.

BEFORE YOU MOVE ON...

1. **Details** How did Galileo's observations change people's understanding of space?

2. **Opinion** Why do you think so many people in the early 1990s wanted to be astronauts?

3. **Inference** Why is a Manned Maneuvering Unit important to an astronaut in space?

---

keen great

potential possible

an outstanding ability a great skill or talent

scientific discipline subject in science

genetic makeup arrangement of genes and chromosomes. Genetic make-up determines one's inherited features.

in excellent condition very healthy

Living in Space

All the things that we do on Earth to stay alive are also done by astronauts in space. Astronauts still need to eat, breathe, sleep, keep clean and healthy, and use the toilet. Everything needed for these activities is transported to, or made in, space. The main difference between life on Earth and life in space is **weightlessness**. Seemingly simple, everyday tasks, such as breathing, need to be carefully thought out. As the astronauts use up oxygen and breathe out carbon dioxide, they are in danger of **suffocating**. Fresh oxygen is circulated through the craft. Water vapor from the astronauts' breath is collected and recycled for use in experiments and for drinking.

What's on the Menu?
Meals are prepared long before launch. Packaged foods may be ready to eat, or need warming, or need water added. Many foods, such as cornflakes, meatballs, and lemon pudding, are similar to those on a supermarket shelf. Fresh foods are eaten at the start of a trip or when delivered by visiting astronauts. Food packages are held on trays.

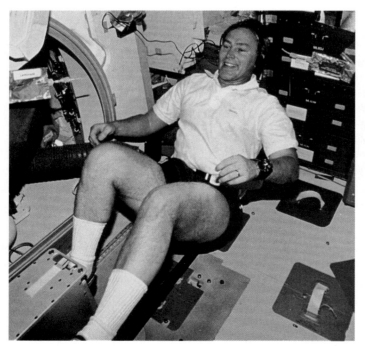

Time in the Gym
The upward movement of fluids in an astronaut's body may cause excretion of more urine by the kidneys, upset of the **body's salt concentration**, and loss of **muscle tissue and function**. About two hours of daily exercise helps to **counteract** this. Here exercise and experiment are combined as the astronaut's condition is monitored.

---

suffocating dying due to lack of oxygen
body's salt concentration amount of salt in the body's fluids

muscle tissue and function fibers that give the body strength and the ability to move
counteract reverse the bad effects of

Astronauts at Work

A working day for astronauts could be spent inside or outside the spacecraft. Inside, **routine monitoring and maintenance** on the craft are carried out alongside **scientific testing and experimentation**. Activities such as **investigating** the effects of space travel on the human body, testing new products for use in space, and doing research in food production will benefit future space generations. Commercial organizations send experiments into space to be performed in weightlessness. Work outside a craft is called Extravehicular Activity (EVA). Out in space astronauts are either tethered to their craft or wear a Manned Maneuvering Unit (MMU), a powered backpack. They might be **deploying satellites**, setting up experiments, or building new space stations.

POINT-BY-POINT

Space Exploration

travelers

chimpanzees

astronauts

live in space
- eat, breathe, sleep
- keep clean
- stay healthy
- use toilet

work in space
- do repairs
- do scientific tests
- do experiments and research

Orders from Below

Astronauts are assigned tasks on a **mission** long before they leave Earth. This can mean working closely with the scientists and engineers who have designed and produced experiments in the months prior to launch. Once the astronauts are in space, the scientists wait anxiously on Earth for the successful completion of the mission. In the meantime, they stay in touch with the scientists on the ground.

investigating finding out
deploying sending into space
mission flight

Steady as She Goes

Astronauts Dale Gardner and Joseph Allen, of the U.S., made the first-ever satellite rescue in November 1984. Wearing an MMU to steer himself, Gardner approached Westar, the second of two communications satellites in incorrect orbits. Once it was captured, he secured it to the space shuttle, to be returned to Earth for refitting and relaunch.

BEFORE YOU MOVE ON...

1. **Main Idea and Details** Give three details that support this main idea: Astronauts must do all the things people on Earth must do in order to stay alive.

2. **Details** If you were an astronaut working in space, what would your day be like? Make a list of your activities.

Space Stations

A space station is a space home. Astronauts can be on board for months at a time. They carry out experiments, make observations, and **collect valuable data** on how humans **cope with** long-term space life. The records for the most hours in space and longest unbroken stay by one person were made on a station called Mir. It was Russia's eighth space station; the earlier ones were all named Salyut. The U.S. had one station in the 1970s, Skylab. In the future astronauts from many different countries will work together on a space station called the International Space Station.

Look After Yourself

For some experiments in the space stations, the astronauts are both the scientists and the subjects of their investigations. Their job is to see how human bodies—their own—cope with the space environment. On Earth, **gravity** pulls things toward its surface and so provides a **visual reference for up and down**. In space, there is no up and down.

Space Union

In June 1995, an American space shuttle, *Atlantis*, docked with Mir for the first time. Together they made the largest spacecraft ever in orbit. On board were the seven astronauts who had arrived on *Atlantis*, and three other astronauts who were already in Mir. These three prepared for re-entry into gravity after more than three months in space. They returned to Earth with the results of the experiments they had done while in space.

---

collect valuable data gather useful information
cope with adapt to

visual reference for up and down way to tell by looking which direction is up and down

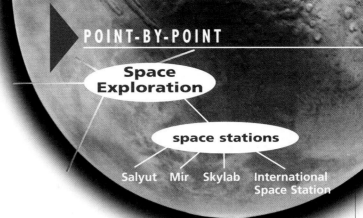

▶ POINT-BY-POINT

Space Exploration

space stations

Salyut   Mir   Skylab   International Space Station

The International Space Station

The United States, Canada, Russia, Japan, the 11 nations in the European Space Agency (ESA), and Brazil are working together to create the International Space Station. This **computer-generated image** shows how it could look in space. Astronauts in the International Space Station will study more about how being in space for a long time affects the human body. They will also test new space technology. What they learn will help prepare people in the future to go to Mars and beyond!

Space Laboratories

There will be several **space laboratories** in the International Space Station. Astronauts will research ways to fight diseases like diabetes, cancer, and AIDS. They will also be able to discover new products and ways to make things. These laboratories will also give the scientists a unique way to observe the Earth and its environment.

BEFORE YOU MOVE ON...

1. **Making Decisions** If you had the chance, would you live in a space station? Why or why not?

2. **Summary** What will the International Space Station be used for?

....

computer-generated image picture made by a computer

Space Technology on Earth

Space industry research is used to benefit our everyday lives. Technologies and techniques designed for use in space have been **transferred to or adapted for** life on Earth, often in fields **totally unrelated to** the original research. An everyday item such as food wrapping was developed from reflective film used on satellites. Car-control systems used by one-handed drivers came from the one-handed technique used in the **Lunar Rover**. Modern **smoke-detection systems** use technology developed for smoke detection on the Skylab space station. Tens of thousands of **spin-offs** have come from space research. Many of them have been adapted for medicine.

Time Under Pressure
Space spin-offs are everywhere in daily life. Watches have digital displays **capable of surviving increased gravitational force**. Clothes are made with lightweight, thermal fabrics. Athletic footwear has stay-dry insoles, and sports helmets and shin guards are lined with shock-absorbing foam.

Bar Code Scanning
A trip to the supermarket means an encounter with space technology—from the food you buy to the scanner that reads bar codes to register the prices. Many of the ready-to-eat and dried meals introduced in the 1980s and 1990s are the result of space research.

---

transferred to or adapted for shifted to or changed for
totally unrelated to completely different from
Lunar Rover moon vehicle

spin-offs new products created from parts or ideas
capable of surviving increased gravitational force strong enough to keep from breaking when there is more pressure from gravity

The Future in Space

Space travel is going to be as familiar in the years ahead as air travel became in the 20th century. Travelers will have the choice of going as a tourist for a short stay in a hotel, or in the more distant future, setting up home in a Moon or Mars base. Astronauts will continue to explore and work from space stations. They will be joined by a new **breed** of robotic space workers operating telescopes and mining equipment on the Moon.

▶ **POINT-BY-POINT**

ready-to-eat and dried meals

digital watches

new fabrics and clothing

food wrapping

products from space technology

Space Exploration

bar code scanners

car-control systems

smoke-detection systems

future in space

holiday resort

Holiday Resort
Japanese businessmen are planning an Earth-orbiting hotel, followed by one on the Moon. It will be a base for spacewalks, sightseeing tours to the Moon, and unique sports and games in weightlessness.

breed type, variety, kind

BEFORE YOU MOVE ON...

1. **Main Idea and Details** Give at least three details that support this main idea: Space research has been used to benefit us in our everyday lives.
2. **Comparisons** Compare the ways ordinary people travel today with the ways they might travel in the future. List the similarities and differences.

ABOUT THE AUTHOR

Carole Stott discovered a favorite topic, astronomy, and now there's no limit to what she shares about that topic with young readers. She has written or edited numerous books to help children explore and understand outer space, including *Observing the Sky, New Astronomer,* and *Images of the Universe.* She wrote *Celestial Charts: Antique Maps of the Heavens,* to show how people viewed the sky long ago.

Respond to the Article
Check Your Understanding

SUM IT UP

Relate Main Ideas and Details Use your notes to add the details that tell more about the main ideas on the diagram.

Tree Diagram

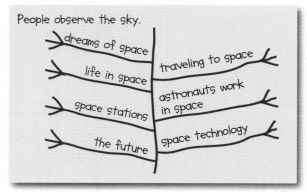

People observe the sky.
- dreams of space
- life in space
- space stations
- the future
- traveling to space
- astronauts work in space
- space technology

Write a Paragraph Turn the words for one main branch into a **main idea sentence**. Use the details to write the rest of the paragraph.

Example:

   People in ancient times dreamed and wondered about outer space. Galileo used a powerful telescope and discovered that Earth was not at the center of the universe. Jules Verne wrote fiction about space. Other people observed the sky and used the movement of the planets to tell time. People still dream about space and they want to learn more about it.

THINK IT OVER

Discuss and Write Talk about these questions with a partner. Write the answers.

1. **Opinion** What do you think are the most important discoveries people have made about space? Explain your answer.

2. **Personal Experience** What kind of discovery would you like to make? Why?

3. **Characters' Motives** Why do people continue to push past the frontier?

4. **Comparisons** Lewis and Clark and the astronauts all had to prepare for their expeditions. How were their preparations alike? How were they different?

EXPRESS YOURSELF
▶DESCRIBE AND PERSUADE

Work with a group to create a radio advertisement for the latest space hotel. Use persuasive language and descriptive details to make your listeners want to stay there.

Language Arts and Literature

USE VERBS

Learn About Verbs An **action verb** tells what the subject does.

> Many people **dream** about space exploration.

A **linking verb** connects the subject of a sentence to a word in the predicate. That word can describe the subject or name it in a different way.

> A space station **looks** futuristic.
> A space station **is** a home in space.

Forms of the verb *be* are linking verbs. *Appear, look, seem,* and *feel* are also linking verbs.

If a verb is made up of more than one verb, the last verb is the **main verb**. It shows the action. The verb that comes before it is a **helping verb**.

> About 350 humans **have traveled** into space.

Identify Verbs Find each verb in this paragraph. Tell what kind of verb it is.

> Work outside a spacecraft looks dangerous. Sometimes the astronauts are tethered to the craft. Other times they wear an MMU.

Practice Write each sentence. Add a verb and write what kind it is.

1. Space research _____ helped our lives.

2. Bar code scanners _____ from space technology.

3. Thermal fabrics _____ space spin-offs.

4. Other inventions _____ life easier.

WRITE A PERSONAL NARRATIVE

Imagine that you went on a vacation to the first space hotel. Tell about the hotel and your experiences there by writing a personal narrative.

1 **Write Your Draft** Look back at "Space Exploration" for ideas. Make a list of the things you could do or see at a space hotel. Pick out one or two to write about. Because a personal narrative is a story that tells about you, write it in the first person.

2 **Edit Your Work** Did you use first-person pronouns? Did you describe what happened and how you felt?

3 **Share Your Work** Tape record your narrative. Play some space-sounding music in the background. Put your tape and a paper copy of your narrative in the listening center. Invite your friends to listen or read along!

Sample Narrative

My Vacation with the Stars

I had a great time at the Hotel Pegasus, which is in orbit near the Deep Space Twelve space station. One of my favorite places at the hotel was the Gravity-Free Room. All of the furniture is bolted to the floor—and to the ceiling! I floated and tumbled all around. It was fun to try to catch a ball without gravity.

Review **pronouns** on Handbook pages 437–440.

Respond to the Article, continued

Content Area Connections

SOCIAL STUDIES
SPEAKING

SIMULATE A SPACE COMMUNITY

Imagine living and working with several other people in an area about the size of your classroom. You're together day and night, maybe for months—with no way out!

Astronauts living aboard a space station have to be able to get along well with each other and work out their differences. Could you live like an astronaut? Try this experiment to find out.

1 Create a Small Space With your group, mark off a section of the classroom with masking tape. Stay together inside the area for an hour. Do all of the things you would usually do—work, play, read, or study.

2 Share the Results Discuss these questions.

- What did you like about being in the small space? What didn't you like?

- How did your group members get along? What did you do when there was a disagreement?

- What suggestions do you have about getting along?

3 Compare Results with an Astronaut Find out how the real astronauts deal with living in space. Go to the NASA Internet home page at **www.nasa.gov**. Then find the link for chatting with an astronaut.

TECHNOLOGY/MEDIA
SCIENCE

RESEARCH SPACE TECHNOLOGY

Find out the latest space technology and write a new section for the "Space Exploration" article.

1 Choose a Topic Look through the selection for ideas, or think of a new topic.

2 Do Your Research Look in the *Readers' Guide to Periodical Literature* for current articles about your topic or try some of these Web sites. Remember that Web sites change frequently. If you can't access one site, try another one.

INTERNET

INFORMATION ON-LINE

Web Sites:
➤ **Space Sites**
- www.nasa.gov/kids.html
- www.challenger.org

Download helpful information and pictures.

3 Write Your Article Combine text and pictures to create your article. Share your article with your classmates.

 Learn to use the **Internet** on Handbook pages 392–393.

Roads Go
Ever Ever On

poem
by J.R.R. Tolkien

Prepare to Read Poetry

THINK ABOUT WHAT YOU KNOW

Draw a Picture Imagine you are traveling on a familiar road, highway, or trail. Draw a picture of it. Add details that show what you see along the way. How do you feel as you travel along?

sea ocean

see look at; understand

sewn worked with a needle and thread

sown sprinkled, scattered

son male child in a family

sun star around which Earth and the other planets revolve

LEARN KEY VOCABULARY

Use Context Clues to Meaning Study the sound-alike words. Tell your partner a sentence that uses one of the words. Can your partner identify which definition of the word you mean? Repeat for all of the words.

LEARN ABOUT SYMBOLISM

A **symbol** is something that stands for a feeling, mood, or idea. Poets use **symbolism** to give their words a deeper meaning. For example, in the poem you will read, the road is a symbol for life's journey.

> ### READING STRATEGY
> **How to Interpret Symbols**
> 1. Read the poem.
> 2. Find the symbols the poet uses.
> 3. Tell what the symbols mean.
> 4. Reread the poem with the symbolism in mind.

As you read "Roads Go Ever Ever On," use a chart to help you think about what the symbols mean.

What the Poet Says	What the Poet Means
Roads go over rock.	Life can be hard.

Roads Go Ever Ever On

from *The Hobbit*

Roads go ever ever on,
    Over rock and under tree,
By caves where never sun has shone,
    By streams that never find the sea;
Over snow by winter sown,
    And through the merry flowers of June,
Over grass and over stone,
    And under mountains in the moon.

— *J. R. R. Tolkien*

Respond to the Poem

Discuss Talk about these questions with a partner.

1. **Rhyme** How does the use of rhyme add to the sense of movement in the poem?

2. **Comparisons** What other things could be used to symbolize life's joys, adventures, and challenges?

3. **Personal Experience** Where do you expect your life's road to lead? What do you look for when you are choosing what road to take?

EXPRESS YOURSELF
▶ CHORAL READING

With your group, decide how to present "Roads Go Ever Ever On" as a choral reading. Practice your reading, and then perform it for your classmates.

ABOUT THE POET

British author **J. R. R. Tolkien** (Tohl-KEEN) wrote "Roads Go Ever Ever On" in his world-famous book *The Hobbit*. He once said, "I am in fact a hobbit in all but size. I like gardens, trees, and unmechanized farmlands." As a child he explored the English countryside. He found an outlet for his creativity by making up languages. As an adult he taught ancient languages and studied the myths and legends of Northern Europe. When he wrote, he drew upon his hobbies and interests to enrich his fantasy worlds.

A Personal Journey

- How is life like a journey? What discoveries can you make about yourself along the way?

- What do you do when you encounter a culture that's different from your own? Why?

- How does your cultural background influence your values and beliefs?

THEME-RELATED BOOKS

Tea with Milk
by Allen Say

The story of a Japanese American who struggles to understand her cultural identity when her family moves to Japan.

NOVEL

In the Year of the Boar and Jackie Robinson
by Bette Bao Lord

Arriving in New York in 1947, a young Chinese immigrant starts to feel at home when she discovers baseball and the Brooklyn Dodgers.

America Street
edited by Anne Mazer

An anthology of contemporary short stories about growing up in America's diverse society.

Build Language and Vocabulary

TELL A STORY

Study the painting and read the saying. What do you think the saying means?

Persistent Sea No. 2, by O. Louis Guglielmi, oil on canvas.

When one door closes, another opens.

— *Traditional saying*

 Now listen to the story.

MAKE A SEQUENCE CHAIN

Think about the doors that have closed and opened in your life. Make a sequence chain to show how one closing led to one or more openings.

Sequence Chain

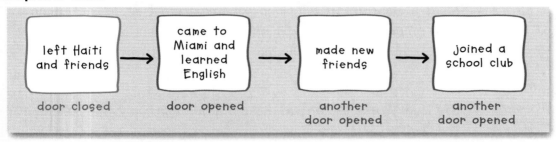

left Haiti and friends → came to Miami and learned English → made new friends → joined a school club

door closed / door opened / another door opened / another door opened

---

BUILD YOUR VOCABULARY

Culture Words When students move from a home country to the U.S., doors open into a new culture. Write the word *culture* and its meaning in your notebook.

> **cul·ture** (kul´chər) *n.* The arts, beliefs, and customs that make up a way of life for a group of people.

Now write as many words and phrases as you can think of that tell what you or a classmate may have discovered about the American way of life. Add to your lists as you go through the unit.

USE LANGUAGE STRUCTURES ▶ COMPLEX SENTENCES

Writing: Tell a Personal Story Think about your encounters with other cultures. Use complex sentences to tell about them. Use words from the **Word Bank**.

Example:
Nina and I were excited **because** we were wearing our fancy dresses for the first school dance. **When** we walked into the gym, we were surprised to see that all of the other girls were wearing jeans.

Word Bank

although
because
if
since
so
until
when
where

Something to Declare

autobiography
by Julia Álvarez

Prepare to Read

THINK ABOUT WHAT YOU KNOW

Make a Class Graph Is looking like everyone else important? Create a bar graph to show your opinions. What conclusions can you draw?

LEARN KEY VOCABULARY

Use New Words in Context Read the words and study the definitions. Then write the paragraph, adding the missing words.

Last night, I watched a beauty _____(1)_____ on TV. Each state had one _____(2)_____ , and every girl was a real _____(3)_____ to look at. We looked for _____(4)_____ to predict the winner. All the contestants looked their best, and every _____(5)_____ of every face was pretty. One contestant _____(6)_____ the judges and had to leave the stage. Another contestant sang a beautiful song and _____(7)_____ me to take singing lessons again. All the contestants had _____(8)_____ feelings of worry as they waited _____(9)_____ to see who would win.

LEARN TO SUMMARIZE

A **summary** tells the most important ideas in a story and helps you remember what you read.

READING STRATEGY
How to Summarize

1. Make a list of important details in each section of the story.

2. Read through your list and put a check next to the details that are most important.

3. Write a summary statement that uses these important details and tells the main idea of the section.

As you read "Something to Declare," collect important details for each section and write a summary statement.

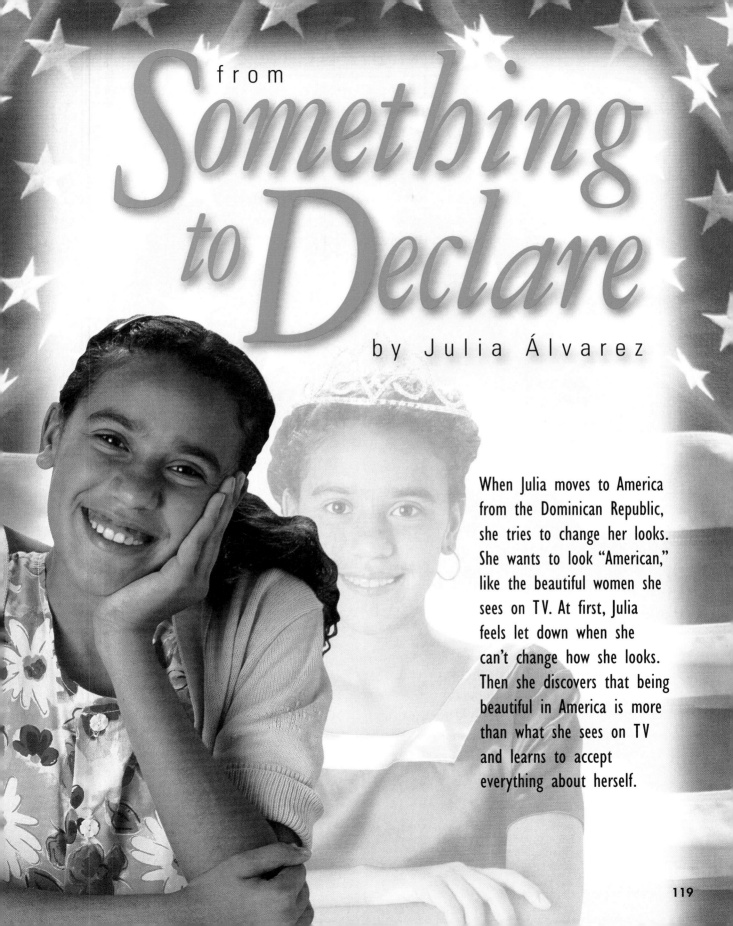

from

Something to Declare

by Julia Álvarez

When Julia moves to America from the Dominican Republic, she tries to change her looks. She wants to look "American," like the beautiful women she sees on TV. At first, Julia feels let down when she can't change how she looks. Then she discovers that being beautiful in America is more than what she sees on TV and learns to accept everything about herself.

Julia and her sisters, who have just arrived in America, watch the Miss America contest on TV. They search for clues that will help them look "American."

As young teenagers in our new country, my three sisters and I searched for **clues** on how to look as if we belonged here. We collected magazines, studied our classmates and our new TV, which was where we discovered the Miss America contest.

Watching the **pageant** became an annual event in our family. Once a year, we all plopped down in our parents' bedroom, with Mami and Papi **presiding** from their bed. In our nightgowns, we watched the fifty young women who had the American look we **longed for**.

The beginning was always the best part—all fifty **contestants** came on for one and only one appearance. In alphabetical order, they stepped forward and enthusiastically introduced themselves by name and state. "Hi! I'm! Susie! Martin! Miss! Alaska!" Their voices **rang with false cheer**. There they stood, fifty puzzle pieces forming the pretty face of America.

We were beginning to feel at home. Our **acute** home-sickness had passed, and now we were like people recovered from a shipwreck, looking around at our new country, glad to be here. "I want to be in America," my mother hummed after we'd gone to see West Side Story, and her four daughters chorused, "OK by me in America."

Our teachers and classmates at the local Catholic schools referred to us as "Porto Ricans" or "Spanish." No one knew where the Dominican Republic was on the map.

No one knew where the Dominican Republic was on the map.

---

presiding being in charge

longed for wished for, wanted

rang with false cheer sounded like they were trying to be happy even though they really were not

"South of Florida," I explained, "in the same general **vicinity** as Bermuda and Jamaica." I could just as well have said west of Puerto Rico or east of Cuba or right next to Haiti, but I wanted us to sound like a vacation spot, not a Third World country, a place they would **look down on**.

Although we wanted to look like we belonged here, the four sisters, our looks didn't seem to fit in. We complained about how short we were, about how our hair frizzed, how our figures didn't curve like those of the bathing beauties we'd seen on TV.

"The grass always grows on the other side of the fence," my mother scolded. Her daughters looked fine just the way they were.

But how could we trust her opinion about what looked good when she couldn't even get the sayings of our new country right? No, we knew better.

In 1960 when Julia came to the U.S., she saw contestants like these in the Miss America pageant. Today's contest includes beautiful American women from many cultural backgrounds.

BEFORE YOU MOVE ON...

1. **Details** Where did Julia and her sisters find clues on how to look?

2. **Character's Motive** Why did Julia choose to say that the Dominican Republic was near Bermuda and Jamaica?

3. **Cause and Effect** Why did the girls feel as if they didn't "fit in"?

---

vicinity area, neighborhood
look down on not have a good opinion about

BECOMING AMERICAN

The four sisters argue with their mother and do
everything they can to change themselves.

We would have to translate our looks into English, iron and tweeze them out, straighten them, mold them into Made-in-the-U.S.A. **beauty**.

So we **painstakingly** rolled our long, curly hair round and round, using our heads as giant rollers, ironing it until we had long, shining shanks, like our classmates and the contestants, only darker. Our skin was **diagnosed** by beauty consultants in department stores as **sallow**; we definitely needed a strong **foundation** to tone down that olive. We wore tights even in the summer to hide the legs Mami would not let us shave. We begged for permission, dreaming of the contestants' long, silky limbs. We were ten, fourteen, fifteen, and sixteen—merely children, Mami explained. We had long lives ahead of us in which to shave.

We **defied** her. Giggly and red-faced, we all pitched in to buy a big tube of hair remover cream at the local drugstore. That night we crowded into the bathroom, and I, the most **courageous** along these lines, offered one of my legs as a guinea pig.

When it didn't become **gangrenous** or fall off as Mami had predicted, we creamed the other seven legs. We beamed at each other; we were one step closer to that runway, those flashing cameras, those oohs and ahhs from the audience.

Mami didn't even notice our smooth legs; she was too busy disapproving of the other changes. Our clothes, for one. "You're going to wear *that* in public!" She'd **gawk**, as if to say, What will the Americans think of us?

---

painstakingly very carefully
diagnosed looked at to see if there is a problem
sallow grayish, greenish, or yellowish in color
foundation thick makeup for the face

courageous brave, fearless
gangrenous diseased
gawk look at us with surprise and without understanding

"This *is* what the Americans wear," we would argue back.

But the dresses we had picked out made us look cheap, she said, like bad, fast girls. She preferred her choices: **fuchsia** skirts with matching vests, flowered dresses with bows at the neck or gathers where you wanted to look slim, everything bright and busy, like something someone might wear in a foreign country.

My mother never seemed to have a favorite contestant. She was an ex-beauty herself, and no one seemed to measure up to her high standards. She liked the good girls who had common sense and talked about their education and about how they owed everything to their mothers. "Tell that to my daughters," my mother would **address the screen**, as if none of us were there to hear her. If we challenged her—how exactly did we *not* appreciate her?—she'd **maintain a wounded silence** for the rest of the evening. Until the very end of the show, that is, when all our disagreements were forgotten and we waited **anxiously** to see which of the two finalists holding hands on that near-empty

We would have to translate our looks into English.

stage would be the next reigning queen of beauty. We were hardly strangers to this **ritual** of picking the beauty. In our own family, we had a running competition as to who was the prettiest of the four girls. We **coveted** one another's best **feature**: the oldest's dark, almond-shaped eyes, the youngest's great mane of hair, the third oldest's height and figure. I didn't have a preferred feature, but I was often voted the cutest, though my oldest sister liked to remind me that I had the kind of looks that wouldn't age well. Although she was only eleven months older than I was, she seemed years older, ages wiser. She bragged about the new kind of math she was learning in high school, called algebra, which she said I would never be able to figure out. I believed her. Dumb and ex-cute, that's what I would grow up to be.

BEFORE YOU MOVE ON...

1. **Details** What did the girls do to try to change their looks?

2. **Inference** Why did Julia's mother feel unappreciated?

3. **Personal Experience** How are Mami's opinions about what to wear in America the same as your parents? How are they different?

---

fuchsia bright, reddish purple
address the screen talk to the television set
maintain a wounded silence not say anything because she felt hurt

ritual tradition, custom
coveted wanted to have

Julia learns that her new life brings change and greater opportunities.
She experiences feelings of discomfort as well as acceptance.

*A*s for the prettiest Miss America, we sisters kept our choices secret until the very end. The range was limited—pretty white women who all *really* wanted to be wives and mothers. But even the small and **inane** set of options these girls represented seemed **boundless** compared with what we were used to. We were being **groomed** to go from being dutiful daughters to being dutiful wives. No stops along the way, no careers, no colleges, no shared apartments with girlfriends, no boyfriends, no social lives. But the young women on-screen, who were being held up as models in this new country, were in college, or at least headed there. They wanted to do this, they were going to do that with their lives. Sometimes there would even be a contestant headed for law school or medical school. If one good thing came out of our watching this yearly parade of American beauties, it was that subtle permission we all felt as a family: a good girl could **excel** outside the home and still be a winner.

Every year, the queen came down the runway in her long gown with a **sash** like an old-world general's belt of ammunition. When she stopped at the very end of the stage and the camera zoomed in on her misty-eyed beauty and the credits began to appear on the screen, I always felt let down.

I knew I would never be one of those girls, ever. It wasn't just the blond, blue-eyed looks or the beautiful, leggy figure. It was who she was—an American—and we were not. We were foreigners, dark-haired and dark-eyed with olive skin that could never, no matter the sun blocks or foundation makeup, be made into peaches and cream.

A good girl could excel outside the home and still be a winner.

---

inane silly, ridiculous
boundless with no limit or end
groomed prepared, taught, trained

excel do well, do something important
sash long ribbon worn across one shoulder and down to the waist

We were not able to see into the future then, beyond our noses, which we thought weren't the right shape; beyond our curly hair, which we wanted to be straight; and beyond the screen, which **inspired** us with **a limited vision** of what was considered beautiful in America. Soon ethnic looks would be in. Even Barbie, that **quintessential** white girl, would suddenly be available in different shades of skin color with bright, colorful outfits that looked like the ones Mami had picked out for us.

....

a limited vision only a part of the view; not the full picture

quintessential best example of a

BEFORE YOU MOVE ON...

1. **Paraphrase** In your own words, tell the one good thing that resulted from watching the Miss America contest.

2. **Character** Describe Julia's feelings when the queen came down the runway.

3. **Predictions** What changes in American culture would later affect Julia's first impressions about who and what was considered beautiful in America?

ABOUT THE AUTHOR

Julia Álvarez left the Dominican Republic with her family and arrived in New York City at the age of 10. In America, she discovered that books helped her adjust to her new homeland and they helped her create a world in which she didn't feel isolated. Even though her traditional Dominican family raised her to be a housewife, she knew that she wanted to be a writer by the time she was in high school. Since 1984, Julia Álvarez has published many award-winning essays, poems, and stories based on her experiences as an immigrant.

Respond to the Autobiography

Check Your Understanding

SUM IT UP

Summarize Each Section Use important details to complete a summary statement for each section of the autobiography.

1 Wanting to Belong	2 Becoming American	3 Coming to Terms
Details	Details	Details
Summary Statement	Summary Statement	Summary Statement

Summarize the Selection Put all your summary statements together to create a summary for the entire autobiography. Combine short sentences into a complex sentence to show how the ideas relate.

Example:

The sisters wanted to belong in America.
They searched for clues on how to look.

▼

Because the sisters wanted to belong in America, they searched for clues on how to look.

THINK IT OVER

Discuss and Write Talk about these questions with a partner. Write the answers.

1. **Summary** What did Julia discover about Americans? How did her discoveries change her life?

2. **Personal Experience** If you could have a conversation with Julia during her first week of school, what advice would you give her about living in America?

3. **Opinion** The saying "Beauty is in the eye of the beholder" suggests that beauty is more than just something you see on the outside. How would you define beauty?

4. **Judgments** How do you think television, radio, and other media influence people's ideas about beauty?

EXPRESS YOURSELF ▶PERSUADE

If you were Julia, how would you persuade Mami to let you wear the latest styles of clothing? Find a partner to play the role of Mami and persuade Mami to let you wear a pair of jeans.

Language Arts and Literature

USE FIGURATIVE LANGUAGE: SIMILES

Learn About Similes Sometimes a writer uses adjectives to describe someone or something.

The girls' hair was **dark**.

To give the reader a better picture, a writer might compare the color to something else.

The girls' hair was **as dark as night**.

The girls' hair was **like night**.

These comparisons, which use the words *like* or *as*, are called **similes**. Similes are one type of figurative language that helps readers see ordinary things in new ways.

Find Similes What two things does the author compare in this sentence?

> Every year, the queen came down the runway in her long gown with a sash like an old-world general's belt of ammunition.

Practice Now add a simile to complete these sentences.

1. The girls thought the Miss America contestants were as _____ as _____.
2. The girls tried to make their curly hair as _____ as _____.
3. They wanted legs that were like _____.
4. The clothes Mami preferred were like _____.

WRITE A JOURNAL ENTRY

Imagine that you are Julia. Choose an event from the story and write a journal entry about it. Use at least one simile.

1 **Write Your Draft** Make a movie in your mind of the event. Write about what happened. Describe what you see. Tell how you feel.

2 **Edit Your Work** Do your similes give a good picture of what things were like for Julia? Also look over your sentences for correct spelling and punctuation.

3 **Share Your Work in a Group** One person can read aloud a journal entry, the group can find the simile, and another person can draw a picture to go with the simile.

Journal Entry

June, 1960

Today Mami and Papi brought home a TV, a delicious treat for our eyes. We're as happy as the winners on the game shows!

Develop your skill in the **writer's craft**. See Handbook pages 414–423.

Respond to the Autobiography, continued
Language Arts and Literature

▶ VIEWING/WRITING

ANALYZE PROPAGANDA TECHNIQUES

Learn About Propaganda Many advertisers use TV to sell their products. They use propaganda techniques to convince you to think or feel a certain way.

- A **glittering generality** uses loaded words like *New! Improved! Powerful!*

- The **transfer** technique uses respected symbols or figures like the Statue of Liberty to make you feel good about a product.

- The **testimonial** technique uses well-known people like actors to try to sell something.

- A company shows **plain folks** in its ads to show that people like you use the product.

- The **bandwagon** technique makes you think everyone else is doing it so you should, too.

- Companies use negative words about the competition. That's called **name-calling**.

Be part of the "Inn" Crowd

With over 2,000 Road Palace Inns from coast to coast, it's no wonder where America's pets are choosing to stay. Every Road Palace Inn offers rooms that are a step above with comfortable beds, large sitting areas and in-room honor bar. Plus, most Road Palace Inns have a great restaurant on premise serving more than just burgers and fries.

So stay where the livin' is easy.   **Road Palace Inn**

Road Palace Inn Hotel Chain

1968 Olympic Gold Medalist Edward Cuthbert wouldn't set foot in Munich without Titans.

Step on it.

Titan Athletic Shoes

The competition only goes where the crowds are. We go where the sun is. A⚓A
NOT THE SAME PORT VISITS · NOT THE SAME CRUISE

Anchors Aweigh Cruise Lines

OAK...lovely floors for lively families

National Oak Floor Manufacturers' Association

We want YOU as a Saver

Benj. Franklin
FEDERAL SAVINGS & LOAN ASSN.

Benj. Franklin Savings and Loan

Identify Techniques Discuss the ads on these pages with a partner. Which propaganda technique does each company use to persuade people to buy its product?

New, improved formula makes your whole wash look and smell cleaner.

Better Than Ever

Vivid

Laundry Detergent

WITH COLOR ENHANCERS

Vivid Laundry Detergent

Practice Think about the propaganda around you.

1. Describe the ads you see on TV or in magazines to your partner. Which ads use which techniques? Which are most convincing?

2. Choose a product. Use each propaganda technique to create ads to sell it.

For tips on **viewing**, see Handbook page 403.

Respond to the Autobiography, continued

Content Area Connections

TECHNOLOGY/MEDIA
SOCIAL STUDIES

REPORT ON AN IMMIGRANT'S CONTRIBUTION

Like Julia Álvarez, immigrants from around the world have made great contributions to the United States. Choose a famous immigrant, research what that person has done, and then prepare a report.

1 Choose a Person Think of a famous immigrant or choose someone from this list.

Madeleine Albright	Iman
Mikhael Baryshnikov	Midori
Liz Claiborne	Frank Oz
Gloria Estefan	I.M. Pei
Patrick Ewing	An Wang

2 Get Organized Make a K-W-L chart to record what you know and what you want to learn about the person.

| K
What I Know | W
What I want
to Learn | L
What I
Learned |
|---|---|---|
| Gloria Estefan is from another country. | Where is she from? | |
| She sings the song "Conga." | What influenced her to sing that kind of music?

What impact has her music had on U.S. culture? | |

3 Gather Information and Take Notes These Web sites might be a good place to start. Remember that new sites appear every day! Use the name of the person as the key word in your search.

INTERNET

INFORMATION ON-LINE

Web Sites
➤ **Sites for Biographies**
 • www.infoplease.com
 • www.biography.com

➤ **Encyclopedia Articles**
 • www.eblast.com
 • www.encarta.com

Download helpful articles and take notes in your K-W-L chart.

4 Prepare a Multimedia Report Organize your notes to present what you've learned about the immigrant's contributions. Make a poster or use a computer design program to illustrate your report.

For tips on using the **Internet**, see Handbook pages 392–393. Learn to use **word-processing software** to write your report on pages 383–389.

Between **two** WORLDS

collection
of poems

Prepare to Read Poetry

THINK ABOUT WHAT YOU KNOW

Quickwrite Your cultural background and the backgrounds of your parents often influence who you are. Do you have one or more cultural backgrounds? Write a sentence or two in your notebook to tell about your background.

free 1. *adj.* not under someone else's control 2. *adj./adv.* without cost

land 1. *n.* part of the Earth's surface that is not covered by water, the ground 2. *v.* bring or come to the shore 3. *v.* come down or bring to rest on a surface

roots 1. *n.* plant parts that grow under the ground 2. *n.* beginnings of a family, ancestry 3. *v.* cheers for people in a contest

LEARN KEY VOCABULARY

Use Context Clues Study the new words and their definitions. Read the paragraph. Use the words around each underlined word to figure out its meaning.

Last summer I discovered a lot about my <u>roots</u> and my family's history. Some of my ancestors were slaves. Others were <u>free</u> farmers who grew crops on the <u>land</u> between the North and the South. Although their lives were different, they all believed in doing what was best for their families.

LEARN TO READ POETRY

Some poets use **free verse,** or lines that do not rhyme and do not have a regular rhythm. Still, the words in the poem flow in an appealing way and communicate the poet's message.

> ### READING STRATEGY
> **How to Read a Free-Verse Poem**
> 1. Preview the poem by looking at its shape and length.
> 2. Read the poem aloud to discover how it sounds.
> 3. Picture what the poet is saying.
> 4. Read the poem again and again until you understand the poet's message.

As you read the poems in "Between Two Worlds," think about each poet's message and how you feel about it.

Between two WORLDS

Three poets, each on a personal journey between two cultures, share their discoveries.

Diana Chang often writes about her Chinese American identity. She was born in the U.S. and is the daughter of a Chinese father and a Eurasian mother. Today Diana Chang lives in Pennsylvania. In this poem, she uses questions and answers to help her share her feelings about her multicultural identity.

Saying Yes

"Are you Chinese?"
"Yes."

"American?"
"Yes."

"*Really* Chinese?"
"No . . . not quite."

"*Really* American?"
"Well, actually, you see. . ."

But I would rather say
yes

Not neither-nor,
not maybe,
but both, and not only

The homes I've had,
the ways I am

I'd rather say it
twice,
yes

—*Diana Chang*

BEFORE YOU MOVE ON...

1. **Summary** What is the poet saying about herself?
2. **Personal Experience** Who would you say you *really* are?

....

not quite not completely
actually in fact, really
rather instead, more willingly

Between Two Worlds   **133**

Arnold Adoff is a well-known author and poet who writes frequently about his interracial family. Arnold Adoff is Jewish, and his wife, author Virginia Hamilton, is African American and Protestant. They have a son and a daughter. In "Still Finding Out," Arnold Adoff describes his children's backgrounds through their eyes.

Still
FINDING
OUT

Finding out that Grandpa Perry
was
born a slave   and died a free
farmer
here in Ohio:
            I am
                free
here in Ohio
        on the Perry land: planting tomatoes
                    on his same land.

I am part Perry
        and
        part still
            finding
            out.

—*Arnold Adoff*

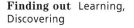

Finding out Learning, Discovering

Roots

I carry
my roots
with me
all the time
rolled up
I use them
as my pillow

—Francisco X. Alarcón

Francisco X. Alarcón grew up in both the United States and Mexico, so he considers himself to be from both countries. His binational background is so important to him that he lives in the United States and visits Mexico regularly.

BEFORE YOU MOVE ON...

1. **Inference** Which of these words describe how each speaker feels about his background? Explain your choices to a partner.

   proud   *comfortable*
   confused   *curious*

2. **Personal Experience** Who is a part of you? What are you still finding out?

Respond to the Poems
Check Your Understanding

SUM IT UP

Draw Conclusions Think about the message in each poem and complete this chart.

Poem Title	Cultural Backgrounds in the Poem	The Message
"Saying Yes"	Chinese American	Be equally proud of all your cultural backgrounds.
"Still Finding Out"		
"Roots"		

Compare Literature Study the chart and write a statement that summarizes what the messages have in common. Write another statement to tell how they are different.

THINK IT OVER

Discuss and Write Talk about these questions with a partner. Write the answers.

1. **Summary** How does each poem represent a personal journey between two or more cultures?

2. **Personal Experience** Which poem means the most to you? Why?

3. **Comparisons** Reread "Saying Yes" and "Roots." Which poet seems more confident about being "between two worlds"? Explain your answer.

EXPRESS YOURSELF ▶RECITE

Choose one of the poems to recite with a partner. Plan which parts of the poem each of you will say. You might want to:

- Read the questions for "Saying Yes" and have your partner read the answers.

- Choose the words or phrases you'll say for "Still Finding Out," and have a partner read the rest.

- Take turns saying one line of "Roots," and then say the last line together.

Practice your poem, and then recite it for the class.

Language Arts and Content Area Connections

WRITE A POEM

Create a Free-Verse Poem Borrow some lines from the poems in this collection and write a new free-verse poem of your own.

Sample Poem

> I carry my birthplace in my heart.
>
> I use it as my foundation for my new life.
>
> I am Japanese. I am American.
>
> Not neither–nor, but both.
>
> I carry my birthplace and my new place in my heart.

▶ SOCIAL STUDIES

EXPLORE GEOGRAPHY

Make a Migration Map Choose an ethnic or racial group mentioned in one of the poems. Use reference materials such as atlases, encyclopedias, and the Internet to find out the answers to these questions:

- Did the group originate in one or more countries? Which one(s)?

- What are the top five countries where members of the group live now?

- Why did these members move?

Sketch a map to highlight the origin of the group and show the migration movements.

▶ REPRESENTING/SPEAKING
▶ SOCIAL STUDIES

PICTURE A MIX OF CULTURES

As the poets have described, people from many cultures have built the face of America.

Follow these steps to make a collage and give a presentation on how a different culture has influenced life where you live.

1 **Focus on a Culture** Start by choosing a culture to investigate. Notice how that culture is represented in your city in artwork, architecture, food, clothing, agricultural practice, and so on.

2 **Create a Collage** Use photographs of places or things in your city that represent the culture. Cut out pictures from magazines and newspapers. Gather artifacts like post cards, brochures, or menus. Arrange them into a collage on a piece of posterboard.

3 **Give an Oral Report** Present your collage to your class. Explain how the culture you selected has influenced everyday life in your city.

Chinatown in Los Angeles, California

Writing That Tells a Story

Narrative writing tells a story. For one kind of narrative writing, the writer makes up characters, a setting, and events. In another kind of narrative writing, the writer tells about real people and real events.

PROFESSIONAL WRITING MODELS

"Lewis and Clark" is a **biography**—a story about a real person's life. It is written in the third person. That means that the writer, or narrator, is not part of the action.

from **"Lewis and Clark"**

On June 20, 1803, President Thomas Jefferson asked his private secretary, Captain Meriwether Lewis, to lead an expedition from the Mississippi River to the West Coast.

Lewis agreed. As co-leader, he chose William Clark, who had once been his commanding officer in the army. On their journey, they would explore ways of opening the fur trade.

A GOAL-AND-OUTCOME NARRATIVE

Many biographies tell how a person reaches a goal. In a goal-and-outcome story, you can learn about a person's goal and the challenges or obstacles the person has to overcome to reach that goal. Sometimes the person reaches the goal, and sometimes there is an unexpected outcome! Study the chart. Discuss the goals and outcomes in "Lewis and Clark."

Goal-and-Outcome Chart

SELECTION	GOALS	OBSTACLES	STRATEGIES	OUTCOMES
Lewis and Clark	explore new territory	raging rivers	built boats	traveled faster by going down the Platte and Missouri Rivers
		winter weather	built forts	survived the winter
		travel through unfriendly territory	York and Sacagawea helped develop good relations with the Indians.	got through Indian lands safely

STUDENT WRITING MODEL

Biography

Christopher Tarpeh: A Boy Who Never Gave Up!

by Vashti Smith

As the rain fell, Christopher and his mom bailed out the water that leaked into their house. They had to, or the house built of mud, sticks, and dry grass would turn into a pile of mud. This was just one of the difficult chores Christopher Tarpeh had to do as he was growing up in an African town called Jacob. Although his life was hard, Christopher was not discouraged. He always dreamed of a better life—one that he could have if he got a good education.

Christopher was born on November 28, 1956. As a child, he worked hard helping his mom on the farm. When he was only 10 years old, he carried cassava and fufu to the marketplace to sell. Then he used the money he earned to buy food which he took home and cooked on the wood stove. After eating, he washed the dishes with water that he had to carry up a steep hill to his house.

Christopher didn't let all this hard work stop him from going to school. Even after chopping wood, he walked to school. The walk to school was difficult, too. It took him three hours each way! All along the way, there were lions and snakes. On one occasion, a hungry lion chased him. Luckily, Christopher outran it! This experience scared him, but he kept going to school anyway.

One of the happiest days of Christopher's life was when he graduated from secondary school. He didn't stop there, though. Christopher went to college to be an historian although he eventually became an electronics engineer. He made his life better by getting an education and by following his own advice: "Learn how to work hard no matter how difficult your life becomes. You must never give up."

BEGINNING
The beginning sentence sparks the reader's interest. The first paragraph tells about Christopher's goal.

MIDDLE
In the middle, examples and details help to describe the obstacles Christopher faced in reaching his goal.

Dates and time words signal when the events took place.

Vashti wrote in the **third person.** She used the pronouns *he* and *they*.

ENDING
The ending tells that Christopher reached his goal and presents a thoughtful idea.

Writing That Tells a Story, continued

The Writing Process

> **WRITING PROMPT**
>
> Now you will write a goal-and-outcome narrative for your class to read. Write a biography about a person you admire.

PREWRITE

1 **Collect Ideas and Choose a Subject** What people could you write about? What are their goals? Brainstorm with a partner. You might want to record the possibilities in a chart.

People	Goals
1. Kim	get on the swim team save her allowance for a computer
2. Chang–Díaz	become an astronaut
3. Aunt Vida	start her own medical practice

Talk over your ideas; then choose a person and a goal to write about.

2 **Unlock the Writing Prompt** Before you begin writing, fill out an **FATP** chart to help guide your writing.

3 **Collect the Details** List details about your subject's goal, the obstacles, and the outcome. Look up information in reference books or on the Internet. If you know the person, you might want to conduct an interview.

4 **Get Organized** You might want to use a Goal-and-Outcome Chart like the one on page 138 to organize your details. Write the details in the order in which they happened or use numbers to show the order.

Wherever I can find a place to sit and write, that is my home.

— Mary Tallmountain

FATP Chart

HOW TO UNLOCK A PROMPT
Form: *biography*
Audience: *classmates*
Topic: *Chang–Díaz*
Purpose: *to tell how he became an astronaut*

Reflect and Evaluate

- How did talking to a partner help you decide what to write about?
- Why do you think writing about a goal is important?
- Do you have enough details to make your writing interesting?

DRAFT

Use your **FATP** chart to help you focus your writing. Write quickly just to capture your ideas, and don't worry about making mistakes.

1 **Write the Beginning** In your first paragraph, describe the goal. Start with a great beginning sentence—one that will catch your reader's attention. Try different ways to start your first paragraph.

Writer's Craft: Introductory Sentence

Express an emotion.

Just OK	Much Better
Franklin has always wanted to be an astronaut.	Franklin's dream of discovering life in outer space has compelled him to keep pushing the limits as an astronaut.

Describe an action or event.

Just OK	Much Better
When Franklin was a boy, he launched model rockets.	"Bam!" Franklin looked up. His model rocket launch was a success, but the rocket tore the rain gutter off the house!

Ask a question.

Just OK	Much Better
Did you know that Franklin Chang-Díaz has been on several space flights?	What would it be like to spend thousands of hours floating in space?

Make a startling statement.

Just OK	Much Better
Franklin could see the Earth through his window.	Franklin gazed at the tiny, round Earth floating outside his window.

2 **Write the Middle** Describe the obstacles and how you or your subject overcame them. Use the details and examples from your chart. Use dates or sequence words to show a logical order of events.

3 **Write an Ending** In your last paragraph remind your readers about your subject's goal and tell the outcomes, both expected and unexpected. End with a strong sentence.

Writer's Craft: Concluding Sentence

Express an emotion or include a thoughtful idea.

"When I'm up orbiting Earth," says Chang-Díaz, "I feel like there is nowhere else I'd rather be."

Reflect and Evaluate

- How do you feel about your draft? Will your audience enjoy reading it?
- Does your draft tell about the goal, the obstacles and the outcome?

Writing That Tells a Story, continued

REVISE

1 **Reread Your Draft** Review your **FATP**. Is your form, audience, topic, and purpose clear? Does your writing tell about a goal and how someone reached the goal?

2 **Conduct a Peer Conference** Talk to a partner or group about your writing. Can you combine any sentences to add variety to your writing? Use the guidelines on Handbook pages 411 and 417 to help you.

Look at the questions a partner asked Vashti during a Peer Conference. Read what Vashti thinks about the changes she will make.

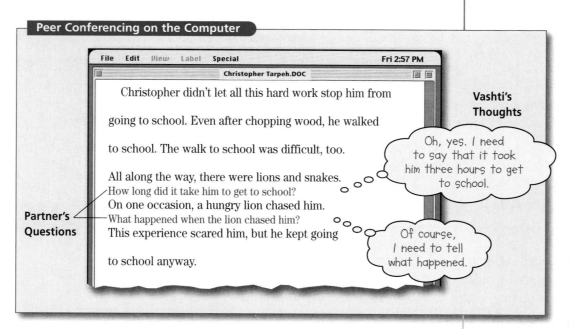

Peer Conferencing on the Computer

| File Edit View Label Special | Fri 2:57 PM |

Christopher Tarpeh.DOC

Christopher didn't let all this hard work stop him from going to school. Even after chopping wood, he walked to school. The walk to school was difficult, too.

All along the way, there were lions and snakes.
How long did it take him to get to school?
On one occasion, a hungry lion chased him.
What happened when the lion chased him?
This experience scared him, but he kept going to school anyway.

Partner's Questions

Vashti's Thoughts

Oh, yes. I need to say that it took him three hours to get to school.

Of course, I need to tell what happened.

3 **Mark Your Changes** Look at your notes and decide how you want to change your writing. Revising Marks appear on Handbook page 411. For editing on a computer, see pages 383–389.

> **Reflect and Evaluate**
>
> • Did your peers like what you wrote? What changes did they suggest?
>
> • Are you pleased with your writing?
>
> • Did you include all the details that you wanted to?

COMPOUND AND COMPLEX SENTENCES

Sentences can be classified, or grouped together, by the number of clauses they have.

A male lion looks fierce, but the female does most of the hunting.

- A **simple sentence** has one independent clause. An independent clause expresses a complete thought. It makes sense by itself.

  Examples: Africa is a large continent.

  Africa has many wild animals.

- A **compound sentence** has two or more independent clauses joined by a comma and a conjunction like **and, but,** or **or.**

  Examples: <u>Africa is a large continent</u>, **and** <u>it has many wild animals.</u>
             independent clause   **independent clause**

                  <u>Many animals eat only plants</u>, **but** <u>some animals are meat eaters.</u>
              independent clause   **independent clause**

Conjunctions in Compound Sentences

and	nor
but	for
or	yet

- A **complex sentence** has an independent clause and one or more dependent clauses. The clauses are joined by a subordinating conjunction. The independent clause expresses a complete thought. The dependent clause does not.

  Example: <u>Meat eaters are fast runners</u> <u>because they must chase their prey.</u>
            independent clause   **dependent clause**

  If the dependent clause comes first, use a comma after it.

  Example: <u>Because they must chase their prey</u>, <u>meat eaters are fast runners.</u>
            dependent clause   **independent clause**

Conjunctions in Complex Sentences

although
because
if
since
until
when
where

Practice Add conjunctions and the correct punctuation to combine each pair of sentences. Make a compound sentence or a complex sentence.

1. A group of lions is called a pride. The pride usually stays together.
2. The females do most of the hunting. The males keep the pride safe.
3. Lions are good hunters. They look lazy during the day.
4. Lions move quickly. They can catch gazelles or antelopes.
5. They like large prey. Sometimes they will eat fish.
6. They hunt before dawn. It is dark and cool out.

Writing That Tells a Story, continued

EDIT AND PROOFREAD

1 **Check for Mistakes** Look through your writing and correct any mistakes in capitalization, spelling, and punctuation. If you need help, use Handbook pages 459–469.

2 **Check Your Sentences** Look for the correct use of conjunctions.

3 **Make a Final Copy** If you are working on a computer, print out the corrected copy of your work. If not, rewrite it and make the corrections you marked.

PUBLISH

Choose one of these ideas for publishing your writing, or come up with your own idea.

- If you are using a desktop publishing program, scan and import a photo or drawing of your subject into your document. Wrap the text around the picture, and include a caption.

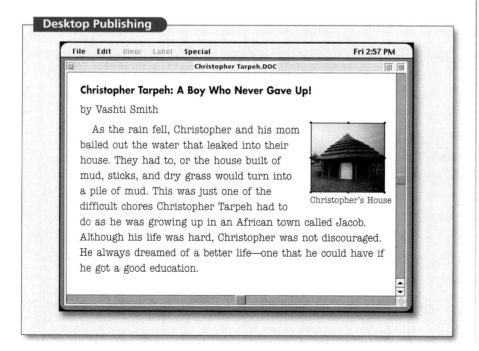

Desktop Publishing

File   Edit   View   Label   Special   Fri 2:57 PM

Christopher Tarpeh.DOC

Christopher Tarpeh: A Boy Who Never Gave Up!

by Vashti Smith

As the rain fell, Christopher and his mom bailed out the water that leaked into their house. They had to, or the house built of mud, sticks, and dry grass would turn into a pile of mud. This was just one of the difficult chores Christopher Tarpeh had to do as he was growing up in an African town called Jacob. Although his life was hard, Christopher was not discouraged. He always dreamed of a better life—one that he could have if he got a good education.

Christopher's House

- Read your biography to your classmates. Play some inspiring music softly in the background as you read.

Key In To **Technology**

After you've checked your spelling, use the spell-check feature on the computer as a double-check.

Reflect and **Evaluate**

- Are you pleased with your narrative? Does it
  - ☑ have a good beginning, middle, and ending?
  - ☑ tell about a real person's goal, obstacles, strategies, and outcomes?
  - ☑ use the third-person point of view?
- What did you like best about your writing? What did you like least?
- Will this work go in your portfolio? Why or why not?

THE FORCE of DISCOVERY

1 ▶ Look Back at the Unit

Rank Discoveries In this unit you read about people who made discoveries. What were the discoveries?

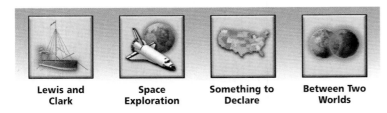

Lewis and Clark **Space Exploration** **Something to Declare** **Between Two Worlds**

Rank their discoveries from most to least important. Support your conclusions. Then, summarize the risks and benefits of each discovery.

2 ▶ Show What You Know

Sum It All Up Expand and organize your ideas on this mind map. Share your ideas about discoveries with a partner.

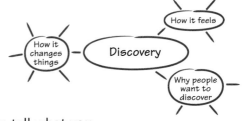

Reflect and Evaluate Finish this sentence to tell what you learned in this unit about discoveries:
When I started this unit, I didn't know that _____, but now I know_____.
Add this statement to your portfolio, along with work from the unit that reflects your accomplishments.

3 ▶ Make Connections

To Your Community Discover a part of your community that is culturally different from your own. Report back to the class on your findings. Share your knowledge of this new part of town.

Wrath

An angry heart.

八　divided

刀　knife

屮　When the heart is divided, anger develops.

Respect

The heart honors others.

廿　twenty

𦥑　pairs of hands

屮　Twenty pairs of hands symbolize twenty generations. When the heart acknowledges the wisdom of twenty generations, respect develops.

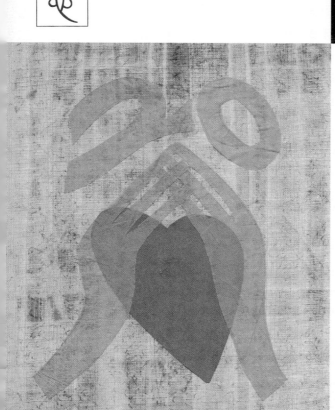

Wrath and *Respect*, Ed Young, mixed media. Copyright © 1997.

Turning
PROBLEMS into
SOLUTIONS

Wrath, or anger, leads to conflict. Respect
leads to resolution. With a group, list other
conflict-and-resolution pairs. Then create
symbols like these. What did you learn about
how to resolve conflicts?

THEME **1**
A More Perfect Union
The United States has laws that protect individual
liberties and a justice system that promotes and
ensures the peaceful resolution of conflicts.

THEME **2**
Getting to the Solution
You can always find more than one way to solve a
problem or end a conflict.

Preamble, Mike Wilkins, painted metal on vinyl and wood. Copyright © 1987.

This collage presents the words of the Preamble to the Constitution of the United States:

We, the people of the United States, in order to form a more perfect union, establish justice, insure domestic tranquillity, provide for the common defense, promote the general welfare, and secure the blessings of liberty to ourselves and our posterity, do ordain and establish this Constitution for the United States of America.

A More Perfect Union

- Why should people have rights?

- What action do you take when you think one of your rights is being abused or ignored?

- How should rights be protected? What is the role of government in resolving conflicts between individuals or groups?

THEME-RELATED BOOKS

The Wagon
by Tony Johnston

A young slave dreams of freedom and of being carried away in the wagon his father built for the master.

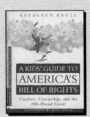

A Kids' Guide to America's Bill of Rights
by Kathleen Krull

How the Bill of Rights affects our daily life, told with short stories and amusing pictures that bring the topic to life.

Big Annie of Calumet
by Jerry Stanley

Story of a woman who fought for justice in the workplace during America's Industrial Revolution.

149

Build Language and Vocabulary
ASK FOR AND GIVE INFORMATION

This statue is the symbol of justice in the United States. What do you think the blindfold, the scales, and the sword represent?

MAKE A SYMBOL OF JUSTICE

What symbol would you use to represent justice?
Draw your own symbol, make a model, or bring
in objects that show your ideas.

BUILD YOUR VOCABULARY

Words About Government The justice system is just one part of the
government. What other words do you know about government? Make
a chart to show the words and their meanings. As you go through the unit,
add more words and their meanings to your chart.

Words About Government	Meanings
justice system	part of a country's government that makes sure everyone is treated fairly
court	place where trials are held
law	says what we can and cannot do
judge	person who decides what's right or wrong

USE LANGUAGE STRUCTURES ▶ RELATIVE CLAUSES

Writing: Explain Your Symbol Have a partner ask questions about your
symbol. Write the answers. Include relative clauses with *who*, *whom*, *whose*,
or *that* in your sentences.

   Example:

   What do the figures in your symbol stand for?
   The figures **that surround the book** show that justice is for everyone.

The Bill of Rights Rap

rhyming chant
by Anne Miranda

Prepare to Read

THINK ABOUT WHAT YOU KNOW

Idea Exchange What do you know about the beginning of the United States? Refer to pages 153–155. Discuss with your group what you know and what you learned.

amendment

Bill of Rights

Constitution

delegate

guarantee

liberty

powers

protect

retain

right

wisely penned

LEARN KEY VOCABULARY

Locate and Use Definitions Study the new words. Use the Glossary to make a personal vocabulary card for each word.

Front

Word: amendment
Definition: change made to a document
Sentence: There are many amendments to the Constitution.

Back

Amendments

LEARN TO CONNECT NEW INFORMATION TO WHAT YOU KNOW

A good way to understand a topic is to connect the new information to what you already know.

READING STRATEGY

How to Connect New Information to What You Know

1. Preview the selection. Look at the title, captions, and pictures for an idea of what it is about.
2. Think about what you already know about the topic.
3. Write questions about what you want to learn.
4. Look for answers to your questions as you read.

Fill in the **K** and **W** columns of a **K-W-L** chart for the Bill of Rights. Then, after you read "The Bill of Rights Rap," complete the **L** column.

Breaking Away from Great Britain 1763–1783

It is 1763 and the people in **colonial** America are ruled by Great Britain. Most of the colonists are content with the government until King George III passes laws that seem unfair. The colonists **protest** and begin the Revolutionary War. In 1776, the colonists write the Declaration of Independence; thus, they **declare** their freedom from British rule.

Declaration of Independence, July 4, 1776, John Trumbull William Strickland, oil on canvas.

1773

Colonists throw British tea into Boston Harbor to protest paying unfair taxes on the tea.

Boston Tea Party, anonymous, hand-colored print, 1773.

1775

Many colonists feel that war is the only way to **resolve** their differences with Great Britain. The first battle of what is later called the Revolutionary War takes place.

1776

Colonists sign the Declaration of Independence. This document states that the colonies do not have to obey the laws of Great Britain or pay taxes to the British government.

1783

The British realize they cannot win the war. They sign a peace **treaty** with the United States of America.

Preliminary Peace Negotiations with Great Britain, Benjamin West, oil on canvas, 1783.

1770   **1780**

colonial the territory called
protest complain about, show their objections to
declare announce

resolve solve, settle
treaty agreement

Gaining Rights for the People
1787–1791

After the Revolutionary War, the United States becomes **an independent nation**. Important leaders meet to plan and organize the new government. They write the **Constitution**, a document that describes the **powers** and **duties** of each part of the federal government. In 1789 it becomes law. A few years later, ten **amendments** called the **Bill of Rights** are added. The Bill of Rights **protects** the individual **rights** and freedoms of every American citizen. Since then, 17 more amendments have been added. The Constitution, including its amendments, is the highest law of our country today.

1787

The delegates sign the Constitution of the United States of America in Philadelphia.

1791

The first ten amendments, the Bill of Rights, are added to the Constitution.

1865

Slavery is abolished under the Thirteenth Amendment.

Signing of the Constitution, Thomas P. Rossiter, oil on canvas, 1787.

1750	1800	1850

---

an independent nation a country that has its own government

duties jobs, tasks, responsibilities

abolished no longer allowed, done away with

Legislative Branch

Senators and members of the House of Representatives write and pass federal laws.

Executive Branch

The President and the Vice President suggest laws, sign bills into law, and make sure the laws are obeyed.

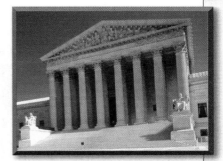

Judicial Branch

Judges and justices decide what the laws mean and if the laws are in agreement with the Constitution.

Under the Constitution, there are three **divisions**, or branches of government. Each branch has certain powers and responsibilities. New issues arise constantly; however, the United States has successfully operated under the Constitution for more than two hundred years.

1920

The Nineteenth Amendment allows for women's suffrage.

The Bill of Rights is a guarantee; consequently, Americans continue to enjoy many rights, freedoms, and privileges.

| 1900 | 1950 | 2000 |

divisions parts, sections
suffrage right to vote

privileges advantages

The Bill of Rights Rap

BY ANNE MIRANDA

The first ten amendments to the Constitution make up the Bill of Rights. These amendments guarantee many of the rights and privileges enjoyed by every American.

The BILL OF RIGHTS guarantees
our freedoms and our **liberty**.

We can go to court to **settle a score**.
That's what our system of law is for.

AMENDMENT I protects our right
to speak, meet, or pray as we like.

★ We can **worship** as we choose,
write opinions, and speak our views.

★ We have the right to meet in peace
without **disturbance** from police.

★ If we think the government's doing wrong,
we can voice our **objections** loud and strong.

AMENDMENT I

Freedom of Religion
People can worship, or not
worship, as they choose.

Freedom of Speech
Individuals can say and
write what they think.

Freedom of Assembly
Groups of people can
gather peaceably.

Freedom of the Press
People can express their ideas
and opinions in printed
documents. People cannot,
however, print things that are
untrue about others.

Freedom of Petition
People can criticize the
government. They can write
or speak to government
officials to ask for changes
or to support ideas.

The artist's inspiration
for this painting came
from a speech by
President Franklin
Roosevelt. This one
shows a man exercising
his freedom of speech.

The Four Freedoms: Freedom of Speech,
Norman Rockwell, oil illustration.
Copyright © 1943.

settle a score solve a disagreement
worship pray, practice religion

disturbance interruption
objections complaints

AMENDMENT 2 keeps our homes from harm,
by allowing the right to **keep and bear arms**.

AMENDMENT 3 was **wisely penned**
to **put breaches of privacy to an end**.

★ It used to be soldiers had the right
to eat our food and stay the night.

★ Now our government must provide
a place for soldiers to **reside**.

If the police come knocking at the door,
then we're protected by AMENDMENT 4.

★ We have the right to our personal things:
our house, our car, and our diamond rings.

★ Before the police can take what they please,
they must have a **warrant to search and to seize**.

★ **Probable cause** must be made for the **quest**,
and the same thing is true to make an arrest.

AMENDMENT 2
The Right to Bear Arms

With permission from the federal or state government, people can own weapons to protect themselves from harm.

AMENDMENT 3
Housing Soldiers

Soldiers cannot come and live in your house unless Congress passes a law that they can.

AMENDMENT 4
Search and Seizure

Police cannot arrest anyone without a good reason. Police usually need a search warrant to search homes, or take belongings to be used as evidence.

BEFORE YOU MOVE ON...

1. **Vocabulary** Work with a group to come up with as many meanings as you can for *bear*. Use each in a sentence.

2. **Conclusions** What old law did Amendment 3 change? Why was this important?

3. **Generalization** What is Amendment 4 about?

---

keep and bear arms have and use weapons to protect ourselves

put breaches of privacy to an end stop forced entries into people's private homes

reside live, stay

warrant to search and to seize legal paper that lets the police look through and take a person's belongings

Probable cause A good reason

quest search

Amendment 5 outlines the way
our **system of justice** works today:

★ A **trial** by **jury** is everyone's right,
   where the truth of the matter can **come to light**.

★ A person found innocent of a crime
   cannot be tried a second time.

★ A person on trial doesn't need to report
   any **self-incriminating facts** in court.

★ Parts of this amendment guarantee,
   other rights to life, liberty, and property.

Amendment 6 makes us all aware
of the rights to a trial that is speedy and fair.

★ A public trial by a jury of **peers**
   cannot drag on for a thousand years.

★ We're allowed to hear all the **evidence,**
   to have a lawyer, plus a good defense.

Amendment 5
Rights of the Accused

- A person cannot be tried more than once for the same crime.
- People do not have to respond to questions about themselves at their trial. They do not have to say anything that might make them seem guilty.
- A person's life, liberty, or property may not be taken except through legal means.
- The government cannot take away someone's property unless it pays a fair price.

Amendment 6
Requirements for a Trial by Jury

- A person charged with a crime must be told about the charges.
- A person accused of a crime has the right to a speedy, public trial by jury.
- An accused person has the right to hire a defense lawyer. If the accused wants a lawyer but cannot afford one, one must be provided by the government.

---

system of justice process of making sure that everyone is treated fairly by law

trial meeting held in a courtroom to decide a case

jury a group of people who listen and make a decision about a court case

come to light be made clear

self-incriminating facts facts that show he or she is guilty

peers people who have similar backgrounds

evidence information about a case, proof

Amendment 7 is really short.
It addresses the rules for the **civil court**.

If we are sued for a minor offense,
we may have a jury and a legal defense.

Amendment 8 protects us while
we're being **sentenced** or waiting for trial.

★ We cannot be **charged excessive bail**
to await our trial outside of jail.

★ Punishment for crimes cannot be cruel
or even **unusual**. That's the rule.

Amendment 9 says the people **retain**
other rights not listed here by name.

Amendment 10, the last in the chain,
addresses other powers that still remain.

Those delegated powers are left for the states
and give power to the people—that's really great!

BEFORE YOU MOVE ON...

1. **Details** Under what circumstances is a person involved in a civil case entitled to a trial by jury?
2. **Inference** Why was Amendment 9 included in the Bill of Rights?

civil court meeting in which disagreements are settled

sentenced told the punishment we get for being found guilty of breaking a law

charged excessive bail asked to pay too much money as a promise that we will return to court at a later time

unusual rare, uncommon

ABOUT THE AUTHOR

To **Anne Miranda**, freedom of speech is the most important feature of the Bill of Rights. "As a writer," she says, "it is important to be able to say what I think." She feels many Americans take freedom of speech for granted. She believes that when the right to speak freely is not protected, people become afraid to speak the truth. She has written more than ten books for young readers, including *Monster Math* and *Night Songs,* and won the Parent's Choice Award in 1999.

Respond to the Chant
Check Your Understanding

SUM IT UP

Connect New Information to What You Know Look at your **K-W-L** chart.

- What new information did you learn about the Bill of Rights? How did it add to or change what you knew before you read the selection?

- Were all of your questions answered?

- Review the **L** column of your chart. Is there more information you want to add?

K What I **K**now	W What I **W**ant to Learn	L What I **L**earned
I can have a trial if I have to go to court.	How else does the Bill of Rights protect me in court?	I don't have to testify against myself. I can't be tried twice for the same crime. I have the right to a speedy, fair trial.

Write a paragraph or record your ideas on tape to tell what you learned. Include any questions you still have about the topic.

Draw Conclusions With a partner, discuss answers for the following questions. Name the amendment that supports your answer.

- Imagine you don't like a new city tax law. What can you do to protest the law?

- Imagine someone you know is arrested for a crime. What rights does that person have?

THINK IT OVER

Discuss and Write Talk about these questions with a partner. Then write the answers.

1. **Details** What are three ways the legal system protects our freedoms listed in the Bill of Rights?

2. **Generalization** Why are school rules important? How do they protect your freedom?

3. **Opinion** Which amendment in the Bill of Rights is the most important to you? Why?

4. **Author's Style** How do the rhythm and rhyme of the selection help get the message across? How do they help you remember the key details?

EXPRESS YOURSELF ▶ RECITE

Choose a portion of the chant to recite with your group. You might want to use instruments, clapping, or movements to make your performance interesting. Also try to vary your tone of voice and volume to go with what you are saying. Practice your chant, and then recite it for the class.

Respond to the Chant, continued
Language Arts and Literature

▶ GRAMMAR IN CONTEXT

USE INDEFINITE PRONOUNS

Learn About Indefinite Pronouns When you are not talking about a specific person or thing, use an **indefinite pronoun.**

> Has **anyone** here read the Bill of Rights?

Some Indefinite Pronouns

anybody	everybody	somebody	nobody
anyone	everyone	someone	no one
anything	everything	something	nothing

These indefinite pronouns are singular. When you use them in the subject of a sentence, also use a singular verb.

> **Everyone** benefits from the Bill of Rights.

Identify Indefinite Pronouns Find two indefinite pronouns in this paragraph.

> In the United States, everybody has important rights. For example, the police can't arrest anyone without a good reason.

Practice Add an indefinite pronoun to complete each sentence.

1. Do you know _____ about the Bill of Rights?

2. I don't know _____ , only some things.

3. The Bill of Rights is important to _____ .

4. _____ will read it at our next meeting.

▶ WRITING/SPEAKING

WRITE AND DELIVER A PUBLIC SERVICE ANNOUNCEMENT

Choose one of the freedoms defined in the first amendment. Write a public service announcement about it.

- Explain what people should know about the freedom and how it affects them.

- Edit your work to make sure it is clear.

- Decide how to deliver your announcement. Will you record it on tape, present it as a rap, or read it aloud?

- Present your announcement to the class, to the school, or to a community group.

▶ VIEWING/WRITING

WRITE A STORY

View the painting on page 157. What is the man doing? Why? Write a story about the event. Include several characters and tell the outcome. Post your final copy in your class.

Sample Story

> Paul Corman stood up and cleared his throat. "Excuse me, Mr. Chairman. But I have to disagree with the highway proposal."

 For tips on **viewing**, see Handbook page 403.

Content Area Connections

SOCIAL STUDIES

RESEARCH THE THREE BRANCHES OF THE UNITED STATES GOVERNMENT

With your group, research one of the branches of the U.S. government described on page 155. Add the results to a class chart.

1 **Gather Information** Use social studies textbooks, print and electronic encyclopedias, and almanacs. Write the notes for the branch you chose in a chart like this one.

Branch: Judicial

Job	Duties	Qualifications	Length of Term
Federal Judge			

2 **Share Your Research** When all the groups are done, display and compare the results of your research. Use your notes to complete a class chart.

WRITING/SPEAKING
SOCIAL STUDIES

EXPLAIN THE HISTORY OF WOMEN'S SUFFRAGE

Find out more about the history of women's right to vote. Then report what you learn.

1 **Choose a Topic** Write about the history of women's suffrage or about someone who was important to the movement.

2 **Gather Information** Research your topic in electronic sources and encyclopedias. Print out helpful information and take notes.

3 **Make an Outline** Organize the information into an outline to guide your writing.

Example:
Carrie Chapman Catt
I. Background
   A. High school principal, school superintendent
   B. Pre-marriage agreement that gave her time to work for women's suffrage

4 **Present Your Report** Write your report. Then tell what you learned in an interesting way. You might give a multimedia report with sound bites and slides, or dress up and act like the person as she describes her contributions.

For more about the **research process,** see Handbook pages 394–399. Learn to make a **multimedia presentation.** See pages 390–391.

AMISTAD RISING

historical fiction
by Veronica Chambers

Prepare to Read

THINK ABOUT WHAT YOU KNOW

Create Symbols What do the words *freedom* and *slavery* make you think of? Create a symbol for each word. Explain your symbols to the class.

---

abolitionist person who wanted to stop the practice of people owning other people

captivity time when you are held against your will

case matter for a court of law to decide

defense argument in favor of the person charged with a crime

deliberate think over carefully to make a decision

illegal against the law

legal allowed by law

prisoner person who is held against his or her will

slave trader person who buys and sells people as property

slavery practice of owning and controlling human beings

LEARN KEY VOCABULARY

Use New Words in Context Study the new words and their definitions. Then write the paragraph, adding the missing words.

The practice of _____(1)_____ began early in America's history. Africans were brought to Virginia and held in _____(2)_____ . A _____(3)_____ would then sell his African _____(4)_____ . In 1777, Vermont made slavery _____(5)_____ . The _____(6)_____ fought to end slavery in all of the U.S. By 1808, it was no longer _____(7)_____ to import slaves, but you could still own them. In a famous court _____(8)_____ , a slave named Dred Scott sued for his freedom. His _____(9)_____ was that if he moved to a free state, he should be a free man. However, the Supreme Court met to _____(10)_____ and ruled against Scott.

LEARN TO RELATE CAUSES AND EFFECTS

The **cause** is the reason something happens. The **effect** is what happens. Relating causes and effects helps you understand the chain of events in a selection.

READING STRATEGY
How to Relate Causes and Effects

1. Look for words that signal causes and effects: *so, because, since*.

2. Ask yourself: What happened? Why did it happen?

3. Think about how the events are related. Does one cause lead to several effects?

As you read "Amistad Rising," write the causes and effects to show the chain of events.

AMISTAD RISING

A STORY OF FREEDOM

An African man, Joseph Cinqué, is taken from his home and put on a slave ship going to North America. He and other Africans land in America where they fight for the right to return home. *Amistad Rising* is based on the true story of Cinqué's fight for justice and freedom.

BY VERONICA CHAMBERS   ILLUSTRATED BY PAUL LEE

Stand here with me on the shores of New London, Connecticut. Feel the cool breeze of the Atlantic Ocean on your face. Feel the dirt beneath your feet; this land is far from ordinary. It is here upon this very soil that Joseph Cinqué set foot in America, bringing with him a group of **renegade slaves** and leaving his mark on history.

This is a story about the changing **winds of fortune**, about a man who was born free, was made a slave, and battled nations to be free again. It is a true story. And like so many stories, it begins not on land but at sea.

Have you ever wondered why the ocean is so wide? It's because it holds so much history. There's not a drop of seawater that doesn't have a secret; not a river or a lake that doesn't whisper someone's name. Ask the ocean about the **legend** of Joseph Cinqué, and this is what you might hear.

renegade slaves slaves who had run away
winds of fortune events in a person's life
legend story told for generations

THE SLAVE SHIPS SAIL

Traders take people from Africa to sell as slaves in North America. Conditions on the ships are horrible.

The year was 1839. Owning slaves was still **legal**, although the stealing of slaves from Africa was not. **Slavery** was a huge business. Many **slave traders** had grown rich from selling human beings, and they **were reluctant** to give it up.

It was nightfall when the slave ship *Teçora* set sail from Sierra Leone, a small country on the coast of West Africa. The water rippled like quicksilver in the moonlight as the ship voyaged toward Cuba. But in the ship's **hold**, more than five hundred Africans were held **prisoner**. There was no toilet, there was no bath, and the **stench** was unbearable. The Africans were chained together in pairs. Heavy iron shackles bound their hands and their feet. Movement was difficult. Escape was impossible. **Disease and malnutrition** claimed the lives of many; others **perished** under the murderous beatings of the slave traders. The dead were tossed overboard without a thought.

After two tempestuous months at sea, the *Teçora* arrived in Cuba. There, fifty-three of the prisoners—including four children—were sold to two Spanish slave traders and forced to board yet another ship to take them to a Cuban **plantation**.

This ship was called *Amistad*, the Spanish word for "friendship."

> **BEFORE YOU MOVE ON...**
> 1. **Characters' Motive** Why didn't the slave traders want slavery to end?
> 2. **Summary** Describe what happened to the slaves on the boat.

---

were reluctant did not want
hold lower part where things are stored
stench bad smell

Disease and malnutrition Sickness and lack of good, healthy food
perished died
plantation large farm

THE PRISONERS ESCAPE

Joseph Cinqué is one of the captured men. After he hears that
the traders will kill them all, the prisoners take over the ship.

Three days into the journey, the *Amistad* sailed through an unexpected storm. The ship was battered by roaring rain and wind. The trip took longer than the crew expected and **provisions** were low. Each slave survived on a daily meal of two potatoes, a banana, and just a little water.

In the hold of the ship, a young man tried to **quell** his unsettled stomach. Fear gripped him as he watched his fellow Africans suffer and starve. He was young and afraid, but destiny had a plan for him. His name was Singbe, although the slavers had given him the Spanish name Joseph Cinqué, and he belonged to a group of people called Mende who lived near Sierra Leone. He had been working on a village road when he was **seized** and sold to the slavers of the *Teçora*.

During the first two months of his **captivity**, Cinqué was disturbed to find that he had begun to forget little things about Africa—the smell of freshly harvested rice, the color of the sunsets, the feel of wet grass

> ## Cinqué demanded to know what would happen.

beneath his running feet. When he closed his eyes he could see these things only as distant and blurry as a dream. But he could never forget the people he had left behind. His wife. His three children. His mother and father.

Every day Cinqué grew more restless, wondering what the Spaniards intended to do with him and the other Africans. Though they were forbidden to speak, his companions whispered questions: What lay ahead? What would slavery mean? Would they simply be transported from ship to ship indefinitely?

Cinqué had to find out.

Occasionally, a few captives were allowed on deck for some air. Cinqué waited for his turn, and when he was finally ushered above, he attempted to coax some answers from Celestino, the cook. The two men communicated with hand gestures, for neither spoke the other's language.

Cinqué demanded to know what would happen to them.

....

provisions food and fresh water
quell calm down
seized taken by force

Celestino smiled devilishly, **intent** on playing a cruel joke. He pointed to barrels of beef and signaled to Cinqué that the slave traders planned to kill the Africans, cut them up, salt them for preservation, and eat them like cured beef.

Fear and anger filled Cinqué. He would not be eaten by the white men who held him captive. He would not.

He decided to **strike** that night. With a loose nail he had found earlier in a deck board, he **picked the lock** on his shackles, freeing himself and then the other prisoners. Once free, they quieted the four children and searched the cargo hold. A box of sugarcane knives was discovered—a **boon**!

Sneaking up to the deck, they took the crew by surprise. In the fight, Celestino, the captain, and one African were killed. Two of the crew jumped overboard. Three men were taken prisoners. Cinqué needed them to **navigate** the ship back toward Africa, back toward home. When the sun rose again, Cinqué and his companions greeted the day as free people.

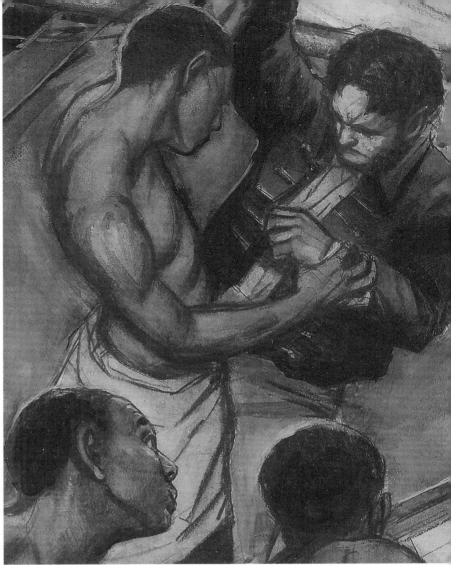

....

intent determined
strike attack, fight
picked the lock got the lock open
boon good thing
navigate show which way to sail

BEFORE YOU MOVE ON...

1. **Inference** Why was Cinqué forgetting things about his home?
2. **Character's Motive** With a partner, make a list of reasons for Cinqué's actions.
3. **Prediction** Do you think that Cinqué and the Africans will make it back to Africa? Why or why not?

CINQUÉ PLEADS FOR FREEDOM

Instead of Africa, the *Amistad* arrives in America. The Africans remain prisoners until Cinqué and his ally, John Adams, win their freedom in court.

But they had **claimed victory** too soon. Cinqué ordered the Spaniards to steer the ship toward the rising sun. They obeyed and sailed the ship east toward Africa during the day, but then at night turned the ship around and sailed northwest toward North America.

For two months the ship **pitched** back and forth across the Atlantic Ocean. Eight more Africans died during that time—some from their battle wounds, some from food poisoning, and some from starvation.

Then on August 27, 1839, the *Amistad* was **escorted** by an American ship into the harbor of New London, Connecticut. Weary, hungry, and hopelessly lost, Cinqué and the others were forced to come ashore.

An American naval lieutenant saw the possibility for quick **profits** in the Africans. But this was the North, and a group of whites and free blacks **campaigning against** the **institution of slavery** was gaining popularity. They called themselves **abolitionists**, and they took on Cinqué and the other Africans as their most important **case**.

The Africans were sent to prison in New Haven, Connecticut, until a decision could be made.

The abolitionists managed to find a translator, and Cinqué told his story in a U.S. court. He was only twenty-five years old, but his experience on the *Amistad* had given him the confidence of a much older man.

---

claimed victory thought they won
pitched rocked
escorted guided, led, accompanied

profits earned money, income
campaigning against trying to convince others to stop
institution of slavery tradition of keeping slaves

The courtroom was crowded, and many were moved by Cinqué's **impassioned words**.

"I am not here to argue the case against slavery," Cinqué said, "though I will say it is a sin against man and God. I am here to argue the facts. The **indisputable**, international law is that the stealing of slaves from Africa is now **illegal**."

"The men who kidnapped us, who beat and tortured us, were—and are—guilty of this crime," Cinqué continued.

"We are a peaceful people. We regret the loss of life caused by our **mutiny**. But we are not savages. We took over the ship to save our lives. We have done no wrong. Allow us to go home."

The weekend before the judge made his decision, Cinqué and his companions waited in the New Haven jail, their hearts filled with fear and hope. The judge held the power to make the Africans slaves or to set them free. On Monday morning, January 13, 1840, they worried no longer. He had decided they should be returned home.

They were free.

> **"We have done no wrong."**

But as Cinqué was soon to learn, the passage to freedom was as winding as the *Amistad*'s journey across the sea. President Martin Van Buren, concerned that freeing the Mende would enrage southern slave holders, ordered the district attorney to **file an appeal** so the case would be heard in the U.S. Supreme Court. And because of this, Cinqué gained his greatest American **ally**: former president John Quincy Adams.

Having heard about the mutineers, Adams came out of **retirement** to argue Cinqué's case. He was seventy-two years old. It had been more than thirty years since he had argued a case in a courtroom, and the thought of bearing the responsibility for this one worried the elderly statesman deeply.

But inspired by Cinqué, whom many of the abolitionists had begun to refer to as the Black Prince, Adams tirelessly prepared his **defense**. In court he spoke on behalf of the Mende for eight and a half hours. Sweat poured from his brow, and his voice filled the packed courtroom as he presented his case.

---

impassioned words speech full of emotion
indisputable not-to-be-questioned
mutiny fight to take over the ship

file an appeal request a new trial
ally friend, supporter
retirement the private life he had since he quit working

There were many **factors at play**: Were the Africans the rightful property of the Spaniards? Were they brutal murderers? Or were they freedom fighters, no different than the men and women who had rebelled against England and founded the United States of America? There was also international pressure. Spain wanted the slaves and the *Amistad* returned to Cuba; could the United States risk **provoking European ire** over the lives of thirty-five surviving Africans?

After Adams made his closing arguments, the Supreme Court **retired** to **deliberate**.

For Cinqué and the others, the fearful process of waiting and praying began again.

A week later, on March 9, 1841, the Supreme Court announced that Adams had **prevailed**.

The Africans were truly free.

It took many months for the abolitionists to raise the money for the Africans' long journey back to West Africa. But at last the ship sailed, and when the African coast was finally in sight, Cinqué gathered everyone together.

"Let us give praise and thanks," Cinqué called out, his voice booming across the deck. "By the strength of our spirit and with the assistance of our ancestors, we are not slaves today. Our children will not be slaves. And their children will not be slaves. We are exactly as God willed us to be. My brothers, my sisters, we are free." **Savoring** the word, he let it melt like sugar on his tongue. He paused and then tasted the word again. "Free," he said, more softly now.

Each person aboard the ship felt the word coming up from their hearts, tasted the sweetness of it in their mouths, then released it into the salty sea air. "Free," they said **in unison**. "We are free."

---

factors at play different things to think about
provoking European ire angering the governments of European countries
retired left the courtroom

prevailed won
Savoring Enjoying, liking
in unison all together

If you stand right here on the New London shore, you can hear the words of the great Joseph Cinqué. His voice is so powerful that it travels across both space and time. If you bend down to the Atlantic, you can hear it in the beating of the waves. The wind whispers it as it blows around your head. And when the rain falls, it's like tears of happiness.

You can hear his words almost anywhere you listen for them: "We are free. Free. Free. Free."

BEFORE YOU MOVE ON...

1. **Simile** Discuss with your partner why the author says that Cinqué's road to freedom "was as winding as the *Amistad*'s journey across the sea."

2. **Details** What were some of the factors Adams wanted the court to consider?

3. **Conclusions** What message did the Supreme Court's decision give Europeans about the court's opinion of the slave trade?

ABOUT THE AUTHOR

Veronica Chambers knows what it is like to come to a whole new country. Her family moved to the United States from Panama when she was very young. She followed her dreams of going to college and then becoming a journalist. Veronica Chambers modestly says, "I've tried everything so it just looks like I've had more successes than failures." Those successes include editing for a number of well-known magazines and writing several books before turning thirty years old.

ABOUT THE ILLUSTRATOR

Paul Lee graduated with honors from the Art Center College of Design and currently lives in Placentia, California. He used acrylic paints on Bristol® board for his illustrations.

Respond to the Story
Check Your Understanding

SUM IT UP

Relate Causes and Effects Complete cause-and-effect charts to show the chain of events in the story.

Cause-and-Effect Chart

Cause:
Slave traders steal people from Africa to sell as slaves.

Effect:
Five hundred Africans are captured and put on a ship at night to go to Cuba.

Effect:
Many Africans die from disease, malnutrition, or beatings.

Effect:
Fifty-three prisoners are sold and put on another ship.

Write a Summary Put a check by the most important details in your charts. For example, knowing that the ship left Africa full of people is an important detail. Knowing that it left at night is not important. Use the important details to write a summary of the selection.

THINK IT OVER

Discuss and Write Talk about these questions with a partner. Then write the answers.

1. **Generalization** Why is personal freedom so important? How are our personal freedoms protected in the United States?

2. **Relevant and Irrelevant Information** Read Cinqué's speech on page 171. What information supports his argument? What information does not support his argument?

3. **Judgment** Is it true that Cinqué and the other mutineers "did no wrong"? Explain your answer.

4. **Conclusions** Why was Cinqué's case so important to the abolitionists?

EXPRESS YOURSELF ▶ PERSUADE

What points do you think John Quincy Adams made at Cinqué's appeal? With a partner, list the points Adams would make. Then write a speech he could have presented to the Supreme Court to persuade them to free Cinqué and the other Africans. Present the speech to your class.

Language Arts and Literature

GRAMMAR IN CONTEXT

USE RELATIVE PRONOUNS

Learn About Relative Pronouns Some sentences include a clause that gives information about a person or thing. These **relative clauses** are introduced by a **relative pronoun**.

> The story is about a man **who was taken from his home in Africa**.

Who, whom, and *whose* are relative pronouns that connect a clause to a person in the sentence.

> This man, **whose name was Joseph Cinqué**, fought for his freedom.

You can use *that* to connect a relative clause to a person or a thing.

> The man **that the slave traders shipped to Cuba** was sold to Spaniards.
> The speech **that Cinqué gave** impressed the jurors.

Practice Write the sentences. Add a relative pronoun to complete each sentence.

1. Adams was inspired by Cinqué, _____ was known as the Black Prince.

2. The defense _____ Adams gave in court was convincing.

3. Adams said the Africans were like the colonists _____ had rebelled against England.

4. The Court agreed that the Mende, _____ rights had been taken, should be free.

WRITING/SPEAKING

WRITE A LETTER

Pretend that you are Cinqué. Write a letter to your family in Sierra Leone while you wait for your trial or to John Quincy Adams after you have safely returned to Africa.

1 **Write Your Draft** Think about your feelings and hopes. Use at least one indefinite pronoun like *someone* or *anybody* in your letter. Include clauses with relative pronouns.

2 **Edit Your Work** Have a classmate evaluate what you wrote. Ask: *How well did I express the thoughts in the "voice" of Cinqué?* Make sure to include the date, greeting, and closing.

3 **Share Your Letter** Make a final copy of your letter; then read it aloud to your group.

Review **pronouns** on Handbook pages 437–440.

A recreation of the *Amistad* is launched after two years of construction.

Respond to the Story, continued
Content Area Connections

▶ TECHNOLOGY/MEDIA
▶ SOCIAL STUDIES

COMPARE PATHS TO FREEDOM

Joseph Cinqué gained freedom through the legal system. Other Africans in America ran away to escape slavery by using the Underground Railroad. With a group, research the Underground Railroad. Then compare the runaway slaves' experience with Cinqué's.

1 Gather Information and Take Notes Try these key words and Web sites to begin your search. Download interesting information.

INTERNET

INFORMATION ON-LINE

Key Words:
Amistad
"Underground Railroad"

Web Sites:
▶ **Underground Railroad**
  • www.beavton.k12.or.us/Greenway/leahy/ugrr/
  • www.nationalgeographic.com

▶ **More About Amistad**
  • www.amistad.mysticseaport.org

2 Compare Notes Make a comparison chart to share with your class. Add any new information you learn. What conclusions can your class make about the experiences of Africans in the United States?

Learn to use the **Internet** on Handbook pages 392–393.

▶ REPRESENTING
▶ SOCIAL STUDIES

RELATE CINQUÉ'S CASE TO THE BILL OF RIGHTS

Work with a partner to trace Cinqué's steps through the United States' justice system. Which steps are related to the Bill of Rights? Choose a visual way to report your findings and ideas. You might create:

• a Web site with links to actual *Amistad* sites

• a series of artist sketches with captions showing Cinqué in court

• a graph showing results of a class poll about how the Bill of Rights applies to Cinqué's trial.

For information about **representing**, see Handbook pages 404–405.

Caged Bird

poem
by Maya Angelou

Prepare to Read Poetry

THINK ABOUT WHAT YOU KNOW

Make a Venn Diagram How are a caged bird and a free bird similar? How are they different? Show your ideas in a Venn diagram.

claim say that something belongs to you, take something you believe is yours

distant far away

fearful frightened

leap jump

long for want

rage anger

seldom not often

stalk walk stiffly and angrily

trill fast, repeating sound

tune music, melody

LEARN KEY VOCABULARY

Relate Words Study the new words and their definitions. Use a thesaurus to find synonyms for each word. Think of other related words and images, too. Record all of your ideas in a chart.

Word	Synonyms	Related Words
distant	far, afar	beyond reach, over there, far away, past the horizon, out of sight, far off

LEARN TO VISUALIZE

Sensory images are words and phrases that describe how something smells, tastes, feels, looks, or sounds. Poets often use sensory images to help readers picture exactly what they mean.

READING STRATEGY
How to Visualize
1. Read the poem once to get a feel for its mood and meaning.
2. Reread the poem. Look for words and details that create powerful sensory images.
3. Use the images to make a picture in your mind. What is the poet saying?

As you read "Caged Bird," use the sensory images to help you "see" the poet's message.

Caged Bird

A free bird leaps
on the back of the wind
and floats downstream
till the current ends
and dips his wing
in the orange sun rays
and dares to claim the sky.

But a bird that stalks
down his narrow cage
can seldom see through
his bars of rage
his wings are clipped and
his feet are tied
so he opens his throat to sing.

The caged bird sings
with a fearful trill
of things unknown
but longed for still
and his tune is heard
on the distant hill
for the caged bird
sings of freedom.

—Maya Angelou

Respond to the Poem

THINK IT OVER

Discuss Talk about these questions with a partner.

1. **Personal Experience** What makes you feel free?

2. **Comparisons** How are the mood and tone of this poem similar to what Cinqué in "Amistad Rising" was probably feeling?

EXPRESS YOURSELF

▶ RECITE A POEM

Meter is the regular pattern of a poem's rhythm. Listen to the poem and clap out the meter. How does the rhythm support the meaning? Then recite the poem, emphasizing the meter.

ABOUT THE POET

Maya Angelou's life reads like a book. In fact, her autobiography *I Know Why the Caged Bird Sings* tells stories about her childhood in the segregated state of Arkansas. Maya Angelou has become one of the most respected authors of our age. She is also a poet, historian, actress, playwright, civil-rights activist, producer and director.

"Civilization is a method of living, an attitude of equal respect for all men" —Jane Addams, 1933,
George Giusti, India ink and gouache on paper. Copyright © 1955.

Getting
to the
Solution

- What happens when you have a conflict with a friend?

- What steps do you take to resolve a conflict? What can you do to make the solution a good one for all sides?

- Which solutions to your own personal conflicts have been the most satisfying? Why?

THEME-RELATED BOOKS

The Woman Who Outshone the Sun
from a poem by Alejandro Cruz Martinez

Villagers learn a lesson after their cruelty drives away a beautiful woman with wonderful powers.

The Warrior and the Wise Man
by David Wisniewski

Twin brothers set out to see who will be first to complete a difficult task. One uses force, the other uses wisdom.

NOVEL

A Different Kind of Hero
by Ann R. Blakeslee

The miners don't want Chinese in their camp. When young Renny stands up for a bright Chinese boy, there's big trouble.

Build Language and Vocabulary

PERSUADE

Listen to the song. What does the songwriter want people to do?

We Are Not Alone

Cooling tower for a nuclear power plant in Oregon.

We are not alone, those of us who care
That the coming generations
Might live free from contamination
We are not alone something tells me
We are not alone.

And we are not afraid to make our feelings known
To help our friends and neighbors
To share in our concern
Won't you listen with your hearts to this song of ours
We are not alone.

We're crying "shut down the spread of atomic waste"
We're crying "shut down the threat of a nuclear haze"
We're saying "no more can we believe that it's safe
To hide our heads in the sand
And pretend not to understand
The poisoning of our land."

For the sake of our children, let us come to our senses
In the name of love, let us come to our senses
In the threat to life, nobody profits
There isn't a moment to lose
While we still have a chance to choose
Where our future goes.

—*Raffi*

MAKE A PROBLEM-AND-SOLUTION CHART

Think of an issue you feel strongly about. Make a problem-and-solution chart to describe the problem and how it could be solved.

Issue: Activities for Teenagers

Problem	Solutions
There's no safe place for teenagers to hang out and have fun in our town.	• Build a recreational center just for teenagers. • Keep the gym at school open on weekends.

BUILD YOUR VOCABULARY

Words Used in Persuasion Some words help you convince someone to do something about a problem. Work with a group to list these persuasive words and phrases.

People have to stop . . . It's not fair that . . . Take action!	You must . . . We can't ignore the fact that . . . This issue is so important that . . .

USE LANGUAGE STRUCTURES ▶ PRESENT PERFECT TENSE

Speaking: Give a Persuasive Speech Take a stand on the issue stated in your problem-and-solution chart. Give a persuasive speech to your class. Include sentences that use present perfect tense verbs.

Example:

Teenagers need a place of their own to be with their friends. My friends **have stated** many times how bored they are on weekends. We must have something to do to stay out of trouble. Seaside **has decided** to build a recreational center for its teenagers. Why can't our town do the same thing?

Dealing with Conflict: Finding Resolution

article and
persuasive letters
by Shirleyann Costigan

Prepare to Read

THINK ABOUT WHAT YOU KNOW

Journal Entry In your journal, describe a difficult problem you or someone you know has encountered. How can the problem be solved?

conflict problem, disagreement

consensus general agreement

diffuse make less strong

dispute argument, quarrel

intervene come between people to settle an argument

mediation act of coming in to try to settle an argument

negotiation talking back and forth between two or more people in order to reach an agreement

peer person who is an equal

resolution something decided on, solution

LEARN KEY VOCABULARY

Use New Words in Context Study the new words and their definitions. Then use the words to complete the word map.

Word Map

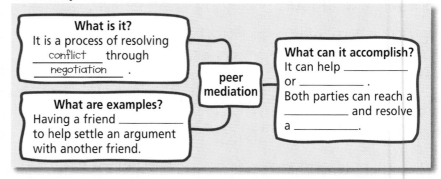

What is it?
It is a process of resolving ___conflict___ through ___negotiation___ .

What are examples?
Having a friend _____ to help settle an argument with another friend.

peer mediation

What can it accomplish?
It can help _____ or _____ .
Both parties can reach a _____ and resolve a _____ .

LEARN ABOUT AUTHOR'S PURPOSE

The **author's purpose** is the reason the author writes something. If you know the author's purpose, you can better evaluate what you read.

READING STRATEGY
How to Identify Author's Purpose

1. Survey the selection. What kinds of information does the author include? Is the selection fiction or nonfiction?

2. Ask yourself: Does the author want to tell me a story? Explain, describe, or express something? Persuade me to do something?

Survey pages 185–193. What are the authors' purposes?

Dealing with
Conflict:
Finding
Resolution

by
Shirleyann
Costigan

Peer mediation is a process in which students, trained to act as mediators, help other students resolve conflicts in school. During a peer mediation session, such as the one described in this article, students in conflict often become more understanding about themselves and each other.

Katrina

José

What is Conflict?

Conflict is a natural part of life. It occurs when two or more people stand in the way of each other's basic **psychological** needs. There are four basic psychological needs.

- The need for belonging means the desire to feel loved, to share, and to get along with others.

- The need for power occurs when someone wants to be recognized and respected for achievement.

- The need for freedom includes wanting to make choices.

- The need for fun means wanting to laugh, play, and enjoy life.

At one time or another in our lives, we all have these needs. In moments of conflict, we don't always know which of our needs is being **threatened**. We only know we are not getting what we want, and that can make us angry.

What is Resolution?

Resolution occurs when people in conflict find **solutions** that **satisfy everyone**. Once they find agreeable solutions, they decide what steps to take to reach them.

Case Study of a Conflict Situation

José wanted to **audition** for a part in the school play. When the director Katrina saw that he was in a wheelchair, she didn't think he looked right for the part. She explained

What is Peer Mediation?

Peer mediation is a **process** that helps kids resolve conflicts. It is conducted by students, for students and that's why it is called *peer* mediation. The process involves **negotiation**, mediation, making decisions by **consensus**, and confidentiality.

✓ Negotiation occurs when the parties in conflict meet to work out the problem and resolve the **dispute**.

✓ Mediation is a process in which a third person states the **ground rules** and guides the two people toward finding solutions.

✓ Decision-making by consensus happens when the people craft a plan of action that everyone agrees to support.

✓ Confidentiality is each person's promise that he or she will not discuss anything said during the session outside of the mediation room.

psychological emotional
threatened put in danger
solutions answers to their problems
satisfy everyone make all people happy

audition try out
process method, series of steps
ground rules basic procedures

that his wheelchair would be difficult to move around the stage. José got angry. Katrina got angry, too. She asked José to leave and tried to move him off the stage, but José put on the brakes and wouldn't **budge**. Finally, the drama coach **intervened**. She suggested that José and Katrina work out the problem through **peer mediation**.

The Peer Mediation Session

On the day of the mediation, José and Katrina met Juan and Alexis, in the Conflict Resolution Team (CRT) office. Juan and Alexis were trained **mediators**. They were skilled at helping people to get the facts out in the open. They would also help José and Katrina express their thoughts and opinions. During the session, they would ask José and Katrina to take turns defining the problem, to repeat, **clarify**, or respond to what the other person had said.

Juan opened the session by explaining the ground rules. Alexis had everyone sign **a Contract of Confidentiality**. Then the process of negotiating began.

Juan: Katrina, tell us what the problem is.

Katrina: He wants to be in my play and I don't think he's good for the part.

Conflict:
José wants to be in the school play. The director Katrina thinks he's not right for the part because he is in a wheelchair.

Juan: José, tell us what you think the problem is.

José: I feel like she is forming an opinion of me unfairly. She doesn't think that I have the ability to play the part, and acting is my main thing, and her doing this is making me feel bad.

Juan: Can you repeat what José said, Katrina?

Katrina: He thinks that I am judging him unfairly because he is in a wheelchair.

Juan: Is that right, José?

José: Yeah.

BEFORE YOU MOVE ON...

1. **Summary** Retell why conflict occurs.
2. **Details** What is involved in the process of peer mediation?
3. **Inference** Why do you think the mediator Juan asks Katrina to repeat what José said?

---

budge move
mediators people who help others talk to each other

clarify make clear
a Contract of Confidentiality an agreement to keep things private

Dealing with Conflict **187**

Alexis: Katrina, how do you feel about the situation?

Katrina: I think that this is my play, and my play is really important to me. I just don't think that José is the person I want. I mean, he doesn't have what I need.

Alexis: José, would you **restate that** please?

José: She doesn't think I have what it TAKES to be in her play. I don't fit in.

Alexis: Is that right, Katrina?

Katrina: Yes.

Alexis: So now, José, how do you feel about the situation?

José: I feel, well, yeah, it's important for her to have a nice play and everything, but, if they're handing out flyers for people to come and join the play, then I say, it's for everybody. It's not right that people who have a disability can't be in it. I want at least a chance to try out and show her what I can do; to just give me a chance before she makes a decision like that. She should be more **open-minded**.

Juan: So you just want a chance to try out and have her see your acting abilities.

José: Yeah. I feel if someone like President Roosevelt can lead a nation from a wheelchair, then, I mean, why can't I do this little tiny thing?

Juan: So you think that since other people have succeeded with their disabilities, and succeeded very well, you should be given **an opportunity** to succeed in whatever you want to do.

José: Yes.

Alexis: Katrina, what do you want this mediation to **accomplish**?

Katrina: Truthfully, I'm really not sure. At first I thought I didn't want him in the play, but really, I'm just kind of afraid of that wheelchair. My brother was in a serious accident recently. He may be disabled for life: the doctors aren't sure

Ground Rules for a Peer Mediation Session:

Work to solve the problem.

Treat each other with **respect**.

Keep this meeting confidential.

Confidentiality Means:

What is said here stays here.

Don't talk about things people said in the session with anyone.

If anyone asks, just say, "We solved it" or "We didn't solve it."

If you think someone has broken confidentiality, report it to the Conflict Resolution Team.

People who break confidentiality rules may be suspended from school.

---

restate that say that again

open-minded willing to see things in a new way

an opportunity a chance

accomplish do, achieve

respect consideration, kindness, courtesy

yet, but he may have to be in a wheelchair. I think I may be **reacting to** that. I mean—my brother's condition is hard for me to deal with. Maybe I thought if José was in the play, it would . . . I don't know.

Alexis: What you're saying is that this is not a personal thing against José, but his disability makes it harder for you to deal with your brother's accident and stuff.

Katrina: Yes.

Alexis: José, would you repeat that please?

José: Yeah. My disability reminds her of her brother and it's hard for her to think about that. That's what caused her reaction when she saw me.

Alexis: Is there anything you want to say about that, José?

José: Well, I didn't know that, and maybe she should have explained it to me earlier, but that's what we are here for, right?

Alexis: So basically you feel better that there's **a reason** why she feels the way she does, and it isn't because she's against you.

José: Yeah, I feel better, but I don't think her reason should keep me from being in the play. I understand how she must feel, but, hey, look at me. I'm in a wheelchair and I deal with it—it's people that try to hold me back.

Juan: Katrina?

Conflict:

José wants to be in the school play. The director, Katrina, thinks he's not right for the part because he is in a wheelchair.

Mediation

Juan and Alexis help José and Katrina discuss the problem in a peer mediation session.

José wants Katrina to be more fair in her decision.

Katrina realizes that José's wheelchair frightens her. That makes her judge him unfairly.

José feels better knowing there is a reason for her feelings, but he still wants to audition for the part.

Katrina: I am sorry. I shouldn't have let my personal problems influence my decision.

Alexis: It seems that you two have a little better idea of what is going on. Do you think that you are ready to come up with some solutions?

BEFORE YOU MOVE ON...

1. **Judgments** Why do you think the ground rules for a peer mediation session are important?
2. **Cause and Effect** Why did Katrina judge José before he auditioned?
3. **Predictions** What do you think Katrina and José will agree to do?

....

reacting to responding to, feeling
a reason an explanation for

Katrina

Alexis

Juan

Concluding the Session

Katrina and José did come up with solutions. José asked to be allowed to audition. He also wanted to see the other kids' auditions so he could compare his performance with theirs. Katrina agreed to that. She promised to base her decision on the person's ability to play the character and nothing else. **Her one request** was that José accept her final decision. José agreed. Then they both signed a contract that stated how they planned to resolve the problem.

Summary

José's basic need for *belonging* and *power* were threatened by Katrina's actions. He felt rejected and **powerless**. On the other hand, José threatened Katrina's *power* as a director, and her *freedom* to choose what she wanted. In the end, Katrina realized that her problem was more about her brother than about the play. Once she admitted that, José felt better. The anger between them was **diffused**. Then they were in a position to work out solutions.

Not all conflicts are so easily resolved. Some are never resolved because two parties cannot let go of their anger. Resolution through mediation requires that the people in conflict are willing to work together. They must be **flexible** and not stick **stubbornly** to their own **point of view**. Only then can they reach a **peaceable resolution** that satisfies their needs.

....

Her one request The one thing she asked
powerless helpless
flexible willing to change

stubbornly firmly
point of view way of seeing things
peaceable resolution calm solution

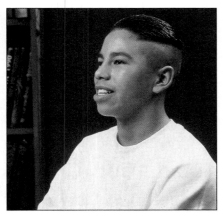

José

Conflict:

José wants to be in the school play. The director, Katrina, thinks he's not right for the part because he is in a wheelchair.

Mediation

Juan and Alexis help José and Katrina discuss the problem in a peer mediation session.

José wants Katrina to be more fair in her decision.

Katrina realizes that José's wheelchair frightens her. That makes her judge him unfairly.

José feels better knowing there is a reason for her feelings, but he still wants to audition for the part.

Resolution

José will audition. Then Katrina will choose someone for the part based on acting ability and not on personal reasons. José will accept what she decides.

BEFORE YOU MOVE ON...

1. **Details** What diffused the anger between Katrina and José?
2. **Personal Experience** Tell a partner about a time that you helped someone solve a conflict.

ABOUT THE STUDENTS

Juan Gonzales, Alexis Sales, José Gutiérrez, and **Katrina Loyola** are student mediators at Watsonville High School in Watsonville, California. They worked with their CRT counselor, Mary Perugini, to bring you this peer mediation session. Because a real peer mediation session is strictly confidential, they acted out a typical conflict situation. Mary Perugini captured their words on audio tape.

Dealing with Conflict   191

Meredith Middle School News

Letters to the Editor

Who Decides?: Pro and Con on Peer Mediation

Meredith Middle School is thinking of setting up a peer mediation program. It would allow students to help other students peaceably resolve conflicts. In our last issue, we asked: *Do you think it's a good idea to have a peer mediation program in our school?* Here are two responses, pro and con.

It Teaches Responsibility

Dear Editor:

I think that peer mediation is a good idea. People are always saying that middle schoolers should take responsibility for their actions. I think we can handle that, and peer mediation teaches us how.

I know of two ways to handle student conflicts. One way is to let an adult decide who is right and who is wrong. Even though it is easier, it doesn't teach us responsibility. The second way is through peer mediation. In peer mediation, student mediators are trained to help us talk through our problems. They can help us decide how to settle the problem so that everybody wins.

I have experienced peer mediation firsthand in another school. When I first went into my peer mediation session, I was angry. But after I listened to the other guy's side, and he listened to mine, we both had a better understanding of what was going on. The mediator helped us make a plan for settling our differences. We followed the plan and now we're friends. I think kids who are angry like I was should have a program like this to help them work things out.

Jan W., 7th grade

It's Unrealistic

Dear Editor:

Peer mediation isn't realistic. It seems like a good idea since students work together to settle conflicts, but the real world isn't like that. Peer mediation gives us a false sense of who's in charge. Our parents, our teachers, our counselors, and other adults tell us what we should or should not do. When we grow up and get jobs, then our boss will tell us what to do. Hey, that's life!

Students are always in conflict over one thing or another. Usually, it blows over, or we just somehow work it out. That's the way it always has been and always will be. So instead of worrying about how to "mediate," I say we should be learning how to work with adult authority! Besides, face it, adults have more experience than we do. They can make decisions that are fair to both sides.

Another reason I'm not for peer mediation is the confidentiality issue. I don't always trust people to keep things to themselves. I've talked to two kids who went to peer mediation sessions in other schools. They both blabbed everything that went on in the session. What's up with that?

I say, if you can't solve a problem with someone your own age by yourself, take your problem to an experienced adult. You may dislike the solution, but chances are it will be fair.

Robert R., *8th grade*

BEFORE YOU MOVE ON...

1. **Fact and Opinion** Give an example of a fact stated in each of the letters.
2. **Judgments** Which letter do you feel is more persuasive? Why?
3. **Making Decisions** If you were a student at Meredith and could vote on the issue of a peer mediation program, would you vote pro or con? Give your reasons.

Respond to the Article and Letters
Check Your Understanding

SUM IT UP

Compare Literature: Fact and Opinion Make a chart to compare the article and the letters. Write the facts in each selection.

	Article	Letters to the Editor
Purpose		
Facts	Includes definitions of conflict.	Jan experienced peer mediation.

Then write the opinions in each selection.

Opinions	Katrina didn't think José looked right for the part.	Peer mediation teaches students to take responsibility.

Evaluate Literature Choose the article or one of the letters. Write a paragraph that evaluates how well the author met his or her purpose for writing. Use the information in your chart.

THINK IT OVER

Discuss and Write Talk about these questions with a partner. Then write the answers.

1. **Judgment** Which of the four psychological needs is most important to you: belonging, power, freedom, or fun? Explain your answer.

2. **Comparisons** If José and Katrina wrote letters to the editor about whether or not peer mediation is a good idea, what do you think their two opinions would be? Why?

3. **Opinion** Do you think peer mediation is a good idea for your school? Why or why not?

4. **Author's Purpose** Think about "The Bill of Rights Rap," "Amistad Rising," and "Caged Bird." What are the authors' purposes for writing each selection?

EXPRESS YOURSELF
▶ DESCRIBE AND CLARIFY A PROBLEM

Getting your point across can be hard, especially if you are upset. Describe a problem to your partner. Have your partner restate what you said. Is what he or she said accurate? If not, explain the problem again using different words. Once your partner correctly retells your problem, switch roles.

Language Arts and Literature

USE CONTEXT CLUES

Learn About Context Clues To figure out the meaning of a new word, use **context clues**, or the words around the new word. Look for different types of context clues.

- **definition clue:**
  A conflict is a disagreement between people.

- **example clue:**
  A conflict like two people wanting to use the computer at the same time can be hard to solve.

- **restatement clue:**
  A conflict can often be solved by talking through it. It is important to resolve arguments.

Find Context Clues What kind of context clue helps you know what *flexible* means?

> They must be flexible and not stick stubbornly to their own point of view.

Practice With a partner, list words you don't understand in the selection. Write the context clues for each word. Tell which type of context clue helps you decide what the word means.

New Word: flexible

Context Clue	Type of Clue
not stick stubbornly to their own point of view	restatement clue

MEDIATE A DISPUTE

Work with your group to act out a peer mediation session.

1 Choose a Conflict to Resolve With your class, brainstorm several conflicts that could arise at school. Choose one to act out with your group, or use one of these ideas:

- Vegetarian students want more choices in the cafeteria, but giving them more choices would cut out others' favorite foods.

- The dance ensemble and drama club both need to use the theater at the same time.

- The tennis and the rugby teams both need new uniforms. There is only enough money in the budget for uniforms for one team.

2 Mediate the Conflict Review the Ground Rules for a Peer Mediation Session on page 188. Decide who will represent each side of the argument and who will be the two peer mediators. Everyone works to find a solution.

3 Share the Resolution Because this is a made-up situation, you can tell the class about your group's session. Share your ideas about how peer mediation works.

Learn to participate in a **discussion**.
See Handbook page 400.

Respond to the Article and Letters, continued
Language Arts and Literature, continued

▶ WRITING/SPEAKING

ANALYZE AND EVALUATE INFORMATION

Write an essay evaluating the arguments in each letter on pages 192–193.

1 Analyze the Letters Complete this chart with your peer-conferencing group.

Type of Information	Examples in Jan's Letter	Examples in Robert's Letter
missing information	gives only two ways to handle student conflicts	
inaccurate information		
facts		
opinions		
exaggerations		

2 Share Your Information Compare notes with your group. List ways that Jan and Robert could make stronger arguments.

3 Write an Essay How strong do you think each letter is in supporting its argument? Write an essay describing your position. Edit it and share the final copy with your group.

Develop your skill in the **writer's craft**, see Handbook pages 414–423.

▶ READING/REPRESENTING

FIND THE HIDDEN AGENDA

Learn About Apparent and Hidden Agendas
The **apparent agenda** is what the purpose of something appears to be, for example, a store has people fill out a form for a contest.

The **hidden agenda** is the real reason for doing it. The store's hidden agenda is to gather people's names and addresses from the forms to add to its advertising mailing list.

Recognizing the hidden agenda will help you understand the author's purpose for writing.

Find the Hidden Agenda Read this letter. What does the author really want?

Letter

> Dear Editor,
>   There is a bare parking strip along Brook Street between Alder and Fifth. It would be the perfect spot to turn into a garden. The Plants Foundation will supply the plants if we can get some teenagers to do the work. I think it would be a wonderful way to get young people involved in our community!
>   Mrs. Eleanor Fisk
>   5270 Brook Street

Practice Review what you learned about hidden agenda. Then write a campaign speech, a TV commercial, or a magazine ad with an apparent and a hidden agenda. See if your classmates can identify both agendas in your work.

Content Area Connections

SOCIAL STUDIES
TECHNOLOGY/MEDIA

WRITE ABOUT THE UNITED NATIONS

One of the main purposes of the United Nations is to keep peace between nations by acting as a mediator in disputes. With a group, find out more about the United Nations' role as a mediator. Then write a magazine article about what you learn.

1 Gather Information What does the United Nations do? When and where has its mediation worked?

These Web site addresses can lead you to sites that will help answer these questions, but remember that Web sites change every day, so follow interesting links.

INFORMATION ON-LINE

Key Words:
+mediation +"United Nations"

Web Sites:
➤ **Sites about the United Nations**
  • www.un.org
  • www.betterworldfund.org

➤ **Encyclopedia Articles**
  • www.eblast.com
  • www.encarta.com

Download helpful information and pictures for your magazine article.

2 Organize Information Reread the information you downloaded. Make an outline of the information you want to include in your article.

3 Prepare Your Article Use a word-processing program to write your article. Edit it by checking for accuracy. Include a headline. Scan in or download photographs and write captions for them. Print out the final version to display in your classroom.

For more about the **research process**, see Handbook pages 394–399. Learn to use **word-processing software** on pages 383–389.

The Truth About Sharks

realistic fiction
by Joan Bauer

Prepare to Read

THINK ABOUT WHAT YOU KNOW

Quickwrite Have you ever been in a situation that made you feel as if you were being treated unfairly? What happened? How did you react? Write about it.

false accusation untrue statement that someone has done something wrong

falsely arrested held by the police for something you did not do

inconvenient troublesome, annoying

merchandise things for sale

misconstrue misunderstand

possession ownership, control

publicly humiliated embarrassed or ashamed in front of other people

security guard someone who protects property, often at a business

shoplifter person who steals from a store

unrighteousness unfairness

LEARN KEY VOCABULARY

Use New Words in Context Study the new words and their definitions. Use the new words as you act out these scenes with your group.

It is very **inconvenient**, but you rush to a store to buy **merchandise** on sale. Then you realize that you have **misconstrued** the ad. The sale is next week!

Your friend is returning a bracelet. A **security guard** sees the bracelet in her **possession** so she is **falsely arrested** as a **shoplifter**. She protests the **unrighteousness** of being **publicly humiliated** by the **false accusation**.

LEARN TO RELATE PROBLEMS AND SOLUTIONS

In many stories, a character has a **problem** to **solve**. Knowing what the problem is and how the character tries to solve it helps you better understand the action.

READING STRATEGY
How to Relate Problems and Solutions

1. Ask yourself: What is the situation? What is the problem?
2. Look for the attempts the character makes to try to solve the problem. How do the attempts affect what happens in the story?
3. Think about what finally happens. Does the character manage to solve the problem? If so, how?

Now read "The Truth About Sharks." Look for the problem and how the character tries to solve it.

The Truth About

Sharks

by Joan Bauer

A teenage girl, falsely accused of shoplifting, uses her head to find a solution to her problem.

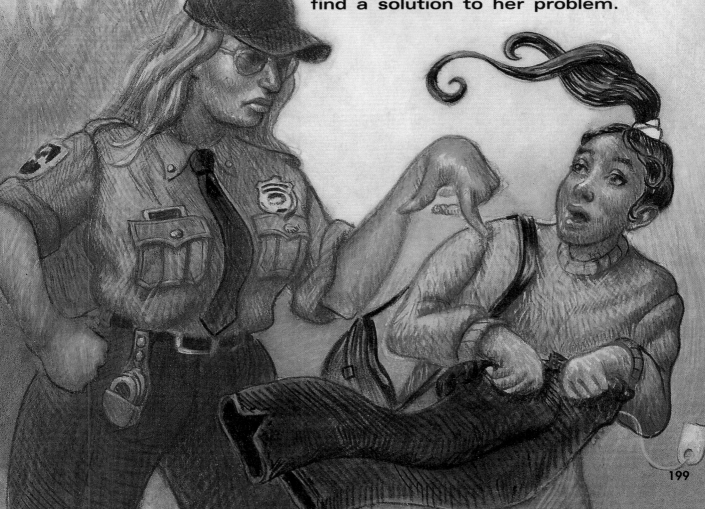

1

ACCUSED OF SHOPLIFTING

A security guard accuses a girl of shoplifting.
The girl tries to explain that she is innocent.

—

Mitchell Gail's was a huge store; five stories, to be exact.

I walked past the **stocky**, **stern security guard**. She glared at me through **frigid**, gray eyes and touched her name tag: MADGE P. GROTON, SECURITY GUARD. The sign above her read, **SHOPLIFTERS** WILL BE **PROSECUTED TO THE FULL EXTENT OF THE LAW**. I should hope so. I headed for the pants section.

I found four pairs of black slacks, size 10, and one pair, size 8. I walked into the dressing room, past another larger, more **threatening** sign—SHOPLIFTERS WILL BE PROSECUTED TO THE FULL EXTENT OF THE LAW—just in case any thieves missed the first warning. A sweet saleswoman showed me to an empty changing room. Her name tag read HANNAH.

"If you need anything I'll help you," Hannah said.

"Thanks."

I tried on the first four pairs. No luck.

I tried the fifth. Not bad. I turned in front of the mirror. Not perfect, but doable.

She was strong. She pushed me past a line of staring customers, into the elevator.

I put on my shoes, left my coat and sweatpants in the changing room with my purse underneath them. I said to Hannah, "I'll take these, but I'm going to keep looking."

"They look nice on you."

They do, don't they? I smiled at the **beckoning** sale sign over a rack of pants right by the elevator that I'd not seen before.

I walked toward the rack and was just reaching for an excellent pair of size 10 black silk pants when a rough hand came down hard on my shoulder and spun me around.

"That's not the way we play the game," Madge P. Groton, Security Guard, barked.

"What?"

"That's not the way we play the game," she repeated, pulling my hands behind my back and pushing me forward.

"*What are you talking about?*"

She was strong. She pushed me past a line of staring customers, into the elevator. She squeezed my hands hard. A cold fear swept through me.

"*What,*" I shouted, "*are you doing?*"

....

stocky big, heavyset
stern strict, harsh
frigid ice cold

prosecuted to the full extent of the law arrested and charged with breaking the law
threatening frightening
beckoning inviting

"You were going into the elevator wearing pants you didn't pay for. We call that shoplifting around here."

"*No, I was—*"

She pressed my hands tighter.

"*You're hurting me!*"

"*Shut up!*"

Tears stung my eyes. My chest was pounding. I had seen a TV show about what to do if you're **falsely arrested**. You don't fight, you calmly explain your **position**. There was an explanation. I would give the explanation to this person at the right time and I would go home. If I panicked now . . .

"Ma'am, **I'm *innocent*,**" I said.

"Yeah, and I'm the Easter Bunny." She opened a door that read SECURITY, and pushed me inside to a **dingy** beige windowless room with the now-familiar sign: SHOPLIFTERS WILL BE PROSECUTED TO THE FULL EXTENT OF THE LAW.

"Please, Ma'am, Ms. Groton . . ."

My whole body was shaking.

"Take them off," she snarled.

"What?"

"Take the pants off. Now."

I stared at her. "You mean here?"

She put her hand on her gun. This was crazy.

"I get a phone call, right?"

"You are in **possession** of stolen **property**."

"Ma'am, I know you're trying to do your job. Just listen to me. I was going to buy these pants. I told this to the saleswoman. I left my coat and my pants and my purse in the changing room. Believe me, this is a big—"

"Take them off." She leaned back in her chair, enjoying her power.

I felt my face shaking like tears were exploding inside. I was sick and terrified. My mind reached for anything.

BEFORE YOU MOVE ON...

1. **Conflict** Describe the conflict that gets the story started.
2. **Inference** What does the security guard mean by saying, "Yeah, and I'm the Easter Bunny"?
3. **Prediction** What do you think the girl will do?

Tears stung my eyes. I was just about ready to cry.
position point of view
I'm innocent I didn't do anything wrong

dingy dirty, shabby
property things, goods

CONVINCING THE POLICE

A policeman arrives. He agrees to find the saleswoman
who will prove the girl's innocence.

I remembered that article I'd read about sharks. If you're swimming in the ocean and a shark comes at you to attack, hit him in the nose, the expert said.

I looked at Madge P. Groton, Security Shark.

"No, Ma'am. Not until I get my pants back."

She leaned toward me; her face was tight and mean. "You do what I tell you."

I took a huge breath and looked at her hard.

"No, Ma'am."

Her face darkened. She punched a button on a large black phone, said into the receiver, "I've got one. Send a car."

Nausea hit. My heart was beating out of my chest. Madge P. Groton, Security Guard, took her handcuffs off her belt and clinked them on the cracked linoleum floor again and again.

"If we could just talk to that saleswoman," I tried, "I think we could clear this—"

"That's not the way we play the game."

"The law says I get to make a phone call."

"You can do it at the **station**."

I started to cry. "I didn't do it."

"Ma'am, my purse and coat and pants are still in the changing room." Nothing.

I checked my watch: 1:10. I lowered my head and started to cry.

"I didn't do it."

I jumped at the harsh knock on the door. A big policeman with leathery skin entered with his hand on his gun. He listened to the security guard's story. I told him she'd made a mistake, but it didn't seem to matter. No one believes prisoners.

The policeman took my arm firmly and we walked out of the store to the waiting police car.

"You have the right to remain silent," he said the sickening words to me. "You have the right to **an attorney**. If you do not have an attorney, one will be appointed for you."

He opened the back door of the **squad** car. I got in crying.

The door shut like a prison gate.

"It wasn't worth it, Miss," he said, got into the front and drove off.

"Officer," I whispered, "I know you're doing your job. I know that security guard was doing hers, but I've got to tell you, if we go back to that store, I've got a **witness**

---

station police department
an attorney a lawyer

squad police
witness person who saw what happened

202 Unit 3 | Conflict and Resolution

who knows that I didn't do it."

This was a definite **gamble**. I didn't know if that saleswoman would remember me.

"Who?" he asked.

I told him about the saleswoman. "Officer, I am really scared and I don't know what else to do. Would you let me try to **prove** I'm innocent?"

He stopped the car and stared at me through the grill.

The policeman searched my face. "Which salesperson?"

"Her name was Helen. No. Hortense. Wait—*Hannah*. Yes! *Please* believe me, Officer."

The officer sighed deeply. "I don't have time for this." He rammed the patrol car into gear, did a perfect U-turn, and headed back toward Mitchell Gail's.

We walked through the front door, past Madge P. Groton, who **nearly dropped her fangs** when she saw us.

"Just checking something out," said the officer to her and kept on walking to the elevator.

The elevator opened at the fourth floor. We got out. My eyes searched for Hannah. The policeman walked up to a gray-haired saleswoman.

"We're looking for Hortense," he said.

"*Hannah!*" I shrieked.

The woman pointed to Hannah. We walked toward her. Remember me? I wanted to shout.

"Do you know this young woman?" the policeman asked Hannah.

Hannah looked at me and smiled. "I waited on her this morning. She left her purse and coat and stuff in the changing room. I've got them for you."

Madge P. Groton **stormed up**. "What's going on?"

"Just clearing a few things up," said the officer.

Madge P. Groton **dug in her spurs**. "This girl is a shoplifter. I caught her trying to leave the store wearing **merchandise!**"

BEFORE YOU MOVE ON...

1. **Character's Motive** Why does Madge Groton call the police?
2. **Vocabulary** List the words on pages 202 and 203 that have to do with crime and legal procedures.

---

gamble chance, risk
prove show without doubt that
nearly dropped her fangs was very surprised

stormed up walked up angrily
dug in her spurs stuck to her original complaint

3

RECEIVING JUSTICE

The girl is proved innocent. The store manager offers compensation for the misunderstanding.

Hannah looked shocked. "Then why would she leave her purse in the changing room?"

Why indeed?

I smiled broadly at Madge P. Groton, Security Guard, whose face had turned a delightful funeral gray.

"And why would she leave her coat?" Hannah continued. "It's worth at least as much as the pants. You made a mistake, Madge."

"Can I see her purse?" asked the officer.

Hannah ran to get it.

"You got a wallet in here?"

I reached deep within and pulled it out. He checked my driver's license. He counted the money. Seventy-five dollars.

"I think," said the officer, "we've got things **straightened out** here, wouldn't you say so, Ms. Groton?"

Madge P. Groton **sputtered** first. Her wide jaw locked. Her thick neck **gripped**. Her nose mole twitched. She turned on her scuffed heel and stormed off. The officer gave me back my purse, coat.

"You're free to go," he said. "Just give the store back the pants."

"I never want to see these pants again. Thank you for believing me, Officer . . . um . . . I don't know your name."

"Brennerman."

I thanked him again.

I thanked Hannah.

I ran into the changing room, put on my dear, old gray grubbies, **drew a penetrating breath of freedom**, and raced toward my mother's car. It was 2:30.

I turned left on Route 1 feeling something wasn't quite right.

The **unrighteousness** of it grew in my soul.

I'd been **publicly humiliated**.

Falsely accused.

I have my rights!

I rammed Mom's car around and headed back for Mitchell Gail's.

I am teenager, **hear me roar**.

I parked the car, stormed into the store past the SHOPLIFTERS WILL BE

> I smiled broadly at Madge P. Groton, Security Guard, whose face had turned a delightful funeral gray.

---

straightened out settled, resolved
sputtered spoke without finishing her sentences, stuttered
gripped tightened up

drew a penetrating breath of freedom took a very deep breath, relieved that I was free
hear me roar see what I can do, I am as strong as a lion

PROSECUTED TO THE FULL EXTENT OF THE LAW sign, right past Madge P. Groton, to the store office.

"Can I help you?" asked a tired receptionist with too red hair.

"Only if you're in charge, Ma'am. I need to see the manager. "

She looked me up and down. "He's busy now." She looked toward the manager's closed office door. The sign read: THOMAS LUNDGREN, STORE MANAGER.

"It can't wait."

"I'm afraid it's going to have to, dear, you see . . ."

"No, Ma'am. You see. I was falsely arrested in this store by Madge P. Groton, and in exactly two seconds I'm going to call a very large lawyer."

"Oh, *Mr. Lundgren!*" the woman's bony hands fluttered in front of her face. She flew into his office. I walked in behind her. "We have a little problem."

Thomas Lundgren, Store Manager, **appraised** my grubby gray sweats, unimpressed. "What problem is that?" he said coarsely, not getting up.

I told him. The policeman, Hannah, Madge, the lawyer.

He got up.

"Sit down," he purred at me. "Make yourself comfortable. Would you like a soda? *Candy?*"

"I'd like an **apology**."

"Well, of course, we at Mitchell Gail's are **appalled** at anything that could be **misconstrued** —"

"—This wasn't misconstrued."

"We'll have to check this out, of course."

I folded my arms. "I'll wait, Mr. Lundgren."

"Call me Tom." He snapped his finger at the receptionist. "Get Madge up here."

I crossed my legs. "I'd call the police, too, Tom. Officer Brennerman. He's probably the most important one, next to the lawyer."

Tom grew pale; the receptionist twittered. "Make this happen, Celia," he barked. Then he smiled at me big and wide. "We certainly **pride ourselves on treating our customers well**."

The phone buzzed and Tom lunged for it.

"I see . . . Yes, Officer Brennerman, it was most unfortunate . . . a **vast misunderstanding** . . . thank you."

Madge P. Groton **had seeped into the hall**. I said, "By the way, Tom, in addition to **false accusations** and public

---

appraised critically looked at
apology admission that you made a mistake
appalled shocked, alarmed

pride ourselves on treating our customers well
feel it is important to be nice to our shoppers
vast misunderstanding very big mistake
had seeped into the hall had come quietly into the hallway

humiliation, your security guard told me to take off my pants in her office."

"Pardon?"

"It was a low moment, Tom."

"Tell me you kept them on."

I nodded as Tom moved shakily to the hall, his arms outstretched. "Madge, what is this I'm hearing?"

He shut the office door.

There were hushed, snarling words that I couldn't make out.

The door opened. Tom grinned. "Madge is truly sorry for the misunderstanding."

Madge **glowered** at me from the hall. She didn't look sorry.

"Mitchell Gail's is terribly sorry for the . . . **inconvenience**," he murmured.

"Um, it was a bit more than an inconvenience."

"We would like you to accept a $250 gift certificate from the store for your trouble."

I thought about that.

"We'd be happy to make it $500 for all your trouble," Tom added quickly.

"I'll think about it, Tom."

"We'd really like to get this worked out here and now."

"I'm sure you would, Tom, but I'm going to think about it."

I walked into the hall, down the stairs and out the door.

Yes!

I decided to not call a lawyer. Tom upped the gift certificate to $650 and had Madge P. Groton **personally apologize to me**, which was like watching a vulture telling a half-eaten mouse that he didn't really mean it.

"I'm sorry for the trouble," she snarled. Tom glared at her.

"It was wrong of me," she added flatly.

"Thank you," I said.

I guess I'd learned the truth about sharks: If one comes **barreling at you**, the best thing to do is hit it on the nose.

BEFORE YOU MOVE ON...

1. **Paraphrase** In your own words, tell what happens after the girl talks to the store manager.

2. **Cause and Effect** What effect does the girl's threat of a lawsuit have?

3. **Personal Experience** Describe an experience you have had in being wrongly accused. Explain how you defended yourself.

ABOUT THE AUTHOR

Joan Bauer based "The Truth About Sharks" on a personal experience that happened when she was nineteen. The outcome of that incident was not as satisfactory as the one she writes in the story, but, she says, "The beauty of fiction is that it can allow the writer to have power over past experiences." Joan Bauer has written many award-winning books for young adults.

---

glowered stared angrily

personally apologize to me tell me directly that she was sorry

barreling at you moving at full speed toward you

Respond to the Story
Check Your Understanding

SUM IT UP

Relate Problems and Solutions Make a problem-and-solution chart for "The Truth About Sharks."

Problem-and-Solution Chart

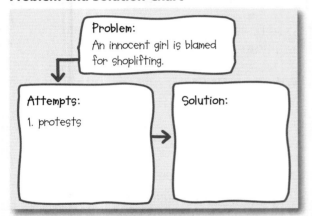

Problem:
An innocent girl is blamed for shoplifting.

Attempts:
1. protests

Solution:

Write a Summary Use your chart to write a summary of "The Truth About Sharks." State the problem in your topic sentence. Use your detail sentences to tell what the girl did about it. Tell how the problem was solved in a concluding statement.

THINK IT OVER

Discuss and Write Talk about these questions with a partner. Write the answers.

1. **Synthesis** Explain what the title "The Truth About Sharks" has to do with the story.

2. **Character's Point of View** Imagine that you are the security guard. Tell the story from your point of view.

3. **Personal Experience** Have you ever had to explain to an adult that he or she was wrong? How did you feel about it? How did the adult react?

4. **Judgment** Why do you think the security guard didn't believe the girl? How does stereotyping like this lead to false accusations?

EXPRESS YOURSELF ▶ RETELL A STORY

Pretend you are the main character and your partner is your best friend. Role-play coming home, calling your friend, and explaining what happened at the store. Then switch roles.

Respond to the Story, continued
Language Arts and Literature

▶ GRAMMAR IN CONTEXT

USE THE PRESENT PERFECT TENSE

Learn About the Present Perfect Tense The **present perfect tense** tells about action that began in the past and is still going on.

> Madge **has worked** at the store for years.

The present perfect tense is formed with *has* or *have* plus the past participle of the verb. The past participle form of regular verbs ends in *-ed*.

> She **has** always **watched** carefully for shoplifters.

Irregular verbs have special forms for the past participle. Study these examples. For more, see Handbook pages 450–451.

Some Irregular Verbs

Verb	be	come	know	stole
Past Participle	been	come	known	stolen

Practice Write each sentence. Use the present perfect tense of the verb in parentheses.

1. Madge _____ to do her job well. (try)

2. She _____ the police before. (call)

3. They _____ to question the suspect. (come)

4. Some of the suspects _____ guilty. (be)

5. The manager _____ Madge for her work in catching these people. (praise)

▶ WRITING

WRITE A CHARACTER SKETCH

A **character sketch** is a short, vivid description of a person. Write a character sketch of the girl in "The Truth About Sharks."

❶ **Prepare to Write** Use a web to record the girl's traits and what she is like.

❷ **Write Your Draft** Use the details to write sentences that tell what the girl is like. Use descriptive words and similes to help your readers picture the girl.

❸ **Check Your Work** Edit your writing to make it more descriptive and interesting. Also check to be sure you used correct spelling, punctuation, and grammar.

❹ **Share Your Work** Read your work in a group, and compare your character sketches.

Learn about **clusters** on Handbook page 370. Develop your skill in the **writer's craft**. See pages 414–423.

Content Area Connections

 SOCIAL STUDIES
WRITING/SPEAKING

LEARN ABOUT HISTORY-MAKERS

Use the Internet or other resources to learn about someone who made a difference by standing up for his or her rights. Then share the information with your class.

1 **Select a Person** Choose one of these people or research another person you know of:

Alexander Solzhenitsyn   Rosa Parks
Galileo Galilei   Nelson Mandela
Ryan White   Crazy Horse
Betty Friedan   Jesse Owens

2 **Gather Information and Take Notes** Use the person's name as key words to begin your search. Download helpful articles and pictures and take notes.

3 **Share Your Information** Try one of these ideas to share what you learned:

speech   mock interview
editorial   photo essay
letter to the editor poem
encyclopedia article rap song
character sketch   portrait with facts

 For more about the **research process**, see Handbook pages 394–399.

SCIENCE
REPRESENTING

FIND OUT ABOUT BODY CHEMISTRY

What takes place physically when a person is frightened? Do research to find out. Then create a visual representation of what you learn.

Research Effects Use the Internet, science books, encyclopedias, and other sources to answer questions like these. Take notes on what you learn.

- What **chemical changes** take place in the **brain** when a person is scared? What **physical changes** occur in the **body**? Why?

- What is the **fight-or-flight reaction**?

- What is the **effect** on the body of repeated stress or fear? What is **post-traumatic stress syndrome**?

Present the Information Use your information to make a chart, diorama, map, board game, fact poster, or graph. Write captions to explain anything that you can't illustrate.

A doctor examines film of the brain.

Writing That Persuades

How does a writer try to persuade readers? The writer takes a position and gives strong support for it. Persuasive writing makes the reader say, "Yes, I see your point and I agree with you!"

PERSUASIVE LANGUAGE IN PROFESSIONAL WRITING

In "Amistad Rising," the character Cinqué tries to persuade a jury to give him his freedom. He uses facts and strong words to support his position. He makes clear what action he wants the jury to take.

The girl in "The Truth About Sharks" uses emotional language and logical arguments to convince the policeman to take her back to the store.

from "Amistad Rising"

". . . I am here to argue the facts. The indisputable, international law is that the stealing of slaves from Africa is now illegal."

". . . We regret the loss of life caused by our mutiny. But we are not savages. We took over the ship to save our lives. We have done no wrong. Allow us to go home."

from "The Truth About Sharks"

"Officer," I whispered, "I know you're doing your job. I know that security guard was doing hers, but I've got to tell you, if we go back to that store, I've got a witness who knows that I didn't do it."

I told him about the saleswoman. "Officer, I am really scared and I don't know what else to do. Would you let me try to prove I'm innocent?"

LOGICAL ORDER IN PERSUASIVE WRITING

Persuasive writing is more effective when writers present their arguments in a logical order. For example, they might present a sequence of benefits that will result from the proposed action. Or, they might present their reasons for taking action in order from least important to most important. Study these diagrams.

Diagrams of Logical Order

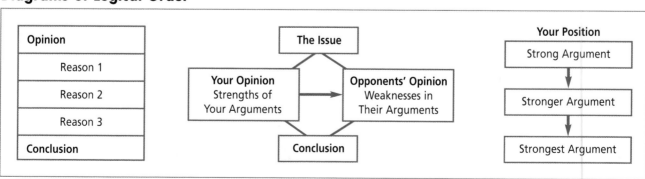

STUDENT WRITING MODEL

Persuasive Essay

We Need School Uniforms

by Magdiel Ramírez and Imara Guerrero

Should school uniforms be required at Oakridge Middle School? We think so. Uniforms should be worn by all the students in our school. If everyone had to wear a uniform, there would be fewer problems with money, discipline, and school pride.

First of all, clothing is expensive. Kids are always asking their parents to buy them shoes and shirts with designer labels. A shirt with a popular designer label costs twice as much as a regular shirt. If students wore uniforms, their parents could save a lot of money. They would only have to buy two uniforms and one pair of shoes. Families would only have two sets of clothes to wash so they could save on their water bills, too.

In addition, wearing uniforms would improve school discipline. Many kids worry that other kids will make fun of the way they dress. So they spend too long trying to find something to wear and are late to school. Some kids even fight over who has the coolest clothes. These things won't be problems if everyone wears the same thing.

Finally, uniforms are a way to show pride in our school. Instead of thinking about being fashionable, students will think about being part of the school community. Clothing shouldn't matter as much as getting an education. School uniforms are a reminder about what is important.

Uniforms would solve some of the problems that we have now and make our school a better place. School uniforms are good for students, our families, and our school. We must tell everyone we can to make uniforms part of our school experience.

INTRODUCTION
The writers **present the issue** and **state their position** in the first paragraph. They get the reader ready for their arguments by mentioning the main reasons for their opinion.

BODY
In the body, the writers **present their arguments** in a **logical order**. Each paragraph presents a different argument. Together, the paragraphs give the benefits of wearing school uniforms.

The writers use **persuasive words** to get their readers to take action.

They include **facts or examples** to support their opinions.

CONCLUSION
The last paragraph sums up the writers' position and asks the reader to take action.

Writing That Persuades, continued

The Writing Process

PREWRITE

1 **Collect Ideas and Choose an Issue** With a partner, brainstorm issues you care about. Try making a cluster to show your ideas.

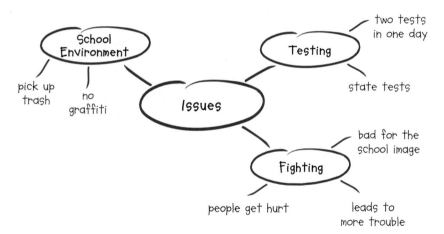

FATP Chart

HOW TO UNLOCK A PROMPT
Form: _persuasive essay_
Audience: _students at our school_
Topic: _why there should be no fighting_
Purpose: _to persuade readers to agree with my opinion_

Choose the issue that matters the most to you for your topic.

2 **Unlock the Writing Prompt** Before you begin writing, fill out an **FATP** chart to help guide your writing.

3 **Decide How to Support Your Position** You might list reasons that something should change. Or, you might list the benefits that can result if your readers take action.

4 **Put Your Ideas in Order** Look at the diagrams on page 210. Decide on the best order for presenting your arguments. Number the ideas in your list or make an outline. See Handbook pages 396–398 for help with making an outline.

Reflect and Evaluate

- How did your partner help you come up with ideas?
- Why do you think your issue is an important one to write about?
- Do you need more supporting reasons to support your position?

DRAFT

Use your **FATP** chart to help you focus your writing. Write quickly to get all your ideas down. Later, you can fix any mistakes and make other changes.

1 **Write the Introduction** State the issue and give your opinion. Briefly mention the main points you'll cover in your essay.

2 **Write the Body** As you write, use persuasive words to convince your readers to agree with you. Add details to support your opinion and show exactly what you mean.

Writer's Craft: Show, Don't Tell

Use dialogue to show what someone or something is like.

This tells:	This shows:
Stronger students pick on weaker students.	I have seen a bully or stronger student push a weaker student to play a trick. "Why did you push me?" the bully says to the innocent student.

Use sensory details to show what something is like.

This tells:	This shows:
Even play fighting is no fun when people get hurt.	Play fighting might seem fun, but what happens if someone hits a little too hard? The person who gets hurt will probably get mad. Too often play fighting leads to real fighting.

Be specific.

This tells:	This shows:
Sometimes a little thing can cause a big fight.	An accidental shove in the hallway can lead first to angry words and then to punching.

Add examples or facts.

This tells:	This shows:
Students get into trouble for fighting at school.	Vice Principal Jefferson suspended five students for fighting in the last three months.

---

3 **Write the Conclusion** In your last paragraph, restate your position and sum up your supporting arguments. End with a strong sentence.

Writer's Craft: Concluding Sentence

Make a request to take action.

Follow my advice and stop the fighting—then everyone will enjoy peace and happiness.

Reflect and Evaluate

- How do you feel about your draft? Will your audience understand your position?

- Are your arguments presented in a logical order?

Writing That Persuades, continued

REVISE

❶ Reread Your Draft Review your **FATP**. The form, audience, topic, and purpose should be clear in your essay. Does the body of your essay include a supporting argument in each paragraph?

❷ Conduct a Peer Conference Talk to a partner or group about your writing. Are there any unimportant details to take out? Are there important details you should add? Use the guidelines on Handbook page 411 to help you with a conference.

Look at the peer reviewer comments about Magdiel and Imara's essay. Read their responses.

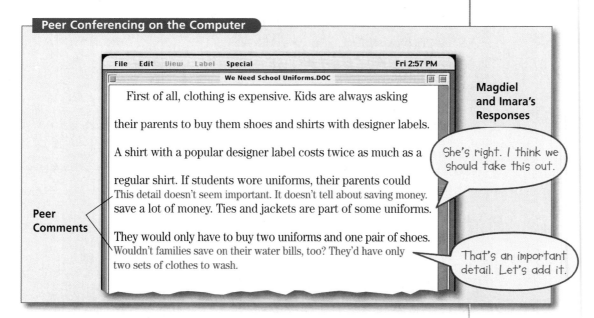

Peer Conferencing on the Computer

File Edit View Label Special   Fri 2:57 PM

We Need School Uniforms.DOC

First of all, clothing is expensive. Kids are always asking

their parents to buy them shoes and shirts with designer labels.

A shirt with a popular designer label costs twice as much as a

regular shirt. If students wore uniforms, their parents could
This detail doesn't seem important. It doesn't tell about saving money.
save a lot of money. Ties and jackets are part of some uniforms.

They would only have to buy two uniforms and one pair of shoes.
Wouldn't families save on their water bills, too? They'd have only
two sets of clothes to wash.

Peer Comments

Magdiel and Imara's Responses

She's right. I think we should take this out.

That's an important detail. Let's add it.

❸ Mark Your Changes Decide what changes you will make. Revising Marks appear on Handbook page 411. For how to make changes on a word-processed document, see Handbook pages 383–389.

> *I write to clear my own mind, to find out what I think and feel.*
>
> — V.S. Pritchett

Reflect and Evaluate

- Did your peers think your essay was persuasive? What changes did they suggest?
- Are you happy with your essay?
- Did you make all the points you wanted to?

> GRAMMAR IN CONTEXT

SENTENCES WITH RELATIVE CLAUSES

A relative clause adds information to a sentence. It begins with a relative pronoun.

Many students wear school uniforms that are stylish.

- An independent clause expresses a complete thought. It makes sense by itself. A dependent clause does not make sense by itself.

    Example: Students will spend less money on clothes if they wear uniforms.
    <u>independent clause</u>   <u>dependent clause</u>

- A **relative clause** is one kind of dependent clause. It begins with a relative pronoun. The relative pronoun connects the clause to a noun or pronoun in the sentence.

    Examples: People spend too much on designer clothes, **which** are expensive.
    <u>independent clause</u>   <u>relative clause</u>

    Many students want shoes **that** are made by popular companies.
    <u>independent clause</u>   <u>relative clause</u>

Relative Pronouns

that
which
who
whom
whose

Use a comma to set off a relative clause when it is not necessary to the meaning of the sentence.

    Example: Bay School, **which** is a new school, asked us to wear uniforms.
    <u>relative clause</u>

If the clause is important to the meaning of the sentence, do not use a comma. Never use a comma with a relative clause beginning with *that*.

    Examples: The person **who** approved the uniforms is the principal.
    <u>relative clause</u>

    He thinks a uniform **that** is simple can look stylish.
    <u>relative clause</u>

Practice Combine each pair of sentences. Use relative clauses to make complex sentences.

1. The boys at Bay School wear uniforms. The uniforms include a jacket and slacks.
2. Each boy must wear a tie and a shirt. The shirt is blue and neatly pressed.
3. The girls at Bay School must wear skirts. The skirts cannot be short.
4. Yvonne Veline attends Bay School. She likes wearing the uniform.
5. Yvonne chose to attend this school. This school is known for its strict rules.

Writing That Persuades   **215**

Writing That Persuades, continued

EDIT AND PROOFREAD

1 **Check for Mistakes** Look through your writing to correct any mistakes in capitalization, spelling, and punctuation. If you need help, use Handbook pages 459–469.

2 **Check Your Sentences** Look for the correct use of relative clauses.

3 **Make a Final Copy** If you are working on a computer, print out the corrected version of your work. If not, rewrite it to make the corrections you marked.

PUBLISH

Choose one of these ideas for publishing your writing, or come up with your own idea.

- Is your essay about a topic of interest to your community? If so, send it by e-mail or in an envelope to your local newspaper. It might be published on the Editorials or Opinions page.

Colton Times

Opinions

State Testing: One Student's Opinion
by Hannah Liu

It's April. Are you starting to feel nervous and anxious? That's probably because it's testing time again! I believe that we should all take a look at how often kids are tested each year.

- Read your essay aloud to classmates. Have them vote by secret ballot to tell whether they agree or disagree with your argument. Make a bar graph to show the results.

- Find a classmate with a different opinion on the same issue. Each of you can read your essay aloud to the class. Then you can ask and answer questions from the audience.

Key In `TO` Technology

Use the **Find** feature to look for a period after each sentence. If the computer skips a sentence, you'll know you've left out a period (unless there's a question or an exclamation mark).

Reflect and Evaluate

- Are you pleased with your essay? Does it
  - ☑ state your position and give supporting arguments?
  - ☑ have an introduction, body, and conclusion?
  - ☑ include arguments in a logical order?
- What do you like most about your essay?
- Will this work go in your portfolio? Why or why not?

TURNING PROBLEMS INTO SOLUTIONS

1 Look Back at the Unit

Rate Selections In this unit you read about how people resolve conflicts. Think about each selection.

Bill of Rights

Amistad Rising

Dealing with Conflict

The Truth About Sharks

Write the title of each selection on an index card. Rate each selection with one to five stars. Give five stars to the best one to indicate how well it was written. On the back of each card, summarize how the problems and solutions were presented.

2 Show What You Know

Sum It All Up Expand and organize your ideas on this mind map. Share your ideas about conflict and resolution with a partner.

Problems

Solutions

Conflict and Resolution

Reflect and Evaluate Write a paragraph to summarize what you have learned about conflict and resolution. Add this writing to your portfolio, along with work from the unit that reflects your accomplishments.

3 Make Connections

To Your Community Is there a problem in your city or town that you think can be solved? Write a letter to the local newspaper with your suggestion.

Finish

Start

It's Up to You!

Take a look at the maze. Use your finger to trace a path from Start to the Finish. Along the way you will have to make choices about which path to follow. What happens when you make the wrong choice? What can you learn from wrong choices? How do your decisions affect reaching your goal?

THEME **1**
A Fork in the Road
Only you can choose which road in life you'll take. There are so many choices along the way!

THEME **2**
An Element of Risk
Sometimes a tough decision involves risk for yourself or others. Risk makes a choice even more difficult.

219

A Fork in the Road

- Before you make a choice, do you always think about the consequences? Why or why not?

- How do your choices affect what happens in your life?

- Why is it important to keep your goal in mind when you are making decisions? Explain.

THEME-RELATED BOOKS

Richard Wright and the Library Card
by *William Miller*

Richard's life changes when he borrows a white man's library card. The books Richard reads become his ticket to freedom.

Beautiful Warrior
by *Emily Arnold McCully*

When Mingui decides to learn kung fu to discourage a brutal suitor, her choice changes her life.

NOVEL

Jacob Have I Loved
by *Katherine Paterson*

Always outshone by her twin sister, Louise struggles to find her own place in the world. Her choice surprises even her.

Build Language and Vocabulary

JUSTIFY

Listen to the first part of the folk tale. What do you think will happpen next?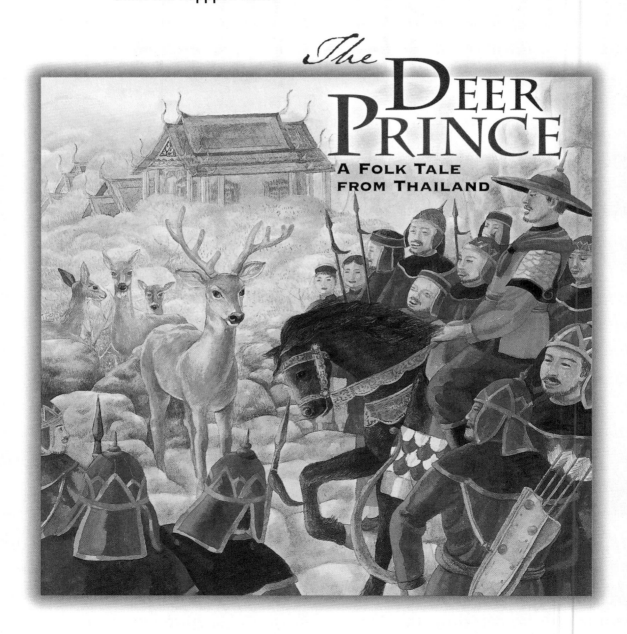

MAKE A DECISION

Imagine that you are the king. What decision would you make about the prince?

BUILD YOUR VOCABULARY

Decision-Making and Justifying Words Make a chart to show the words you used to make the decision and your reasons. Add to your chart as you read the selections in this unit.

Decision-Making Words	Justifying Words
choice	I have proof that . . .
decision	I had to because . . .
advantages and	I feel strongly that . . .
disadvantages	There was no other
The pros are . . .	choice.
The cons are . . .	It was a risk, but I . . .

USE LANGUAGE STRUCTURES ▶ PAST PERFECT TENSE

Speaking: Justify a Decision Tell a partner the story of "The Deer Prince." Be the king, and explain and justify your decision. Use the past perfect tense in some of your sentences.

Example:

Before the Deer Prince made an agreement with the king, the king **had killed** many deer.

I decided not to kill the prince. I felt I should be generous to him because he **had shown** pity for the doe.

Now listen to the end of the folk tale to find out what decision the king did make and why.

The Lady, or the Tiger?

short story
by Frank R. Stockton

Prepare to Read

THINK ABOUT WHAT YOU KNOW

Share Your Experiences Tell your group about a time you helped someone make a choice. Discuss how your feelings affected your advice.

accused blamed

crime something that is against the law

cruel very mean

guilty responsible for doing something wrong

innocent blameless, free from fault

judge determine to be right or wrong

justice fairness, decision based on the law

ordinary usual, typical

punished made to suffer for doing something wrong

rewarded given something in return for something done

LEARN KEY VOCABULARY

Use New Words in Context Study the words and their definitions. Then write a paragraph to explain the events in the flow chart.

Flow Chart

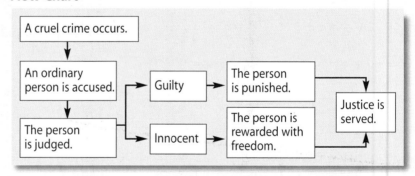

LEARN TO MAKE AND CONFIRM PREDICTIONS

When you make a **prediction**, you say what you think will happen. This helps you focus on each new event in the story.

READING STRATEGY
How to Make and Confirm Predictions

1. Review what you've read or seen so far. You might make a prediction chart to list the details.
2. Think about what you know from your experience.
3. Write what you think will happen next.
4. Read to see if your prediction is correct.

As you read "The Lady, or the Tiger?" stop to make predictions.

The Lady, or the Tiger?

ADAPTED FROM A CLASSIC SHORT STORY

BY FRANK R. STOCKTON

A king has an unusual form of justice. A person accused of a crime must choose between two closed doors. If that person chooses the door that opens to a tiger, the person is guilty. If the accused chooses the door that opens to a woman, the person is innocent. When the princess's beloved has to choose his fate, he looks to the princess for help. Only she knows what is behind each door.

1

THE KING'S JUSTICE

A king punishes the man who loves his daughter by making him choose between two doors that will mean the difference between life and death.

In the very olden times, there lived a king who did things **according to his own fancy**. Some of **his methods** were strange and even **cruel**, but since he was king, he could do as he liked and his subjects had to obey. One of his strangest **notions** was the way he **dispensed justice**, for instead of **judging** whether or not a person committed a **crime**, the king left that decision to **chance**.

When a subject was **accused** of a crime that seemed sufficiently important, a public notice announcing the day of judgment was sent throughout the kingdom. On the appointed day, all the king's subjects would crowd into the king's arena, a huge amphitheater built especially for these events. When everyone was assembled, the king gave a signal. The accused person stepped out from a prison cell located under the arena, bowed to the king, then walked toward two doors that were built into the circular walls of the amphitheater.

These two doors, side by side and exactly alike, held the secret of the prisoner's **fate**, for he and only he could choose which door to open. Behind one door stood a beautiful lady. Behind the other waited a hungry tiger. If the prisoner chose the door to the lady, he would be judged **innocent** and would be **rewarded** with the lady for his wife, whether he wanted to marry her or not. If he were already married, he had to put his wife and family aside to marry the lady, for the king commanded it. If he chose the door to the tiger, he would be judged **guilty** and would be **punished** with a horrible death. Only the doorkeeper knew behind which door stood the lady or the tiger. The fate of the prisoner was decided completely by chance, which greatly satisfied the king's notion of justice.

Behind one door stood a beautiful lady. Behind the other waited a hungry tiger.

---

according to his own fancy the way he wanted to

his methods the ways he did things

notions ideas

dispensed handed out, carried out, provided

chance luck

fate future, destiny

Everyone in the kingdom loved this **form** of justice as well, for when they attended these events, they did not know whether they would see a bloody killing or a happy wedding. Either way, it was exciting, and no one could say the king's method was unfair since the accused person chose which door to open.

The king had a beautiful daughter whose soul was as **fanciful** and **untamed** as his. She was **the apple of her father's eye**, and the king loved her above all humanity. It so happened that this beautiful princess fell in love with a young man who was extraordinarily handsome and brave, but he was not of **royal** blood. That did not matter to the **willful** princess. She loved him with her entire heart and soul, and the young man loved her in return.

The romance **blossomed and deepened** for several months, until the day the king found out about it. He became furious. He raged against the romance, saying he would never let an **ordinary** person marry his royal daughter. He threw the youth into jail for the crime of loving the princess, and for winning the princess's love. Then he **appointed** a day for the young man's judgment in the arena.

BEFORE YOU MOVE ON...

1. **Details** Explain the decision that an accused person would have to make.

2. **Character** What kind of person was the princess? Describe her.

3. **Character's Point of View** Why does the king think the young man is wrong to love the princess?

---

form type, kind
fanciful full of dreams
untamed wild
the apple of her father's eye her father's favorite, her father's treasure

royal kingly, noble
willful stubborn
blossomed and deepened grew stronger and more serious
appointed set, scheduled

2

THE PRINCESS'S CHOICE

The princess knows what is behind each door and
helps the accused man make a choice.

The king ordered his men to find the hungriest, most savage tiger in the land to put behind one door, and the loveliest, most charming lady to put behind the other. Now the king was especially pleased with his **unusual** form of justice, because no matter which door the youth chose, he would be out of his daughter's life forever: he would be either married or dead.

On the morning of the event, so many people wanted to be in the arena that they filled all the seats and pressed against the doors outside. The king and his court sat in their places, opposite the silent twin doors.

All was ready. The signal was given. A door into the arena opened and out walked the youth. The crowd whispered among themselves. They had not known that **a man so fair** lived among them. What a terrible thing for him to be there!

The young man turned to bow to the king. He saw that the princess was sitting to the right of her father. Some young ladies would not want to be at such an event, but remember, the princess had a passionate side to her nature. Her intense soul would never want to miss an occasion in which she was so personally involved, no matter how horribly it might end.

Ever since **her beloved** was put in jail, she thought about nothing else. In the end, she had done what no other person ever had. She went to the arena and spoke to the man who knew the secret of the doors. She paid him a great deal of gold to learn which door concealed the tiger and which concealed the lady.

She not only found out which door concealed the lady, she learned who the lady was—one of the fairest **damsels** in the kingdom. The princess hated her. She had often seen this fair woman **glance lovingly** at her beloved, and there were times when she thought her beloved returned these

---

unusual strange, odd
a man so fair such a good-looking man
her beloved the man she loved

damsels young ladies
glance lovingly look with love in her eyes

glances. She had seen them walking together, only for a moment, but long enough, she thought, for two people to speak a few **tender** words.

Needless to say, the princess was **jealous**. The thought that her beloved might marry the fair lady tormented her as much as the thought of him dying. She would lie sleepless at night, picturing the horrible sight of a tiger leaping toward her young man, tearing him apart with its cruel fangs. More often, she pictured him at the other door, staring with happiness at the fair lady who secretly loved him. She imagined the crowds cheering and the wedding bells ringing. She imagined how happy they would be together, even though she would be crying many tears. She thought it would be better for him to die, and that part of her which shared the cruel side of her father's nature, **willed that it be so**; yet she hated to think about the tiger, the **ghastly shrieks**, and all the blood.

Now the time of choosing had arrived. Soon the youth would choose either life or death. As he bowed to the king, he glanced at the princess. The lovers did not speak. They knew each other so well that they could almost read each other's thoughts. The young man knew right away that the princess had learned the secret behind the doors. He had only a moment to find out the truth. She raised her right hand. Because everyone was staring at him, he was the only one to see her signal.

Now remember, reader, the princess had several weeks to think about her own choice: would she give her beloved to the tiger, or to the lovely lady? You must think about how people act when they feel love and when they feel terrible jealousy. How would she choose?

---

tender kind, loving
Needless to say Clearly, Obviously
jealous wanting to have her beloved to herself, possessive

willed that it be so hoped for that to happen
ghastly shrieks horrible screams

Trusting in her love, the young man turned and walked quickly across the empty space. Throughout the arena, every heart stopped beating, every breath was held, every eye stared at the tall, beautiful young man. What, they wondered, would be his fate? Which door would he choose? Without a pause, he went to the door on the right, and opened it.

Now the point of the story is this: Which came out of the opened door—the lady, or the tiger?

BEFORE YOU MOVE ON...

1. **Character's Motive** Why did the king think his form of justice was perfect for the accused man?

2. **Details** How did the princess learn which door concealed the tiger and which concealed the lady?

3. **Making Decisions** If you had been the princess, would you have given your beloved to the lady or to the tiger? Explain.

ABOUT THE AUTHOR

Frank R. Stockton (1834–1902) wrote children's books, novels, and short stories. He quickly gained fame after "The Lady, or the Tiger?" was published. He said he let his readers speculate on the choice of the princess so that they might "think it out for themselves." This story was so popular, it was said that Frank Stockton received fan letters for the rest of his life.

Respond to the Story
Check Your Understanding

SUM IT UP

Predict the Outcome With a partner, use your prediction charts to review the story. From what you know about the princess, what choice would she make? Make a new chart to show your prediction.

Details and Information	Prediction
The princess loved the young man. She knew what was behind each door.	

Write an Ending Use your ideas to write an ending that tells how the princess had been feeling about her decision, what she had decided to do, and how the crowd had reacted. Use past perfect verbs like *had felt* and *had decided*.

THINK IT OVER

Discuss and Write Talk about these questions with a partner. Then write the answers.

1. **Judgment** Is the king's form of justice fair? Explain your answer.

2. **Character's Point of View** The young man is standing at an important "fork in the road." Why does he trust the princess's advice?

3. **Opinion** Which emotion do you think is stronger, love or jealousy? Explain your answer.

4. **Author's Purpose** Why do you think the author left the ending up to your imagination?

EXPRESS YOURSELF ▶JUSTIFY

Imagine that you are an advisor to the princess and your partner is the princess. Justify reasons why your partner should tell the young man to choose the door with the tiger. Then justify reasons to tell the young man to choose the door with the lady.

Language Arts and Literature

ANALYZE STORY STRUCTURE: RISING AND FALLING ACTION

Learn About Story Structure In some stories, the most important event is called the **climax**. The events before the climax are the **rising action**. The events after the climax are the **falling action**.

Study a Story Map How does this story map show rising and falling action?

Map of Rising and Falling Action

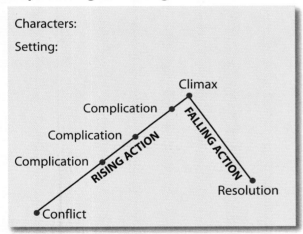

Practice Make a map to show the rising and falling action in "The Lady, or the Tiger?" Use the story ending you and your partner wrote for the resolution.

WRITE IN RESPONSE TO LITERATURE

What did "The Lady, or the Tiger?" help you learn about yourself and the choices you make? Write an essay about the self-discoveries you made as you read the selection.

1 **List Details** Write down what this story helped you discover about yourself.

2 **Make a Draft** Use a strong topic sentence that tells what you discovered. Then write detail sentences that support your idea.

3 **Check Your Work** Use a computer spell-check program or dictionary to check your spelling. Revise any sentences that are incomplete or unclear.

4 **Share Your Work** Read your essay to your group. Discuss your classmates' discoveries.

Sample Essay

> I discovered that I really like stories that don't give all of the answers because they make me think for myself. After I read "The Lady, or the Tiger?" I couldn't stop thinking about the story.

Develop your skill in the **writer's craft**. See Handbook pages 414–423.

Respond to the Story, continued

Content Area Connections

TECHNOLOGY/MEDIA
SOCIAL STUDIES

COMPARE CULTURES THROUGH ARCHITECTURE

Make a Comparison Report The trial in this selection takes place in an arena.

- Learn about the architecture of ancient arenas and how ancient cultures used them.

- Look up modern U.S. arenas and how our culture uses them.

Start with these Web sites and then use key words and look for links. Download helpful information and take notes.

INTERNET

INFORMATION ON-LINE

Key Words:
arena
amphitheater
Colosseum

Web Sites:
➤ **Ancient Arenas**
   • www.eblast.com
   • www.pbs.org

Make a comparison chart that shows the similarities and differences between ancient and modern arenas. Then present your chart as part of a report to the class.

DRAMA

PRESENT A PLAY

Follow these steps to turn "The Lady, or the Tiger?" into a play your group can perform for the class. You can also look at the steps and example of a play on pages 66–67.

① **Rewrite the Story** Turn the story into a script. Make up dialogue for all of the characters. You'll also need lines for a narrator to say.

② **Get Ready to Perform** Decide who will do the different jobs.

- Actors and the director practice the play.

- Costume designers create costumes.

- Set designers plan how the stage and scenery look.

③ **Rehearse and Perform** Practice the play with all of the scenery and in costume. Present your play to the class.

 For tips on **telling a story**, see Handbook page 402.

The Road Not Taken

poem
by Robert Frost

Prepare to Read Poetry

THINK ABOUT WHAT YOU KNOW

Create a Word Web Think about an important choice you made. Create a web to show the effects of your choice.

played better — I joined the school band.

pep rally

Carlos — made great friends

Meagan

mall

performed

---

fair 1. *adj.* pleasing, beautiful 2. *adj.* clear, not stormy 3. *adj.* not favoring one over another, just

lead 1. *v.* guide or direct 2. *v.* go toward

way 1. *n.* road or path 2. *n.* manner or style of doing something

wear 1. *v.* have on as clothing 2. *n.* use

wood 1. *n.* hard part of a tree 2. *n.* small forest

LEARN KEY VOCABULARY

Use Context Clues to Meaning Study the new words and their definitions. Read the paragraph. Use the words around each underlined word to help you figure out its meaning.

> We stood under the trees in the <u>wood</u>. We tried to decide which <u>way</u> would <u>lead</u> to the <u>fair</u> little lake we had heard about. None of the paths we saw showed any signs of <u>wear</u>.

LEARN TO VISUALIZE AND PARAPHRASE

When you **visualize** what you read, you picture in your mind what the words describe. When you **paraphrase**, you retell something in your own words.

READING STRATEGY
How to Visualize and Paraphrase a Poem
1. Read the poem.
2. Picture the scene in your mind.
3. Tell the poem in your own words.

As you read "The Road Not Taken," visualize the place that the poet describes and paraphrase each stanza.

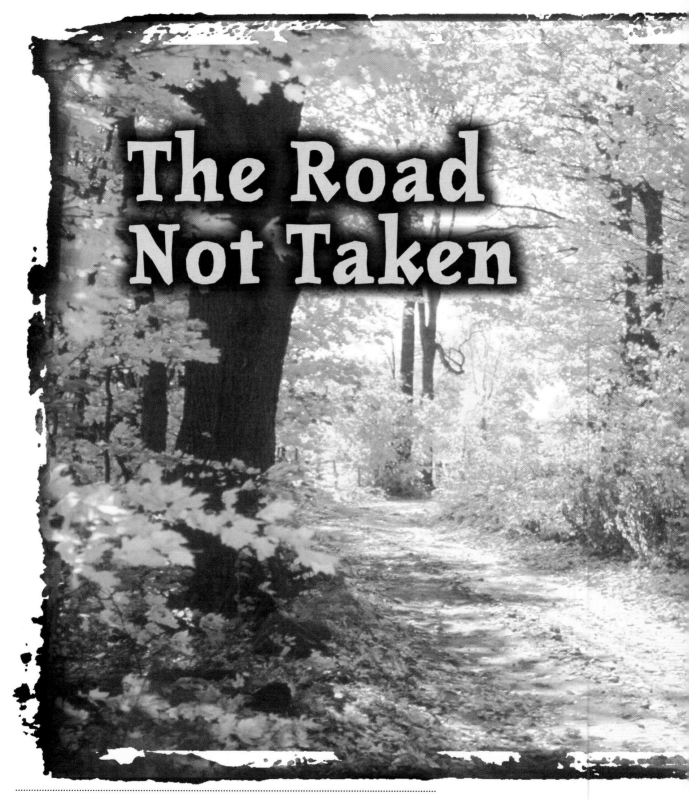

The Road Not Taken

diverged separated
undergrowth bushes, low plants
passing evidence of people going

trodden beaten, pounded
ages and ages hence many years from now

Respond to the Poem

Two roads diverged in a yellow wood,
And sorry I could not travel both
And be one traveler, long I stood
And looked down one as far as I could
To where it bent in the undergrowth.

Then took the other, as just as fair,
And having perhaps the better claim,
Because it was grassy and wanted wear;
Though as for that, the passing there
Had worn them really about the same.

And both that morning equally lay
In leaves no step had trodden black.
Oh, I kept the first for another day!
Yet knowing how way leads on to way,
I doubted if I should ever come back.

I shall be telling this with a sigh
Somewhere ages and ages hence:
Two roads diverged in a wood, and I—
I took the one less traveled by,
And that has made all the difference.

—Robert Frost

THINK IT OVER

Discuss Talk about these questions with a partner.

1. **Comparison** What makes one road better than another? Which road would you have chosen? Why?

2. **Conclusion** At the end, does the poet sigh with regret, or with satisfaction? Explain.

EXPRESS YOURSELF ▶ RECITE

Learn About Rhyme Scheme and Meter Read one stanza of the poem with your group. Clap out the beat of the poem and discuss which words rhyme.

Recite the Poem Practice with your group, and recite your stanza as part of a group reading.

ABOUT THE POET

Robert Frost is one of America's most popular 20th century poets. His talent earned him four Pulitzer Prizes. Robert Frost once said that his ambition in life was to write "a few poems it will be hard to get rid of." Most would agree that he succeeded.

AIMEE MULLINS

biography
by Johnette Howard

Prepare to Read

THINK ABOUT WHAT YOU KNOW

Brainstorm Possibilities Think of something that you really want to do but think you can't do. Work with a partner to come up with ideas to reach your goal.

able-bodied person

capable

coach

dash

deuce

disabled athlete

double below-the-knee amputee

event

personal-best

prosthesis

single-leg amputee record

test of will

track meet

LEARN KEY VOCABULARY

Locate and Use Definitions Study the new words. Write each word in a chart and guess what it means. Check the definition in the Glossary.

Term	Guess	Definition	✓
able-bodied person	someone who isn't sick	someone with a strong, healthy body	✓

LEARN TO MONITOR YOUR READING

When you **monitor your reading**, you stop from time to time to be sure you understand the text.

READING STRATEGY
How to Monitor Your Reading

1. Clarify the information. Find out the meanings of unfamiliar words or ideas.

2. Ask yourself questions about the information.

3. Summarize what happens. Think about the most important events and when they happen.

4. Use what you know so far to make predictions about the rest of the article.

Use all of these strategies as you read each section of "Aimee Mullins."

AIMEE

WORLD-CLASS ATHLETE

MULLINS

BY JOHNETTE HOWARD • WITH TEXT SUPPORT BY NAT PRITCHARD

Although **AIMEE MULLINS** has no legs below her knees, she has never let her physical condition limit her choices in life. With her prosthetic legs, she ran in track and field events around the country. Aimee is now a model and a public speaker.

Aimee surges ahead to win this race in San Diego, California.

efore Aimee Mullins was one year old, her parents Brendan and Bernadette learned that their tiny child did not have **fibulas**, which meant that she had no use of her lower legs. They had to decide whether to have Aimee's legs **amputated** so that she could wear **prosthetic legs**, or to leave her legs as they were and confine her to a wheelchair. Even if they chose the surgery, there would be no guarantee that she could ever walk. So began the first of the many extraordinary choices Aimee and her parents would have to make.

SHE WANTS TO RUN

Georgetown track coach Frank Gagliano says he doesn't remember if he was **shuffling through** papers on his desk or "whatever" when the call came to his office **out of the blue**—he just knows that the details of what the caller was saying **didn't register**. In 37 years of coaching track and field, Gagliano had trained Olympians such as Steve Holman, Kevin McMahon, and John Trautmann. He **fields a lot of calls**. So when the caller that day in August 1995 introduced herself as Aimee Mullins and said that she was a **double below-the-knee amputee** and that she wanted to run track, it was completely **in character** for Gagliano to say, "Fine. Meet me at the track at noon."

Not until Mullins, then a **junior** at Georgetown University, showed up did Gagliano realize that each of her **shins** ended about six inches below the knee

---

fibulas bones between her knees and her feet

amputated removed by a doctor

prosthetic legs legs made of plastic or man-made materials

Georgetown track coach Georgetown University's running trainer

shuffling through looking at

out of the blue unexpectedly

didn't register did not stay in his memory

fields a lot of calls talks to a lot of different people on the telephone

in character normal, typical

junior third-year student

shins lower legs

and that she ran on **prostheses**. Mullins told him she wanted to train for the August 1996 **Paralympics** in Atlanta, and Gagliano said, "O.K. Well, let me see you run."

Earlier, Mullins had tried training herself for a few weeks on a gravel high school track in northwest Washington, D.C. She knew **no drills**. Before phoning Gagliano, she had competed in one **track meet**, an **event** for **disabled athletes** in Boston a few weeks earlier. She had told hardly anybody of her plans when she signed up for the long jump and the 100- and 200-meter **dashes**. To her **astonishment** she won all three.

In the spring of 1996, Mullins was a member of the Georgetown women's track team, competing against able-bodied athletes whose times in the 100 beat hers by almost four seconds. At her first collegiate meet, at Duke University, Mullins ran the 100 in a **personal-best** 16.70 seconds. Three weeks later at the Big East Championships at Villanova University, she was **mortified** when one of her brand-new sprint legs, which are held onto her stumps by thick silicone sleeves, nearly slipped off because

she was sweating. She **pleaded** with Gagliano to **scratch her** from the 200: What if one of her legs flew off? The crowd would, in her words, "freak out." She would fall. Aimee says, "And you know what? Gagliano growled, 'If your leg flies off during the **deuce**, hey—it flies off. So what! You fall down. Put it back on. Then you finish the race.'"

POINT-BY-POINT

MILESTONES IN AIMEE'S LIFE

1 Aimee's legs are amputated before she is one year old.

2 She decides to compete in the Paralympics. Coach Gagliano agrees to train her.

3 She competes on her college track team.

BEFORE YOU MOVE ON...

1. **Cause and Effect** What was Aimee able to do because of her parents' decision when she was a baby?
2. **Character's Motive** Why did the coach refuse to pull Aimee out of the race?
3. **Vocabulary** List all of the words and phrases from these two pages that are about Aimee's running experiences.

....

Paralympics Olympics for the physically disabled
no drills no training workouts
astonishment surprise, amazement
mortified very embarrassed
pleaded begged
scratch her take her off the list of competitors

Aimee Mullins **241**

Aimee Mullins competes in the long jump.

NOTHING STOPS HER

Mullins ran. She finished. In the **ensuing** year her times dropped to 15.77 in the 100 and 34.06 in the 200, both **unofficial world records** in her class. Her best long jump is 11' 4 ½", a U.S. mark and just seven inches off the **single-leg amputee record**. She is the only double below-the-knee amputee to have competed on a Division I track team. At the 1996 Paralympics she was one of more than 3,300 athletes from 127 countries, but she was the only double-leg amputee in the women's 100 or long jump.

Gagliano says he **never doubted** Mullins would make the 1996 U.S. team. Asked why, he drops his **wise-guy** voice into **a stage whisper** and says, "Because the kid **was on a mission** see? Desire. To take a bus to practice? Get a ride from a friend? Ride a bike? Desire. So I had no doubt she'd go all the way to the Paralympics." He leans forward in his office chair and adds, "You know, she's not like everyone else."

He and his staff only treated her that way. When his assistant, Ron Helmer, introduced Mullins to her teammates that first day, he said, "This is Aimee Mullins. She's from Allentown, Pennsylvania. She's **a transfer student** from George Washington University. And she's gonna run.'"

If you ask Mullins what she loves about running, she'll say it's not just the thrill of being in motion—that **sensation** when "you're sprinting fast and your legs almost throw you down the track." More than anything, Mullins loves to compete. She says, "Every single meet when they say, 'On your mark'—that feeling in my stomach and my throat, it's like the first time I ever ran. I always think, Why am I doing this? It's so **nerve-racking**. I can't sleep the night before. And as soon as the race is over?"—here she smiles—"I can't wait to do it again. Running is like a **test of will**."

That's especially true for Mullins. A single-leg amputee requires 30% to 40%

---

ensuing coming, next
unofficial world records the fastest times in the world, but not recognized as such
never doubted always believed
wise-guy smart-aleck
a stage whisper a clear but quiet voice

was on a mission determined to get something done
a transfer student a student coming from another college
sensation feeling
nerve-racking frightening

more oxygen **to perform** the same activity as an **able-bodied person**. Those figures are even higher for a double-leg amputee. The custom-made Flex-Foot sprint legs she wears—**state-of-the-art** carbon-graphite creations that look like upside-down question marks sprouting below her knees—**require** great balance and strength.

Yet Mullins insists she finds nothing amazing about herself. As a kid she played softball and soccer. She skied competitively. The first time her parents took her to the beach, at age 7, she ran straight into the surf—only to be driven underwater by a crashing wave. When she came back up she had already taken off her **buoyant** wooden legs and tucked one under each arm. "And then I just kinda hung out that way, just floating," she says, laughing.

POINT-BY-POINT

MILESTONES IN AIMEE'S LIFE

4 Aimee competes in the 1996 Paralympics.

5 She sets several track records.

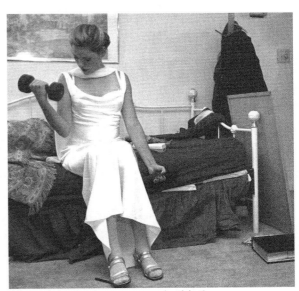
Aimee is both glamorous and athletic.

BEFORE YOU MOVE ON...

1. **Main Idea and Details** State a main idea supported by these details: Some of Aimee's track times are unofficial world records. Her long jump is close to a record.

2. **Character's Point of View** Why does Gagliano think that Aimee is "not like everyone else"?

3. **Prediction** From what you know about Aimee so far, how do you think she will meet challenges in the future?

---

to perform to do
state-of-the-art the latest, the newest
require need, demand
buoyant floatable, unsinkable

In this photo, Aimee is wearing her life-like silicone legs.

Aimee also chose to pursue a career in modeling. She says, "One reason I want to model is to do projects that challenge people's idea of beauty and the myth that disabled people are less **capable**, less interesting. I want to **expose people to** disability as something that they can't pity or fear or closet, but something that they accept."

She sends out the message every chance she gets. Already, she is a **riveting** public speaker: self-deprecating, unflinchingly personal and unsentimental, with a delightfully provocative streak. (As a kid she enjoyed jolting her substitute teachers by flipping a bolt and turning her prosthetic feet backward when the teachers weren't looking.) She has been known to plunk one of her prosthetic legs atop a chair minutes

THAT'S NOT ALL SHE DOES!

Aimee considers athletics important but adds, "there are so many things I want to explore." She's conversant in Italian. She's an **accomplished** painter. In 1993 she was among the three **full-ride college scholarship** winners the U.S. Defense Department selects annually on the basis of academic performance, SAT scores, writing samples, and a panel interview. She was a dean's list senior majoring in history and diplomacy at Georgetown's **rigorous** School of Foreign Service.

ABOUT THOSE LEGS...

Aimee owns 6 pairs of legs, each for a special purpose! Each pair was made specifically for her and cost several thousand dollars. Her "leg collection" includes:

- A pair of C-shaped, carbon-fiber Sprint Flex III for running.

- A pair of silicone legs for around the town. These legs match her skin tone perfectly and have formed ankles and molded toes.

- A pair of legs especially for swimming.

- A pair of sculpted wooden prosthetic legs for her runway modeling debut.

accomplished expert, skillful, talented
full-ride college scholarship all college costs paid for
rigorous difficult

expose people to help people see
riveting fascinating, interesting, appealing

into a speech and roll up her pants leg so the audience can get a better look. She insists that no question about her disability is too dumb or **offensive**.

The ways she affects people are extraordinary. On Memorial Day Mullins was in-line skating on the Mall in Washington, D.C. when she was stopped by a Vietnam veteran named Phill Hebert. Hebert asked a friend to hand him his tattered camouflage jacket and told Aimee, "I want you to have something." Mullins looked down to see that he had pinned his Purple Heart on her shirt.

"I kept telling him, 'I can't take this medal,'" Mullins says. "But he kept **insisting**. He said, 'You have more courage than most people I know.'

"I think, We didn't ask for this. So how can it be courage that we go on? What else are we supposed to do? Give up? No. No. You don't give up till your heart stops beating."

> ## POINT-BY-POINT

MILESTONES IN AIMEE'S LIFE

1. Aimee's legs are amputated before she is one year old.

2. She decides to compete in the Paralympics. Coach Gagliano agrees to train her.

3. She competes on her college track team.

4. Aimee competes in the 1996 Paralympics.

5. She sets several track records.

6. Aimee becomes a model.

7. She encourages others through her public speaking.

BEFORE YOU MOVE ON...

1. **Details** List three activities or careers, other than athletics, that Aimee has explored.

2. **Personal Experience** Describe a goal you set for yourself and tell how you have worked to achieve it.

3. **Paraphrase** In your own words, tell what happened when Aimee met Phill Hebert.

ABOUT THE AUTHOR

Johnette Howard is a newspaper and magazine sports columnist. In her almost 20 years of reporting, she has written about all sorts of sports events including basketball, baseball, hockey, and the Olympics. Her writing has won several national and state awards.

---

offensive insulting
insisting saying she had to

Respond to the Biography

Check Your Understanding

SUM IT UP

Sequence Information What important choices did Aimee and her parents make? When were those decisions made? Make a time line to show the order of their choices.

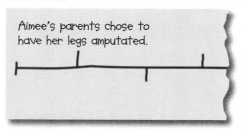

Time Line

Aimee's parents chose to have her legs amputated.

Evaluate Your Reading How did monitoring your reading help you create the time line? Which strategy helped you the most? Write a paragraph to explain how you will use these strategies when you read a new selection.

Wheelchair athlete in the Paralympics

THINK IT OVER

Discuss and Write Talk about these questions with a partner. Then write the answers.

1. **Evidence and Conclusions** How would Aimee's life have been different if she had been in a wheelchair?

2. **Opinion** What would it be like to train with Aimee on the track team?

3. **Character's Point of View** How does Aimee view things that many others would find too difficult?

4. **Personal Experience** What lessons have you learned for yourself after reading about Aimee's choices and those of her parents?

EXPRESS YOURSELF ▶ PERSUADE

Imagine you are a reporter for a magazine and your partner is your managing editor. Convince your partner that you should include Aimee in an article about beautiful people.

Language Arts and Content Area Connections

▶ VOCABULARY

USE STRUCTURAL CLUES: GREEK AND LATIN ROOTS

Learn About Greek and Latin Roots Many English words are made up of Greek and Latin roots with other word parts added. Knowing the meaning of the roots helps you understand the meaning of the entire word.

Root	Meaning	Example
aud	to hear	audience
fer	to carry	transfer
graph	to write, draw	graphics
loc	place	local
path	sensitive, suffering	sympathy
phon	sound	telephone
spir	to breathe	respiration

Practice What do you think the underlined words mean? Use the list of roots to make a guess and then look up the word in the dictionary.

> I heard a story about Aimee Mullins on <u>audiotape</u>. I was so <u>inspired</u> by her courage. It would be great to have her <u>autograph</u>. I'm going to try to <u>locate</u> more information about her.

▶ WRITING

WRITE JOURNAL ENTRIES

Aimee had to make a lot of choices that changed her life. Make a journal entry about the important choices you have made.

- Write the date.
- Tell what decision you made.
- Describe the consequences of your decision. Were the consequences positive or negative?

▶ SCIENCE

RESEARCH SYNTHETIC MATERIALS

Scientists use special materials for Aimee's different legs so that she can use her energy most efficiently for whatever she is doing. Use print and electronic sources to find out why her various legs are made of certain materials. Make a poster that lists the characteristics of the different materials.

For more about the **research process**, see Handbook pages 394–399.

In June 1989, thousands of Chinese
students protested against the Chinese
government by gathering in Tiananmen
Square in Beijing, China. Military tanks
were sent in to try to stop the protest.
One man stood in front of the tanks to
stop them from moving forward. Not only
was this a risk because the tanks might
not have stopped, but it was also a great
risk for him to disobey his government.

An Element of Risk

- When is a risk worth taking?

- When is a risk too great?

- How might the choices you make—and the risks you take—affect the lives of others?

THEME-RELATED BOOKS

Drummer Boy
by *Ann Turner*

A thirteen-year-old boy joins the Yankee Army as a drummer boy and risks his life to lead troops into battle.

Cupid and Psyche
by *M. Charlotte Craft*

When Psyche loses Cupid through her lack of faith, she must perform three dangerous tasks to win him back.

If You Could Be My Friend
Presented by *Litsa Boudalika*

Actual letters are carried secretly back and forth between two young women who lived on opposite sides of the Middle East conflict.

Build Language and Vocabulary

EXPRESS NEEDS, INTENTIONS, AND OPINIONS

Listen to the tape as you view the photograph.

Workers struggle to keep a small child from falling
into rushing flood waters during a rescue attempt.

DESCRIBE THE EVENTS

What happened during the rescue? Make a chart to show what the people needed, what they planned or intended to do, and what opinions they expressed.

Needs	Intentions	Opinions
Rescuers need rope.	Man on bank throws rope for rescuers to catch.	Man thinks rescuers can catch rope.

BUILD YOUR VOCABULARY

Words About Risk and Courage Now discuss this quote with your partner. What does it mean?

> Courageous risks are life-giving; they help you grow, make you brave, and better than you think you are.
> — *Joan L. Curcio*

Use some of the words in the quote and others you know to start a collection of words about risk and courage. Add more words to your collection as you read this unit.

USE LANGUAGE STRUCTURES ▶ FUTURE PERFECT TENSE

Speaking: Give a Speech Give a speech to thank Miguel and Luis for rescuing the child. Tell what your intentions are and what the community needs to do for them. Give your opinion about what they did. Use future perfect tense verbs.

Example:
I intend to see that by this time next year, Luis and Miguel **will have received** the community's award for outstanding courage. We all should be grateful and proud that we have such caring citizens among us.

PASSAGE TO FREEDOM

biography
by Ken Mochizuki

Prepare to Read

THINK ABOUT WHAT YOU KNOW

Quickwrite Take a minute to list what you know about World War II and the Holocaust. Share your ideas with your group.

diplomat person living in one country, representing another country's government

Holocaust murder of 6 million Jews and others during World War II

issue provide

Jew person whose religion is Judaism

Nazi soldier member of Hitler's German army

official written permission document signed by a person in charge that allows you to do something

refugee person who leaves a country to escape danger

survivor person who lives through a difficult situation

visa signature or stamp needed to enter another country

LEARN KEY VOCABULARY

Relate Words Study the new words and their definitions. Write the word *visa* in the center of a box. In the corners, write the new words that go with it. Complete another box of words for *Holocaust.*

Word Boxes

visa
issued by
an embassy

Holocaust

LEARN TO RELATE PROBLEMS AND SOLUTIONS

In some stories, the problems and solutions are stated clearly. In other stories, you have to use what you know to figure out what the problems and solutions are.

READING STRATEGY
How to Relate Problems and Solutions
1. Ask who has the problem.
2. Look for the details that tell you what the problem is.
3. Think about what else is happening that is not in the text.
4. Describe the solution. Provide evidence from the text or use what the author tells you about the characters and setting.

As you read "Passage to Freedom," think about the problems the characters face and the steps they take to solve them.

PASSAGE TO FREEDOM

by Ken Mochizuki
with an afterword by Hiroki Sugihara

illustrated by Dom Lee

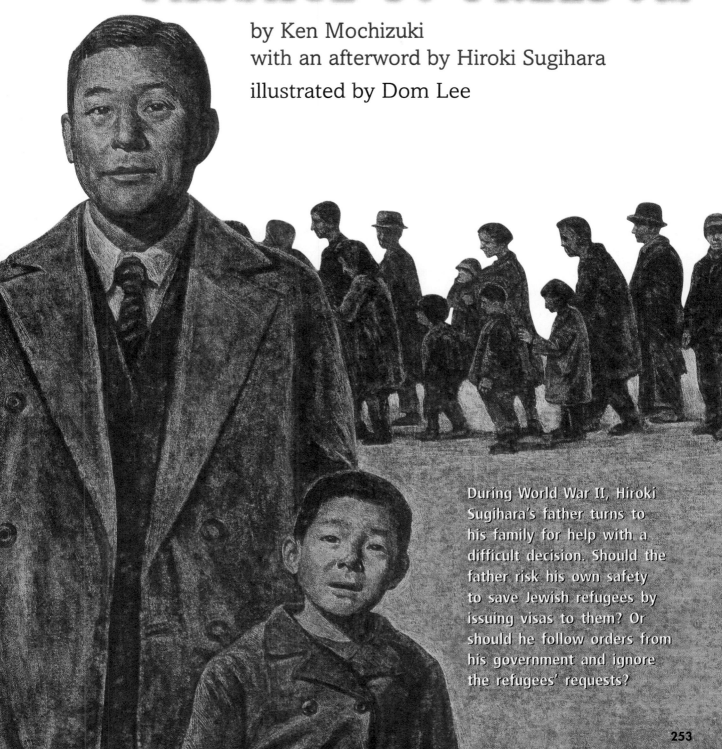

During World War II, Hiroki Sugihara's father turns to his family for help with a difficult decision. Should the father risk his own safety to save Jewish refugees by issuing visas to them? Or should he follow orders from his government and ignore the refugees' requests?

1

WAR TOUCHES THE SUGIHARAS

Hundreds of Jewish refugees come to the Japanese embassy
to ask the Sugiharas for help.

———

There is a saying that **the eyes tell everything about a person**.

At a store, my father saw a young Jewish boy who didn't have enough money to buy what he wanted. So my father gave the boy some of his. That boy looked into my father's eyes and, to thank him, invited my father to his home.

That is when my family and I went to a **Hanukkah celebration** for the first time. I was five years old.

In 1940, my father was a **diplomat representing** the country of Japan. Our family lived in a small town in the small country called Lithuania. There was my father and mother, my Auntie Setsuko, my younger brother Chiaki, and my three-month-old baby brother, Haruki. My father worked in his office downstairs.

In the mornings, birds sang in the trees. We played with girls and boys from the neighborhood at a huge park near our home. Houses and churches around us were hundreds of years old. In our room, Chiaki and I played with toy German soldiers, tanks, and planes. Little did we know that the real soldiers were coming our way.

Then one early morning in late July, my life changed forever.

My mother and Auntie Setsuko woke Chiaki and me up, telling us to get dressed quickly. My father ran upstairs from his office.

"There are a lot of people outside," my mother said. "We don't know what is going to happen."

In the living room, my parents told my brother and me not to let anybody see us looking through the window. So, I **parted** the curtains a tiny bit. Outside, I saw hundreds of people **crowded around** the gate in front of our house.

The grown-ups shouted in Polish, a language I did not understand. Then I saw the children. They stared at our house through the iron bars of the gate. Some of them were my age. Like the grown-ups,

> "There are a lot of people outside," my mother said. "We don't know what is going to happen."

---

the eyes tell everything about a person you can know everything about someone by looking into her or his eyes

Hanukkah celebration Jewish festival celebrated in December

representing serving, working for

parted opened

crowded around standing close together by

their eyes were red from not having slept for days. They wore heavy winter coats—some wore more than one coat, even though it was warm outside. These children looked as though they had dressed in a hurry. But if they came from somewhere else, where were their suitcases?

"What do they want?" I asked my mother.

"They have come to ask for your father's help," she replied. "Unless we help, they may be killed or taken away by some bad men."

Some of the children held on tightly to the hands of their fathers, some **clung** to their mothers. One little girl sat on the ground, crying.

I felt like crying, too. "Father," I said, "please help them."

My father stood quietly next to me, but I knew he saw the children. Then some of the men in the crowd began climbing over the fence. Borislav and Gudje, two young men who worked for my father, tried to keep the crowd **calm**.

My father walked outside. **Peering** through the curtains, I saw him standing on the steps. Borislav translated what my father said: He asked the crowd to choose five people to come inside and talk.

My father met downstairs with the five men. My father could speak Japanese, Chinese, Russian, German, French, and English. At this meeting, everyone spoke Russian.

BEFORE YOU MOVE ON...

1. **Inference** What does Mr. Sugihara's encounter with the young Jewish boy tell you about Mr. Sugihara's character?

2. **Details** Why did the crowd of people want Mr. Sugihara's help?

3. **Making Decisions** Imagine that you are Hiroki Sugihara and you see a crowd of people gathered outside your home. What would you do?

---

clung held tightly
calm quiet, still
Peering Looking

A CONFLICT ARISES

Sugihara's government won't help the refugees. He must choose
to obey his superiors or his own judgment.

I couldn't help but stare out the window and watch the crowd, while downstairs, for two hours, my father listened to frightening stories. These people were **refugees** —people who ran away from their homes because, if they stayed, they would be killed. They were **Jews** from Poland, escaping from the **Nazi soldiers** who had **taken over** their country.

> People ran away from their homes because, if they stayed, they would be killed.

The five men had heard my father could give them **visas — official written permission** to travel through another country. The hundreds of Jewish refugees outside hoped to travel east through the Soviet Union and end up in Japan. Once in Japan, they could go to another country. Was it true? the men asked. Could my father issue these visas? If he did not, the Nazis would soon catch up with them.

My father answered that he could **issue** a few, but not hundreds. To do that, he would have to ask for permission from his government in Japan.

That night, the crowd stayed outside our house. **Exhausted** from the day's excitement, I **slept soundly**. But it was one of the worst nights of my father's life. He had to make a decision. If he helped these people, would he put our family in danger? If the Nazis found out, what would they do?

But if he did not help these people, they could all die.

My mother listened to the bed squeak as my father tossed and turned all night.

The next day, my father said he was going to ask his government about the visas. My mother agreed it was the right thing to do. My father sent his message by **cable**. Gudje took my father's written message down to the **telegraph office**.

I watched the crowd as they waited for the Japanese government's reply. The five representatives came into our house several times that day to ask if an answer had been received. Any time the gate opened, the crowd tried **to charge inside**.

---

taken over gained control of
Exhausted Very tired
slept soundly slept deeply

cable a system of wires that carry telephone or telegraph messages
telegraph office place where messages were sent through wires
to charge inside to push forcefully through the gate

Finally, the answer came from the Japanese government. It was "no." My father could not issue that many visas to Japan. For the next two days, he thought about what to do.

Hundreds more Jewish refugees joined the crowd. My father sent a second message to his government, and again the answer was "no." We still couldn't go outside. My little brother Haruki cried often because we were running out of milk.

I grew tired of staying indoors. I asked my father **constantly**, "Why are these people here? What do they want? Why do they have to be here? Who are they?"

My father always took the time to explain everything to me. He said the refugees needed his help, that they needed permission from him to go to another part of the world where they would be safe.

"I cannot help these people yet," he calmly told me. "But when the time comes, I will help them all that I can."

My father **cabled his superiors** yet a third time, and I knew the answer by the look in his eyes. That night, he said to my mother, "I have to do something. I may have to **disobey** my government, but if I don't, I will be disobeying God."

The next morning, he brought the family together and asked what he should do. This was the first time he ever asked all of us to help him with anything.

BEFORE YOU MOVE ON...

1. **Cause and Effect** Why did the refugees come to Mr. Sugihara and not to someone else?

2. **Character's Motive** When Mr. Sugihara could not get official permission to issue visas for the refugees, why did he ask his family for help?

3. **Prediction** What do you think the Sugiharas will decide to do?

---

constantly over and over again
cabled his supervisors sent a message by wire to his bosses in Japan
disobey go against, not follow the orders of

3

A DECISION IS MADE

The family chooses to help the refugees. Sugihara writes
many visas until the family has to leave Lithuania.

My mother and Auntie Setsuko had already **made up their minds**. They said we had to think about the people outside before we thought about ourselves. And that is what my parents had always told me—that I must think as if I were in someone else's place. If I were one of those children out there, what would I want someone to do for me?

I said to my father, "If we don't help them, won't they die?"

With the entire family in agreement, I could tell **a huge weight was lifted off my father's shoulders**. His voice was **firm** as he told us, "I will start helping these people."

Outside, the crowd went quiet as my father spoke, with Borislav translating.

"I will issue visas to each and every one of you to the last. So, please wait patiently."

The crowd **stood frozen** for a second. Then the refugees burst into cheers.

Grown-ups embraced each other, and some reached to the sky. Fathers and mothers hugged their children. I was especially glad for the children.

My father opened the garage door and the crowd tried to rush in. **To keep order**, Borislav handed out cards with numbers. My father wrote out each visa **by hand**. After he finished each one, he looked into the eyes of the person receiving the visa and said, "Good luck."

Refugees camped out at our favorite park, waiting to see my father. I was finally able to go outside.

Chiaki and I played with the other children in our toy car. They pushed as we rode, and they rode as we pushed. We chased each other around the big trees. We did not speak the same language, but that didn't stop us.

---

made up their minds decided
a huge weight was lifted off my father's shoulders my father felt his worries were gone
firm steady, determined

stood frozen did not move
To keep order To organize the people
by hand in his own handwriting

For about a month, there was always a line leading to the garage. Every day, from early in the morning till late at night, my father tried to write three hundred visas. He **watered down** the ink to make it last. Gudje and a young Jewish man helped out by stamping my father's name on the visas.

My mother offered to help write the visas, but my father insisted he be the only one, so no one else could get into trouble. So my mother watched the crowd and told my father how many were still in line.

One day, my father pressed down so hard on his **fountain pen**, the tip broke off. During that month, I only saw him late at night. His eyes were always red and he could hardly talk. While he slept, my mother massaged his arm, stiff and cramped from writing all day.

Soon my father grew so tired, he wanted to quit writing the visas. But my mother encouraged him to continue. "Many people are still waiting," she said. "Let's issue some more visas and save as many lives as we can."

While the Germans approached from the west, the Soviets came from the east and took over Lithuania. They ordered my father to leave. So did the Japanese government, which **reassigned him** to Germany. Still, my father wrote the visas until we **absolutely** had to move out of our home. We stayed at a hotel for two days, where my father still wrote visas for the many refugees who followed him there.

Then it was time to leave Lithuania. Refugees who had slept at the train station crowded around my father. Some refugee men surrounded my father to protect him. He now just issued permission papers—blank pieces of paper with his signature.

As the train pulled away, refugees ran alongside. My father still handed permission papers out the window. As the train **picked up speed**, he threw them out to waiting hands. The people in the front of the crowd looked into my father's eyes and cried, "We will never forget you! We will see you again!"

I **gazed** out the train window, watching Lithuania and the crowd of refugees fade away. I wondered if we would ever see them again.

"Where are we going?" I asked my father.

"We are going to Berlin," he replied.

Chiaki and I became very excited about going to the big city. I had so many questions for my father. But he fell asleep as soon as he **settled** into his seat. My mother and Auntie Setsuko looked really tired, too.

Back then, I did not fully understand what the three of them had done, or why it was so important.

I do now.

---

watered down added water to
fountain pen ink pen with a metal tip
reassigned him told him to move
absolutely really

picked up speed went faster
gazed looked
settled sat back

Afterword

Each time that I think about what my father did at Kaunas, Lithuania, in 1940, my appreciation and understanding of the **incident** continues to grow. My father **remained concerned** about the fate of the refugees, and at one point left his address at the Israeli Embassy in Japan. Finally, in the 1960s, he started hearing from "Sugihara **survivors**," many of whom had kept their visas, and **considered** the worn pieces of paper to be family treasures.

In 1969, my father was invited to Israel, where he was taken to the famous **Holocaust** memorial, Yad Vashem. In 1985, he was chosen to receive the "Righteous Among Nations" Award from Yad Vashem. He was the first Japanese person to have been given this great honor.

In 1992, six years after his death, a monument to my father was dedicated in his **birthplace** of Yaotsu, Japan, on a hill that is now known as the Hill of Humanity. In 1994, a group of Sugihara survivors traveled to Japan to re-dedicate the monument in a **ceremony** that was attended by several **high officials** of the Japanese government.

BEFORE YOU MOVE ON...

1. **Characters' Motive** Why did the Sugiharas decide to issue the visas? Why did Mr. Sugihara refuse to let his wife help?

2. **Details** Name two of the ways in which Mr. Sugihara was honored after the war ended.

ABOUT THE AUTHORS

Ken Mochizuki has written a number of books about the experiences of Japanese-Americans.

Chiune Sugihara is one of his heroes because of Sugihara's willingness to risk losing his life and career in order to save the lives of others. He says, "I've dedicated *Passage to Freedom* to those who place the welfare of others before themselves. Courageous, unselfish actions need to be applauded and reinforced."

Hiroki Sugihara now travels worldwide to tell about his father's story. Chiune Sugihara's actions helped save over 6,000 lives, the second largest number of Jews rescued from the Nazis. Hiroki Sugihara says the lesson from this story is simple: "This is a story about one human being who helped other human beings."

ABOUT THE ILLUSTRATOR

Dom Lee has illustrated a number of Ken Mochizuki's books. In *Passage to Freedom*, he paints with beeswax and oil paints in brown and sepia tones. The idea is for the illustrations to look like old photographs. Both he and his wife also teach art to children.

---

incident event, happening
remained concerned was still worried
considered thought

birthplace hometown; the city where he was born
ceremony formal occasion
high officials important members

Respond to the Biography
Check Your Understanding

SUM IT UP

Relate Problems and Solutions Make a chart of the problems and solutions in "Passage to Freedom."

Problem-and-Solution Chart

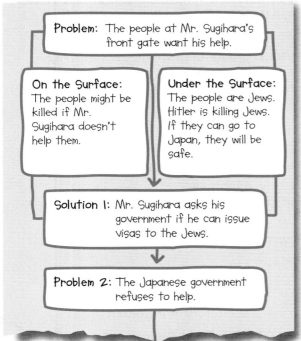

Problem: The people at Mr. Sugihara's front gate want his help.

On the Surface: The people might be killed if Mr. Sugihara doesn't help them.

Under the Surface: The people are Jews. Hitler is killing Jews. If they can go to Japan, they will be safe.

Solution 1: Mr. Sugihara asks his government if he can issue visas to the Jews.

Problem 2: The Japanese government refuses to help.

Write Summary Paragraphs Use your chart to write a summary paragraph for each problem in "Passage to Freedom." State the main problem in your topic sentence. Turn your details into sentences to tell what Mr. Sugihara did to solve the problem. Explain Mr. Sugihara's solution in your concluding statement.

THINK IT OVER

Discuss and Write Talk about these questions with a partner. Then write the answers.

1. **Character** How does the author show Mr. Sugihara's feelings about other people? Find examples in "Passage to Freedom."

2. **Inference** Why didn't the Japanese government want Mr. Sugihara to give visas to all the refugees?

3. **Conflict** Did Mr. Sugihara take a risk when he went against the orders of his government? Explain.

4. **Personal Experience** Tell about another person you've read about or heard of who took great risks to help others.

EXPRESS YOURSELF
▶ EXPRESS INTENTIONS AND OPINIONS

Work in groups of three. Take the roles of Mr. Sugihara, his wife, and Hiroki. Act out the scene in which Mr. Sugihara tells the crowd what he plans to do. Mrs. Sugihara and Hiroki then share their opinions about the decision.

Respond to the Biography, continued
Language Arts and Literature

USE CONDITIONAL SENTENCES

Learn to Express Conditions Sometimes you want to tell how one thing depends on another. The verbs in each clause work together to express your meaning.

> If the Nazis **find** out, what **will** they **do**?
>
> If the Nazis **found** out, what **would** they **do**?
>
> If the Nazis **had found** out, what **would** they **have done**?

Words like *if, unless,* and *as long as* can help you set up the condition in one clause. When the verb in this clause is in a perfect tense, make the verb in the other clause agree.

> If Sugihara **had refused** to issue the visas, the refugees **might have died**.
>
> The Jews **could** not **have escaped** unless Sugihara **had issued** the visas.

Practice Write each pair of sentences. Add the verb to finish the second sentence. Use *could, would,* or *might* as part of the verb.

1. If the refugees got visas, they could escape. If the refugees had gotten visas, they _____.

2. If I were Sugihara, I would issue the visas. If I had been Sugihara, I _____.

3. The Nazis might kill the refugees if Sugihara does not issue the visas. The Nazis _____ if Sugihara had not issued visas.

LEARN ABOUT POINT OF VIEW

Learn About Narrator's Point of View
"Passage to Freedom" is written as if Hiroki Sugihara is speaking to you about the story, or from his **point of view**. The writer tells Hiroki's personal thoughts, memories, and feelings.

Find Examples Notice how the writer expresses his point of view about the story.

> Back then, I did not fully understand what the three of them had done, or why it was so important.

Rewrite a Story Scene Choose one of these characters:

- a Jewish refugee at the gate
- one of the refugees invited in to talk
- another member of the Sugihara family.

Then rewrite the scene from your character's point of view. Tell what your character remembers about the events, what he or she saw and hoped for, and how he or she felt at the time.

Sample Scene

> I knew that if I did not get out of Lithuania, I would be killed. I stood out on the porch of the house where the Japanese family lived. Mr. Sugihara was my only hope. When he finally came to the door, he looked sad, but he looked strong.

Content Area Connections

SOCIAL STUDIES
REPRESENTING/SPEAKING

EXPLORE GEOGRAPHY

Make Maps Use print and electronic sources to find and illustrate a series of maps.

- Choose a section of the world like Europe or Asia. Show which countries the Nazi and Japanese troops occupied at different stages of World War II between 1939 and 1945.

- Draw borders and label the countries.

- Give your maps titles.

- Compare and discuss your maps with the class.

 For more information about the **research process**, see Handbook pages 394–399.

TECHNOLOGY/MEDIA
SOCIAL STUDIES

RESEARCH WORLD WAR II

Choose a country and research its role in World War II. Make a fact sheet using what you learn.

1 **Choose a Country** Select a country you'd like to research or use one of the following:

England	Switzerland	Russia
Sweden	United States	Canada

2 **Gather Information** Start with these Web sites, but remember that new sites appear every day. Use the country's name and "World War II" as key words. Download helpful articles and take notes.

INTERNET

INFORMATION ON-LINE

Web Sites:
➤ **World War II History**
  • www.historyplace.com
  • www.ushmm.org/outreach

➤ **Information about a Country**
  • www.eblast.com
  • www.encarta.com

3 **Make a Fact Sheet** Organize your notes onto a fact sheet. Add captions to photos. Display the fact sheet in your classroom.

 Learn to use the **Internet** on Handbook pages 392–393.

Melba's Choice

memoir
by Melba Pattillo Beals

Prepare to Read

THINK ABOUT WHAT YOU KNOW

Idea Exchange Study the photographs and captions on pages 265–267. In your group, take turns describing two events from the Civil Rights movement.

alternative different choice

consider think over carefully

decision final choice

endanger put in the way of harm

option one of two or more choices

reason think about facts and then draw conclusions

regret feel sorry about

risk chance of harm or loss

setback something that stops or reverses progress

LEARN KEY VOCABULARY

Use New Words in Context Study the new words and their definitions. Choose at least two words that go together, and write them in the same sentence.

I know I am taking a risk, but I do not regret my decision.

LEARN TO USE A DECISION MATRIX

To help you evaluate decisions, you can use a graphic organizer like a **decision matrix**.

CHOICE:	
PROS:	CONS:
DECISION:	

READING STRATEGY
How to Use a Decision Matrix
1. List the pros, or good things about someone's decision.
2. List the cons, or bad things about the decision.
3. Evaluate the pros and cons.
4. Describe the final decision.

As you read "Melba's Choice," fill out a decision matrix for each decision she makes.

THE STRUGGLE FOR CIVIL RIGHTS 1954-1956

It's the early 1950s. Many states in America still segregate blacks and whites. A Supreme Court decision inspires many people to protest the unfair treatment in various ways.

Segregation Laws

Since 1896, African Americans have lived under laws that say there can be "**separate but equal**" facilities for them.

Segregated drinking fountain

Brown v. *Board of Education*, Topeka, Kansas

When Linda Brown is not allowed to go to a nearby school because she is black, her father **files suit** against the Board of Education. In 1954, the Supreme Court **unanimously** decides that it is illegal for schools to separate black students from white students.

The attorneys who argued the case, 1954

Montgomery Bus Boycott

In 1955, Rosa Parks is arrested because she would not give up her seat to a white man. African Americans boycott, or refuse to ride the buses for over a year, until bus policies change. Later the Supreme Court **rules** that bus **segregation violates** the Constitution.

Rosa Parks, 1955

separate but equal apart but the same
files suit took legal action
unanimously all together

rules decides
segregation separation of African Americans and whites
violates goes against, disregards

THE STRUGGLE FOR CIVIL RIGHTS 1957-1965

Even though some people try to stop them, African Americans continue to fight for their rights.

Central High, 1957

School Integration

In 1957, soldiers are called in to protect nine black students as they **integrate** Central High School in Arkansas. In 1962, the enrollment of James Meredith at the University of Mississippi causes **riots**.

Sit-ins

In 1960, when black students in North Carolina are **refused service** at a local lunch counter, they remain until the store closes. They return day after day and soon others join them at that store and at stores throughout the country. The **sit-ins** continue until the counters are integrated.

Lunch-counter sit-in, 1960

Freedom Rides

Beginning in May of 1961, several black students and white students ride buses through the South where **bus terminals** are still segregated. The buses are firebombed, tires are **slashed**, and the riders are beaten. In September the Interstate Commerce Commission orders that the bus terminals be integrated.

Firebombed bus, 1961

integrate work to mix black and white students
riots violent, public disorder
sit-ins acts of occupying seats in a segrated establishment as an act of protest

refused service not waited on
bus terminals the beginning or ending point of a bus route where tickets are sold
slashed cut

March on Washington, 1963

March on Washington

On August 28, 1963, Martin Luther King, Jr., and over 250,000 people **peacefully march** into Washington, D.C., to support a new **civil rights bill**. King gives his famous "I Have a Dream" speech. He says that he hopes that his children will "one day live in a nation where they will not be judged by the color of their skin but by **the content of their character**."

Birmingham, Alabama, 1963

Birmingham, Alabama

In 1963, groups of children peacefully **demonstrate** against unfair treatment. Police send out police dogs and spray the children with fire hoses. The water pressure is strong enough to break bones. The nation is **outraged**.

Freedom March, 1965

March from Selma to Montgomery, Alabama

In 1965, thousands of people gather to march 54 miles to present a **petition** for voting rights to the Alabama Governor. By the time the march is over, 25,000 people have joined in.

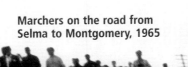
Marchers on the road from Selma to Montgomery, 1965

LET US ALL HOPE THAT THE DARK CLOUDS OF RACIAL PREJUDICE WILL SOON PASS AWAY AND THE DEEP FOG OF MISUNDERSTANDING WILL BE LIFTED FROM OUR FEAR-DRENCHED COMMUNITIES AND IN SOME NOT TOO DISTANT TOMORROW THE RADIANT STARS OF LOVE AND BROTHERHOOD WILL SHINE OVER OUR GREAT NATION WITH ALL OF THEIR SCINTILLATING BEAUTY.

— *Martin Luther King, Jr., from Letter from Birmingham City Jail*

---

peacefully march lawfully walk as a group
civil rights bill proposed law to ensure one's constitutional freedoms
the content of their character what they are like inside

demonstrate protest
outraged greatly offended and angered
petition formal written request

Melba's Choice

from *Warriors Don't Cry*

by Melba Pattillo Beals

Melba volunteers to be one of the African Americans to integrate Central High School in Little Rock, Arkansas. As she and eight other black students prepare for the school year, she realizes how dangerous her decision is. Every day she has to choose if she will continue to go forward or turn back.

Jefferson Thomas

Ernest Green

Minnijean Brown

Carlotta Walls

Terrence Roberts

Gloria Ray

Thelma Mothershed

Elizabeth Eckford

Melba Pattillo

ACCEPTING A CHALLENGE

Melba volunteers to be a student who integrates Central High.
Along with eight other students, she gets much attention.

The daily papers were full of news about the *Brown* v. *Board of Education* case. I couldn't imagine Little Rock's white people would ever change their minds and allow their children to go to school with me, no matter what laws those men on the Supreme Court made. But on May 24, 1955, the newspapers said the Little Rock school board had adopted a plan to **limit integration** to Central High School. They weren't going to allow it to actually begin, however, for two years—not till September, 1957.

When my teacher asked if anyone who lived within the Central High School District wanted to attend school with white people, I raised my hand. As I signed my name on the paper they passed around, I thought about all those times I'd gone past Central High wanting to see inside. I was certain it would take a miracle to integrate Little Rock's schools. But I **reasoned** that if schools were open to my people, I would also **get access to other opportunities** I had **been denied**, like going to shows at Robinson Auditorium, or sitting on the first floor of the movie theater.

Grandma India and Mother Lois followed the story closely; but when we discussed it over dinner, the talk about white people doing bad things to us kept me from telling them I had signed the list to go to Central High.

The NAACP (National Association for the Advancement of Colored People) filed suit to make the schools integrate immediately. Federal Judge John Miller **dismissed** the NAACP suit for immediate school integration, saying it was all right for the school board to integrate gradually. Central High seemed to be just one more place I wasn't going to see the inside of.

> "...I reasoned that if schools were open to my people, I would also get access to other opportunities I had been denied..."

---

limit integration not allow very many African American students to go

get access to other opportunities be allowed to do other special things

been denied not been given or been offered

dismissed ruled against, rejected

About that time, I decided to quit worrying about whether I should tell my parents I had signed up to go to Central. My brother Conrad, Mother, Grandma, and I were about to go North. We were driving to Cincinnati, Ohio, to visit my great-uncle Clancey.

For me, Cincinnati was the **promised land**. After a few days there, I lost that Little Rock feeling of being choked and kept in "my place" by white people. I felt free, as though I could **soar** above the clouds. I was both frightened and excited when the white neighbors who lived across the street invited me for dinner. It was the first time white people had ever wanted to eat with me or talk with me about ordinary things. Over the dinner table, I found out they were people just like me. They treated me like I was an **equal**, like I belonged with them.

I was wondering how I could tell Mama I wasn't ever going back to Little Rock. I planned to beg and plead with Uncle Clancey to let me live with them and finish high school in Cincinnati. I thought I had a pretty good chance of having things go my way until one evening when we sat watching the national news.

"That was your father on the phone." Mother appeared to be annoyed as she spoke. "He said to pay close attention to the news because he got a call today saying Melba's been **assigned** to go to Central High with the white people."

Mother was pale, her lips drawn tight as she glared at me. All of them circled around me. With horrified expressions, they looked at me as though I had lied, or sassed Grandma, or grown a second nose. I stood in the middle of the room, hoping the floor would swallow me up as they **grilled me**.

Melba and her family travel from their home in Little Rock, Arkansas, to Cincinnati, Ohio. There, Melba is treated as an equal by white people for the first time in her life.

---

promised land best place to live
soar fly
equal person just as good as they were

assigned chosen
grilled me asked me questions over and over again

> **"We hurried home to begin living a life I had never imagined in my wildest dreams."**

When had I planned on telling them? Why did I sign my name to the paper saying I lived near Central and wanted to go, without asking their permission? Did I **consider** that my decision might **endanger** our family? All the while I was trying to back away from their **harsh inquisition**. I no longer cared the least bit about Little Rock; I just wanted to live right there in Cincinnati.

That was the end of my vacation. We hurried home to begin living a life I had never imagined in my wildest dreams.

I was suddenly drowning in **unfamiliar** activities and sounds—the sound of the constantly ringing telephone, of people talking loudly in my ear and expressing their views about integration, of reporters' **urgent** voices describing what integration might do to the city and the South, and of official-looking adults lecturing me about integration for hours in closed meetings.

During one of those first meetings, members of the school administration made it clear that it would be better if we changed our minds and returned to our own school. Right away they warned us that we would not be permitted to participate in any **extracurricular activities**. Although we all were **startled** by their declaration, we took only a moment to reply. We would continue no matter what.

The only good thing about the meetings was that they allowed me to visit with my friends—the other students who would be integrating Central. I had known most of them all my life. At one point there had been sixteen others, but some of them chose not to participate because of **threats of violence**. It frightened me to see our number **dwindling**. Still, I was delighted with those I knew were definitely going.

In the end, there were nine of us: Ernest Green, Terrence Roberts, Jefferson Thomas, Elizabeth Eckford, Thelma Mothershed, Minnijean Brown, Carlotta Walls, Gloria Ray, and I.

BEFORE YOU MOVE ON...

1. **Character's Motive** Why did Melba want to attend Central High?
2. **Figurative Language** Melba said that she hoped "the floor would swallow me up." Discuss with a partner other ways to say the same thing.
3. **Conflict** How did the school administration react to the black students?

---

harsh inquisition difficult, repeated questions
unfamiliar strange, new
urgent eager, demanding
extracurricular activities activities done after school

startled surprised
threats of violence people expressing a wish to do physical injury
dwindling getting fewer and fewer, dropping

2

STARTING THE FIRST DAY

An angry crowd greets Melba at Central.
When Melba's friend is threatened, the crowd cheers.

By Wednesday morning, September 4, I could hardly believe it was really happening—I was going to Central High School.

Every radio in the house was tuned to the stations that gave frequent news reports. The urgent voices grabbed our attention whether we wanted them to or not.

As we ate, I hoped no one noticed that I pushed my food about my plate because my stomach didn't want breakfast. Mother spoke my name softly, and I looked up at her. "You don't have to integrate this school. Your grandmother and I will love you, no matter what you decide."

"But I have no choice if we're going to stay in Little Rock," I said. I couldn't stop hoping that integrating Central High School was the first step to making Little Rock just like Cincinnati, Ohio. Besides, we had been told students of Little Rock's richest and most important white families **attended** there. They were also probably very smart. As soon as those students got to know us, I had total faith they would realize how wrong they had been about our people.

"A lot has changed in the two years since you signed up to go to Central. You were younger then," Mother said with a frown on her face. "Maybe it was a **hasty** decision—a decision we'll all **regret**."

"I have to go," I said. "I've given my word to the others. They'll be waiting for me."

"You have my permission to change your mind at any time. This has to be your decision. No one can go into that school each day for you. You're on your own."

Before Mama Lois could say another word, the phone rang. As Mother held the phone to her ear, she stood **motionless** and

The News From Little Rock

"Hundreds of Little Rock citizens are gathered in front of Central High School awaiting the arrival of the Negro children. We're told people have come from as far away as Mississippi, Louisiana, and Georgia to join forces to halt integration. Governor Faubus continues to predict that blood will run in the street if Negroes force integration in this peaceful capital city of just over a hundred thousand citizens."

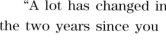

---

attended went to school
hasty quickly-made

motionless without moving

Elizabeth Eckford being yelled at by the angry crowd.

silent and her face grew **ashen and drawn**. Then she slowly **replaced** the receiver in its cradle and said, "It's time to go!"

We hurried up the block lined with wood-frame houses and screened-in porches. In the distance, large crowds of white people were lining the curb directly across from the front of Central High. As we approached behind them, we could see only the clusters of white people that stretched for a distance of two blocks along the entire span of the school building.

The sun beat down on our heads as we made our way through the crowd searching for our friends. Most people ignored us, **jostling** each other and craning their necks to see whatever was at the center of the **furor**. Standing on our toes, we stretched as tall as we could to see what everyone was watching.

It was my friend Elizabeth. The anger of that huge crowd was directed toward her as she stood alone, in front of Central High, facing the long line of soldiers, with a huge crowd of white people screeching at her back.

As Elizabeth walked along the line of guardsmen, they did nothing to protect her from **her stalkers**. When a crowd of fifty or more closed in like diving vultures, the soldiers stared straight ahead, as if posing for a photograph. Once more, Elizabeth stood still, stunned, not knowing what to do. The people surrounding us shouted, stomped, and whistled as though her **awful predicament** were a triumph for them.

Ever so slowly, we **eased our way** backward through the crowd, being careful not to attract attention.

BEFORE YOU MOVE ON...

1. **Making Decisions** If you had been in Melba's place, would you have changed your mind about going to the school? Explain.
2. **Inference** Why do you think the guardsmen did not protect Elizabeth Eckford?
3. **Viewing** Look at the photograph on page 273. Discuss with a partner how the different people are feeling and acting.

---

ashen and drawn pale and tense-looking
replaced put back
jostling bumping, pushing
furor excitement

her stalkers the people who wouldn't leave her alone
awful predicament horrible problem
eased our way carefully went

3

TAKING RISKS

Although the danger frightens Melba, she decides
that going back to Central High is the right thing to do.

We **gained some distance** from the center of the crowd and made our way down the block. But when I looked back, I saw a man following us, yelling, "They're getting away!" Pointing to us, he **enlisted** others to join him. Now we were being chased by four men, and their number was growing.

One of the men closest to me swung at me with a large tree branch but missed. I felt a **surge** of strength and a new wind. As I turned the corner, our car came into sight. I ran hard—faster than ever before—unlocked the door and jumped in.

I swung open the passenger door for Mother and **revved the engine**. Barely waiting for her to shut the door, I shoved the gearshift into reverse and backed down the street with more speed than I'd ever driven forward.

Turning left, we gained speed as we drove through **a hail of shouts and stones** and glaring faces. But I knew I would make it because the car was moving fast and Mama was with me.

"I think I want to go back to Horace Mann High School," I told my grandmother.

"At least I'll have assignments and friends and all sorts of wonderful first school day things to do."

"One little **setback**—and you want out," she said. "Naw, you're not a quitter."

from Melba's Diary

> September 4, 1957
>
> I was disappointed not to see what is inside Central High School.
> I don't understand why the governor sent grown-up soldiers to keep us out.
> I don't know if I should go back.
> But Grandma is right, if I don't go back, they will think they have won. They will think they can use soldiers to frighten us, and we'll always have to obey them. They'll always be in charge if I don't go back to Central and make the integration happen.

---

gained some distance got away
enlisted asked, encouraged
surge sudden feeling

revved the engine hit the gas
a hail of shouts and stones a lot of people yelling at us and throwing stones

Melba Pattillo Beals, far left, and her fellow students meet with Thurgood Marshall (later to become a Supreme Court Justice) and Mrs. C. Bates, president of the Little Rock NAACP, on the steps of the Supreme Court.

In thinking back on her experience, Melba remarks:

Yet even as I **wince** at the terrible **risk** we all took, I remember thinking at the time that it was the right decision—because it felt as though the hand of fate was **ushering us** forward. **Naive and trusting**, adults and children alike, we kept thinking each moment, each hour, each day, that things would get better, that these people would come to their senses and behave. So we headed down a path from which there was no turning back, because when we thought of **alternatives**, the only **option** was living our lives behind the fences of segregation and passing on that **legacy** to our children.

BEFORE YOU MOVE ON...

1. **Cause and Effect** What caused Melba to think about going back to her old school?
2. **Character's Motive** Why did Melba's grandmother say, "Naw, you're not a quitter."?
3. **Making Decisions** According to the author, African Americans in the late 1950s had two alternative courses of action. What were they?

---

wince flinch, think about with pain
ushering us helping us go

Naive and trusting Innocent and accepting
legacy gift from our generation

September 1957.
Federal troops outside
Central High School.

Integrating
Central High

September 1957

On the 23rd, the nine students return but are met by another angry mob. They go in through a side door, but have to leave that afternoon due to the violence.

Two days later President Eisenhower sends soldiers to protect the nine students. The soldiers walk with each of them to class. Even so, they are all subject to incredible violence.

November 1957

The federal troops all leave. The violence continues.

February 1958

Minnijean Brown is suspended and then expelled for dumping soup on a boy who was taunting her. She moves to New York to finish her school year.

April 1958

Melba's mother is fired. Her superiors tell her she can have her job back if Melba withdraws from Central.

May 1958

Ernest Green graduates from Central.

September 1958

Governor Faubus closes all of Little Rock's high schools.

September 1959

Melba goes to Santa Rosa, California, to finish high school.

September 1960

The NAACP forces Little Rock to reopen the high schools. Carlotta Walls and Jefferson Thomas eventually graduate.

ABOUT THE AUTHOR

Melba Pattillo Beals started writing *Warriors Don't Cry* soon after she left Central High, but it took almost 40 years before she could tell the story the way she wanted to. She wants to say clearly that "to assume that you ever have the right to mistreat another human being is wrong." Although she left Arkansas and became a reporter and then a writer in California, her family stayed in Little Rock. In fact, her brother Conrad became the first black U.S. Marshal in the history of the South.

Respond to the Memoir
Check Your Understanding

SUM IT UP

Analyze and Evaluate Literature Use your charts to review the decisions Melba made. Do you agree with her choices? Do you feel the risk was worth it? Write what you would have done.

CHOICE: Melba has to decide whether she will volunteer to integrate Central High School.	
PROS: She wants to see the inside of the school. If schools were open to African Americans, other opportunities might be, too.	**CONS:**
DECISION:	
What I would have done:	

Draw Conclusions Imagine that you have interviewed Melba Pattillo Beals. Write a newspaper article that sums up your interview. Use your charts to help you. Include how her choices have changed U.S. schools today.

Example:
Students from all over the U.S. have felt the effect of Melba Pattillo Beals's brave determination. I spoke with Ms. Beals about her experience at Central High.

THINK IT OVER

Discuss and Write Talk about these questions with a partner. Then write the answers.

1. **Character's Motive** Why did Melba keep going back to Central despite the huge risk?

2. **Character's Point of View** How did Melba's mother feel about Melba's decision to go to Central? How did her feelings compare to the grandmother's feelings?

3. **Character** Imagine you were one of the soldiers who protected the nine students. How would you have felt? What would you have done?

EXPRESS YOURSELF ▶ JUSTIFY

Imagine you are Melba and your partner is Melba's mother. Justify to your partner your decision to go to Central High. Then switch roles.

Respond to the Memoir, continued
Language Arts and Literature

▶ GRAMMAR IN CONTEXT

USE THE PERFECT TENSES

Review the Perfect Tenses Verbs in the perfect tenses use the helping verbs *has, have, had,* or *will have* and a form of the main verb called the **past participle**.

The **present perfect tense** of a verb can tell about an action that began in the past and may still be going on.

> I **have known** about Melba's actions for a long time.

The **past perfect tense** tells about an action completed before another action in the past.

> Melba **had volunteered** to go to Central High before she talked with her family.

The **future perfect tense** tells about an action that will be completed at a specific time in the future.

> By the end of the summer, Melba **will have talked** to many people about the integration.

Practice Write each sentence. Choose the correct perfect tense verb.

1. Before Central High was integrated, it <u>has been / had been</u> an all-white school.

2. Melba <u>had decided / have decided</u> to volunteer before she knew there would be trouble.

3. By the time new students enter Central, they <u>have heard / will have heard</u> about Melba's courage.

▶ WRITING/SPEAKING

DELIVER A NEWSCAST

Imagine you are a news reporter in Little Rock in the 1950s or 1960s. Report the facts about integrating Central High. Make sure you don't include personal opinions!

1 **Write Your Draft** Choose an episode from "Melba's Choice."

First collect the facts:

Who	What	Where	When	Why

Then write a newscast that tells both sides of the story.

2 **Edit Your Work** Be sure that you have reported the facts fairly. Replace any words that sound like an opinion. Make sure you use the correct verb tense, too.

3 **Share Your Work** Pretend you are facing a TV camera as you deliver your newscast.

Example:
Nine black students had prepared to begin classes at Central High School in Little Rock today, but Governor Faubus called out the National Guard to prevent the students from entering the school.

Review **verbs** on Handbook pages 444–454. For tips on giving an **oral presentation**, see pages 401–402.

Content Area Connections

▶ SPEAKING
▶ SOCIAL STUDIES

EVALUATE SOURCES OF INFORMATION

"Melba's Choice" is written from Melba's point of view. The story might be different if someone else told it. Look up some articles about Civil Rights and compare the information you find.

1 **Evaluate Articles** Focus on a specific event during the Civil Rights Movement. With a group, read and evaluate magazine and newspaper articles from various parts of the country in the 1960s. You can find the articles at your library.

2 **Compare Information** How do the facts vary from source to source? What conflicting information and inconsistencies do you notice? Identify the author's biases, exaggerations, and judgments. Discuss your findings with a group.

Learn to participate in a **discussion**. See Handbook page 400.

▶ MUSIC
▶ SOCIAL STUDIES
▶ LISTENING/SPEAKING

ANALYZE PROTEST SONGS

There were many songs in the 1960s that related to the Civil Rights Movement, equality, and nonviolence. Compare them to more modern political songs.

1 **Listen to Songs** Search in the library or on the Internet using the key words "Civil Rights" to find the names of songs and musicians from that time. Listen to the songs. Read the lyrics, too.

2 **Compare the Songs** Use a Venn diagram to compare the topics, lyrics, and style of music to some of today's political songs. Discuss with a group how they are alike and different.

Learn about **diagrams** on Handbook pages 373–374.

A man plays and sings a protest song.

Writing for Personal Expression

In expressive writing, writers share their personal thoughts and feelings about a subject or events. Often they tell about events from their own past by writing journal entries or memoirs.

PROFESSIONAL WRITING MODEL

"Melba's Choice" is a **memoir**. Melba Pattillo writes in the first person to express her feelings about an experience in her past. How can expressing your feelings help readers understand events in your life?

from "Melba's Choice"

> As we ate, I hoped no one noticed that I pushed my food about my plate because my stomach didn't want breakfast. Mother spoke my name softly, and I looked up at her. "You don't have to integrate this school. Your grandmother and I will love you, no matter what you decide."
>
> "But I have no choice if we're going to stay in Little Rock," I said. I couldn't stop hoping that integrating Central High School was the first step to making Little Rock just like Cincinnati, Ohio.

A PROBLEM-AND-SOLUTION MEMOIR

Memoirs often show how real people face problems and try to solve them. In a problem-and-solution memoir, writers express personal feelings as they tell about a problem that happened in the past and how it was solved. Study the chart. Discuss the problem and solution in "Melba's Choice." Talk about Melba's feelings during each event.

Problem-and-Solution Chart

"MELBA'S CHOICE"
Problem:
African American students are not allowed to go to the all white Central High School.
Events:
1. The NAACP tries to make schools integrate right away, but a federal judge dismisses the suit.
2. Melba's teacher asks if anyone wants to go to Central High anyway and nine students sign up to go.
3. When the students try to enter the school, a huge crowd yells at them and threatens them.
4. The students try again, but threats from the angry mob force them to leave early.
Solution:
President Eisenhower sends soldiers to protect the students and walk them to class.

STUDENT WRITING MODEL

Memoir

I Remember Friendship

by Ha Nguyen

I came to the United States from Vietnam when I was eight years old. My father had lived here for four years before Mother and I arrived. Because my father knew English, he enrolled me in school.

Although that first day was bright and sunny, I felt very lonely and uncomfortable. Everyone was a stranger. The teacher was nice enough, though. She asked me my name, and then showed me where to sit. Soon all the other students came into the room. I was surprised at how loud they were. I saw quickly that there were no other Vietnamese children. After everyone stopped talking, the teacher introduced me. She spoke my name in a way that I didn't recognize, and some of the kids laughed. I didn't know any English then and didn't realize that my name sounds like a laughing sound in English. I thought they were laughing at me! That was one of the worst feelings in the world.

At recess, everyone seemed to have something to do but me. I thought about my friends in Vietnam, and hot tears filled my eyes. Then a girl from my class tapped me on the shoulder. "Come play dodgeball," she said. I didn't know how to play, but I tried anyway. It wasn't hard to figure out the game. All you had to do was throw the ball, catch the ball, and try to hit someone in the middle.

The girl who helped me was Alicia. She became my friend and helped me get through my first American year. Then she moved away. By that time, I had learned a lot of English and was feeling more comfortable at school. However, I will never forget the day Alicia tapped me on the shoulder and asked me to join in.

Time order words signal when the events happened.

Throughout her memoir, Ha used different **forms of past tense verbs** to show when the action took place.

PROBLEM

Ha describes a **problem**. She didn't understand English and didn't know how to join in with the other students at her new school.

Ha tells about her own experiences and feelings, using the **first-person** point of view.

SOLUTION

Ha tells about the events that help her solve the problem.

Writing for Personal Expression, continued

The Writing Process

> **WRITING PROMPT**
>
> Now you will write a memoir to share with your teacher and classmates. In your memoir, you will tell about a problem you had and how it was solved. Tell about your feelings, too.

PREWRITE

1 Collect Ideas and Choose a Topic Think about experiences in your past. Was there a particular time when you were worried about something? Was there a problem that you had to solve? Make a list.

> **Problems I Remember**
>
> fighting at the playground
>
> sending a valentine to Nikki
>
> getting lost in the subway
>
> having to leave our apartment

Think about each item on your list. Then choose the one you remember the most about.

2 Unlock the Writing Prompt Before you begin writing, fill out an **FATP** chart to help guide your writing.

3 List Events and Feelings Think about your experience. What happened? What was the problem? List the details and your feelings about the events.

4 Organize Your Details Make a plan to tell about your experience in an organized way. You might want to write the details in order in a chart like the one on page 280.

FATP Chart

HOW TO UNLOCK A PROMPT
Form: _memoir_
Audience: _my teacher and classmates_
Topic: _getting lost in the subway_
Purpose: _to show what happened and how I felt_

Reflect and Evaluate

- What helped you decide what to write about?
- Do you remember enough about the experience to make your writing interesting?
- Why will your readers be interested in your problem?

DRAFT

Write quickly just to get your ideas down. Use your FATP chart to remind yourself of what and why you are writing.

1 **Write the Beginning** Start out by telling your readers when and where things happened. That way they'll better understand what your problem was and how it was solved.

2 **Tell About Events and Feelings** Use some of these ways to make your writing flow smoothly and help your readers follow along.

Writer's Craft: Effective Paragraphs

Stick to the first-person point of view.

> Riding on the subway wasn't ~~Roberto's~~ *my* favorite thing to do for a long time. That's because when I was only five, I got lost in the New York City subway.

Use the same verb tense.

> Seven years ago, I was a tiny five-year-old with a big, scary problem. One Saturday, we got up early. Mom ~~decides~~ *decided* that we should go to Brooklyn to visit my cousins.

Use transition words to connect your paragraphs.

> That day, the subway was jammed with people. People bumped me the whole way, but I held tight to my mom's hand.
>
> **However,** when I stepped off the train, I looked up to see a woman that I didn't know! I was really scared.

Use time order words.

> **After** I stopped crying, the nice woman took me to the transit police. **Just as we got there,** the police were talking to Mom on the phone. **Finally,** the police gave me a ride in a police car right to my cousins' house!

---

3 **Tell the Solution** At the end of your memoir, tell what finally happened and how the problem was solved. Also tell how your feelings changed. Your readers will want to know why your experience was important and memorable.

Reflect and Evaluate

- How do you feel about your draft?
- Does it tell about a problem and how it was solved?
- Will your audience understand how you felt about the experience?

Writing for Personal Expression, continued

REVISE

1 Reread Your Draft Did you follow your **FATP**? Does your memoir tell about a problem and solution and how you felt about an experience?

2 Conduct a Peer Conference Talk to a partner or group about your writing. Use the guidelines on Handbook page 411 for help.

Look at the suggestions a partner made after reading Roberto's memoir. What changes will he make?

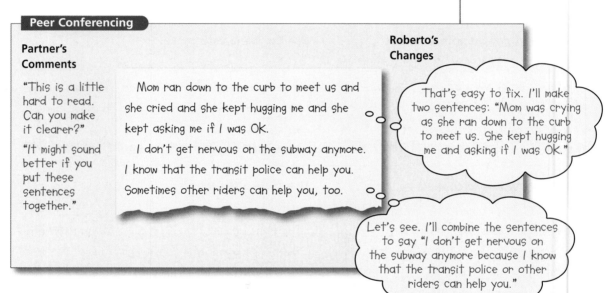

Peer Conferencing

Partner's Comments

"This is a little hard to read. Can you make it clearer?"

"It might sound better if you put these sentences together."

Mom ran down to the curb to meet us and she cried and she kept hugging me and she kept asking me if I was OK.

I don't get nervous on the subway anymore. I know that the transit police can help you. Sometimes other riders can help you, too.

Roberto's Changes

That's easy to fix. I'll make two sentences: "Mom was crying as she ran down to the curb to meet us. She kept hugging me and asking if I was OK."

Let's see. I'll combine the sentences to say "I don't get nervous on the subway anymore because I know that the transit police or other riders can help you."

3 Mark Your Changes Decide how to improve your writing. Revising Marks appear on Handbook page 411. To make changes to a word-processed document, see Handbook pages 383–389.

Key In TO Technology

On the computer, you can save different versions of your writing. Use the **Save As** command from the File menu and add a number to the document name. Then you can look back and choose the version you like best.

Reflect and Evaluate

- Did your peers like what you wrote? What changes will you make?

- As you read over your memoir, did you think of more details to add?

- Does your memoir give a clear picture of your experience and how you felt?

> GRAMMAR IN CONTEXT

VERB TENSES

The tense of a verb shows when an action happens.

The train arrives at the station.

- **Simple verb tenses** tell if an action happens at a time in the present, past, or future.

  Examples:

  Present: People **gather** on the platform. The train **stops.**
  The action happens now or is happening all the time.

  Past: The passengers **stepped** inside. A woman **found** the last seat.
  The action happened earlier, or in the past.

  Future: The doors **will close** soon. The train **is going to speed** away.
  The action will happen later, or in the future.

- **Perfect verb tenses** are formed with *has, have,* or *had* and the past participle of the main verb.

  Examples:

  Present perfect: The train **has stopped** at this station every day for years.
  The action began in the past and is still going on.

  Past perfect: There was no room for new passengers because everyone **had crowded** into the train at the last stop.
  The action was completed before some other action in the past.

  Future perfect: In about 15 minutes, that train **will have arrived** at the next station.
  The action will be completed at a specific time in the future.

Practice Complete each sentence. Write the verb in the tense shown.

Verb and Tense	Sentence
reach, past	1. I _____ out and held my mother's hand.
take, past perfect	2. Suddenly I realized I _____ the hand of a stranger.
happen, past	3. "What _____ to my mother?" I thought.
close, future perfect	4. "Oh, no! In a second the doors _____ and I will be left here without her."
realize, past	5. Luckily, the woman _____ that my mother was still on the train.
enjoy, present perfect	6. I _____ telling this story often.

Writing for Personal Expression   **285**

Writing for Personal Expression, continued

EDIT AND PROOFREAD

1 **Check for Mistakes** Look through your writing to correct any mistakes in capitalization, spelling, and punctuation. If you need help, use Handbook pages 459–469.

2 **Check Your Sentences** Look for the correct use of verb tenses. Ask a peer to read any sentences with verbs you are uncertain about.

3 **Make a Final Copy** If you are working on a computer, print out the corrected version of your memoir. If not, rewrite it and make the corrections you marked.

PUBLISH

Choose one of these ideas for publishing your writing, or come up with your own idea.

- Make an audio recording of your memoir. Practice first so that you will read clearly and with expression.

- Contribute your memoir to your school's Web site. Add a brief note about who you are and what viewers will discover if they read your memoir.

- Use a bound journal or notebook to begin a collection of memoirs for different times in your life.

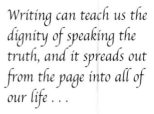

Writing can teach us the dignity of speaking the truth, and it spreads out from the page into all of our life . . .

— Natalie Goldberg

Reflect and Evaluate

- Does your memoir
  - ☑ tell about a problem and solution?
  - ☑ clearly show when things happen?
  - ☑ stick to the first-person point of view?
  - ☑ express your personal thoughts and feelings?
- What do you like best about your memoir? What could still be improved?
- Will this work go in your portfolio? Why or why not?

It's Up to You!

1 ▶ Look Back at the Unit

Grade the Characters In this unit you read about people who made choices. What choices did they make? How do you think they arrived at their decisions?

The Lady, or the Tiger?

Aimee Mullins

Passage to Freedom

Melba's Choice

Write a character report card for the princess, Aimee Mullins, Mr. Sugihara, and Melba Pattillo Beals. Base their grade on the types of choices they made. Then think about the choices you would have made in their situations.

2 ▶ Show What You Know

Sum It All Up Expand and organize your ideas on this mind map. With a partner share your thoughts about choices.

Reflect and Evaluate Make a list of new words you have learned in this unit. Add this list to your portfolio, along with the work from the unit that reflects your accomplishments.

Choices
Impossible
Very Hard
Hard
Easy

3 ▶ Make Connections

To Your Community Find out about the people who founded your city or town. What difficult choices did they have to make? How have their choices affected you and your community?

In 1989 and 1990, after almost 30 years, the wall that divided Berlin into two separate cities was destroyed. Finally, the people of East and West Berlin united as one city.

BREAK THROUGH THE BARRIERS

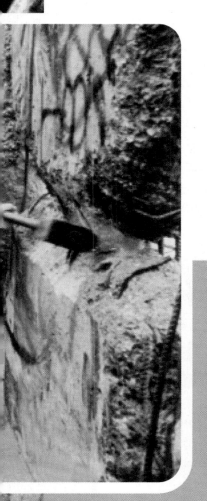

Talk about the photographs with a partner. Then fold a piece of paper into four squares. In each square, name a barrier that stops you from doing or learning something. Discuss ways to break through each barrier, then tear its square from the paper. How do you feel when you tear down each barrier?

THEME **1**

Making It Through Tough Times

Sometimes events are out of your control. Hard work can help you triumph over those tough times.

THEME **2**

Moving Forward

Knowing what's really important in your life is a triumph. Only then can you move forward.

YEARS OF DUST

DUST STORM
FARMERS FLEE

RESETTLEMENT ADMINISTRATION
Rescues Victims
Restores Land to Proper Use

During the Great Depression many farm workers
were unemployed. The Resettlement Administration
tried to help farmers pay their debts.

Making It Through Tough Times

- What events in people's lives can affect their survival? What are examples of tough times?

- What qualities and traits do you need to make it through the tough times?

THEME-RELATED BOOKS

The Babe and I
by David A. Adler

During the depression, a boy and his father develop a bond of understanding when they learn each other's secrets.

Skylark
by Patricia MacLachlan

When drought comes to their prairie home, Sarah takes the children to Maine while Jacob stays behind to wait for rain.

NOVEL

Treasures in the Dust
by Tracey Porter

Violet and Annie May cling to their friendship through drought, separation, and the Great Depression.

Listen to this song written during the Great Depression  in the United States. What is the songwriter's message?

BROTHER, CAN YOU SPARE A DIME?

They used to tell me I was building a dream,
and so I followed the mob,
When there was earth to plow, or guns to bear,
I was always there right on the job.
They used to tell me I was building a dream,
with peace and glory ahead,
Why should I be standing in line,
just waiting for bread?

Once I built a railroad, I made it run,
made it race against time.
Once I built a railroad; now it's done.
Brother, can you spare a dime?
Once I built a tower, up to the sun,
brick, and rivet, and lime;
Once I built a tower, now it's done.
Brother, can you spare a dime?

— *lyrics by E.Y. Harburg*
— *music by Gorney Harburg*

TAKE NOTES ABOUT THE DEPRESSION

 Listen to what people say about the Great Depression and take notes.

BUILD YOUR VOCABULARY

Words About the Great Depression Share your notes with a partner. Then create a semantic map to record the words and phrases that tell about the Great Depression. Collect more words to add to your map as you read the selections in this unit.

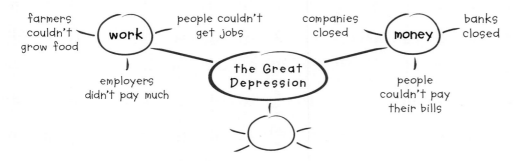

USE LANGUAGE STRUCTURES ▶ SENTENCES WITH CLAUSES

Writing: Elaborate on the Topic Rewrite the paragraph. Add clauses that give more information about the topic. Use a variety of sentences: compound, complex, and compound-complex. Choose words from the Word Bank to begin the new clauses.

> The Great Depression was a difficult time. Banks closed. People lost their jobs. People couldn't pay their bills. Some people found new jobs. Employers couldn't pay them much. Farmers couldn't grow crops. There was no rain.

Example:
The Great Depression was a difficult time **for everyone who lived in the United States in the 1930s.**

Word Bank

Coordinating Conjunctions

and	nor
but	or
for	yet

Subordinating Conjunctions

although
because
if
since
so
until
when
where

Relative Pronouns

who	that
whom	which
whose	

THE DIRTY THIRTIES

historical account
by Jerry Stanley

Prepare to Read

THINK ABOUT WHAT YOU KNOW

Compare Storms Look at the dust storm photographs in this selection. Use a Venn diagram to compare a dust storm and a rain storm.

bankruptcy

barren

borrow

collapse

decline

drought

Great Depression

Panhandle

stock market

unemployment

LEARN KEY VOCABULARY

Locate and Use Definitions Study the new words. Then write sentences to show how sets of words go together. Use a dictionary to look up any words you don't know.

> Words that Go Together
> barren, drought
> Sentence: When a drought occurs, there is no water for the crops, and the land becomes barren.

LEARN TO USE SQ3R

SQ3R stands for Survey, Question, Read, Recite, and Review. This strategy helps you focus on and remember new information.

READING STRATEGY

How to Use SQ3R

1. Survey the selection. Look at the graphics, charts, and photos.
2. Question yourself about what you expect to learn. Change the titles and headings into questions.
3. Read the selection slowly and carefully.
4. Recite the most important information for each section in your own words.
5. Review what you read. Take notes to answer your questions.

Use SQ3R as you read and take notes about "The Dirty Thirties."

THE DIRTY THIRTIES

Tough Times and Even Tougher People

from *Children of the Dust Bowl*
by Jerry Stanley

Life has never been easy for the farmers of the Oklahoma Panhandle. They struggle to hold on after the stock market crash of 1929 drastically decreases the value of their crops. Then, when years of drought and dust storms change their farmland into a "dust bowl," it takes every ounce of strength and resourcefulness to turn their lives around.

Life of the Oklahoma Farmer

Life had always been hard on the farmers who lived in Oklahoma, and in the 1930s it was especially hard on those who lived in the **Panhandle**, a **barren stretch of** rock and red soil sandwiched between Texas, Kansas, and New Mexico. These people owned small family farms of forty to eighty acres and were "dry farmers." They had no **irrigation system**, no **reservoirs** to store water, no **canals** to bring water to their farms. When there was enough rain, the Okies in the Panhandle grew wheat and corn and raised cattle. When there wasn't enough rain, they were forced to sell their livestock and farm machinery and **borrow** money from the bank. Every year they gambled with their lives, hoping for enough rain to get by.

1931: The Year the Rain Stopped

In 1931 it stopped raining in the Panhandle. The sky became bright and hot, and it stayed that way every day. Cornstalks in the fields **shriveled** from the sizzling heat. Shoots of wheat dried up and fell to the ground. The farmers **were caught in an impossible situation**. They were already suffering from the effects of the **Great Depression**, which had started in 1929 when the **stock market collapsed**. The Depression caused the price of wheat and corn to fall so low that it made growing these crops **unprofitable**.

Annual Rainfall at Goodwell, Oklahoma: 1931-1940

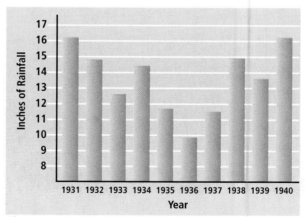

The average annual rainfall for this period was 13.52 inches. The average annual rainfall for the preceding decade (1921-1930) was 17.86 inches.

---

stretch of area made up of
irrigation system way of delivering water to crops
reservoirs lakes made by humans
canals ditches, waterways

shriveled became dried up and wrinkled
were caught in an impossible situation were in a very difficult position
unprofitable not worth enough money to cover expenses

Farming in Oklahoma. **Drought** and wind have ruined the field behind the farmer.

POINT-BY-POINT

CAUSES AND EFFECTS: 1929-1931

The stock market crashes. The Great Depression begins.

Farmers cannot pay their bills. Banks take back control of the farms.

Most farmers had borrowed money to buy their land and had borrowed again **against their land** in **lean years**. When the prices for their crops fell, many couldn't **make payments** to the banks that held **title** to their land. By 1932 one thousand families a week in Texas, Oklahoma, and Arkansas were losing their farms to the banks. And now it had stopped raining in the Panhandle, and the crops themselves were failing.

BEFORE YOU MOVE ON...

1. **Details** What is a "dry farmer"?

2. **Conclusions** Were the Panhandle farmers wealthy or poor? What makes you think so?

3. **Summary** What factors led to the loss of so many farms in 1932?

....

against their land by using their land as the guarantee that they would pay back the money

lean years the years when farmers couldn't sell enough crops to make money

make payments come up with the money they owed

title ownership papers

1936: The Year the Dust Came

Then when it seemed that things couldn't get any worse, they did. The year was 1936. It hadn't rained more than a few drops in the Panhandle for five straight years. One day the wind started to blow, and every day it blew harder and harder, as if nature were playing a cruel joke on the **Okies**. The wind blew the dry soil into the air, and every morning the sun rose only to disappear behind a sky of red dirt and dust. The wind knocked open doors, **shattered** windows, and **leveled** barns.

It became known as the great Dust Bowl, and it was centered in the Panhandle near Goodwell, Oklahoma. From there it stretched to the western half of Kansas, the eastern half of Colorado, the northeastern **portion** of New Mexico, and northern Texas. In these areas, and especially in the Panhandle, the dry winds **howled** for four long years, from 1936 to 1940. Frequently the wind blew more than fifty miles an hour, carrying away the **topsoil** and leaving only hard **red clay**, which made farming impossible.

Skies As Red As Blood

In the flatlands of the Panhandle people could see the dust storms coming from many miles away. The winds made the sky "boil red, blood red," said Horace Ray Conley of Foss, Oklahoma. "You could see the **northers** coming," he recalled. "It carried that old red dirt, and the whole sky would be red. They were mean clouds, ugly clouds." As a child, Horace walked to school backward to keep the dirt from scraping him in the face. He remembered he was often let out of school to go to the family **storm cellar** where he would be safe.

As the clouds rose and **roiled** each day, thousands of birds and rabbits raced in front of the **approaching** storms. That was the signal to the Okies to hurry before it was too late. They had to **herd** their cows into the barn quickly, tie down farm equipment and whatever supplies they had outside, then run for cover. Cracks around windows and doors were taped or stuffed with wet towels, but it was impossible to escape the dust.

The Dust Bowl, 1936-1940

Okies farmers from Oklahoma
shattered broke, smashed
leveled destroyed, flattened
portion part
howled blew so hard it made a crying noise
topsoil loose, rich dirt good for growing crops
red clay fine particles of soil that stick together like glue

northers fierce winds from the north
storm cellar room below ground used for protection during a bad storm
roiled moved around like they were being stirred
approaching coming, advancing
herd lead, gather, drive

CAUSES AND EFFECTS:
1932–1936

The drought continues.
Farmers cannot grow crops.

Without crops, the topsoil
dries up. Dust storms blow
the dry soil away.

March 1936: A dust storm rises over the Texas Panhandle. Horace Ray Conley of Foss, Oklahoma, said storms like this made the sky "boil red, blood red."

The Dirty Thirties   **299**

An Oklahoma farmer and his son raised the height of a fence to keep it from being buried by drifts of blowing soil.

At night families slept with wet washcloths or sponges over their faces **to filter out** the dust, but in the morning they would find their pillows and blankets caked with dirt, their tongues and teeth coated with **grit**.

Dust Storms Take Their Toll

Every morning the house had to be cleaned. Everett Buckland of Waynocka said, "If you didn't sweep the dust out right quick between the storms, you'd end up scooping it out with a shovel." And every morning someone had to go check the animals. The **fierce gales** half-buried chickens, pigs, dogs, and occasionally cattle. Children were assigned the task of cleaning the nostrils of cows two or three times a day.

The Dust Bowl killed people who stayed out too long without shelter. Roland Hoeme of Hooker almost lost his grandmother to one storm. "I remember my grandmother hanging on to a fence post," he said. "The wind was blowin' so hard she looked like a **pennant in a breeze**." However, more people died from "dust **pneumonia**"—when the dust caused **severe damage** to the lungs. Bessie Zentz of Goodwell **summed up** the nightmare experienced by the "Dust Bowlers," as they came to be called: "The dust storms scared us to pieces," Bessie said. "It was dark as the middle of the night, and it stayed that way all day."

Farmers Face Desperate Times

The storms ended most hope of farming in the Panhandle. The Okies planted mulberry trees for **windbreaks** and plowed furrows deep in the ground to help keep the soil in place. But the wind sometimes still blasted the seeds from the furrows and whipped the crops from the earth. To survive, farmers took to hunting jackrabbits, and the

---

to filter out to keep out
grit sand, coarse dirt
fierce gales very strong winds
pennant in a breeze flag or banner moving in a gentle wind

pneumonia sickness which makes breathing difficult
severe damage horrible injury
summed up said in a few words
windbreaks barriers against the wind

Panhandle diet became **biscuits**, beans, and "**fried jack**." Others took to hunting coyote, not to eat but to **collect the bounty** offered by the state for each one killed.

It was a time of **desperation**. From 1930 to 1940 the number of farmers and agricultural workers in the Dust Bowl states **declined** by **approximately** 400,000; by 1937 the **unemployment** rate in Oklahoma, Arkansas, and Texas had risen to 22 percent. Most of the Okies had lost their farms or were about to; nearly 50 percent of Oklahoma's farms changed hands in **bankruptcy** court sales in the 1930s.

When a farmer couldn't pay the bank, a tractor was sent to knock down his farmhouse as a way of forcing him to leave the land— "tractored out," they called it. The Okies were broke, they were without land, and they were hungry. And still the wind blew day and night, scraping all life from the earth. It's little wonder that Okies named this period in their lives the Dirty Thirties.

▶ **POINT-BY-POINT**

CAUSES AND EFFECTS: 1936–1940

The drought and dust storms continue. Most farmers lose their farms.

Abandoned farm in the Dust Bowl, Oklahoma

Percent of Unemployment: 1930-1935

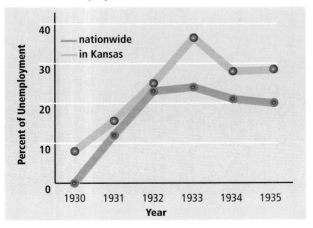

BEFORE YOU MOVE ON...

1. **Details** Where exactly was the Dust Bowl located?
2. **Vocabulary** How did Horace Ray Conley describe the dust storms? What do his words tell you about his feelings?
3. **Cause and Effect** What were some of the things the Okies did in response to the dust storms?

biscuits small, hard pieces of bread
fried jack cooked jackrabbit
collect the bounty get the payment

desperation hopelessness, great sadness
approximately about

1931–1940: The Dust Bowl Migration

The Okies **drew strength** from the winds that blew them out of the Panhandle. Penniless, **broken by hardship and poverty**, they were **determined to conquer adversity**. Crowding around campfires on the open prairie amid the ruins of their farmhouses and fields, they started to talk about a distant place where, it was reported, there was food, work, sunshine—and clear skies.

California! California! California! To the Okies the word "California" was magical, describing a place where they could go to better their lives.

Above all, the Dust Bowlers believed they would find work in California—if they could get there. They believed this because growers in California sent thousands of **handbills** to Oklahoma and the other Dust Bowl states, handbills that said things like: 300 WORKERS NEEDED FOR PEACHES—PLENTY OF WORK—**HIGH WAGES** and 500 MEN FOR COTTON—NEEDED NOW—START WORK RIGHT AWAY!

When the Okies read these advertisements nailed on trees and old telephone poles, there was but one thing to do. As one man in Porum, Oklahoma, put it, "All you could hear was 'Goin' to Californ-I-A! Goin' to Californ-I-A!' Nobody talked about nothin' else 'cept goin' to Californ-I-A!"

PACIFIC OCEAN

CALIFORNIA · NEVADA · UTAH · COLORADO · NEBRASKA · KANSAS · ARIZONA · NEW MEXICO · OKLAHOMA · TEXAS

1935-1940 Over 1,000,000 people migrated to California

---

drew strength got power

broken by hardship and poverty feeling sad due to the tough times and little money

determined to conquer adversity set on making it through the hard times

handbills small printed advertisements

high wages good salaries. When you make a lot of money for your work, you are getting high wages.

Migrant families sold many of their possessions and packed the rest into old cars and trucks for the journey west.

The advertisements for workers led to what is called the Dust Bowl migration. It was the largest migration of people in U.S. history. Between 1935 and 1940 over one million people left their homes in Oklahoma, Texas, Arkansas, and Missouri and moved to California.

On the Road to California

And what a sight it was! The Okies sold what few **valuable possessions** they still had—an old tractor, a plow, perhaps a cow that had survived. Then aunts and uncles, brothers and sisters, parents and grandparents, **pooled** their money to buy an old **jalopy**, or a beat-up flatbed truck. Soon the vehicle would be loaded down with tools, pots, pans, **bulging** suitcases, guitars, washtubs, and mattresses. And always, **straddling** the ten-foot-high mountain of family possessions, there were children, often six or more, whose job it was to make sure the ropes stayed tight and nothing was lost.

For others there was nothing to sell, nothing to pack. Many of these Okies **"rode the rail"** to California, **sneaking aboard** empty railroad boxcars heading west.

The Okies worked along the way. They might pick cotton in Twitty, Texas, to earn enough money to get to Wikieup, Arizona, in time for the lettuce and carrot harvest. If their truck broke down or they ran out of money for gas, which happened often, some of the men would hitchhike to the nearest town, get **an odd job** and maybe earn fifty cents, enough money for repairs or gas for the next day.

Always they kept up hope: hope that the truck wouldn't overheat again, hope that the tires would last one more day, hope that there would be enough food and water for tomorrow, hope that they would eventually **"light"** in California, and above all, hope that they could find a job when they got there.

valuable possessions things worth money
pooled put together
jalopy run-down automobile
bulging overly full
straddling sitting with legs wide apart on top of

rode the rail took the train
sneaking aboard hiding in; getting on without anyone knowing
an odd job only part-time, temporary work
light arrive, land

Reaching the Fields of Green

The winding stream of Dust Bowl jalopies eventually reached Tehachapi Grade. It is a beautiful road that **snakes gently** through the Tehachapi Mountains of California, then shoots straight down to the San Joaquin Valley like a dangerous ski slope. For the Okie families who **descended the grade**, it was a time of **rejoicing** and laughter. All of their troubles suddenly seemed to disappear, for now they could see with their own eyes what they had only dreamed about for months, sometimes years. From two thousand feet above sea level they saw a vast stretch of orchards, **endless fields** of grapes, cotton, and tomatoes, and as far as the eye could see in any direction, green—so much green it was hard to believe after life in the Panhandle.

When Patsy Lamb's family saw the valley for the first time through the windshield of their old Model A Ford, her father pulled the car off to the side of the road on a high bluff. Patsy and her four brothers and sisters got out of the car and stood in a line on the edge of the bluff, where they stared at the sea of green below them **as if in a trance**. Patsy was ten years old at the time. When she turned away from the bluff, she saw their mother standing behind her crying. Then Patsy started to cry, and soon everyone was crying.

Disappointment in a Land of Promise

From 1935 to 1940 **an endless stream** of **ramshackle** cars and trucks rolled down Tehachapi Grade. Patsy Lamb's family and the other migrants from the Dust Bowl states poured into the agricultural towns in the southern end of the San Joaquin Valley—

Agricultural workers in the San Joaquin Valley

---

snakes gently goes back and forth
descended the grade went down the mountain
rejoicing happiness
endless fields planted land as far as they could see

as if in a trance as if they were asleep with their eyes open, as if they were hypnotized
an endless stream a never-ending line
ramshackle broken-down

Delano and Bakersfield, where the advertisements said grape pickers were needed; Wasco and Shafter, where it was said **field hands** were needed for potatoes; Arvin and Lamont, where **rumor had it** that work could be found harvesting cotton, carrots, and beans. But the Okies soon discovered they had been **misled** about California. They started seeing signs at the edge of every town they approached: NO JOBS HERE! IF YOU ARE LOOKING FOR WORK—KEEP OUT! 10 MEN FOR EVERY JOB!

Everywhere they went it was the same— too many workers and not enough jobs. The growers in California had advertised for more workers than they actually needed, so there was a **surplus** of farm labor. What California had to offer the Okies was more hunger and misery.

▶ POINT-BY-POINT

CAUSES AND EFFECTS: 1935-1940

California growers advertise for workers. Over one million people migrate to California in search of jobs.

The Dust Bowl migrants do not find jobs in California and continue to live in poverty.

Dorothea Lange, 1936

Oklahoma farmers, who arrived in California, would not find work and suffered from life in temporary migrant camps.

BEFORE YOU MOVE ON...

1. **Inference** Why did Patsy Lamb and her family cry when they saw the San Joaquin Valley?
2. **Conclusions** Why did the Okies face more hunger and misery in California?
3. **Opinion** How would you characterize the attitude of the Okies who headed to California?

---

field hands people who work in the fields
rumor had it many people had heard
misled told the wrong thing
surplus excess, oversupply

Many people were out of work until the government helped them by creating jobs.

Epilogue

When Franklin Delano Roosevelt became President of the United States in 1933, he began to create programs to help the millions of Americans who were out of work and out of luck. These programs came to be known as "The New Deal." Farmers began to receive the financial help they needed to save their farms.

The Civil Conservation Corp (CCC) provided jobs to over 3 million single men between the ages of 17 and 23. Workers lived together in camps in the nation's forests, and were paid $30 a month for digging ditches, planting trees, and building reservoirs. At the CCC camps, many workers had a warm bed and three meals a day for the first time in years. Over 8.5 million adult men and women found employment in another government program—the Works Progress Administration (WPA)—that put people to work building roads and bridges, public parks and buildings.

The New Deal marked the beginning of the end of the Okies' suffering. Government-supported education programs allowed many people to **learn a trade** or profession. Patsy Lamb was able to graduate from college as a **nutrition specialist**. Carlton Faulconer, another Dust Bowl migrant who ended up in California, became the owner of an **insurance company**. Looking back on the Dirty Thirties, he said, "I'm not ashamed of where I came from. I'm proud of my family. I'm proud of what I did. And I'm proud of where I am today."

BEFORE YOU MOVE ON...

1. **Inference** Why do you think the programs Roosevelt created were called "The New Deal"?
2. **Conclusions** How were programs like the WPA good for both the country and its citizens?
3. **Personal Experience** What would you have done if you lived in the Dust Bowl during the Dirty Thirties? Would you have stayed on your land, gone to California, or tried something else?

---

learn a trade receive training for an occupation
nutrition specialist person knowledgeable about proper diet

insurance company business which guarantees another against loss

Abandoned farmhouse in Dalhart, Texas, 1938.

POINT-BY-POINT

CAUSES AND EFFECTS: 1929-1940

The stock market crashes. The Great Depression begins.

Farmers cannot pay their bills. Banks take back control of the farms.

The drought continues. Farmers cannot grow crops.

Without crops, the topsoil dries up. Dust storms blow the dry soil away.

The drought and dust storms continue. Most farmers lose their farms.

California growers advertise for workers. Over one million people migrate to California in search of jobs.

The Dust Bowl migrants do not find jobs in California and continue to live in poverty.

President Roosevelt creates the New Deal, which helps the Okies find jobs and get out of poverty.

ABOUT THE AUTHOR

Jerry Stanley, his wife, and four children live in Bakersfield, California, where many of the "Okies" came to live. He teaches California history to college students and has written several award-winning books. He says, "My best guess is that I became a writer because I had to—I'm not happy unless I'm writing something." He especially likes to write about real people, such as the "Okies," who overcame tough times and gained personal strength.

Respond to the Historical Account
Check Your Understanding

SUM IT UP

Relate Causes and Effects Use your notes to complete a cause-and-effect chart for each section of "The Dirty Thirties." Write a main idea statement for each section.

Section 1

What happened? Crops died.	Why? It stopped raining in 1931.
Main Idea: Because it stopped raining in 1931, many crops died.	

Generate the Main Idea Share your main idea statements with your group. Then work together to write one main idea statement for the entire selection.

THINK IT OVER

Discuss and Write Talk about these questions with a partner. Then write the answers.

1. **Cause and Effect** Do you think that a Great Depression could happen again in the United States? Why or why not?

2. **Comparisons** Compare how the people of the Dust Bowl and Melba in "Melba's Choice" dealt with hardship. How did hardship make them tougher people?

3. **Evidence and Conclusions** Give three or more reasons why the 1930s were called the "Dirty Thirties."

4. **Inference** Many Okies moved to California, but some stayed on their farms. Why did these people stay?

EXPRESS YOURSELF ▶ELABORATE

With your group, act out a scene in which an Oklahoma family emerges from a farmhouse after a dust storm, watches as their farm is "tractored out," or starts west on the road to California.

Have another group act as news reporters and interview you by asking questions such as: *What happened? How do you feel? What will you do now?* Answer each question, and then tell more to elaborate on your answer.

Language Arts and Literature

USE ADJECTIVES THAT COMPARE

Learn About Comparatives and Superlatives
A **comparative adjective** shows how two things
are alike or different. To form the comparative,
add **-er**. If the adjective is long, use **more** or **less**.

> Life was **harder** in the 1930s than it is today.
> It was **more difficult** to pay debts than it had
> been before.

A **superlative adjective** compares three or more
things. To form the superlative, add **-est**. If the
adjective is long, use **the most** or **the least**.

> For many people, it was the **hardest** time in
> their lives. The Dust Bowl was one of **the
> least comfortable** places to live at that time.

Identify Adjectives What comparative and
superlative adjectives are used in these sentences?

> In Goodwell, Oklahoma, it was drier in 1935
> than in 1934. It was the driest in 1936.

Practice Write each sentence. Add a
comparative or superlative adjective.

1. It was always difficult to grow wheat. When
   the rain stopped, it was even _____ .

2. The price of wheat was low, but then it
   dropped to the _____ price of the decade.

3. The wind was strong at first, and then it grew
   even _____ .

4. Everything was dusty. In fact, homes were the
   _____ they had ever been.

WRITE ABOUT A CONFLICT

Learn About Conflict in Literature Conflicts
occur when two things don't agree. Three types
of conflicts are: person against person, person
against society, and person against nature.

In a chart, list the conflicts in "The Dirty Thirties."
If there were resolutions, write them, too.

Type of Conflict: person against nature

Person	Nature	Resolution
Farmers need good top soil to grow crops.	The wind blows the soil away.	

Write a Letter Pretend you are living in the
Oklahoma Panhandle during the 1930s. Write a
letter to a friend that tells about two conflicts
you are facing and your plans to resolve them.
In your writing, use adjectives that compare.

Sample Letter

> May 6, 1935
>
> Dear Andrew,
>   Last night was the most ferocious wind
> storm yet. We are waging war against this
> stubborn enemy. I wonder sometimes who
> will win: the wind or us?

Review **adjectives** on Handbook
pages 441–443.

Respond to the Historical Account, continued
Content Area Connections

▶ SOCIAL STUDIES
▶ REPRESENTING/SPEAKING

RESEARCH THE GREAT DEPRESSION

With your group, find out how the Great Depression affected the people living in one area of the United States. Then, with your class, make general statements about the effects of the Great Depression.

1 Research an Area Select an area of the country like southern California or New York City. Use the name of the area and the "Great Depression" as key words in your search through library books and encyclopedias.

2 Make Visuals and Share Results Make charts or diagrams to illustrate what you learn. Deliver a report to the class. Listen to and look at all the information other groups present.

3 Form Generalizations Use what you learned to brainstorm a list of general statements about the depression with your class.

Example:
When a region has economic problems, unemployment is usually high.

▶ TECHNOLOGY/MEDIA
▶ REPRESENTING/VIEWING

MAKE A DEPRESSION-ERA POSTER

Images from the Great Depression often tell a story without saying a word. Find and label photos from that time to share with your class.

1 Gather Information Use these Web sites to get started, but remember that new ones appear every day.

INTERNET

INFORMATION ON-LINE

Key Words:
"Great Depression"
"Dust Bowl"

Web Sites:
➤ **Pictures of the Great Depression**
 • memory.loc.gov/ammem/fsahtml/
 • www.fdrlibrary.marist.edu/photos.html

Download helpful images.

2 Make a Poster Display the images on posterboard. Write a caption for each photo and tell how it helped you better understand what people faced during the Great Depression.

3 Have a Poster Session Put your poster in your classroom. Circulate and read other students' posters. Discuss what you learned about the Great Depression.

Learn to use the **Internet** on Handbook pages 392–393.

Out of the Dust

journal of poems
by Karen Hesse

THINK ABOUT WHAT YOU KNOW

Chart the Effects With a group, make a chart to show the effects of the Great Depression and the drought on a farming family in Oklahoma. Include effects on their finances, health, feelings, and social life.

comfort feeling of relief

debt something owed

diversification use of several different things

feud argue

flee run away

slip move quietly, glide

sorrow sadness, grief

spindly long and thin

steady unchanging, constant

sustain keep going, support

LEARN KEY VOCABULARY

Use New Words in Context Study the new words and their definitions. Then write the paragraph, adding the missing words.

Every day we have to _____(1)_____ with the Earth. The winds are _____(2)_____ and continue to blow. We'd like to _____(3)_____ away, but we cannot _____(4)_____ from the dust. We tried _____(5)_____ by planting different vegetables and grains. However, the plants are still _____(6)_____ and weak. They can't even _____(7)_____ a hungry mouse! How will we pay our _____(8)_____ to the bank? It fills me with _____(9)_____ to think about it. At least there is _____(10)_____ in knowing that it will rain some day.

LEARN TO MAKE COMPARISONS

When you **compare** two selections, you look for how they are alike and how they are different.

READING STRATEGY
How to Compare Literature
1. Ask yourself: What is each author's purpose?
2. Think about how each author gets the point across.
3. Think about the ideas in the selections. Are they the same or different?

As you read "Out of the Dust," compare the characters' experiences and feelings to the facts and events in "The Dirty Thirties."

Out of the Dust

by Karen Hesse

Billie Jo and her family live on a farm in Oklahoma where the drought has killed any hope for things to get better. She decides to run away. Sharing stories with a stranger, Billie Jo realizes that she needs to go back home and make it through this tough time with her family.

1

FIGHTING THE DUST

It hasn't rained for years and another dust storm arrives.
Daddy still tries to grow wheat.

Debts

Daddy is thinking
of taking a loan from Mr. Roosevelt and his men,
to get some new wheat planted
where the winter crop has spindled out and died.
Mr. Roosevelt promises
Daddy won't have to pay a dime
till the crop comes in.

Daddy says,
"I can turn the fields over,
start again.
It's sure to rain soon.
Wheat's sure to grow."

Ma says, "What if it doesn't?"

Daddy takes off his hat,
roughs up his hair,
puts the hat back on.
"Course it'll rain," he says.

Ma says, "Bay,
it hasn't rained enough to grow wheat in
three years."

Daddy looks like a fight brewing.
He takes that red face of his out to the barn,
to keep from feuding with my pregnant ma.

I ask Ma
how,
after all this time,
Daddy still believes in rain.

"Well, it rains enough," Ma says,
"now and again,
to keep a person hoping.
But even if it didn't
your daddy would have to believe.
It's coming on spring,
and he's a farmer."

March 1934

Migrant family walking along the
highway in Oklahoma, June 1938.

---

spindled out grown thin
roughs up runs his hand through
It's coming on Soon it's going to be, It's turning into

Dust storm overtakes houses.

Fields of Flashing Light

I heard the wind rise,
and stumbled from my bed,
down the stairs,
out the front door,
into the yard.
The night sky kept flashing,
lightning danced down on its spindly legs.

I sensed it before I knew it was coming.
I heard it,
smelled it,
tasted it.
Dust.

While Ma and Daddy slept,
the dust came,
tearing up fields where the winter wheat,
set for harvest in June,
stood helpless.
I watched the plants,
surviving after so much drought and so much wind,
I watched them fry,
or
flatten,
or blow away,
like bits of cast-off rags.

....
cast-off thrown out, rejected

It wasn't until the dust turned toward the house,
like a fired locomotive,
and I fled,
barefoot and breathless, back inside,
it wasn't until the dust
hissed against the windows,
until it ratcheted the roof,
that Daddy woke.

He ran into the storm,
his overalls half-hooked over his union suit.
"Daddy!" I called. "You can't stop dust."

Ma told me to
cover the beds,
push the scatter rugs around the doors,
dampen the rags around the windows.
Wiping dust out of everything,
she made coffee and biscuits,
waiting for Daddy to come in.

Sometime after four,
rubbing low on her back,
Ma sank down into a chair at the kitchen table
and covered her face.
Daddy didn't come back for hours,
not
until the temperature dropped so low,
it brought snow.

Ma and I sighed, grateful,
staring out at the dirty flakes,

but our relief didn't last.
The wind snatched that snow right off the fields,
leaving behind a sea of dust,
waves and
waves and
waves of
dust,
rippling across our yard.

Daddy came in,
he sat across from Ma and blew his nose.
Mud streamed out.
He coughed and spit out
mud.
If he had cried,
his tears would have been mud too,
but he didn't cry.
And neither did Ma.

March 1934

BEFORE YOU MOVE ON...

1. **Setting** When and where do these poems take place?
2. **Comparisons** What did Daddy think about planting a crop that year? What did Ma think about the idea?
3. **Mood and Tone** What mood or feeling does "Fields of Flashing Light" convey to you?

---

a fired locomotive a railroad engine moving quickly forward

ratcheted loudly tapped

union suit long, one-piece undergarment with shirt and pants attached

grateful pleased, thankful

our relief our feeling that everything was better

rippling moving in waves

streamed out poured out

Many people leave their homes to go west.
Billie Jo decides to go, too.

Migrants

We'll be back when the rain comes,
they say,
pulling away with all they own,
straining the springs of their motor cars.
Don't forget us.

And so they go,
fleeing the blowing dust,
fleeing the fields of brown-tipped wheat
barely ankle high,
and sparse as the hair on a dog's belly.

We'll be back, they say,
pulling away toward Texas,
Arkansas,
where they can rent a farm,
pull in enough cash,
maybe start again.

We'll be back when it rains,
they say,
setting out with their bedsprings and mattresses,
their cookstoves and dishes,
their kitchen tables,
and their milk goats
tied to their running boards
in rickety cages,

setting out for
California,
where even though they say they'll come back,
they just might stay
if what they hear about that place is true.

Don't forget us, they say.
But there are so many leaving,
how can I remember them all?

April 1935

Oklahoma dust bowl refugees stalled on the highway, May 1937.

---

straining pulling tightly
sparse few

running boards steps or platforms beneath the car doors

These hobos ride empty freight cars to Southern California. While several dangle their feet over the side, others lie in the shade behind them.

Out of the Dust

This is not a dream.
There's no comfort in dreams.
I try to contain the ache as I leave my bed,
I try to still my heart as I
slip from my room with my kerchief of dimes.
Moving slowly down the stairs,
I cross through the kitchen, taking only some
biscuits,
and leave my father's house.
It's the middle of the night and I hear every sound
inside me, outside me.
I go,
knowing that I'll die if I stay,
that I'm slowly, surely
smothering.

I walk through the calm night,
under the stars.
I walk to

where the train stops long enough
for a long-legged girl to latch on
and as my heart races
I feel the earth tremble beneath me and then
the sound of sharp knives,
metal against metal,
as the train pulls up to the station.

Once I might've headed east,
to Mr. Roosevelt.
Now I slip under cover of darkness
inside a boxcar
and let the train carry me west.
Out of the dust.

August 1935

BEFORE YOU MOVE ON...

1. **Characters** How do you think Billie Jo's neighbors felt about leaving? What makes you think so?

2. **Making Decisions** If you were Billie Jo, would you have left? Explain why or why not.

---

contain stop, hold back
still my heart keep calm, keep my heart from beating too quickly

smothering dying from not getting enough air
latch on get onto
tremble shake

A man tells Billie Jo about leaving his family.
She realizes she needs to be with her father.

Something Lost, Something Gained

He climbs into my car.
He's dirty and he has a sour smell.
His eyes are ringed by the soil that comes from riding trains.
But there's a deeper shadow to those eyes,
like ashes,
like death.
He needs a hair comb and a shave,
and a mending needle applied to his pants.

He speaks to me,
"Where you from, miss?" he wants to know.
He shows me a picture of his family.
A wife. Three boys.
The photograph is all he carries.
That and the shredding, stinking clothes on his back.
I feed him two of the stale biscuits I've been hoarding
and save the rest.
I'll be hungry tonight,
what with giving my day's biscuits away.
But I can see the gaunt of hunger in his cheeks.
He asks if I have water and I shake my head,

my tongue thick with thirst.
He eats the biscuits.
He doesn't care they're caked with dust.

He finishes eating and crumbs stick to his mustache.
He's staring hard at me and his eyes water.
"I've done it again," he says.
"Taken food from a child."
I show him my cloth bag with more biscuits.
"At home," he said, "I couldn't feed them,
couldn't stand the baby always crying.
And my wife,
always that dark look following me.
Couldn't take no more.

Lost our land, they tractored us out so's we had to leave,
rented awhile, then moved in with Lucille's kin.
Couldn't make nothing grow."

I nodded. "I know."

We talked as the train rocked,
as the cars creaked,
as the miles showed nothing but empty space,
we talked through the pink of the setting sun,

---

a mending needle applied to his pants the tears in his pants sewn up
shredding falling apart, ragged
stale dried out

hoarding keeping, saving
the gaunt of hunger in his cheeks that he is very thin from not eating
kin relatives

and into the dark.
I told him about Ma dying.
I told him about my father,
and how the thing that scared us both the most
was being left alone.

And now I'd gone and left him.
I told him about the piano,
and Arley Wanderdale,
and how I wasn't certain of the date,
but I thought it might be my birthday,
but he was sleeping by then, I think.

He was like tumbleweed.
Ma had been tumbleweed too,
holding on for as long as she could,
then blowing away on the wind.

My father was more like the sod.
Steady, silent, and deep.
Holding on to life, with reserves underneath
to sustain him, and me,
and anyone else who came near.
My father
stayed rooted, even with my tests and my temper,
even with the double sorrow of
his grief and my own,
he had kept a home
until I broke it.

When I woke,
the man was gone, and so were my biscuits,
but under my hat I found the photograph of his
family,
the wife and three boys.

Maybe the photograph was
left in trade for the biscuits,
maybe it was a birthday gift,
the one thing he had left to give.
The children in the picture were clean and serious,
looking out with a certain longing.
The baby had his eyes.
On the back of the photograph,
in pencil,
was the address of his family in
Moline, Kansas.
First chance, I'd send the picture back,
let his wife know he was still alive.

I got off the train in Flagstaff, Arizona.
A lady from a government agency saw me.
She gave me water and food.
I called Mr. Hardly from her office and asked him to
let my father know . . .
I was coming home.

August 1935

This man, carrying everything he owns, walks along the highway toward Los Angeles.

Dorothea Lange, 1937.

---

tumbleweed a dried out bush that blows along in the wind

sod grass-covered ground

reserves stored energy

grief deep sadness

longing wanting, hoping

The wind made the loose soil pile up like snow banks.

Finding a Way

Daddy
started talking
about planting
the rest of the acres in wheat,
but then said, No,
let's just go with what we've got right now.

And I've
been playing
a half hour
every day,
making the skin stretch,
making the scars stretch.

The way I see it, hard times aren't only
about money,

or drought,
or dust.
Hard times are about losing spirit,
and hope,
and what happens when dreams dry up.

The tractor's busted,
we don't have the cash to fix it,
but there's nothing saying Daddy can't do the work
by hand.
It can't be any harder than digging a hole
forty by sixty by six feet deep.

Daddy bought a second mule with Louise's help.
Her betrothal gift to him.
He walks behind the team,

---

busted broken, not working
betrothal gift engagement present

step by step, listing the fields to fight the wind.
Maybe the tractor lifted him above the land,
maybe the fields didn't know him anymore,
didn't remember the touch of his feet,
or the stroke of his hand,
or the bones of his knees,
and why should wheat grow for a stranger?
Daddy said he'd try some sorghum,
maybe some cotton,
admitting as how there might be something
to this notion of diversification folks were
talking about,
and yes, he'd bring the grass back
like Ma wanted,
where he wasn't planting anything else.
He'd make new sod.
And I'm learning, watching Daddy, that you can stay
in one place
and still grow.

I wipe dust out of the roasting pan,
I wipe dust off Ma's dishes,
and wait for Daddy to drive in with Louise,
hoping she'll stay a little later,
a little longer,
waiting for the day when she stays for good.

She wears a comical hat, with flowers,
in December,
and when she smiles,
her face is
full enough of springtime, it makes

her hat seem just right.
She brings apples in a sack,
perfect apples she arranges
in a bowl on the shelf,
opposite the book of poetry.
Sometimes, while I'm at the piano,
I catch her reflection in the mirror,
standing in the kitchen, soft-eyed, while Daddy
finishes chores,
and I stretch my fingers over the keys,
and I play.

December 1935

BEFORE YOU MOVE ON...

1. **Details** What was the stranger's solution to making it through the tough times? Why did he do this?

2. **Vocabulary** List the words and phrases that Billie Jo uses to describe Louise. From this description, do you think that Billie Jo likes her or not?

3. **Opinion** Do you agree with Billie Jo that you can stay in one place and still grow as a person? Explain.

---

listing the fields leaning toward the ground
admitting finally saying, acknowledging

ABOUT THE AUTHOR

Karen Hesse won the Newbery Medal in 1998 for *Out of the Dust*. Since the age of ten, she knew she was good with words. It took her more than thirty years, however, to get published. She says, "I never gave up dreaming of publication." She has worked as a waitress, a nanny, a farm worker, and a librarian. All those experiences have given her ideas for poems, stories, and books.

Respond to the Journal of Poems
Check Your Understanding

SUM IT UP

Sequence Information Make sequence chains to show the events in "The Dirty Thirties" and "Out of the Dust." Then draw lines between events that appear in both selections.

Sequence Chains

Compare Literature Look at the events that are similar. How does each selection describe the event? Use comparative adjectives to compare elements such as the authors' purposes, mood, tone, theme, and writing style.

Example:

"The Dirty Thirties" is **more direct** than "Out of the Dust" because it tells the facts about the farmers' struggles.

THINK IT OVER

Discuss and Write Talk about these questions with a partner. Then write the answers.

1. **Inference** Look at the first poem, "Debts." Why does Ma say "your daddy would have to believe"? What does it mean to really believe in something?

2. **Comparisons** Look for similes and other descriptions of the man on the train and Billie Jo's father. How are the men different?

3. **Character** List three examples from the poems that show Billie Jo's father was a dedicated man.

4. **Predictions** Based on what you know about the time period, what do you think will happen to Billie Jo and her family after her last journal entry? Explain.

EXPRESS YOURSELF ▶READ ALOUD A POEM

Choose one of the poems to read aloud. Practice with a partner. Pay attention to how the rhythm of the stanzas affects the meaning. Notice how the sensory details add to the meaning and mood. Read the poem you selected to your group.

Language Arts and Content Area Connections

LITERARY ANALYSIS

USE LITERARY DEVICES: SIMILES, PERSONIFICATION, AND ONOMATOPOEIA

Learn About Literary Devices Literary devices help create images and set the mood. They give you a clear picture of the characters, setting, and events.

- A **simile** is a literary device that uses *like* or *as* to make a comparison.

  Daddy looks **like a fight brewing**.

- **Personification** gives human qualities or characteristics to animals, objects, or ideas.

  The wind **snatched** the snow.

- **Onomatopoeia** uses words or phrases that imitate sounds.

  The dust **hissed**.

Find Literary Devices Look on the following pages in "Out of the Dust." Find and name the literary device used to describe each thing.

- page 314: lightning and wheat
- page 315: dust
- page 319: the stranger

Practice Use literary devices to write descriptions.

1. Use a simile to describe swirling dust.

2. Use personification to describe a truck.

3. Use onomatopoeia to describe blowing wind.

SPEAKING/LISTENING
SOCIAL STUDIES

HAVE A DEBATE

During the Great Depression, the government started federal programs to help people. Use print and electronic sources to find out about government agencies and relief programs. Then discuss this question with your group: *Should the government intervene when people need help? Why or why not?* Conduct a debate with another group to express your point of view.

SCIENCE
WRITING

INVESTIGATE DIVERSIFICATION

When farmers diversify, they plant a variety of crops to help preserve and replenish the soil. With a partner, form questions about diversification such as: *How did diversification help restore farming to the Dust Bowl?* Use electronic and print sources to find the answers. Write a paragraph to share what you learned.

A farmer in his field

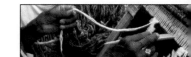

Moving Forward

- Think about the people close to you. What can you learn from them? How does this keep you moving forward?

- What types of experiences or ideas in someone's past might keep him or her from moving forward?

- Why might it be difficult to let go of something in your past?

THEME-RELATED BOOKS

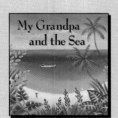

My Grandpa and the Sea
by Katherine Orr

A woman remembers how her grandpa found a way to move on after he could no longer be a fisherman.

Great Expectations
by Charles Dickens

An orphan boy helps a former convict and years later, his great expectations are fulfilled.

Ryan White
by Ryan White and Ann Marie Cunningham

When Ryan is banned from school because he has AIDS, he fights back, then moves on to educate people about AIDS.

Build Language and Vocabulary

NEGOTIATE

View the photograph. Then read the poem. What do they tell you about growing and maturing?

You, the child thinking in front of his home!
You will grow up one day.
You too will have a living room, your threshold will hold shoes
You too will have a house you clean with a broom.

—*Ali Cengizkan*
Translation by *Yusuf Eradam,* from
"For the Photographs of Constantine Manos"

ROLE-PLAY THE DIALOGUE

What are the people in the photograph saying to each other? Role-play the conversation with your partner. Did you come to an agreement?

BUILD YOUR VOCABULARY

Words About Growing Up Have you ever felt like the younger child in the photograph? How do you feel now? List words and phrases you know that describe what it's like to grow up. Keep adding to your list as you read the selections in this unit.

> ### What It Is Like to Grow Up
>
> learn to be responsible
> care about how someone else feels
> stand up for yourself
> avoid fighting
> try to accept new ideas
> solve a problem so that everyone is happy

USE LANGUAGE STRUCTURES ▶ SENTENCES WITH PARTICIPIAL PHRASES

Writing: Negotiate a Solution Imagine that your class has raised money at a car wash. How will you spend it? Write one possibility and give it to your partner. Have your partner reply. Continue until you reach an agreeable solution. Use participial phrases in your sentences.

Example:
Considering the sad state of our library, I think we should spend the money on books.

I disagree. The computers **sitting in the computer lab** need to be upgraded.

The Dance

realistic fiction
by Judith Ortiz Cofer

Prepare to Read

THINK ABOUT WHAT YOU KNOW

Brainstorm Changes How do people make changes or "move forward" in their lives? Record your ideas in a chart.

admit agree that something is true

disappointed unhappy that something did not happen

fascinated charmed, interested greatly in something

mature become fully grown or developed

miserable very unhappy

radiant beaming with joy

serious having deep and sincere feelings

stupor dazed condition, not knowing fully what is happening

widow woman whose husband has died

LEARN KEY VOCABULARY

Use New Words in Context Study the new words. Read the paragraph, and then use the new words to rewrite it from Grandma's point of view.

> Mother had to **admit** I have begun to **mature**. I really take care of Grandma now that she is a **widow**. Mother is **fascinated** by how **serious** I am about helping Grandma when she seems **miserable** or in a sad **stupor**. I want to transfer all of my love to her to keep her from being **disappointed** about anything. Grandma looks so **radiant** when she is happy!

LEARN ABOUT CHARACTERIZATION

Characterization is how a writer develops a character. Good writers use a variety of ways to bring a character to life and keep you interested in a story.

> ### READING STRATEGY
> **How to Recognize Characterization**
> 1. Look for descriptions of the character's physical appearance and personality.
> 2. Ask yourself how the character thinks, feels, and acts.
> 3. Think about the character's dialogue. What does it tell you about the character?
> 4. Read what others think and say about the character.

As you read "The Dance," record the clues about each character in a character map.

The Dance

from Don José of La Mancha
by Judith Ortiz Cofer

Yolanda's mother has a new man in her life, Don José. Although Don José makes her mother very happy, Yolanda worries that her dead father has been forgotten. Yolanda struggles to accept that she and her mother might move forward and have a normal life again.

A NEW MAN IN MAMI'S LIFE

Yolanda's papi is dead, but she still resents that
Mami is seeing a new man, Don José.

"**H**ey, Yolanda, you're gonna miss *Betrayed by Love Again*. It's a hot episode tonight," Maricela yells out at me as she lugs a bag of groceries and drags her little kid up the front stairs. She's rushing 'cause it's almost time for the evening soap opera.

I'm sitting on the front stoop of El Building instead of watching the ***telenovela*** with my mother because of her new boyfriend, Don José. *Don* is not his first name, it means Mr. or Sir, or Your Majesty, or something. All I know is that my mother wants me to treat the guy with *R-E-S-P-E-T-O*. She actually spelled it out for me.

Mami has started seeing a man. I thought she had **settled down to** being a **widow**. It's really been rough for both of us since Papi was killed. Then, one night Mami and I had just started lighting candles to Papi's memory in the bathtub—El Building is a **towering inferno** waiting to happen, so I talked my mother into this **arrangement**.

> There stands this guy who looks like he's just stepped off the airbus from the Island.

She was so **impressed** that she said, "Yolanda, I think you are really **maturing**." Anyway, we hear a knock at the door. I open it and there stands this guy who looks like he's just stepped off the **airbus** from the Island. Clothes are all wrong. And a tan he didn't get from sunbathing at the beach. I mean, you can tell if someone is new to the ***barrio***. It's because of what they call ***la mancha*** around here. It means "the stain." There's no hiding it.

He'd come to sell us tickets to a salsa dance at St. Mary's, where he's the custodian. Standing in our doorway with a straw hat in his hands, he tells us he's from a mountain town in Puerto Rico, a widower with no children who wanted to see *Nueva* York. He sounds like he's from the mountains. He keeps saying, "***Ay, caramba***," after every other word. I was gonna inform him that he's in New Jersey, not *Nueva* York, but my mother pinches my

....

telenovela television soap opera (in Spanish)
settled down to gotten used to
towering inferno fire trap
arrangement way of doing things
impressed pleased
airbus airplane

barrio neighborhood (in Spanish)
la mancha the stain on your hands from peeling plantains (in Spanish)
Nueva New (in Spanish)
Ay, caramba Oh, my gosh (in Spanish)

arm lightly. She seems to be **fascinated** by his **singsongy** talk. She buys two tickets and he finally leaves, but not before she asks him over to watch the *telenovela* on Monday night.

"His pants are too short," I tell her.

"Yolanda, Don José lived in the *campo*, the countryside, of the island all his life. His clothes are old-fashioned—"

"Mami, he dresses like a hick."

"What does this word *hick* mean, *hija*?"

I search my brain for the word I'd heard her use before to describe out-of-it people: "*Jíbaro*," I say. "He acts like a *jíbaro*."

"To some people that's not an insult, Yolanda," she says. "When I was a little girl on the Island, the *jíbaros* were the backbone of our country—the good, simple people who farmed the land." She doesn't look too happy with me for having called him a *jíbaro*. But it's from listening to her gossip with her friends about people just up from the Island that I learned about *jíbaros* with *la mancha*. It comes from the idea that people who grow their own food on the island always had plantain stains on their clothes. Now it means that they dress and act funny—like they've never been in a city before.

So for the last two weeks he's been coming over to our place every night. And lately he brings his guitar and sings *jíbaro* songs to her. I secretly taped the songs so she could hear how ridiculous he sounds.

"*Ay, ay, ay, ay,*" he always starts out like a cat wailing, "I come to sing you this song." Both he and his guitar sound like they're crying. My mother actually does when she listens to him sing the old songs. And when I play the tape for her, instead of agreeing with me, she asks me for it so she can listen to it again. That's when I know she's getting **serious** about this guy.

....

singsongy flowing, rhythmic

hija daughter (in Spanish)

Jíbaro peasant, poor farmer (in Spanish)

THE BLOSSOMING ROMANCE

As Mami and Don José become more involved,
Yolanda worries that Papi will be forgotten.

I've gotta **admit** it, though, Don José has **given me a break from** worrying about my mother. It's been tough seeing her so lonely and **miserable**. She had even stopped caring how she looked, wearing an ugly housedress when she wasn't dressed for work in an even uglier cashier's **smock**. The last few days she's been fixing herself up, though, just to sit down and watch TV with Don José.

I come in during a commercial and catch them laughing at something. I had forgotten what she looked like, happy.

"José tells me that he has won trophies for his salsa dancing, Yolanda. Can you believe it?"

"No, I can't." He springs to his feet, bows to me, and says, "*¿Bailamos, señorita?*"

"You've gotta be kidding me," I say. I just give him a look I hope lets him know what I think of him.

When I go through the living room again, they're sitting quietly on the sofa, one on each end, watching TV. But I can tell by

> "Do you miss Papi?" I ask her, trying to get her to remember.

their eyes that they're not really seeing what's on the screen, they're looking at something inside their own heads.

Later after Don José leaves, my mother barely answers me when I say "Good-night, then ***Buenas nochas***," kind of loud. This is really strange because it's like we've traded places: she's acting like I do when I'm mad at *her*, and I'm acting like she does when she's trying to get me to talk to her.

My next step in trying to get Mami **back to reality** is to take out the photo album one day and start asking her about pictures of Papi. He was a good-looking guy who had been born in San Juan—not some hick mountain town. Mami looks at the pictures with me, but she doesn't get **depressed** like she used to.

"Do you miss Papi?" I ask her, trying to get her to remember how she felt about him before Don José and his guitar took over

---

given me a break from helped me stop
smock apron
¿Bailamos, señorita? Shall we dance, miss? (in Spanish)

Buenas nochas Good-night (in Spanish)
back to reality to see the truth, to remember the past
depressed really sad

our sofa. I hold the album open to a picture of Papi in his brand-new security guard uniform that he was so proud of.

She held the album in her hands for a few minutes; then she said, "Yes, *hija*, I miss your papi very much. But I believe that he would want us to start living a normal life again."

That's when Mami tells me we're going to the St. Mary's salsa dance that night.

"I'm not going," I say to her. I think things are moving a little too fast between her and Don José.

"*Está bien*, Yolanda. You can stay home if you like." She doesn't sound mad, just **disappointed**. Then she spends the afternoon primping. She dyes the gray out of her hair. She takes a bath that lasts at least an hour. I hear her singing one of the *jíbaro* songs while she rolls her hair.

He comes to the door dressed in a pin-striped suit, wing-tip shoes, and a hat that he takes off when my mother comes out of her room. His eyes get big when he sees her in her tight green dress and wearing makeup—which she hadn't done since Papi died. It's like she washed ten years off her when she took that hour-long bath.

"You look like a *primavera* on our emerald Island," Don José says to my mother. And she actually **blushes**. Then he offers her his arm.

"So when are you going to be home?" I ask her, yawning and sounding bored so she doesn't think I really care.

"I don't know," she says, smiling up at Don José. I hear them laughing as they go down the stairs.

BEFORE YOU MOVE ON...

1. **Inference** Yolanda says, "they're looking at something inside their own heads." What does she mean?

2. **Character's Motive** Why did Yolanda take out the photo album?

3. **Character's Point of View** Why wouldn't Mami answer Yolanda when she said "Good-night"?

Está bien Okay (in Spanish)
primavera spring bloom (in Spanish)
blushes turns red from embarrassment

YOLANDA'S NEW VIEW

Although he will never replace Papi, Yolanda realizes that Don José makes Mami very happy.

Saturday night television is pretty bad. I try to watch an old movie. Then, out of the blue, I start worrying about my mother. What if this Don José is just pretending to be **an innocent** *jíbaro* so he can get her alone? Now that Papi is dead, I'm responsible for Mami's safety. She doesn't have street smarts like I do. I remember when the cops came to tell us that Papi'd been shot. He was working as a security guard in a fancy uptown store. Mami got hysterical, and I was the one that had to take her by taxi to the hospital even though I was just thirteen years old. I waited outside the **morgue** while she identified the body; and I sat up with her that night when she didn't want to close her eyes because she said she kept seeing Papi covered in blood.

By now, I'm **pacing** back and forth like the lion at the Bronx Zoo. I imagine her in an **alley**, her throat cut, her green dress torn.

I've made myself sick. I try to sit down

> It had been a long, long time since I'd seen her smile.

and relax. When I switch channels, I get **caught up** in a news-channel special on violent crimes in American cities. That does it. I grab the keys and run down the stairs, **double-time it** in the direction of St. Mary's.

The barrio is really jumping tonight. There's a domino championship at Cheo's ***bodega*** and the place is packed.

I don't stop, especially since I can hear a police siren somewhere ahead and I just know they've found her body. I run faster even though my lungs feel like they're going to burst.

I'm right in front of the church before I slow down. The dance is in the **basement**. I push through the sweaty people and finally squeeze in.

It's a strange sight.

My mother is doing this **tango** with Don José. They are looking into each other's eyes

---

an innocent a harmless
morgue place where the dead are kept before being identified and released for burial
pacing walking
alley dark, narrow side street

caught up interested
double-time it go very fast
bodega grocery store (in Spanish)
basement bottom floor underground
tango dramatic dance from Argentina

as if **hypnotized**. He dips her right, and then left, until her head almost touches the ground. Their movements **are in perfect tune to** the music, and when they do one of their **fancy** turns some people clap. My mother's face is **radiant**.

When the song ends, people clap and whistle. But they don't seem to notice. It's like they're alone in the middle of the crowd. He's still holding her hands. She looks up at him and smiles. He raises her fingers up to his lips and kisses them. That's when I turn around and start pushing my way out of the basement.

I keep seeing my mother's face out there on the dance floor and wishing she had been looking up at Papi when she smiled. But that can't happen anymore. And that makes me feel like I'm choking on a chicken bone. But then, it'd been a long, long time since I'd seen her smile at all.

I race up the stairs and plop down in front of the TV. I'm sort of in a **stupor** by the time I hear the voices saying good-night in Spanish outside the door. Then there's a minute or so of quiet before she puts the key in the lock.

She comes in smiling and eases in next to me. I try to move away, but she gently pulls me closer and kisses the top of my head, holding me for a long time. I get the feeling that she's trying to transfer something to me, something she's feeling— love, happiness, whatever it is, it feels good, so I just close my eyes to try to enjoy it. But glued to the back of my eyelids is a picture of Papi, looking sharp in his white shirt and tie. Don't forget me, he whispers in my head. Don't forget.

---

hypnotized   dazed, overcome
are in perfect tune to   match the rhythm and the beat of
fancy   skillful

ABOUT THE AUTHOR

Award-winning author **Judith Ortiz Cofer** was born in Puerto Rico and moved to New Jersey when she was young. In addition to her fictional stories about life in the barrio, she  writes about her family. She says, "In tracing their lives, I discover more about mine. [Puerto Rico] becomes a metaphor for the things we all must leave behind; [adjusting to life in the United States] is the coming into maturity by accepting the terms necessary for survival."

Respond to the Story
Check Your Understanding

SUM IT UP

Analyze Characters Share your character maps with your partner. Then add sections to your maps that tell the problem each character faces and how it is resolved.

Character Map

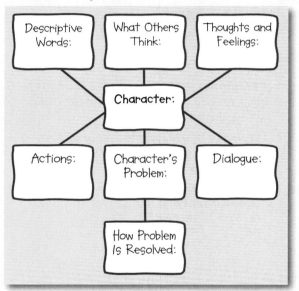

Descriptive Words:

What Others Think:

Thoughts and Feelings:

Character:

Actions:

Character's Problem:

Dialogue:

How Problem Is Resolved:

Evaluate Literature How well do you think the author developed the characters in "The Dance"? Give the author a grade and use examples from the selection to explain your reasoning to your group. Then write a paragraph that tells how you feel the characterization affected the quality of the story.

THINK IT OVER

Discuss and Write Talk about these questions with a partner. Then write the answers.

1. **Character's Point of View** Imagine you are Mami. Retell the story from her point of view.

2. **Conflict** What is causing the tension between Yolanda and Mami? How do you think Mami feels about Yolanda's attitude?

3. **Opinion** Do you think Yolanda's behavior is reasonable? Explain your answer.

EXPRESS YOURSELF ▶ EXPRESS OPINIONS

How does "The Dance" fit the theme of moving forward? Find examples from the selection that support the theme and share your ideas during a class discussion.

Language Arts and Content Area Connections

GRAMMAR IN CONTEXT

USE PROGRESSIVE FORMS OF VERBS

Learn More About Verbs The progressive form of a verb describes action that is in progress or happened over a period of time.

These verbs use a form of the helping verb *be* to tell the tense. The main verb ends in *-ing*.

Tense	Example of the Progessive
Present	They **are dancing** now.
Past	They **were dancing** yesterday.
Future	They **will be dancing** tomorrow.
Present Perfect	They **have been dancing** for a long time.
Past Perfect	They **had been dancing** before I came home.
Future Perfect	They **will have been dancing** by tomorrow evening.

Practice Use a progressive form of the main verb in parentheses to complete each sentence.

1. Right now I _____ on the front stoop. (sit)

2. Mami _____ herself up the last few days. (fix)

3. Inside they _____ television together. (watch)

4. Ever since Mami met Don José, I _____ about Papi. (think)

SOCIAL STUDIES
SPEAKING/LISTENING

EXPLORE GEOGRAPHY

Learn About an Island Work with a group to research and prepare a presentation about an island in the Caribbean.

1 Choose an Island and Gather Information Here are some islands you can learn about:

Bahamas	Barbados
Cayman Islands	Guadeloupe
Dominica	Grenada
Martinique	Haiti
Jamaica	Montserrat
Puerto Rico	Trinidad
Virgin Islands	Dominican Republic

Use print and electronic encyclopedias and almanacs to find out about the island's language, terrain, population, cities, countryside, and culture.

2 Plan a Multimedia Presentation Make a chart or a web to organize the information. Decide if you'll prepare a travel brochure, poster, illustrated chart, or travelogue. Consider including a recording like the national anthem or a video clip of life on the island.

3 Present Your Findings Practice to make sure everyone knows what to say and when to display the appropriate visual. Give your presentation to the class.

Windrider's Dream

historical fiction
by Laurence Yep

Prepare to Read

THINK ABOUT WHAT YOU KNOW

Team Word Web Make a web to show what your group knows about the history of flight.

compensation something that makes up for something else

dignity self-respect

dubious uncertain, doubtful

flying machine airplane

noble magnificent, impressive

petty unimportant

pride self-importance

pursue follow or chase something

superior of the highest quality, exceptional

suspicious distrustful; questionable

LEARN KEY VOCABULARY

Use New Words in Context Study the new words and their definitions. Use the new words as you act out this scene with a partner.

A man has **pursued** his dream and created his own **flying machine**. It is a **noble** device, but his uncle is very **dubious** that it will work. The uncle says building it was such a **petty** way to spend time. He is also **suspicious** that his nephew spent too much money and will never get **compensation** for it. The nephew works hard to maintain his **dignity** as his uncle expresses his concerns. The nephew knows that he used a **superior** design, and the plane will fly. He realizes that this uncle's **pride** is at risk if the machine does not work.

LEARN ABOUT THEMES IN LITERATURE

The **theme** is a story's message about life or human nature.

READING STRATEGY
How to Identify a Story's Theme
1. Think about what the main character learns about life.
2. Look for sentences and passages that tell about people or life in general. What is the author saying?
3. Look at the title of the story. What is its message?
4. Use what you've learned to decide what the theme is.

As you read "Windrider's Dream," make notes in your journal about the characters and events to help you identify the theme.

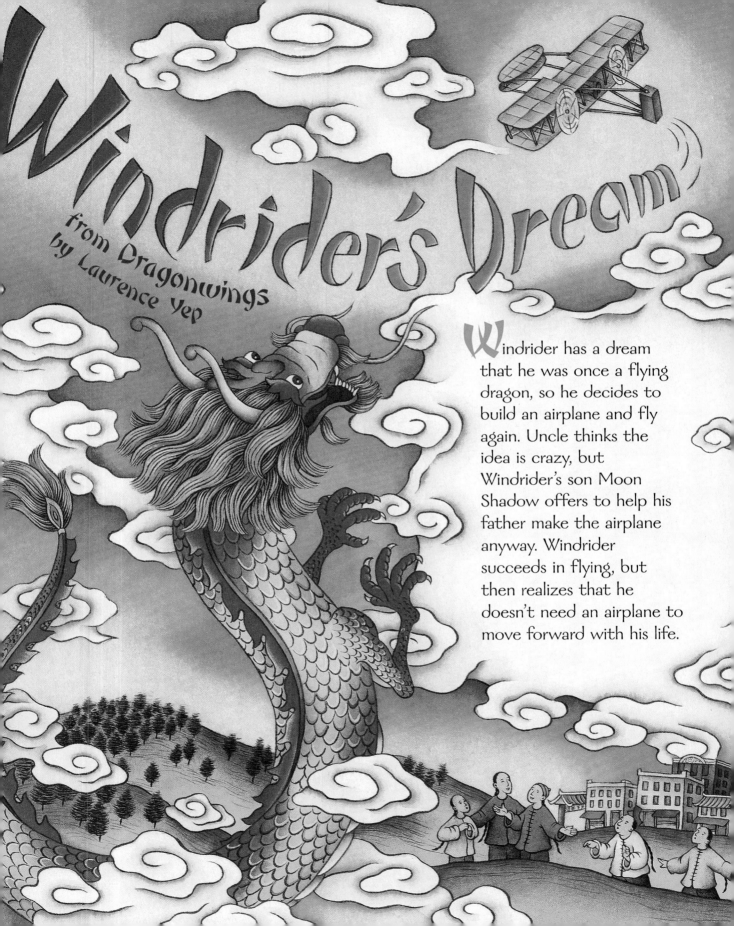

Windrider's Dream

from Dragonwings
by Laurence Yep

Windrider has a dream that he was once a flying dragon, so he decides to build an airplane and fly again. Uncle thinks the idea is crazy, but Windrider's son Moon Shadow offers to help his father make the airplane anyway. Windrider succeeds in flying, but then realizes that he doesn't need an airplane to move forward with his life.

In the early 1900s, Moon Shadow travels from China to join his father Windrider in San Francisco, California. They work in a laundry with others in the "Company": Uncle, Lefty, Hand Clap, and White Deer.

Windrider tells his son about a dream he had of flying with the Imperial Dragon. In the dream, Windrider learned that he was once a dragon and can become one again if, as a human, he passes certain tests.

Because of that, Windrider decides to leave the Company. He is determined to build and fly an airplane he calls Dragonwings. While Moon Shadow believes in his father's dream, Uncle thinks the dream is simply foolish.

FOLLOWING A DREAM

Windrider wants to build an airplane. Uncle thinks it is foolish,
but Moon Shadow offers to help.

Father got Uncle alone and I sat down by them. "This life is too short to spend it **pursuing** little things. I have to do what I know I can and must do."

Uncle banged his fist on the arm of his chair. "Not that dumb dream again."

"Dream or not, I can fly," Father said matter-of-factly. "I can build a **flying machine**."

Uncle looked grim. "Even **assuming** you can build a flying machine and then make money flying it, what will you and your family eat while you're building the machine?"

"It's time I thought of myself," Father **asserted**.

"A **superior** man admits the truth," Uncle snapped. I could see Father was beat. He hung his head for the longest time, staring down at his hands.

"I want to fly too, Father," I said. "We should build the flying machine. Maybe you can make a living doing it. And while we're

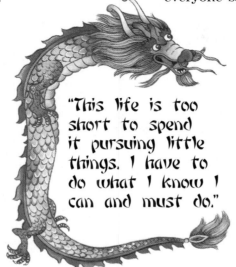

"This life is too short to spend it pursuing little things. I have to do what I know I can and must do."

building it, we'll both get jobs. We'll all manage somehow."

Father straightened a little. "Despite what everyone says?"

"A superior man can only do what he's meant to do," I said.

Uncle laughed **scornfully**. "Don't give me that nonsense."

"He's the only one I hear talking sense," Father said.

"Don't expect to come back here, either of you," Uncle warned us. He was hurt by our leaving him. "I won't have anything to do with fools."

Uncle shoved his chair away from us and got up. "Get away from me," he said.

I was sad about Uncle, but with Father's arm around me, I felt a warm glow inside of me even so. He was Windrider and I was his son.

BEFORE YOU MOVE ON...

1. **Opinion** Do you think Windrider's decision to follow his dream was foolish? Why or why not?

2. **Personal Experience** Have you ever followed your dream even though others thought it was foolish? Tell a partner about your experience.

---

assuming if, supposing
asserted said firmly
scornfully disrespectfully

HANDLING SURPRISES

The plane is built, but there is no money left. Unexpectedly,
Uncle and the Company come to help.

It took three years to build Dragonwings, because we never seemed to have much money to go around. But by the end of the summer of 1909, we were ready.

It was a good thing we finished it when we did, because we were **just about broke**. Up until now, we had always tried to pay our rent, food, and expenses out of our earnings, but little by little we had to **dip into our savings**. Now we had only enough left to pay the rent for next month and hire a team of horses and a wagon to **haul** Dragonwings up to the top of our hill and fly it.

One day when I got home, I found my Uncle's **estranged son** Black Dog there. He put a knife to my throat and demanded that I give him our money. Just then, Father arrived. Despite my protests, Father found our roll of money and gave it to Black Dog. Black Dog snatched it and ran off.

We were going to lose our Dragonwings.

Our rent money had been in that roll, as well as the money we had planned to use for renting a wagon and team of horses. What we were going to do for money, I didn't know.

The next day when the landlord came around for his rent, he got mad at Father when Father asked him for **an extension**. He gave us three days to come up with the money or he'd claim everything inside the place.

We had to go, but how? We would be able to take away only what we could carry. We were going to lose our Dragonwings.

Father did not say anything when I put on my boots and hat and went down to the town through the rain to use the telephone. I had to call our friend Miss Whitlaw who had been planning to come see us the next day.

"Why hello, Moon Shadow," Miss Whitlaw said. "How are you?"

---

just about broke almost out of money

dip into our savings use money that we had been saving

haul carry

estranged son boy with whom he no longer had contact

an extension a few more days to pay the rent

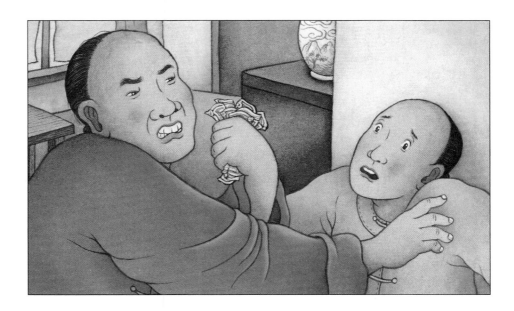

"Fine. I'm afraid you won't be able to come down tomorrow. We're . . . we're moving."

"Well, let us give you a hand."

"No, no. I couldn't think of it."

"Nonsense, there's always work to be done. Expect us there right after church."

"No please, you mustn't come," I said desperately.

There was a **pause** at the other end of the line. "Is there something wrong?" she finally asked.

"No, no. Everything's just fine."

"Well, then, why can't we come over?" she demanded.

"We'll just be busy."

"So busy you don't need help?" Miss Whitlaw asked **suspiciously**.

"Yes, that's it," I said, and hung up before she could ask me anything else.

I do not know when I fell asleep, but it was already way past sunrise when I woke up. Father lay **huddled**, rolled up in his blanket. He did not move when the knock came at our door. I crawled out of the blankets and opened the side door.

Hand Clap stood there as if he had appeared by magic. He bowed.

"There you are." He turned and called over his shoulder. "Hey, everybody, they're here."

Toiling up the hill was our old horse Red Rabbit, and behind him I saw Uncle on the wagon seat. Behind the wagon came the Company, with coils of ropes over their shoulders and baskets of food. I ran down the hill, my feet pounding against the hard, damp earth. I got up on the seat and almost **bowled** Uncle over. For once Uncle did not worry about his **dignity** but caught me up and returned my hug.

---

pause short silence
huddled curled up

Toiling Moving or pulling with difficulty
bowled knocked

"Am I ever glad you're here," I said. "Poor Father—"

Uncle held up his hands. "We know. That's why we came."

"But how? Why?" I was bursting with a dozen questions all at once.

"Why, to help you get that thing up to the top of the hill," Uncle said. "Why else would we close up our shop and take a boat and climb this **abominable** hill, all on the coldest, wettest day ever known since creation?"

"But you don't believe in flying machines."

"I still don't," Uncle said **sternly**. "But I'll be there to haul your machine up the hill, and I'll be there to haul it back down when it doesn't fly. Now." He clapped his hands together. "Come, I'm getting cold."

Uncle and I went into the barn.

"I didn't know you were going to come," Father said.

"Of course, you didn't. Neither did I until last night, and how were we supposed to get word to you when you live off in the wilds?"

Uncle walked past Father, **ducked under** some models and, slipping between the wall and the wing, eyed Dragonwings critically. "How will that thing ever carry you?"

"If you just came to laugh—" Father began, **bristling**.

"I came to help," Uncle snapped. "Not because I believe in your crazy dream. Call it an old man's **whim** if you like." But then Uncle **relented** for a moment. "And we didn't come to laugh."

"All of them, Father," I said. "All the Company came."

"Well, we'll get to see Dragonwings fly once before we lose it," Father said with a laugh.

"Don't worry about losing it either," Uncle said. "We'll give you the money to pay your rent too. Call it a loan, a **compensation**." He wagged a finger at Father. "And don't give me any pigheaded reasons why you can't take it. **Pride** has always been the great sin of our family."

BEFORE YOU MOVE ON...

1. **Making Decisions** If you were Windrider, would you have given Black Dog the money? Why or why not?

2. **Character's Motive** Why do you think Uncle came to Windrider's and Moon Shadow's aid?

3. **Inference** How was Uncle's offer for help an example of "moving forward"?

---

abominable awful, horrible
sternly firmly
ducked under lowered his head to walk under

bristling getting angry
whim sudden crazy idea
relented gave in, softened

3
FLYING

With everyone's help, the airplane is ready to fly.
Then, Windrider takes off.

Father considered that for a moment. "It's not a shameful thing to take money from friends, and you are my friends. I thought I ought to go it alone with just my son, but I was wrong. I'll **own up to it**."

"Good," Uncle said. "Because we dropped the money off on the way up."

"But how did you know the amount, or where my landlord lived?" Father asked. "And how—?"

"We have our ways," Uncle said with a secret smile. "Now show the others this magnificent machine that's about to carry you to the moon."

It was not until two hours later that we got to start.

Hand Clap backed the wagon into the barn, and we put the tailgate down and **propped** some boards against the wagon bed so we could use them like a ramp. Then, using a system of ropes and pulleys hung from the **rafters**, we hauled Dragonwings onto the wagon bed. I could only compare the heavy weight of Dragonwings to the light pair of wings that Father had worn during his visit to the dragon kingdom.

Gently, **coaxingly**, Hand Clap made Red Rabbit head out of the stable. Father pointed up the hill. "We'll go to the very top."

Uncle looked **dubiously** up the steeply **inclined** hill. "This hill," he noted, "is a very steep hill."

"Maybe we'd better hire a team of horses," Father said to Uncle.

Father pointed up the hill. "We'll go to the very top."

"Didn't I say the Company would take your machine up to the hilltop?" Uncle said. It would have made much more sense to have hired a team or even two teams of horses, but it was a point of honor now with Uncle for the Company itself to take the flying machine up to the hilltop. And perhaps Uncle wanted to make up to us for all the time we had been living out here like this, trying to prove he was wrong about our never being able to fly. Uncle added, "I'll get your machine up to the top of the hill if I have to carry it on just my back."

---

own up to it say it is true, admit it
propped put, set
rafters boards that support the roof

coaxingly with encouragement
inclined angled, sloping

When everything was ready, we took our places.

"Ready?" Father asked.

The Company chorused they were.

"Then let's go," Father said.

We strained at the ropes. Slowly, ever so slowly the wagon began to creep up the hill. And Dragonwings, its wings waving over either side of the wagon, **lurched** forward. Foot by foot, we pushed and pulled the wagon with Dragonwings up the hill, its wings dipping and bobbing as if it were **tensing** itself.

Uncle began a chant. And the rest of us, hauling in rhythm to his chant, began to find it was easier. I would say, too, that Uncle pulled the hardest of any of us. And all of a sudden I saw that if life seems awfully **petty** most of the time, every now and then there is something **noble** and beautiful and almost pure that lifts us suddenly out of the pettiness and lets us share in it a little. It did not matter whether Father flew or not. It was enough that the Company had come.

I do not know how, but we managed to get Dragonwings to the top of the hill. For a long time, nobody said anything. We were all too busy trying to **get back our wind**.

"Someone is coming," Lefty called.

We saw the heavily clothed figures tromp up the hill. Miss Whitlaw's face lit up when she saw all of us gathered on the top.

....

lurched moved quickly, jerked
tensing tightening
get back our wind breathe normally again

"Thank goodness," she puffed. "I thought we were going to be late." Beside her, helping to support her arm, was her niece Robin. Father came down the road and took Miss Whitlaw's other arm. "How did you know we were flying?"

"Oh," Miss Whitlaw said **gaily**, and glanced at Uncle, "a little birdie told me."

"Did you tell them?" Father demanded of me.

"No, sir."

Miss Whitlaw had not understood our conversation, but she could get the meaning of it just from Father's angry tone. "Now you just blame a **snoopy** old lady, Mr. Lee. I just had to know what was wrong, so I had my employer, who knows your landlord, call him and find out what was the matter. And then I got hold of your friend, Mr. Deerfoot, over in the City, and he gave a message to your Uncle for him to call me up. And so we worked out everything between us," Miss Whitlaw said.

Father grinned down at Robin. "It's a good thing you got here."

We untied Dragonwings then and **eased it down** the ramp by sheer muscle power. Then, lifting, pulling, and pushing, we rolled it to the **crest** of the hill.

Then Father clapped his hands together nervously. "Well, it's time to start." With a nod to Robin and me, he headed for Dragonwings.

Robin took her place before the left propeller with her hands resting on the blade. I took my place beside the right propeller. Father himself lay belly-down on the bottom wing.

"All right, Moon Shadow, Robin," Father said. We both pulled down at the propellers and backed away. The motor beside Father coughed into life, turned over, and caught. It was as if Dragonwings had finally woken.

The wooden wheels made crisp, crunching sounds as they crushed the weeds. Dragonwings seemed to **teeter** for a moment, balancing on the very edge of the hillside.

The nose of Dragonwings suddenly **tilted** up like some bird scenting the wind that would carry it home. The wind roared over the hilltop, seeming to gather beneath the wings. Dragonwings seemed to leap into the air about five feet and hang **suspended**. I held my breath. Slowly, ever so slowly, Father began to control his flight! He was free in the sky.

BEFORE YOU MOVE ON...

1. **Paraphrase** Write two or three sentences describing how Dragonwings was taken to the top of the hill.

2. **Details** How did Uncle find out that Windrider needed help?

3. **Context Clues/Vocabulary** What is the meaning of *sheer* in the phrase "sheer muscle power"? Look up other meanings of *sheer*.

---

gaily happily
snoopy overly curious
eased it down carefully helped it go down
crest top

teeter move back and forth
tilted faced, headed
suspended in the air without moving

The plane crashes. Windrider recognizes that
his family is more important than an airplane.

Everyone cheered **spontaneously**. I raced along beside Dragonwings for a moment, my legs pumping, my head dizzy, my heart filled with pride. "Father, you did it. You did it."

We watched him fly for perhaps four minutes while we stood knee-deep among the flowers.

"Look at him," Uncle shouted. He was as excited as a little boy. "Look at him. Just look."

Father had just completed another **circuit** and his nose at the time was pointed toward the hillside. I heard a shrill, high, singing sound as the bolt that held the right propeller to the frame snapped. Horrified, I saw the propeller spinning away from Dragonwings in a lazy **arc**.

Dragonwings leaned forward and **burrowed** nose first into the hillside. The body swung back and forth drunkenly and then hung at an odd angle.

I raced toward Dragonwings. Father lay on his back. I took his wrist. He still had a pulse.

Puffing, Uncle joined me. The others gathered around, catching their breaths. Finally Uncle straightened and looked around, relieved. "I think his right leg is broken and maybe two of his right ribs. That's all."

"You mean he'll live?" I asked.

"For now, yes, until he tries his next flying machine." Uncle shook his head.

We **cannibalized** Dragonwings to make a stretcher for Father out of the wooden poles and canvas.

Uncle and White Deer set his leg—there was plenty of wood for that—and we **bound** up his sides tight with some old lengths of cloth. Miss Whitlaw sent Robin after a doctor. By the time she got back with one, we had lifted Father onto the wagon and taken him straight into the stable.

After the doctor left, we waited for Father to wake up. "I wish," Miss Whitlaw

Dragonwings leaned forward and burrowed nose first into the hillside.

---

spontaneously without thinking, as a reaction
circuit circle around the property
arc half-circle

burrowed buried itself
cannibalized tore apart
bound wrapped

said, "that I had never had my employer begin making inquiries."

"I don't think Father would have wanted it any other way." I added, "Neither do I. It . . . it just had to be."

Father **stirred** then and groaned and sat up, leaning on his elbows. He winced and looked at his sides.

I got some tea for him. "Dragonwings is a **wreck**. We'll have to build another one."

Father sipped his tea and set the cup down carefully on the dirt floor. "I'm not going to build another Dragonwings. When I was up there on it, I found myself wishing you were up there. And I realized I couldn't have the two of them together: my family and flying. And just as I saw the hill coming at me, I realized that my family meant more to me than flying. It's enough for me now to know that I can fly."

"But what about becoming a dragon?"

"Ah, well, there's more to being a dragon than just flying," Father said. "Dragons have **immense** families too. It would be nice to live long enough to see my great-grandchildren. And it may be that my final test is to **raise a brood** of superior women and men."

"Humph," Uncle said. "Maybe that crash knocked some sense into you."

"Maybe it did." Father leaned over from his mat and picked up his tea again, moving very slowly because of his bandaged sides.

Uncle glanced at White Deer and Hand Clap. "It'll make it easier to suggest what we were thinking of, then. I think we could use a **levelheaded** partner."

I held my breath. Father turned and winked at me as if to say, "What can we do?" To Uncle, Father said, "We accept and thank you all."

BEFORE YOU MOVE ON...

1. **Details** How long did Dragonwings stay in the air?
2. **Cause and Effect** What caused Dragonwings to crash?
3. **Conflict/Character's Point of View** What choice did Windrider feel he had to make? What did he decide to do? Why?

---

stirred moved
wreck destroyed airplane, ruin
immense very big
raise a brood bring up a family
levelheaded reasonable, sensible

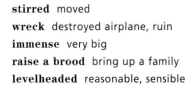

ABOUT THE AUTHOR

Laurence Yep wrote award-winning *Dragonwings* to honor an actual inventor, Fung Joe Guey. To write the book, he had to combine facts with his sense of how people grow and learn. He says he wanted to show that Windrider and Moon Shadow are looking for "that power in each of us to grasp with the mind and heart what we cannot immediately grasp with the hand."

Respond to the Story
Check Your Understanding

SUM IT UP

Identify the Theme What is the theme of "Windrider's Dream"?

- Review your notes.

What the Story Says	What It Means
"Because of that (his dream of flying with the Imperial Dragon), Windrider decides to leave the Company."	Windrider thinks his dream is more important than working with the Company.

- Write a theme statement based on your notes.

- Meet with other students who have written a similar theme statement. Discuss the examples in the story that support your statement.

- Have one person share your group's ideas with the class. Listen to other groups' ideas and the examples they give to support them.

- Use any new ideas to re-think your theme statement and make notes to support it.

Compare Themes in Literature Follow the steps above to come up with a theme statement for "The Dance." Write an essay that compares the themes of the two selections. Do you think these themes are universal or timeless? Why or why not?

THINK IT OVER

Discuss and Write Talk about these questions with a partner. Then write the answers.

1. **Personal Experience** If you were Moon Shadow and had worked very hard to build Dragonwings, how would you have felt when you didn't get to fly in it? Why?

2. **Inference** Uncle says that pride is a great sin in the family. Name two examples from the story that show how a character's pride got in the way of his moving forward.

3. **Conclusions** How did Uncle and Windrider each "move forward"?

EXPRESS YOURSELF ▸NEGOTIATE

Pretend that you are Windrider. You have just been offered a little money from the local "Dream Defender Foundation," but you would like more. Negotiate with a partner, who can be the foundation's representative, to get more funding. Tell what you will do in exchange for their money.

Example:

If you give us more money, we will paint your name on the plane.

Language Arts and Literature

GRAMMAR IN CONTEXT

WRITE SENTENCES WITH PARTICIPIAL PHRASES

Learn About Participial Phrases A group of related words that begins with the *-ed* or *-ing* form of a verb is called a **participial phrase**. It is used to tell more about a noun.

> **Determined to follow his dream,** Father left the laundry.

A participial phrase should be placed next to the noun it tells about.

Use participial phrases to combine ideas from shorter sentences.

> Father spoke carefully. He told us his dream.
> **Speaking carefully,** Father told us his dream.

Identify Participial Phrases in Sentences What participial phrases are in this paragraph?

> Laughing scornfully, Uncle said, "Don't give me that nonsense." Then he stood up, shoving the chair away angrily.

Practice Use a participial phrase to combine the two shorter sentences.

1. Hand Clap appeared. He bowed deeply.
2. Red Rabbit toiled up the hill. He pulled the old wagon.
3. The Company followed the wagon. They carried ropes and food.
4. Uncle forgot his dignity. He returned my hug.

LITERARY ANALYSIS
WRITING

WRITE A LITERARY CRITIQUE

Although **historical fiction** is made-up, the events happen in a real time and place in the past. Compare historical facts with the historical details in "Windrider's Dream." How accurate is the selection?

1 Research Facts Use print and electronic sources like encyclopedias and the Internet to find out more about Chinese American life in San Francisco in the 1900s.

2 List Details Record the historical details and details from "Windrider's Dream."

Details from History	Details from "Windrider's Dream"
Some Chinese Americans had laundry businesses in Chinatown.	Moon Shadow and his father worked in a laundry.

3 Write a Draft Write a thesis statement about the accuracy of the selection. Then write sentences and paragraphs to support it. Include the details from your research.

4 Edit and Share Your Essay Read your essay and make any corrections. Then post your final copy in the classroom.

For more about the **research process**, see Handbook pages 394–399. Develop your skill in the **writer's craft**. See pages 414–423.

Respond to the Story, continued
Content Area Connections

TECHNOLOGY/MEDIA

SOCIAL STUDIES

CREATE A DOCUMENTARY ABOUT FLIGHT

Dreamers like Windrider have made air travel and space exploration possible. Find out about the technological developments made in the history of flight. Then give a multimedia report.

❶ Gather Information and Take Notes Try these Web sites first, but remember that the Internet changes daily! Search for more sites by using the key words.

INTERNET

INFORMATION ON-LINE

Key Words:
"history of flight"
aviation
"Wright Brothers"

Web Sites:
➤ **History of Flight:**
 Information and Photos
 • www.historychannel.com
 • www.museumofflight.org
 • www.nasa.gov
 • www.nasm.si.edu

Download articles and photos. Bookmark Web sites with film clips and sound bites that you can include in your report.

❷ Plan and Organize Your Information
Create a storyboard to help you plan your presentation. Make notes and sketches to show information you'll share and visuals you'll use like photos, movies, or time lines.

Storyboard

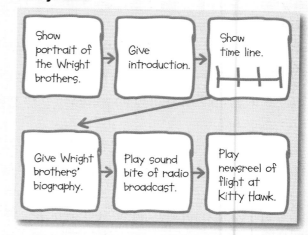

Show portrait of the Wright brothers.
→ Give introduction.
→ Show time line.

Give Wright brothers' biography.
→ Play sound bite of radio broadcast.
→ Play newsreel of flight at Kitty Hawk.

❸ Prepare a Multimedia Report Create the visuals you need. Prepare your film clips or sound bites so you can access them easily as you give your report. Practice giving the report. Then present your report to your class.

Learn to use the **Internet** on Handbook pages 392–393. For help with **multimedia presentations**, see pages 390–391.

Dreams and *Youth*

poems
by Langston Hughes

Prepare to Read Poetry

THINK ABOUT WHAT YOU KNOW

Journal Writing Where do you see yourself going as you get older? Write some sentences in your journal to tell about your plans and dreams for the future.

hold fast hang on tightly

LEARN KEY VOCABULARY

Use New Words in Context Study the new phrase and its definition. Choose two items from the list. Explain to your partner why and how you would **hold fast** to the items.

- your goals
- your beliefs
- your backpack in a crowd
- your surfboard when you surf
- your family values
- your cultural values

LEARN TO INTERPRET FIGURATIVE LANGUAGE

Poets often use **comparisons** in their poems to paint pictures with words. The comparisons help readers create images in their minds.

> **READING STRATEGY**
> **How to Interpret Figurative Language**
> 1. Look for similes. A simile compares one thing to another using *like* or *as*: *The lake is **as clear as glass**.*
> 2. Look for metaphors. A metaphor makes a comparison by saying one thing *is* another thing: *The sun **is a yolk in the robin's egg sky**.*
> 3. When you are reading and see a comparison, think about the image it suggests. Restate the comparison in your own words.

As you read "Dreams" and "Youth," look for comparisons to help you picture what the poet means.

Dreams

Hold fast to dreams
For if dreams die
Life is a broken-winged bird
That cannot fly.

Hold fast to dreams
For when dreams go
Life is a barren field
Frozen with snow.

—Langston Hughes

Youth

We have tomorrow
Bright before us
Like a flame.

Yesterday
A night-gone thing,
A sun-down name.

And dawn-today
Broad arch above the road we came.

We march!

—Langston Hughes

Respond to the Poem

THINK IT OVER

Discuss Talk about these questions with a partner.

1. **Personal Experience**
   What would life be like without dreams?

2. **Theme** How are the messages in these two poems related?

⟩ WRITING)

WRITE A POEM

Write a poem with at least one metaphor or simile. Start with:

> *Hold fast to dreams,*
> *For if dreams soar . . .*

or

> *We have today*
> *Bright before us . . .*

Use other literary devices such as rhyme, alliteration, personification, or onomatopoeia.

ABOUT THE POET

Langston Hughes was one of the most popular writers of the Harlem Renaissance. Through his poetry, Hughes captured the oral traditions of the black culture, including everyday speech. He also emphasized that, despite our differences, both white and black Americans are equally entitled to justice and opportunity. Langston Hughes' message of hope for future generations is expressed in both "Dreams" and "Youth."

Writing to Explain and Narrate

Sometimes the same topic can be used for expository and narrative writing. In expository writing, a writer uses facts to inform readers about a topic. In narrative writing, a writer makes up a story based on facts.

PROFESSIONAL WRITING MODELS

"The Dirty Thirties" is a historical account. The writer explains what happened to Oklahoma farmers who lived in the Dust Bowl during the Great Depression.

"Out of the Dust" is a narrative poem, made up about one family who lived in the Dust Bowl. The narrator is a girl who tells how her family copes with the events described in the historical account.

COMPARING EXPOSITORY AND NARRATIVE WRITING

For a historical account or report, a writer uses dates, facts, and statistics to help readers understand the importance of what happened during a certain period of history. For a narrative, the writer wants you to feel what it was like to live during that time. The writer makes up the characters, but uses a real place and time for the setting. Study the Venn diagram to see how the types of writing compare.

from "The Dirty Thirties"

> In these areas, and especially in the Panhandle, the dry winds howled for four long years, from 1936 to 1940. Frequently the wind blew more than fifty miles an hour, carrying away the topsoil and leaving only hard red clay, which made farming impossible.

from "Out of the Dust"

> While Ma and Daddy slept,
> the dust came,
> tearing up fields where the winter wheat,
> set for harvest in June,
> stood helpless.

Venn Diagram

"The Dirty Thirties"

purpose—to help readers understand what happened to Oklahoma farmers in the 1930s

gives facts about how the Great Depression and weather affected farmers

has photos with captions, graphic aids

told in third person

Both

headings
photos
specific dates

about Oklahoma farmers in the 1930s who face drought, bankruptcy, and dust storms

tells about people who migrate to California

mentions President Roosevelt

"Out of the Dust"

purpose—to help readers imagine what it was like to be a part of a farming family in Oklahoma in the 1930s

made-up narrator and details about a family's experience and how they felt

has photos with captions

told in first person

STUDENT WRITING MODELS

Report

Hank Aaron Goes for the Home-Run Record

by Aurelian Janvier

When I think of home runs, I think of Hank Aaron. He holds the record for career home runs. His total was 755.

Hank did well in baseball, even at a young age. After two years in the minor leagues, he joined the Milwaukee Braves. He was 20 years old. In 1955, his first full season, he hit 27 home runs.

By 1972, sports writers were talking about Hank beating the record of 714 career home runs. By the end of 1972, Hank had already reached a total of 673 home runs. The next season, Hank hit number 713 on September 29.

It was 1974, and Hank needed one home run to tie the record and one to beat it. On April 4, he hit number 714. Four days later, the now Atlanta Braves (formerly the Milwaukee Braves) played the Dodgers. Hank walked the first time up. He was at bat again in the fourth inning. Hank swung at the second pitch and the ball sailed over the fence. Running the bases, Hank watched the screen flash 715. The crowd went wild!

Hank Aaron continued to play two more years, as a designated hitter for Milwaukee. But he will always be remembered for that hit and that magic number—715.

INTRODUCTION
The title and first paragraph identify and introduce the **topic** of your report. They get your reader interested.

BODY
Each paragraph in the body begins with a **topic sentence** that tells one main idea.

The supporting details include **facts** from at least two reliable sources. Aurelian gathered her information from two baseball encyclopedias and a book about Hank Aaron.

CONCLUSION
In the final paragraph, Aurelian sums up the report and reminds the reader why Hank Aaron is important.

Story

Hank Aaron Does It Again!

by Aurelian Janvier

My name is Robbie Rojas. In 1974, I was bat boy for the Atlanta Braves. I got to hand baseball bats to the amazing Hank Aaron. All over Atlanta, all over the United States, all over the *world*, everyone knew Hank Aaron. He was going to beat Babe Ruth's record!

I woke up Sunday morning, April 8, still thinking about the game with the Dodgers. Hank needed just one home run. As my mother drove me to Atlanta Stadium, I couldn't keep still.

"He's going to do it today, Mom," I said. "I can feel it."

STORY ELEMENTS
Aurelian's narrative is based on real people, places, and events.

Aurelian makes up two of the characters and parts of the plot. She tells the story from Robbie's point of view.

Writing to Explain and Narrate, continued

The Writing Process

> **WRITING PROMPT**
>
> **Now you will write a report to inform your classmates about a time in history. After you finish your report, use the facts and details to make up a story.**

PREWRITE

1 **Collect Ideas and Choose a Topic** Think about a time in recent history or long ago. What would you like to learn more about? Brainstorm with your partner and record your ideas in a web or a list. Talk over your ideas, then choose a topic.

2 **Unlock the Writing Prompt** Before you begin writing, fill out an FATP chart to help guide your writing.

3 **Collect Information** Research your topic and take notes. Use at least two sources to get information on your topic. Keep a list of your sources, so you can prove your facts are accurate.

4 **Make an Outline** Use your notes to make an outline. It will help you organize the main ideas and details for each paragraph of your report.

FATP Chart

HOW TO UNLOCK A PROMPT
Form: _report_
Audience: _classmates_
Topic: _Alexander the Great_
Purpose: _give facts about Alexander and his empire_

Alexander the Great: King of Macedonia

I. A royal son
   A. Father was Philip II, a Macedonian king
   B. Mother was a princess from Greece
II. Alexander's childhood
   A. Taught by a famous philosopher, Aristotle
     1. Loved plants and animals
     2. Studied literature and philosophy
   B. Stopped school at 16

Look on Handbook pages 390–395 for help with doing research, taking notes, and making an outline.

Reflect and Evaluate

- How did your partner help you choose a topic?

- Could you find enough information about your topic? If not, try another topic.

DRAFT

Refer to your **FATP** chart to keep you focused on what and why you are writing. Write quickly and try to include as much information as you can from your notes.

1 **Introduce the Topic** Use the title from your outline to begin your report, then write an introduction.

2 **Write the Body** Write a topic sentence for each main idea on your outline. Then turn your details into sentences. As you write, add information to make your writing clear and interesting.

> *If you read good books, when you write, good books will come out of you.*
>
> — Natalie Goldberg

Writer's Craft: Elaborate

Add sensory details to tell what things were like.

Just OK	Much Better
Alexander's mother was a princess from Greece.	Some historians say that Alexander's mother was a brilliant, but hot-tempered princess from Greece.

Tell what came before or after.

Just OK	Much Better
Alexander had to stop his education when he was just 16.	King Philip needed his son to help him rule Macedonia. So, Alexander had to stop his education when he was just 16.

Add examples and specific details.

Just OK	Much Better
Alexander was trained to be strong.	Alexander's education included training in sports, physical fitness, and warfare.

Add dialogue or quotations.

Just OK	Much Better
Alexander the Great was a king and a general.	As King of Macedonia, Alexander conquered the Persian Empire. A noted historian called him "the greatest general in history."

3 **Write a Conclusion** Include a summary of all your main ideas in the last paragraph. Don't be afraid to appeal to your readers' emotions!

> It's amazing that such a young ruler could accomplish so much in 13 years. In that short time, Alexander had carved out one of the largest empires in world history. If anyone deserves to be called "the Great," it is the mighty Alexander.

Reflect and Evaluate

- Are you happy with your draft? Will your audience think your report is interesting?
- Did you include facts to support your main ideas?

Writing to Explain and Narrate, continued

REVISE

1 **Reread Your Draft** Look at your **FATP**. Is your audience, topic, form, and purpose clear? Does your report contain accurate facts and well-organized paragraphs?

2 **Conduct a Peer Conference** Talk to a partner or group about your report. Can you combine sentences to add variety to your writing? Use the guidelines on Handbook page 411 to help you.

> You say that Alexander nearly died from an injury. You should tell more about that.

> That's a good idea. I can say "Alexander nearly died while marching through India. An arrow struck him and pierced his lung."

> I agree. I'd like to know how he got hurt and where it happened.

3 **Mark Your Changes** Review your notes and decide what you want to change. You may need to go back to your original notecards. To make your changes, use the Revising Marks on Handbook page 411, or the word-processing guidelines on pages 383–389.

EDIT AND PROOFREAD

1 **Check for Mistakes** Reread your report and correct any mistakes in capitalization, spelling, or punctuation. For help, refer to Handbook pages 459–469.

2 **Check Your Sentences** Did you add information to your sentences to tell more about your topic? Look to see that you have used commas, conjunctions, and phrases correctly.

3 **Make a Final Copy** Neatly copy your report, or print out a final copy if you are working on a computer.

> **Reflect and Evaluate**
>
> - Did your peers find your report interesting and informative? What changes did they suggest?
>
> - Did you elaborate by adding more details or facts to your report?

> GRAMMAR IN CONTEXT

SENTENCES WITH PARTICIPIAL PHRASES

A participle is a verb form that ends with *-ed* or *-ing*.
A participial phrase is a group of words that includes a participle.

Alexander became a great warrior.

- A participial phrase does not have a subject or a predicate.

    Examples: becoming a king   running an empire   admired by his subjects

- A participial phrase is used as an adjective. It can be added to a sentence to tell more about a noun.

    Examples: Commanding the cavalry, Alexander helped defeat Greece.
    <u>participial phrase</u>

    Alexander ruled over a large empire conquered by his armies.
    <u>participial phrase</u>

Place a participial phrase next to the noun it tells about. That way it will be clear which noun you want to describe.

    Example: Marching through India, Alexander nearly died on the battlefield.
    <u>participial phrase</u>

    Not: Alexander nearly died on the battlefield marching through India.
    <u>participial phrase</u>

Practice Combine each pair of sentences. Use participial phrases to tell about the nouns.

1. Alexander gained power at age 20. Alexander began to carve out an empire.
2. Alexander left Macedonia. Alexander led his armies across Asia.
3. In Persia, Alexander fought a war. The war was originally planned by his father.
4. Alexander had beaten the Persians. Alexander moved east.
5. Alexander marched into Egypt. Alexander was welcomed by the people.
6. Alexander established a town. The town was named Alexandria.

Writing to Explain and Narrate, continued

WRITING PROMPT

Now use the information in your report to write a fictional narrative about the same topic for your classmates to read. Follow the steps in the Writing Process.

PREWRITE, DRAFT, AND REVISE

Remember that in a fictional narrative, the writer tells a story using made-up characters and a real setting. Adjust your **FATP** chart and use it as a guide for your narrative.

Use your report to remind yourself about the historical details.

- Write a beginning that grabs your readers' interest.
- Write a middle that tells about the events. Add dialogue to show what your characters are like. As you write, let your personal voice and style shine through! Use your favorite words and elaborate with details to keep your writing interesting and exciting.
- Write a satisfying ending.
- Read your draft, have others read it, then make revisions.

EDIT AND PROOFREAD

Check your story for mistakes. Use what you learned about participial phrases to vary your sentences.

PUBLISH YOUR REPORT AND STORY

Think of a way to publish your report and story. You might make a home video of you reading your report and your story. Or, create a portable display to set up in your classroom or carry to another classroom. Arrange your writing in an interesting way.

Reflect and Evaluate

- Does your report
  - ☑ have a topic sentence for each paragraph?
  - ☑ use facts to support each main idea?
  - ☑ have an introduction, body, and conclusion?
- Does your story
  - ☑ have a setting that is true to history?
  - ☑ have made-up characters that seem real?
  - ☑ have a beginning, middle, and end?
- Will your work go in your portfolio? Why or why not?

BREAK THROUGH THE BARRIERS

▶1 Look Back at the Unit

Quotes and Votes In this unit you read about people who had to break through barriers. How did they triumph over tough times?

The Dirty Thirties

Out of the Dust

The Dance

Windrider's Dream

Work with a partner to find a quote from each selection that best describes the idea of triumphs. Then vote as a class on which quote best summarizes the concept.

▶2 Show What You Know

Sum It All Up Expand and organize your ideas on this mind map. Share your ideas about triumphs with a partner.

Barriers → Breaking Through → Triumphs

Reflect and Evaluate Write a paragraph about the triumph in this unit that meant the most to you and why. Then add this writing to your portfolio, along with the work from the unit that reflects your accomplishments.

▶3 Make Connections

To Your Community Invite a speaker to come to your class to share his or her experience of breaking through a barrier and how that triumph changed his or her life.

HIGH POINT

Handbook

Strategies for Learning Language

These strategies can help you learn to use and understand the English language.

1 Listen actively and try out language.

WHAT TO DO	EXAMPLES
Repeat what you hear.	You hear: *Way to go, Joe! Fantastic catch!* You say: *Way to go, Joe! Fantastic catch!*
Recite songs and poems.	**When the Ground Shakes** When the ground shakes along the street, There's something happening beneath your feet. Earth layers are shifting, Slipping, Sliding, Bumping together. Shock waves are rising! *When the ground shakes along the street,...*
Listen to others and use their language.	You hear: "When did you know that something was missing?" You say: "I knew that something was missing when I got to class."
Add chunks of language to your speech.	You hear: "You can send the invitation by e-mail or snail mail." You think: *Snails move very slowly, and e-mail is much faster than regular mail. Snail mail must be regular mail.* You say: *I'll send it by snail mail. There's plenty of time, and I have the invitation all written out on special paper.*
Rehearse ways of speaking that match the social situation.	Formal: "Hello, Ms. Taylor. How are you?" "Fine, thank you. And how are you today?" Informal: "Hey, Paco. How's it going?" "Okay. And you?"

WHAT TO DO	EXAMPLES
Use the language you learn in one subject area in other subject areas and outside of school.	**You read this in Social Studies:** After almost two centuries of struggle, the Voting Rights Act of 1965 guaranteed all U.S. citizens the right to vote. **You write this in your reading journal:** *I wonder if The Secret of Gumbo Grove has something to do with voting rights. It'll be interesting to see what Raisin Stackhouse uncovers in the cemetery!* **At home, you might say:** Mom, did you vote? You're guaranteed the right to vote.
Explore different ways of saying things.	**All of these mean the same thing:** My teacher helps me push my thinking. My teacher makes me think before I make up my mind. My teacher helps me stretch my mind to see different viewpoints. Before I make a decision, my teacher suggests I role-play different choices in my mind.

2 Ask for help and feedback.

WHAT TO DO	EXAMPLES
Interrupt politely.	Excuse me. Please explain what the word "habitat" means. **Other options:** "Pardon me, but could you say that again?" "Could you help me? I don't understand the phrase 'how precious life is.'"
Ask questions about how to use language.	Did I say that right? Did I use that word in the right way? Which is correct, "bringed" or "brought"?
Use your native language or English to ask for clarification.	**You say:** "Wait! Could you go over that point again, a little more slowly, please?" **Other options:** "Does 'have a heart' mean to be kind?" "Is 'enormous' another way to say 'big'?"

Strategies for Learning Language, continued

❸ Use nonverbal clues.

WHAT TO DO	EXAMPLES
Use gestures and mime to get across an idea.	*I will hold up five fingers to show that I need five more minutes.*
Look for nonverbal clues.	*María wants me to go to the Subhumans' concert, but I think their music is awful—and downright insulting.* *I'm not sure what she said about the Subhumans' music, but I can tell she doesn't like it. Just look at her!*
Compare nonverbal and verbal clues.	*Let's give him a hand.* *Everyone is clapping. "Give him a hand" must mean to clap for him.*

❹ Verify how language works.

WHAT TO DO	EXAMPLES
Test hypotheses about language.	**You try out what you learned:** I can add *-ation* to the verb *observe* to get the noun *observation*. So maybe I can make a noun by adding *-ation* to all verbs that end in *-e*. Let's see. *Prepare* and *preparation*. Yes, that works! *Preserve* and *preservation*. That works, too. *Compare* and *comparation*. That doesn't sound right. I'd better see what the dictionary says... Now I see — it's *comparison*.

4 Verify how language works, continued

WHAT TO DO	EXAMPLES
Use spell-checkers, glossaries, and dictionaries.	You just finished your draft of a story, so you think: *Now I'll run the spell-check to see what words I need to fix.*
Analyze the situation to determine the appropriate language to use.	**Formal:** "Thank you, Mr. Giacometti, for helping me enter the science fair." **Informal:** "Mom, thanks for getting the jars for my science fair exhibit." "Hey, Roberto, that was cool of you to help me set up."

5 Monitor and evaluate your learning.

WHAT TO DO	EXAMPLES
Assess your own language development.	*Did I use the right words? Was it correct to use "they" when I talked about my grandparents?* *Were my words all in the correct order?* *Was I polite?*
Keep notes about what you've learned. Use your notes to practice using English.	**How to Ask Questions** • I can turn a statement around to make it a question: It is a nice day. Is it a nice day? • I can put the question at the end of a statement: It is a nice day, isn't it? • If I want more than a "yes" or "no" answer, I should use "who," "what," "where," "when," "how," or "why" at the beginning of my question: What will the weather be like today?

Graphic Organizers

You can use graphic organizers to highlight important points in your reading, to organize your ideas before writing, or to represent information for your readers.

CLUSTERS

Clusters help you connect information. You can use a cluster to show

▶ **How Words or Ideas are Related**

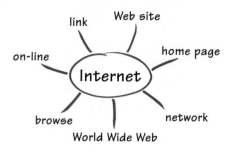

▶ **Details of an Event**

CHARTS

Charts have rows, columns, and labels to display information. Use a chart to

▶ **Picture Data**

Music Preferences Among Eighth Graders	
Rap/Hip-hop	22
Rhythm & Blues	12
Swing	10
Rock	27
Reggae	13

▶ **Relate Ideas**

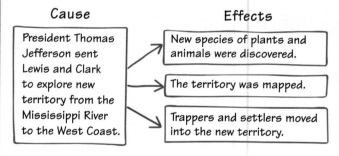

▶ **Compare and Contrast**

Stringed Instruments

Instrument	Number of Strings	How to Play	Relative Size
banjo	4, 5, or 6	pluck or strum	medium
cello	4	use bow	large
double bass	4	use bow or pluck	largest
guitar	6 or 12	pluck or strum	medium
violin	4	use bow	smallest

Record Observations

Location:	Tide pools, Seaside Beach 11/15/00 10:45 a.m.
Sights:	Starfish, sea anemones, seaweed, barnacles
Sounds:	Seagulls calling, waves splashing against rocks
Smells:	Tangy salt air, seaweed
Textures:	Grainy sand, rough rocks, slimy seaweed
Comments:	The tide was out. We walked on the rocks and looked in the tidepools. Some waves splashed into the tidepools, so the living things in the pools were always wet.

Show the Steps in a Process

How to Make a Mask

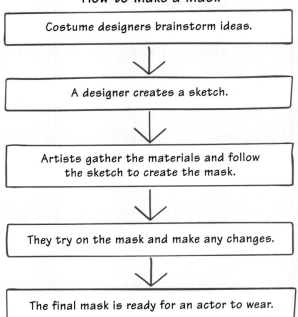

Costume designers brainstorm ideas.

↓

A designer creates a sketch.

↓

Artists gather the materials and follow the sketch to create the mask.

↓

They try on the mask and make any changes.

↓

The final mask is ready for an actor to wear.

Show What You Know, What You Want to Learn, and What You Learned

Topic: The Revolutionary War		
K **What I Know**	**W** **What I Want to Learn**	**L** **What I Learned**
The war was between England and the American colonies. The colonies won and formed the United States.	When was it? What started it? How did the colonies defeat such a powerful country?	Fill in this column after you read.

Show Organization or Classification

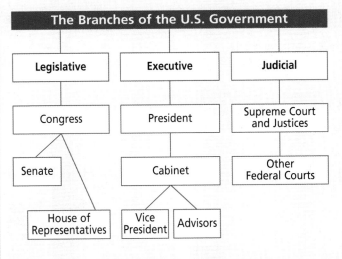

The Branches of the U.S. Government

Legislative — Congress — Senate — House of Representatives

Executive — President — Cabinet — Vice President, Advisors

Judicial — Supreme Court and Justices — Other Federal Courts

Graphic Organizers, continued

GRAPHS

Graphs use words, numbers, lines, and other shapes to picture data. A graph can show

▶ **Parts of a Whole**

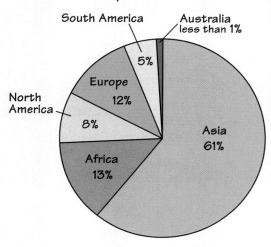

World Population Distribution

▶ **How Something Changes Over Time**

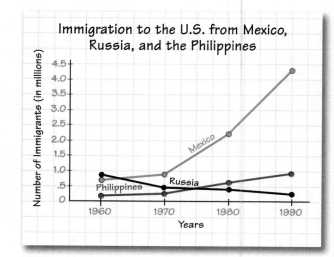

▶ **Comparisons**

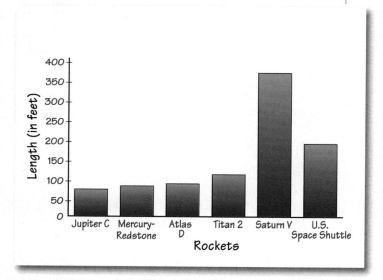

DIAGRAMS

Diagrams combine drawings and text to show where things are, how something works, or when something happens. Use a diagram to

▶ Show When Events Happen

The Founding of the English Colonies in America

1607	Virginia
1630	Massachusetts Bay
1634	Maryland
1636	Rhode Island, Connecticut
1638	New Hampshire
1663	North and South Carolina
1664	New York, New Jersey
1681	Pennsylvania
1704	Delaware (split from Pennsylvania)
1732	Georgia

▶ Show Parts of Something

The Parts of a Guitar

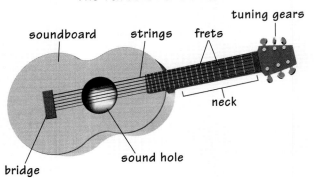

▶ Explore the Meaning of Words

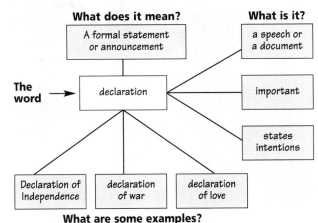

▶ Show a Process that Repeats

The Carbon Dioxide-Oxygen Cycle

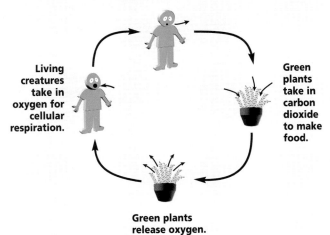

Graphic Organizers, continued

▶ Show Similarities and Differences

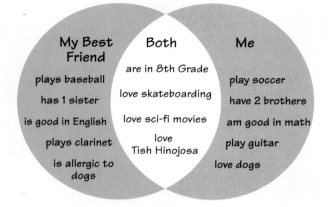

My Best Friend

plays baseball

has 1 sister

is good in English

plays clarinet

is allergic to dogs

Both

are in 8th Grade

love skateboarding

love sci-fi movies

love Tish Hinojosa

Me

play soccer

have 2 brothers

am good in math

play guitar

love dogs

▶ Narrow or Develop a Topic

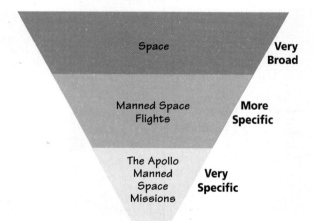

Space — Very Broad

Manned Space Flights — More Specific

The Apollo Manned Space Missions — Very Specific

▶ Organize Details Related to the Main Idea

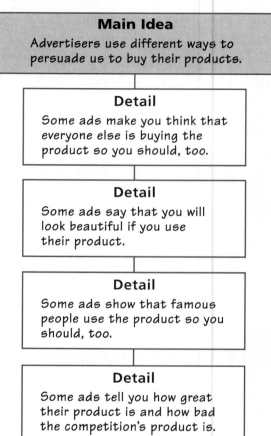

Main Idea
Advertisers use different ways to persuade us to buy their products.

Detail
Some ads make you think that everyone else is buying the product so you should, too.

Detail
Some ads say that you will look beautiful if you use their product.

Detail
Some ads show that famous people use the product so you should, too.

Detail
Some ads tell you how great their product is and how bad the competition's product is.

STORY MAPS

Story maps show how a story is organized.

▶ **Beginning, Middle, and End**

Title: User Friendly

Author: T. Ernesto Bethancourt

Beginning

Kevin's computer, Louis, started asking Kevin questions, just like a real person.

↓

Middle

1. Kevin was upset when Ginny called him a nerd. He went home and told Louis.
2. Louis make creepy calls to Ginny by using its modem.
3. Ginny and her brother got upset about the calls. Kevin warned Louis to stop.
4. The next day, Ginny told Kevin about more problems her family had faced. Kevin knew Louis was responsible.

↓

End

Kevin asked his dad to help. His dad had already reformatted Louis, but he did not understand a strange print–out signed "Louise."

▶ **Goal and Outcome**

Title: Island of the Blue Dolphins

Author: Scott O'Dell

Goal

Karana, alone on her island when her people are killed or taken away, wants to leave.

Event 1

Karana builds a canoe, but it leaks and she has to return to her island.

Event 2

Karana finds a wounded wild dog that becomes her friend.

Event 3

Karana decides it is all right to live alone.

Outcome

Years later, a ship stops by the island and takes Karana to the mainland.

Graphic Organizers, continued

▶ Problem and Solution

Title: The House of Dies Drear

Author: Virginia Hamilton

> **Characters:** Thomas Small, Thomas' family, Pluto Skinner, Mayhew Skinner, Pesty, "Mac" Darrow, the Darrow family, Mr. Carr
>
> **Setting:** an old house that was once a stop on the Underground Railroad

> **Problem:** Thomas' family moves to an old house that seems to be full of secrets.

> **Event 1:** When his family arrives at the house, Thomas' brothers start crying, as if they know the house is haunted.
>
> **Event 2:** Pluto, the caretaker, rearranges the family's furniture, upsetting the family.
>
> **Event 3:** Thomas falls into a hole and discovers a tunnel under the house.
>
> **Event 4:** Someone enters the house at night and leaves mysterious triangles on the door frames.
>
> **Event 5:** The kitchen is vandalized while the Smalls are at church.

> **Solution:** Thomas and his father confront Pluto and learn about the treasure hidden in the house. They agree to help keep the secret of the House of Dies Drear.

▶ Causes and Effects

Title: A Wrinkle in Time

Author: Madeleine L'Engle

Characters: Meg Murry, Charles Wallace, Calvin, Mrs. Whatsit, Mrs. Which, Mrs. Who, Mrs. Murry, Mr. Murry

Causes	Effects
Meg, her friends, and Charles Wallace travel to a planet in search of Mr. Murry.	The group learns that they must overcome the dark thing that is holding Mr. Murry.
The group goes to another planet where everyone acts like a robot.	An evil force called "IT" influences Charles Wallace, and he begins to act like a robot.
Charles Wallace leads them to where Mr. Murry is trapped. Charles says Meg must join "IT" to help free Mr. Murry.	Meg resists and uses Mrs. Who's glasses to free Mr. Murry.
Meg, Mr. Murry, and Calvin leave the planet, but Meg must go back to rescue Charles.	Meg goes back alone with everyone's love and blessings.
Meg's love helps her to overcome and destroy "IT." She rescues Charles.	Everyone goes back to Earth to join their family and friends.

▶ Story Staircase

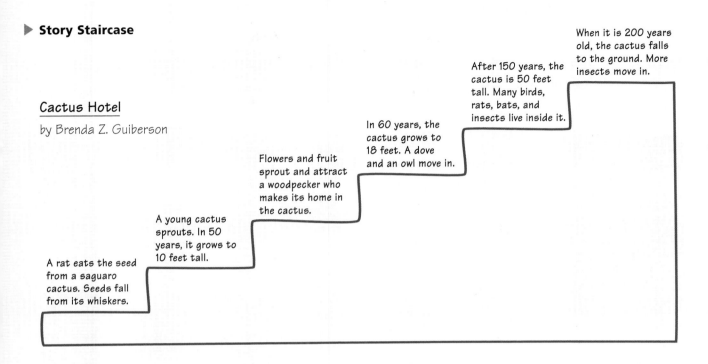

Cactus Hotel
by Brenda Z. Guiberson

A rat eats the seed from a saguaro cactus. Seeds fall from its whiskers.

A young cactus sprouts. In 50 years, it grows to 10 feet tall.

Flowers and fruit sprout and attract a woodpecker who makes its home in the cactus.

In 60 years, the cactus grows to 18 feet. A dove and an owl move in.

After 150 years, the cactus is 50 feet tall. Many birds, rats, bats, and insects live inside it.

When it is 200 years old, the cactus falls to the ground. More insects move in.

▶ Rising and Falling Action

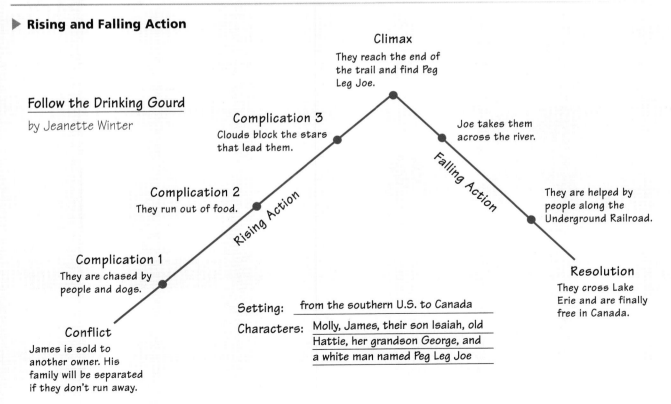

Follow the Drinking Gourd
by Jeanette Winter

Climax
They reach the end of the trail and find Peg Leg Joe.

Complication 3
Clouds block the stars that lead them.

Complication 2
They run out of food.

Rising Action

Complication 1
They are chased by people and dogs.

Conflict
James is sold to another owner. His family will be separated if they don't run away.

Falling Action

Joe takes them across the river.

They are helped by people along the Underground Railroad.

Resolution
They cross Lake Erie and are finally free in Canada.

Setting: from the southern U.S. to Canada

Characters: Molly, James, their son Isaiah, old Hattie, her grandson George, and a white man named Peg Leg Joe

Technology and Media
Technology in Pictures

Technology is used every day in schools, offices, and homes. This section will help you recognize and use machines and electronic tools.

CALCULATOR

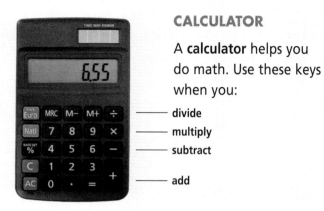

A **calculator** helps you do math. Use these keys when you:

—— divide

—— multiply

—— subtract

—— add

CASSETTE PLAYERS

A **cassette player** records and plays audiocassettes.

audiocassette tape
Use this to play or record sound.

headphones
Use these to listen alone.

buttons
Use these to play, stop, and move the tape forward or back.

microphone
Use this to record sound. Some players have built-in microphones.

COMPACT DISC PLAYER

A **compact disc (CD) player** plays compact discs with music or other sounds.

display screen
This shows information about which **track**, or selection, the machine is playing.

buttons
Use these to play, pause, or stop the recording, and to choose the track you want to hear.

compact disc
Use this to play or record music or other sounds.

FAX MACHINE

A **fax machine** uses phone lines to send or receive a copy of pages with pictures or words.

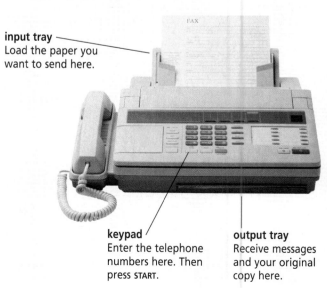

input tray
Load the paper you want to send here.

keypad
Enter the telephone numbers here. Then press START.

output tray
Receive messages and your original copy here.

WIRELESS TELEPHONE

A **wireless telephone** lets you talk to people wherever you are.

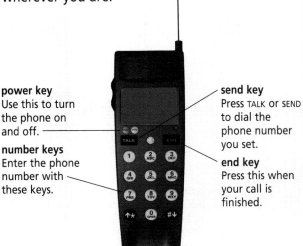

power key
Use this to turn the phone on and off.

number keys
Enter the phone number with these keys.

send key
Press TALK or SEND to dial the phone number you set.

end key
Press this when your call is finished.

CAMCORDER

A **camcorder** is a hand-held video camera. It records pictures and sounds on videotape. You can watch the videotape on a television.

view finder
Use this to see the picture as you record.

microphone
This records sound.

lens
Aim this at the action you want to record.

videotape
Use this or smaller tapes to record or play pictures and sounds.

VIDEOCASSETTE RECORDER

A **videocassette recorder (VCR)** records and plays videotapes through a television. You can record television programs or watch videos that you make, buy, rent, or check out from the library.

television
Use this to watch programs.

remote control
Use this to control the television and other machines from far away.

VCR and **videotape**
Use these to record and watch programs.

DIGITAL VIDEODISC PLAYER

A **digital videodisc (DVD) player** plays discs that have very clear pictures and sounds. You can watch movies by connecting a DVD player to a television or a computer.

digital videodisc
This holds recordings of programs.

Technology and Media, continued
Technology in Pictures, continued

THE COMPUTER

A **computer** is an electronic tool that helps you create, save, and use information.

Compact Disc Read-Only Memory (CD-ROM)
Use this to read or play CD-ROMs with text, sound, video, photographs, and computer software.

monitor and **screen**
These show the text and pictures that are in the computer.

digital camera
Use this to take photographs you can use on the computer. You can view, print, or work on your pictures.

scanner
Use this to take a picture of words or pictures that are already on a page. You can view, print, or work on whatever you scan into your computer.

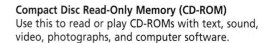

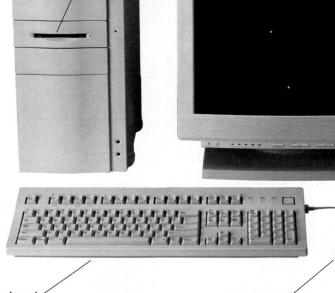

keyboard
This has letter, number, symbol, and function keys. Type here to add information and give commands to the computer.

mouse
Use this to choose and move things on your screen.

printer
Use this to make a paper copy of the information on your computer.

THE COMPUTER KEYBOARD

Use the **keys** on the **keyboard** to write, do math, or give the computer commands. Keyboards may look different, but they all have keys like these:

escape key
Press here to quit a job you are doing.

tab
Press this key to indent for a new paragraph.

function keys
Press these keys to give the computer commands.

delete or **backspace key**
Press here to erase the character to the left of the flashing cursor. You can also erase text that you highlight.

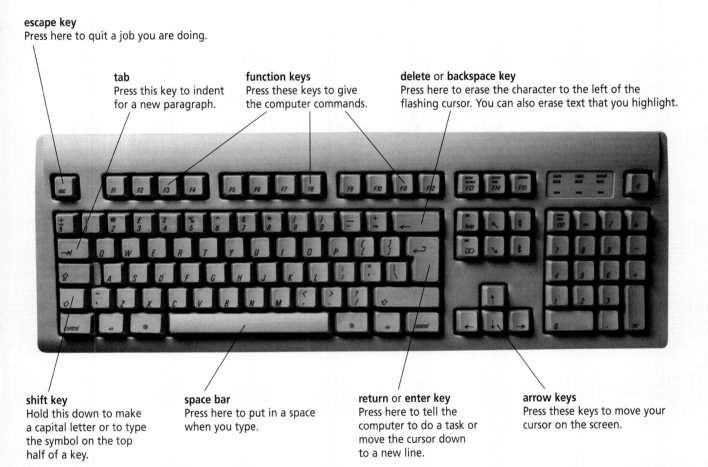

shift key
Hold this down to make a capital letter or to type the symbol on the top half of a key.

space bar
Press here to put in a space when you type.

return or **enter key**
Press here to tell the computer to do a task or move the cursor down to a new line.

arrow keys
Press these keys to move your cursor on the screen.

Technology and Media, continued
How to Send E-mail

E-mail is electronic mail that can be sent on-line from one computer to another. Anyone who has an e-mail address can send and receive messages. E-mail can travel around the classroom or around the world.

You can use e-mail to:

• write messages to one or more friends at a time
• send computer files
• save money on postage and telephone calls
• send and receive messages almost instantly.

To send an e-mail message:

1. Open the e-mail program.

2. Open a new message.

3. Enter this information:

• Type the recipient's e-mail address in the "To" box.
• Type a short title for your e-mail in the "Subject" box.
• Type your message.

4. Send your message.

Each e-mail program is different. Here is one example of a "mailbox:"

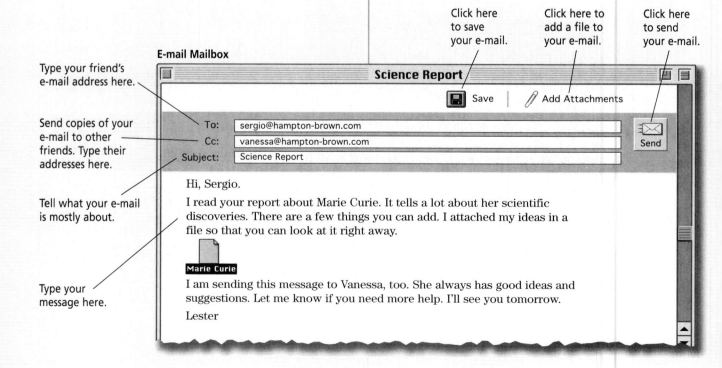

Click here to save your e-mail.

Click here to add a file to your e-mail.

Click here to send your e-mail.

E-mail Mailbox

Type your friend's e-mail address here.

Send copies of your e-mail to other friends. Type their addresses here.

Tell what your e-mail is mostly about.

Type your message here.

Science Report

Save | Add Attachments

To: sergio@hampton-brown.com

Cc: vanessa@hampton-brown.com

Subject: Science Report

Send

Hi, Sergio.

I read your report about Marie Curie. It tells a lot about her scientific discoveries. There are a few things you can add. I attached my ideas in a file so that you can look at it right away.

Marie Curie

I am sending this message to Vanessa, too. She always has good ideas and suggestions. Let me know if you need more help. I'll see you tomorrow.

Lester

How to Use a Word-Processing Program

A **computer program** is a set of directions that tells a computer what to do. A **word-processing program** helps you create and store written work. You can use it to:

- store ideas, outlines, plans, and papers
- write drafts of your work
- revise, edit, and proofread your writing
- format and publish your work
- make written work look neat and organized.

There are many kinds of word-processing programs. There are also different ways to use the computer to make each job easier. This section of the Handbook will give you some ideas. Ask your teacher or classmates for other ways they have found to use your school's word-processing program.

Working on the computer

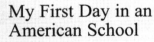

My First Day in an American School

by Marco Quezada

My first day of school in the United States was very scary because I didn't speak English. I didn't know how I was going to talk to people. I didn't have any friends. I tried to understand the teacher, but I couldn't. I felt like a chair.

Suddenly, a very loud bell rang. The teacher opened the door, and all the kids jumped up and rushed out the door.

Why was everyone leaving? In Haiti, we stayed in the same classroom all day. I followed the class, and we went into a new room. A stranger gave me a book and some papers. I was really puzzled. Fortunately, the man spoke some Creole and explained that he was my science teacher.

Finally, I understood. In America, there are special teachers for science, music, and gym. Students also move to new classrooms. At first, it was very confusing, but now I like having different teachers for my subjects.

Technology and Media, continued
How to Use a Word-Processing Program, continued

GET STARTED

1 **How to Set Up a File** Before you start to write, make a **file**—a place to keep your work. Follow these steps:

1. Click **File** to see the **File Menu**. A **menu** gives you a list of choices.

File Menu and New

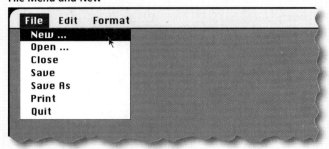

2. Click **New** to create a new document. A blank page will appear.

New Document

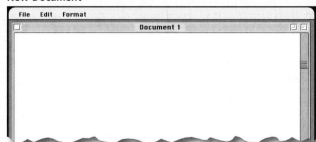

To save your new file in a folder, click **Save As** on the **File Menu**.

File Menu and Save As

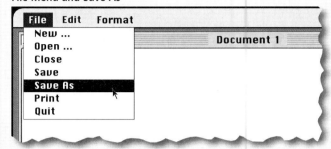

A **dialogue box** will appear to ask for information.

1. Type a short name for your file.
2. Make sure that the file name and folder are correct. If you don't have a folder for your work, ask your teacher for help to start one.
3. Click **Save** to save your file.

Save Dialogue Box

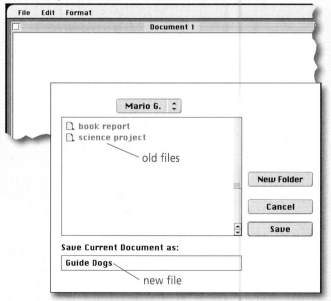

CREATE DOCUMENTS

1 How to Type a Document Now you are ready to type. Your work will appear in front of a flashing cursor. The **cursor** shows where you are working on the page.

Cursor

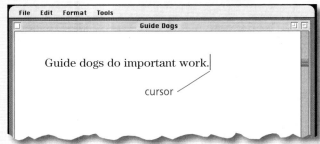

As you type, the **indicator box** shows where you are in the document. You can use the **scroll bar** to move up and down in your file.

- Click and hold the **up arrow** to move toward the top of the screen.
- Click and hold the **down arrow** to move toward the bottom of the screen.

Scrolling

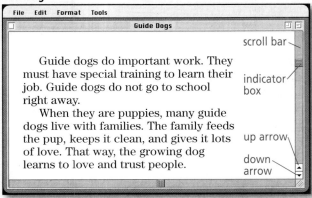

2 How to Save Your Work Remember to save your work as you write. If you do not save, you may lose the work you have done on your file. Remember:

✔ Save your work every 10 minutes!
✔ Save before you leave your computer.
✔ Save before you **Print**.
✔ Save before you **Quit**.
✔ Save, save, save!

To save your work, click **Save** in the **File Menu**.

Save

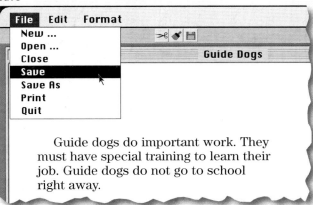

Or, click the **save icon** on the **toolbar**.

Toolbar Icons

toolbar   save icon

Technology and Media, continued
How to Use a Word-Processing Program, continued

MAKE CHANGES TO YOUR WORK

1 **How to Add Words** It is easy to add words to your work.

1. Use your mouse to move the cursor to the place where you want to add words.
2. Click the mouse once. The cursor will start to flash.

Add Words (before)

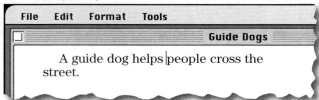

3. Type the new words.

Add Words (after)

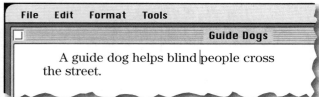

2 **How to Delete Words** When you **delete**, you take words out. Before you delete, you need to highlight the words you want to remove.

1. To remove one word, put the cursor on the word. Click the mouse twice.

Delete Words (before)

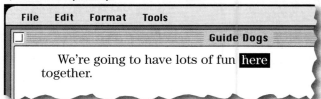

2. You can also **click and drag** to highlight and remove words.
   - Click and hold the mouse and slide it over all the words you want to take out. The words will be highlighted.

Delete Words (after)

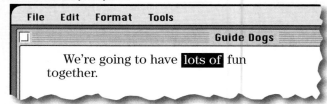

   - After the words are highlighted, press the **delete key**. The words will disappear from the screen.

Delete Words (after)

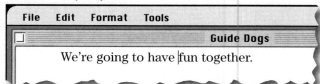

3 **How to Cut and Paste** You can **cut and paste** to move sentences or paragraphs to a different place in your paper.

When you **cut** text, the computer takes out the highlighted words. The words are not deleted. They are stored in the computer's memory to be placed somewhere new.

To cut text, click **Cut** from the **Edit Menu**.

Cut (before)

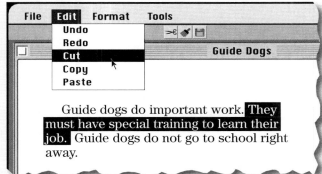

Or, click the **cut icon** on the **toolbar**.

Toolbar Icons

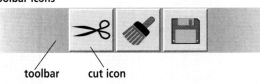

Your text will look like this:

Cut (after)

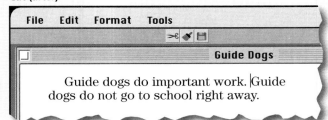

When you **paste** text, the cut words are placed at the flashing cursor. To paste text, move the cursor to where you want the text and click **Paste** from the **Edit Menu**.

Paste (before)

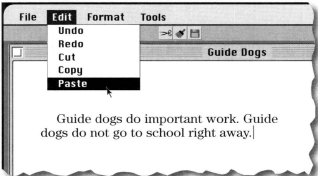

Or, click the **paste icon** on the **toolbar**.

Toolbar Icons

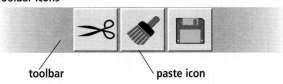

Your text will look like this:

Paste (after)

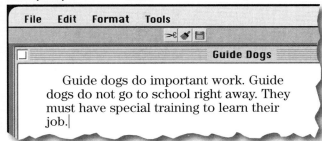

Technology and Media, continued

How to Use a Word-Processing Program, continued

4 **How to Check Your Spelling** Most word-processing programs have tools to check your spelling. Follow these steps:

1. Open the **Tools Menu** and choose **Spelling**. The computer will show you a highlighted word from your text.
2. Choose the correct spelling from the list of suggestions. If the word is not listed, check a dictionary.

Spell Check

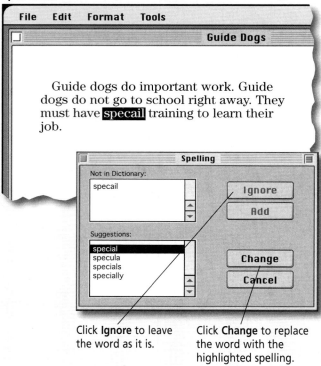

Click **Ignore** to leave the word as it is.

Click **Change** to replace the word with the highlighted spelling.

5 **How to Find Synonyms** Use the computer's thesaurus to find synonyms for words you use.

1. Highlight the word you want to change. Then open the **Tools Menu** and choose **Thesaurus**.
2. Some words have different meanings. Choose the correct one from the list of Meanings.
3. Look at the list of synonyms for that meaning. Highlight the word you want.

Thesaurus

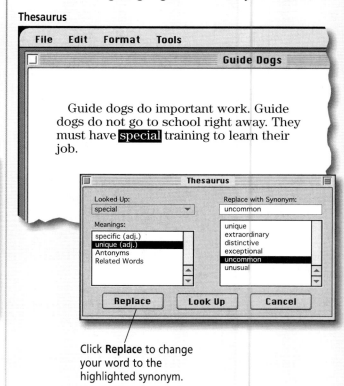

Click **Replace** to change your word to the highlighted synonym.

FORMAT YOUR PAPER

When you **format** your work, you make it look neat and organized. Here are some ways to format, or arrange, your paper.

1 **How to Change the Font, Style, and Size**
A **font** is a unique style for the letters and numbers that you type. Follow these steps:

- Highlight the section you want to change.
- Open the **Format Menu** and choose **Font**, or click the font, style, and size icons on your toolbar.

| bold | italic | underline |

- Choose the font, word style, and word size you want for your text. Then click **OK**.

You can choose from many fonts. For class work, choose a font that is clear and easy to read. If you are writing to friends, you can choose more fun styles! Here are some examples:

Fonts

good for reports	good for essays
good for a friendly letter	*great for your journal*

Styles

normal	*italic*
bold	underlined

Sizes

12	14	16	18

2 **How to Change Text Alignment** When you set **text alignment**, you choose how words will line up on the page. You may want to put a title in the center of the page, or put your name in the right-hand corner. Follow these steps:

- Highlight the text you want to align.
- Click the icon that shows where you want the text placed. For example:

| align left | center | align right | justify |

3 **How to Set Spacing** You can choose the **spacing**—how much space comes between each line you type. Follow these steps:

- Open the **Edit Menu** and choose **Select All**.
- Click the correct spacing icon:

| single space | 1.5 line | double space |

Ask your teacher or your friends for more ideas about how to format your work. Soon, your work will have a new style that is unique and attractive.

Technology and Media, continued
How to Create a Multimedia Presentation

A **multimedia presentation** uses technology to present ideas. Your audience can read, see, and hear your work.

LEARN ABOUT MEDIA

There are many ways to share information. Choose media that fit your purpose. Here are some possibilities:

▶ **Visuals**

- Use a computer to create slides of important points, outlines, or quotations.
- Scan tables or diagrams to show information.

▶ **Photographs**

- Scan photographs.
- Download pictures from the Internet.
- Use pictures from a CD-ROM.

▶ **Video and Animation**

- Use videos from the news.
- Create animation to show how something changes.
- Make a videotape of yourself or others.

▶ **Sounds**

- Play music on a cassette, CD, or CD-ROM.
- Make a recording of yourself or others.
- Download sound files from the Internet.

MAKE A MULTIMEDIA PRESENTATION

Follow these steps to give your own multimedia presentation.

1 Plan Think about how you can present your ideas creatively.

- Put your ideas into a logical order.
- Ask yourself: What pictures, videos, and sounds will help the class understand my ideas? What technology can I use?
- Use a **graphic organizer** to put the steps of your presentation in order. Here is one example:

Flow Chart

```
┌──────────────────────────────────┐
│        Show title slide:         │
│   Democracy in Ancient Greece.   │
└──────────────────────────────────┘
                 ↓
┌──────────────────────────────────┐
│    Talk about Greek city-states. │
└──────────────────────────────────┘
                 ↓
┌──────────────────────────────────┐
│   Show slide of map of ancient   │
│     Greece on the computer.      │
└──────────────────────────────────┘
                 ↓
┌──────────────────────────────────┐
│        Play 2-minute video       │
│       of Greek elections.        │
└──────────────────────────────────┘
```

2 Practice Rehearse your presentation until you are comfortable with your speech and the technology you will use.

- Practice in front of your family and friends. Ask them for ideas and suggestions.
- Unexpected things can happen when you work with technology. Before your presentation, test your equipment to be sure it works.

3 Present Remember that your goal is to give an effective presentation.

- Speak slowly and clearly.
- Give your audience time to understand the ideas you are sharing.
- Have fun!

Technology and Media, continued
How to Use the Internet

The **Internet** is an international network, or connection, of computers that share information with one another. The **World Wide Web** allows you to find, read, go through, and organize information. The Internet is like a giant library, and the World Wide Web is everything in the library including the books, the librarian, and the computer catalog.

The Internet is a fast way to get the most current information about your topic! You'll find resources like encyclopedias and dictionaries on the Internet and amazing pictures, movies, and sounds.

WHAT YOU WILL NEED

To use the Internet, you need a computer with software that allows you to access it. You'll also need a modem connected to a telephone line.

HOW TO GET STARTED

You can search the Internet in many different ways. Ask your teacher how to access the Internet from your school. Usually you can just double click on the **icon**, or picture, to get access to the Internet and you're on your way!

HOW TO DO THE RESEARCH

Once the search page comes up, you can begin the research process. Just follow these steps.

1 **Type in Your Subject** Enter your key words in the search box and then click on the Search button. You'll always see a toolbar at the top of the screen. Click on the **icons** to do things like print the page.

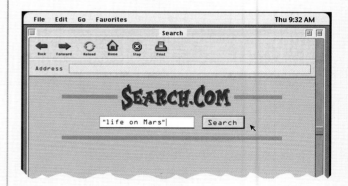

Try different ways to type in your subject. You'll get different results!

- If you type in **Mars**, you'll see all the sites that have the word *Mars* in them. This may give you too many categories and sites to look through!
- If you type in **"Mars exploration,"** you'll see all the sites with the exact phrase, or group of words, *Mars exploration*.
- If you type in **Mars+exploration**, you'll see all the sites with the words *Mars* and *exploration* in them.

2 Read the Search Results All underlined, colored words are links, or connections, to other sites. They help you get from page to page quickly.

- If you want to go directly to a Web page, click on a site.
- Click on a category to see more options for information related to your topic.
- Read the descriptions of the sites to save time.

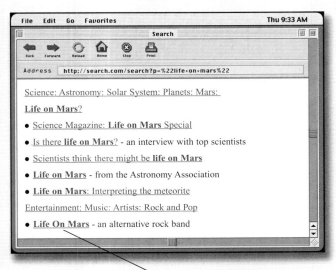

This site could be very interesting, but it probably won't help with your report.

3 Select a Site and Read You might want to pick a new site or start a new search. If so, click on the **Back** arrow to go back a page to the search results. If you want to go to another Web page, click on a link.

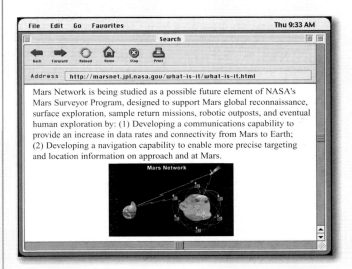

4 Locate More Resources If you already know the **URL (Uniform Resource Locator)**, or address, of a Web site, you can type it in the address box at the top of the screen.

Remember that information on Web sites changes frequently. Sometimes Web pages are not kept up. If you can't access one Web site, try another one.

The Research Process

When you research, you look up information about a topic. You can use the information you find to write a story, article, book, or research report.

➊ CHOOSE A TOPIC

Think of something you want to learn more about and something that interests you. That will be your research **topic**. Pick a topic that is not too general. A specific, or smaller, topic is easier to research and to write about. It is also more interesting to read about in a report. Look at these topics:

Outer Space
This is a big topic! There are a lot of things in outer space: stars, suns, planets, moons, and black holes. That would be too much to research or write about in one report.

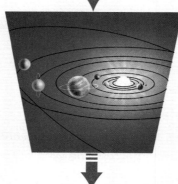

Planets
This topic is better, but it's still too big. There are nine planets in our solar system! You could do a report on the planet Mars. But what is it you want to know about Mars?

Life on Mars
The topic "Life on Mars" is more specific than "Mars." Finding out if Mars has water, plants, animals, or Martians could be VERY interesting!

➋ DECIDE WHAT TO LOOK UP

What do you want to know about your topic? Write down some questions. Look at the most important words in your questions. Those are **key words** you can look up when you start your research.

Is there life on Mars?

Is there water or oxygen on Mars?

Can people, plants, or animals live on the surface of Mars?

Have space missions studied Mars?

Did anyone find proof of Martian life forms?

➌ LOCATE RESOURCES

Now that you know what to look up, you can go to different **resources** to find information about your topic. Resources can be people, such as librarians, teachers, and family members. Resources can also be books, magazines, newspapers, videos, or the Internet. You can find resources all around you.

Whatever your topic is, try exploring the library first. There you'll discover a world of information!

❹ GATHER INFORMATION

When you gather information, you find the best resources for your topic. You look up your key words to find facts about your topic. Then you take notes.

How to Find Information Quickly Use alphabetical order to look up words in a list. In many resources, the words, titles, and subjects are listed in **alphabetical order**.

Look at these words. They are in order by the **first** letter of each word.

> asteroid
> moon
> planet
> sun

If the word you are looking up has the same first letter as other words in the list, look at the **second** letters.

> Mars
> Mercury
> mission
> moon

If the word you are looking up has the same first and second letters as others in the list, look at the **third** letters.

> magnetic
> map
> Mars
> mass

Skim and scan the text to decide if it is useful. When you **skim** and **scan**, you look at text quickly to see if it has the information you need. If it does, you can take the time to read it more carefully. If it doesn't, go on to another source.

To skim:

- Read the title to see if the article is useful for your topic.
- Read the **beginning sentences** and **headings** to find out more about an article's topic.
- Skim the ending. It often sums up all the ideas in the article.

To scan:

Look for **key words** or **details** in dark type or italics. If you find key words that go with your topic, you'll probably want to read the article.

PLANETS, STARS, AND SPACE TRAVEL

LOOKING FOR LIFE ELSEWHERE IN THE UNIVERSE

For years scientists have been trying to discover if there is life on other planets in our solar system or life elsewhere in the universe. Some scientists have been looking for evidence based on what is necessary for life on Earth—basics like water and proper temperature.

WHAT SCIENTISTS HAVE LEARNED SO FAR

Mars and Jupiter. In 1996, two teams of scientists examined two meteorites that may have come from **Mars** and found evidence that some form of life may have existed on Mars billions of years ago. In 1997, in photographs of Europa, a moon of **Jupiter**, scientists saw areas with icy ridges and areas without ice. It seemed that underneath the ice there might be water—one of the essentials of life.

New Planets. In 1996, astronomers believed they found several new planets traveling around stars very far away (many light-years away) from our sun. Scientists do not think life exists on these planets, because they are so close to their sun that they would be too hot. But scientists are hoping to find other stars with planets around them that might support life.

AND THE SEARCH CONTINUES

NASA (the National Aeronautics and Space Administration) has a program to look for life on Mars. Ten spacecraft are to be sent to Mars over the next ten years. Some will fly around Mars taking pictures, while others will land on Mars to study the soil and rocks and look for living things. The first two, *Mars Pathfinder* and *Mars Global Surveyor*, launched in 1996, were scheduled to reach Mars in 1997.

Another program that searches for life on other worlds is called **SETI**. SETI (an acronym for Search for Extraterrestrial Intelligence) uses powerful radio telescopes to look for life elsewhere in the universe.

Question: Is there life elsewhere in the universe? **Answer:** No one knows yet.

The Research Process, continued

④ GATHER INFORMATION, continued

How to Take Notes Write down important words, phrases, and ideas while you are reading and researching. These notes will help you remember **details**. They'll also help you remember the **source**. The source is where you got the information.

Set up your notecards in the following way so you can easily put your information in order when you write.

1. Include your **research question.**

2. Write down the **source** so you can remember where you found your facts.
   - For a book, list the title, author, and page number.
   - For a magazine or newspaper article, list the name, date, volume, and issue number of your source. Also, write the title of the article in quotation marks.

3. List the details and facts in your own words. Use **quotation marks for exact words** you copy from a source.

Notecard for a Book

> Is there life on Mars ?
>
> Mars by Seymour Simon, page 27
>
> —Viking spacecraft supposed to find out if there's life
> —some think experiments showed there isn't
> —others believe experiments were the wrong kind; maybe scientists looked in wrong places

Notecard for a Magazine or Newspaper

> Is there life on Mars ?
>
> Time for Kids, Sept. 13, 1996
>
> Vol. 2, No. 1 "Next Stop: Mars"
>
> —maybe—Mars has some features like Earth. **"It has volcanoes and giant canyons."**
> —hard to prove, but maybe space missions like Pathfinder can find something

⑤ ORGANIZE INFORMATION

Make an Outline An outline can help you organize your report. Follow these steps to turn your notes into an outline.

1. Put all the notecards with the same research question together.

2. Turn your notes into an outline.
- First, turn your question into a **main idea.** Each main idea follows a Roman numeral.

> I. **Life on Mars**

- Next, find details that go with the main idea. Add them to your outline. Each **detail** follows a capital letter. Each **related detail** follows a number.

> I. Life on Mars
>   A. How Mars is like Earth
>   1. Volcanoes
>   2. Giant canyons

3. Write a **title** for your outline. The title tells what your outline is all about. You can use it again when you write your report.

Sample Outline

Mars: Is Anyone Up There?

I. Life on Mars
  A. How Mars is like Earth
    1. Volcanoes
    2. Giant canyons
  B. Fact-finding missions
    1. Viking
    2. Pathfinder

II. Signs of life on Mars
  A. Studied by David McKay's team
  B. Meteorite
    1. Might contain bacteria fossils
    2. Found in Antarctica
    3. Probably from Mars

III. Continued search for life on Mars
  A. Look underground
  B. More study
    1. Mission planned for near future
    2. Gases in atmosphere
    3. What rocks are made of

The Research Process, continued

❻ WRITE A RESEARCH REPORT

Now use your outline to write a **research report**. Turn the main ideas and details from your outline into sentences and paragraphs.

Write the Title and Introduction Copy the title from your outline and write an interesting introduction to tell what your report is mostly about.

Outline

Mars: Is Anyone Up There?

Title and Introduction

Mars: Is Anyone Up There?

You've probably seen some pretty creepy outer space creatures in movies and on TV. Do they really look like that? Are there really living beings up there?

Write the Body Use your main ideas to write a topic sentence for each paragraph. Then use your details and related details to write sentences about the main idea.

Outline

I. Life on Mars
  A. How Mars is like Earth
    1. Volcanoes
    2. Giant canyons

Topic Sentence and Details

People have always wondered if there is **life on** other planets, especially **Mars**. **Because Mars is similar to Earth** with features like **volcanoes and giant canyons,** it seems possible that there is life on Mars. There are lots of missions to Mars, like the spacecrafts Viking and Pathfinder, so it seems like we might find out soon!

Write a Conclusion Write a sentence for each main idea in the last paragraph of your report.

Outline

I. Life on Mars

II. Signs of life on Mars

III. Continued search for life on Mars

Conclusion

Basically, no one knows if there is or isn't life on Mars. It is possible that life does or did exist there. Spacecrafts that go to Mars in the future will give us more proof. Hopefully, the mystery will be solved soon for all of us!

A good research report gives facts about a topic in an organized and interesting way.

Mars: Is Anyone Up There?

You've probably seen some pretty creepy outer space creatures in movies and TV. Do they really look like that? Are there really living beings up there?

People have always wondered if there is life on other planets, especially Mars. Because Mars is similar to Earth, with features like volcanoes and giant canyons, it seems possible that there is life on Mars. There are lots of missions to Mars, like the spacecrafts Viking and Pathfinder, so it seems like we might find out soon!

David McKay and his team of scientists discovered possible signs of ancient Martian life. They think they found bacteria fossils in a meteorite that crashed into Antarctica thousands of years ago. They believe the meteorite is from Mars because it has the same chemicals in it as the Martian atmosphere. They think the fossils, which are a lot smaller than the width of a human hair, were alive on Mars from 3 to 4 billion years ago. At that time, there was water on the planet. Since the fossils were deep in the center of the meteorite, McKay's team feels that the fossils were definitely from Mars and not from Earth.

No one has seen a live Martian, but some scientists feel that we need to keep looking. Since no one has found water on the surface of Mars, maybe Martians live underground where there is water. A mission to look for Martian life and bring soil samples back to Earth is planned for the near future. Until then, scientists will continue to study the other aspects of Mars like the gases in its atmosphere and what its rocks are made of.

Basically, no one knows if there is or isn't life on Mars. It is possible that life does or did exist there. Spacecrafts that go to Mars in the future will give us more proof. Hopefully, the mystery will be solved soon for all of us!

INTRODUCTION
The **title** and **introduction** tell what your report is about. They get your reader interested.

BODY
The **body** of the report presents the facts you found. Each paragraph begins with a **topic sentence** that tells one main idea from your outline. The other sentences give **details** and **related details**.

CONCLUSION
The **conclusion** is a summary of the most important information about your topic.

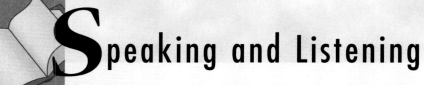

Speaking and Listening

You talk, or speak, to others every day. That's how you express your ideas. You also listen to others to learn about new ideas.

HOW TO BE A GOOD LISTENER

Good listeners listen carefully to what others say.

How to Be a Good Listener

- Pay attention. Open your eyes and ears. Look at the speaker as you listen. That way you'll "hear" more.
- Be quiet while the speaker is talking.
- Don't interrupt unless you need the speaker to talk louder.
- Save your questions until the speaker is finished.

HOW TO PARTICIPATE IN A DISCUSSION

Sometimes you will discuss ideas as a class, in a group, or with a partner. You may also have a conference with a teacher or a peer to talk about your writing. Discussions are good ways to find information, check your understanding, and share ideas.

How to Participate in a Discussion

- Use good listening skills.
- Give each speaker a chance to make a statement. Wait until someone has finished speaking before you respond.
- Make positive comments about the ideas of others. Respect everyone's ideas and feelings.
- Think about the topic. Offer ideas about only that topic and not something else.
- Ask questions if you need more information.

HOW TO LISTEN CRITICALLY

There are many reasons to listen carefully. You can find out how to do something or learn more about a topic. You can also use what you hear to help you decide how you think and feel. As you listen:

- Think about what you are hearing. Try to relate what you hear to what you already know.
- Listen for key words and important details. Take notes to help you remember the ideas.

  Example:
  ecosystem: things in nature and how they
                  work together

- Ask yourself: What is the speaker's purpose? Does the speaker want to inform or entertain the audience? Does the speaker want to persuade me to do something?
- Pay attention to the speaker's tone of voice, gestures, and expressions. What do they tell you about how the speaker feels about the topic?
- Think about who is speaking. Is the speaker an expert on the topic?
- Summarize what the speaker says in your own mind. Do you agree or disagree? What new information did you learn?

HOW TO GIVE AN ORAL PRESENTATION

What would you like to share with others? Choose an interesting topic. Then decide if you want to make a speech, give a report, recite a poem, or give a performance to share your ideas. Follow these steps to prepare your presentation.

1 Plan Your Presentation Think about your audience. What ideas do you want to share? What is the best way to present your ideas?

- Organize your information. You might use a graphic organizer to show the details and the order in which you'll present ideas.

  Example:
  I. Ecosystem
     A. Is like a community
     B. Includes all living things in nature
  II. Food Chain
     A. Is different in different places
     B. Has a sequence
        1. Microorganisms in soil
        2. Plants grow
        3. Animals eat plants

- Think of a way to grab the audience's attention and introduce your topic. You might use a quote, make a startling statement, or ask a question.

- Write your main points on notecards. Use them as you speak to help you remember what to say.

  Beginning of food chain
  —microorganisms in the soil create food for plants
  —plants grow

- Use visuals and technology to support your ideas. Organize them to match your notes.

Food Chain Poster

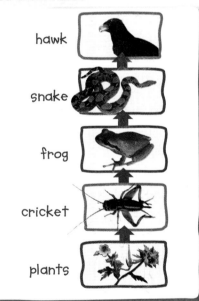

- Use your notecards, visuals, and technology to practice your presentation in front of a mirror or your family. Videotaping or tape recording your presentation may give you ideas about how to improve.

Speaking and Listening, continued

2 **Choose Appropriate Language and Tone**
Are you speaking to your friends, to young kids, or to adults you don't know? Think about your topic, audience, and purpose to help you decide how to give your presentation.

To give a persuasive speech:
- Use a strong, clear tone of voice. Change your tone to emphasize important points.
- Use formal language to present the facts. Use persuasive words to give opinions.

To tell a story:
- Use informal language to make the characters seem real. Change your voice to show when a new character is speaking.
- Use facial expressions, gestures, and other movements to show the characters' feelings and the action.

To give a formal report:
- Use formal language to present the facts and information.
- Speak slowly and clearly so everyone can understand the information.
- Present the information in a logical order.
- Use examples and visuals that support your main points.

Use formal language to give a report.

3 **Give Your Presentation** Now you can stand up and be heard! As you present your ideas:
- Stand up straight.
- Make eye contact with the audience.
- Speak slowly and clearly in a loud voice so everyone can hear you.
- Use expressions and movements that go with the information you are presenting.
- Point to or hold up any visuals so your audience can follow along.
- Try to stay calm and relaxed.
- Thank the audience when you're done. Ask for questions when you are finished.

Viewing and Representing

You can get information from the things you see, or view. You can also use visuals to help you communicate and represent your ideas.

HOW TO EVALUATE WHAT YOU SEE

There are many things to view—photographs, videos, television commercials, graphs and charts, Web sites, and people who use gestures and movements to send messages without words. Here's how to evaluate what you see. Try out the process with the visual below.

1 **View and Look for Details** Take a minute or two to study the visual. Ask yourself:

- Who or what does the image show? Are there other details that tell when, where, why, or how?
- How does the visual make me feel? Do I enjoy looking at it? Does it scare me, make me laugh, or give me a good feeling?
- Do I like the colors? How does the size or shape of the visual affect me?

2 **Think About the Purpose and the Message** What you see can influence the way you feel about a topic. Ask yourself:

- What message does the visual convey?
- Why did the artist create the visual? Does it make me want to do something? Does it give me new information?
- Does the visual represent the complete picture of the topic, or was it chosen to control my understanding of the topic?

3 **Look for Stereotypes** A stereotype is a general opinion that doesn't consider individual differences. It's like saying that because one dog is mean, all dogs are mean. Try to identify any stereotypes in the visual.

Persistent Sea No. 2, by O. Louis Guglielmi, oil on canvas.

Viewing and Representing, continued

HOW TO REPRESENT YOUR IDEAS

There are many resources that can help you make your point more clearly. Choose media that match your purpose and your topic. Strong visual images will make a strong impression.

A beautiful **illustration** can add creativity and make a story come alive.

Illustration

A **flow chart** can show steps in a process.

Flow Chart

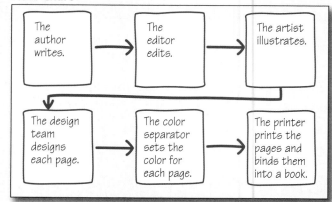

A **chart** or a **graph** can show comparisons.
Look for more graphic organizers on pages 370–377.

Chart

Number of Endangered Species in the United States

Classification	Number of Species
Mammals	61
Birds	75
Reptiles	14
Fishes	69
Insects	28

Graph

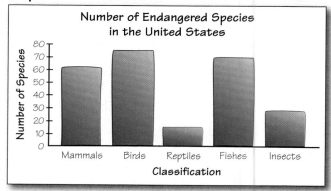

HOW TO MATCH MEDIA TO YOUR MESSAGE

Choose the best media to help you get your point across. It will help you get your audience's attention. Take a look at the different media you can use on Handbook pages 378–381. Here are a few examples.

1 **To Entertain** Include props, illustrations of the setting, or slides for a backdrop. Create a film strip, animation, or a video.

2 **To Inform** Include maps and charts to support your topic. You might make a time line to show chronological events or use a transparency to display information on an overhead projector.

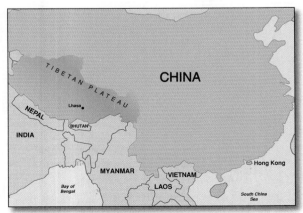

Most Giant Pandas originated in China.

3 **To Persuade** Show images that will change people's opinions. You might use slides or photographs that appeal to people's emotions.

Fewer than 1,000 pandas live in the wild.

Strategies for Taking Tests

These strategies will help you learn how to take tests and show what you know.

MULTIPLE-CHOICE TEST

For a multiple-choice test, you will mark the best answer from a list of choices.

1 Read the Directions Carefully The test directions tell you what you need to do. Words like *best*, *always*, *only*, *all*, and *never* will help you find the correct answer. There may be more than one correct answer, but only one is the "best" answer.

> **Directions: Read each question. Circle the best answer.**
>
> **4.** Which type of transportation causes the least air pollution?
>   **A** a bus   **C** a bike
>   **B** a car   **D** a motorcycle

2 Mark Your Answers You may need to fill in a bubble on an answer sheet, circle an answer, or write your answer on a separate sheet of paper. When you use an answer sheet, be sure to match the item number on the test to the item number on the answer sheet.

> **Read the sentence. Mark the answer that gives the best meaning for the underlined word.**
>
> **5.** People can <u>recycle</u> to help save the Earth.
>   **F** use products over again
>   **G** go backwards on a bicycle
>   **H** throw away all their trash
>   **J** keep trash in a special place

> **4.** Ⓐ Ⓑ Ⓒ Ⓓ
> **5.** Ⓕ Ⓖ Ⓗ Ⓙ

3 Plan Your Time Skip over any hard questions. Don't spend too much time on one question. If you have time, you can go back to it later.

4 Read Items Again If you are not sure about an answer, read the item again. Think about all the answer choices. Which one seems best?

TRUE-FALSE TEST

In a true-false test, you will decide if a statement is true or false.

1 Read Carefully If *any* part of the statement is false, the answer is false. If you're still not sure after reading an item, make your best guess!

2 Look for Key Words Watch for words like *never*, *always*, *all*, and *no*. Statements with those words will often be false.

> _false_   **1.** Businesses never monitor the dirty air from their factories.

SHORT-ANSWER TEST

Often a test item will ask for a short answer. Look for key words like *who* or *what* that tell you the information to include in the answer.

> **12.** What do farmers put on their crops to kill insects? _____pesticides_____

ESSAY TEST

For an essay test, you will need to write one or more paragraphs to answer a question.

1 **Study the Item and Key Words** Read the question at least two times. Look for key words that tell you exactly what to do. You might see prompts like these on an essay test:

- Compare the rainforest and the tundra.
- Summarize how the transcontinental railroad influenced western expansion.
- Describe the main events that led to the Civil War.

2 **Plan Your Answer** Think about the key words and the topic. Write facts or details you know in a web, chart, or another graphic organizer. Add numbers or make an outline to show how you will organize your writing.

3 **Write the Essay** Use the words in the prompt to help you write an introduction. Then use your notes and details to write your essay.

- Write a topic sentence for each paragraph.
- Include all the important details.
- Sum up your essay with a concluding sentence.
- Before you turn in your essay, read it over. Be sure that you have written about what was described in the prompt.

Prompt

> **1.** Explain three ways that people can reduce air pollution.

Sample Answer

> People can reduce air pollution in three main ways. One way is to carpool. If people share rides, they can reduce the amount of car exhaust. A second way is to walk or ride a bicycle for short trips. That doesn't cause any air pollution! Finally, people can encourage businesses to stop the air pollution caused by their factories. If we do these things today, we'll have cleaner air in the future!

The Writing Process

Writing is one of the best ways to express yourself. The steps in the Writing Process will help you say what you want to say clearly, correctly, and in your own unique way.

PREWRITE

Prewriting is what you do before you write. During this step, you collect ideas, choose a topic, make a plan, gather details, and organize your ideas.

1 Collect Ideas Writing ideas are everywhere! Think about recent events or things you've read or seen. You can brainstorm more writing ideas with your classmates, friends, and family. Collect your ideas in a computer file, a notebook, or a journal. Then when you're ready to write, check your idea collections.

2 Choose a Topic Sometimes you have a lot of ideas you want to write about. Other times, your teacher may give you a **writing prompt**, or a writing assignment. You will still need to decide exactly what to write about. Make a list of possible writing ideas. Then circle the one that is the most important or interesting to you. That idea will be your **topic**.

I could write about...

a concert my friends and I went to

when my grandparents arrived in the U.S.

why we need more school dances

why the eagle is a popular symbol

3 Plan Your Writing An **FATP** chart can help you organize your thoughts and focus on the details that you'll need for your writing.

FATP Chart

HOW TO UNLOCK A PROMPT
Form: _personal narrative_
Audience: _my teacher and classmates_
Topic: _when my grandparents arrived in the U.S._
Purpose: _to describe a personal experience_

Here are the ways an **FATP** chart can help you:

- The **form** tells you the type of writing. Study examples of the form to help you decide how to craft your writing.

- If you know your **audience**, you can choose the appropriate style and tone. For example, if you are writing for your friends, you can use friendly, informal language.

- A specific **topic** will help you collect only those details you need.

- The **purpose** is why you are writing. Your purpose can be to describe, to inform or explain, to persuade, or to express personal thoughts or feelings.

For more about writing for a specific audience or purpose, see pages 414–415.

4 Gather Details To write about a personal experience, you can just list the things you remember about an event. For other kinds of writing, you may need to talk about your topic with others or do research to gather information.

There are many ways to show the details you've gathered. You can

- make charts, lists, or webs
- draw and label pictures
- take notes on notecards
- make a story map
- use a gathering grid to write down answers to your questions

Gathering Grid

Topic: Vietnam	Get to Know Vietnam (book)	Internet
What is the population?		
What fuels the economy?		

Show your details in a way that works best for you and for your topic.

5 Get Organized Review your details and plan an interesting way to write about your topic. Put the details in the best order for your writing.

- Sometimes you can organize the details as you write them down.
- Other times, you can use numbers to order events in time sequence or to order the details from most to least important.
- You could also make an outline to show main ideas and supporting details.

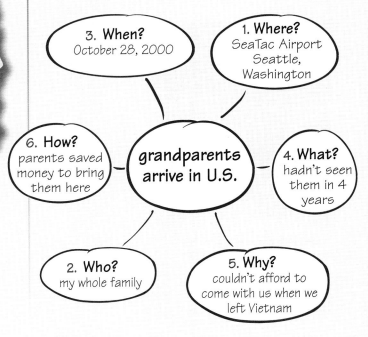

3. **When?** October 28, 2000

1. **Where?** SeaTac Airport Seattle, Washington

6. **How?** parents saved money to bring them here

grandparents arrive in U.S.

4. **What?** hadn't seen them in 4 years

2. **Who?** my whole family

5. **Why?** couldn't afford to come with us when we left Vietnam

The Writing Process, continued

DRAFT

Now you are ready to start writing. At this stage, don't worry about making mistakes—just get your ideas down on paper! Turn your details into sentences and paragraphs. As you are writing, you'll probably think of new ideas. Add those to your draft.

Trang Bui's Draft

> My family stood by the windows and watched the plane land at SeaTac Airport in Seattle on October 28, 2000. We were so excited to see the plane. The people started coming through the door. We lined up so we could see. I had to lift my little sister up so she could see.
>
> Suddenly everyone was hugging and crying. "I see them," my mother cried. My little sister tried to hide. My sister didn't know my grandparents. She was feeling shy.

Write your ideas in a first draft.

REVISE

A first draft can always be improved. When you revise a draft, you make changes to it.

1 Read Your Draft As you read your draft, ask yourself questions about the most important ideas. Make sure your ideas are clear, complete, and presented in the best way.

Revision Checklist

☑ Did I follow the plan on my FATP chart? Is the language appropriate for the writing form and audience? Did I stick to the topic?

☑ Is my writing interesting? Did I use different kinds of sentences? Did I vary the sentence beginnings?

☑ Does my writing have a beginning, a middle, and an ending?

☑ Are my details organized in the best way? Should I change the order of any details?

☑ Did I include details to make my ideas clear? Should I add or cut any details?

☑ Did I use the best words to say what I mean? Did I avoid using the same words over and over again?

2 **Discuss Your Writing with Others** Arrange a time to meet with your teacher to talk about your writing. Ask for suggestions for what you can do to improve it. Make any changes your teacher suggests, and then meet again to see how you are doing.

You might also have a **peer conference** with your classmates. Their comments can help you identify things that you might not notice yourself.

Guidelines for Peer Conferences

When you're the writer:

1. Tell your purpose for writing. Then read your writing aloud, or give copies to the group.

2. Ask for help on specific points:
   • Should I add any details about…?
   • Does the ending make sense?
   • Did I leave anything out?

3. Listen carefully to suggestions and take notes. Use the comments that you think will improve your writing.

When you're the reader:

1. Read the writing twice, or listen once and read it once. Make notes as you read. If you don't understand something, ask questions.

2. Look for the strongest parts of the writing. Why do they work? Tell the writer:
   • I like the way you…
   • One part you described well was…
   • You caught my interest when you wrote…

3. Make specific suggestions. Tell how the writer can improve the details, sentences, or organization.

---

3 **Mark Your Changes** What changes do you want to make to your draft? Use the Revising Marks or special features in your computer's word-processing program to show the changes.

Trang Bui's Revisions

My family stood by the ^big, glass^ windows and watched the plane land at SeaTac Airport in Seattle on October 28, 2000. We were so excited ~~to see the plane.~~ ^When the passengers^ ~~The people~~ started coming through the door, we lined up so we could see. I had to lift my little sister up so she could ~~see~~ ^look over the heads of the people in front^.

Suddenly everyone was hugging and crying. ("I see them," my mother cried.) My little sister tried to hide ^because she^ ~~My sister~~ didn't know my grandparents ^and^ ~~She~~ was feeling shy.

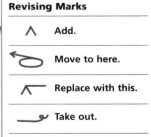

Revising Marks

∧	Add.
↶	Move to here.
∧	Replace with this.
⌣	Take out.

The Writing Process, continued

EDIT AND PROOFREAD

After you revise your draft for content, it's time to check it for mistakes.

1 **Check Your Sentences** When you edit, check that your sentences are clear, complete, and correct. Ask yourself:

- Does each sentence have a subject and a predicate?
- Did I break up run-on sentences?
- Are there any short sentences that I can combine into longer sentences?

2 **Check for Mistakes** Proofread to find and correct errors in capitalization, punctuation, grammar, and spelling. Look especially for:

- capital letters, end marks, apostrophes, and quotation marks
- subject–verb agreement
- use of pronouns
- misspelled words.

3 **Mark Your Corrections** Use the Proofreading Marks to show your corrections or make the corrections when you find them in your document on the computer.

4 **Make a Final Copy** Rewrite your work and make the corrections you marked. If you are using a computer, print your corrected copy. For more ideas about formatting your paper, see page 389.

Trang Bui's Proofread Draft

¶ When we left vietnam, my grandparents had to stay behind. "We are too old to go someplace new," my grandfather said. My grandmother cooked a special *an incredible* dinner for us before we left, but *she* he could not eat. We didnt know how long it would be before we would see each other again.

Proofreading Marks	
∧	Add.
⩕	Add a comma.
⊙	Add a period.
≡	Capitalize.
／	Make lowercase.
⭒	Take out.
¶	Indent.

PUBLISH

Now that you have corrected your work, share it with others! Here are just a few ideas for publishing your writing.

- E-mail it to a friend or family member.
- Make a home video of you reading it.
- Put it on a poster, add pictures, and display it in your classroom.
- Send it to your favorite magazine for publication.

The Best Day of My Life
by Trang Bui

My family stood by the big, glass windows and watched the plane land at SeaTac Airport in Seattle on October 28, 2000. We were so excited! When the passengers started coming through the door, we lined up so we could see. I had to lift my little sister up so she could look over the heads of the people in front.

"I see them," my mother cried. Suddenly everyone was hugging and crying. My little sister tried to hide because she didn't know my grandparents and was feeling shy.

When we left Vietnam, my grandparents had to stay behind. "We are too old to go someplace new," my grandfather said. My grandmother cooked an incredible dinner for us before we left, but she could not eat. We didn't know how long it would be before we would see each other again.

My family came to Seattle to start a new life. My parents worked in the donut shop and sent some of the money they earned each month to my grandparents. It took four long years, but my grandparents finally arrived, and we're all together again.

EVALUATE YOUR WRITING

Save examples of your writing. Date them and collect them in a **portfolio**. Look through your portfolio from time to time to see how you are doing as a writer.

❶ Organize Your Portfolio Try putting all your writing in order by date. Or, make special sections for works written for the same purpose or same audience. You might also group your writing by form—stories, research reports, or poems, for example.

❷ Survey the Work in Your Portfolio Each time you add new work to your portfolio, ask yourself:

- How does this writing compare to other work I've done?
- Am I getting better in certain areas? What are they?
- Are there things that I didn't do as well this time? Why?

❸ Think About How You Write As you look over your writing, think about the words you like to use, the kinds of sentences you write, and what you like to write about. All of those things together are your writing style. That is what makes you a super writer with a style all your own!

I write with Style!

The Writer's Craft

Good writers are always working on their writing. You can use the ideas in this section to make your writing the best it can be.

HOW TO WRITE FOR A SPECIFIC PURPOSE

Good writers change how and what they write to fit their main purpose.
The **purpose** is why you are writing.

PURPOSE	EXAMPLES	
To describe	You could write a description with lots of descriptive details to help your reader "see" what you are describing. My guitar is awesome. The body is a metallic black, and the new strings shine like silver.	For a poem, use colorful verbs to describe what something does. Sounds of A Guitar Strum, strum the silver strings, And sweet notes fill the air.
To inform or to explain	You might give directions to explain how to do something. To play the guitar, hold the neck with your left hand. Then curl your fingers over the frets. Use your right hand to strum or pick the strings over the sound hole.	Or, you could write a paragraph to give your readers important facts about a topic. An electric guitar has a solid body and six strings. The points under the strings change the vibrations into electronic signals. The signals are magnified by an amplifier and sent to loudspeakers where they are converted into sounds.
To persuade	In an advertisement, you can use persuasive words and phrases to convince someone to buy something. **Electric Guitars** Is excellent sound quality what you want? Then come on over to Guitar World. We've got the best brands at the best prices! Guitar World 101 Main Street 555-8931	In an editorial, give your opinion and use persuasive words to change the way things are. I think the school board should vote to keep our music program. I love music, and so do many of my friends. As a matter of fact, we try to finish our homework just so we can get to music class.

PURPOSE	EXAMPLES
To express your thoughts and feelings	Write a journal entry to tell about your personal thoughts and feelings. June 10, 2001 I just saw the Top Dogs in concert. I wish I could play like their lead guitarist!
To entertain	You could write a joke to make your readers laugh. What did the old guitar say to the new one? Don't fret. I'll carry the tune for you!
To learn	It helps to write things down when you are learning about a topic. That way you can see what you already know—and what you don't know. Listening to music can help you relax. Now I want to know how it affects your brain and your body.

HOW TO WRITE FOR A SPECIFIC AUDIENCE

Who will read what you write? Your **audience**. Knowing your audience will help you decide what words to use and what kinds of details to include.

AUDIENCE	EXAMPLES
Adults and people you don't know	Use formal language and details to help them understand what they might not know. I did very well at my guitar lesson today. I learned how to press the tips of my fingers on top of the strings to play different notes.
Your friends	Use informal language because they'll probably understand exactly what you mean. My guitar lesson was great. Now I can jam with any band!
People younger than you	Use simple language so they'll understand. My guitar lesson was fun. Now I can play a song.

The Writer's Craft, continued

HOW TO CHOOSE THE RIGHT WORDS

To help your readers really see what you are writing about, use just the right words.

1 **Use Specific Nouns** Choose nouns that say exactly what you mean.

Just OK	Much Better
The boat went across the water.	The sailboat sped across the lake.

2 **Use Colorful Verbs** Choose verbs that give the best picture of the action.

Just OK	Much Better
The wave came up on the beach.	The wave crashed on the beach.

3 **Add Sensory Words** Use words that tell what you see, hear, smell, taste, and touch to help your readers imagine they are there!

Just OK

Mark sat on the beach by the water. He pushed the sand around. The sun shone down on his skin.

Much Better

Mark sat on the beach by the crashing waves. He sifted the soft, white sand through his fingers. The hot sun beat down on his parched skin, and he could almost taste the salty air.

4 **Use Words with Just the Right Meaning** Some words seem similar in meaning but may give readers a different feeling.
Negative Connotation: skinny
Positive Connotation: slim, slender

5 **Use Figurative Language** Figurative language can help your readers "see" ordinary things in new ways.

- Try using a **simile** with *like* or *as* to make comparisons.

  The man dove like a dolphin into the waves.

- Use a **metaphor** to tell what something is like, without using the words *like* or *as*:

  The man was a playful dolphin.

- Use **personification** to give human qualities to a non-human thing:

  Seagulls laughed overhead.

- You might want to use **hyperbole,** or an exaggeration, to add humor to your writing.

  The squawking gulls could be heard around the world.

HOW TO IMPROVE YOUR SENTENCES

1 **Combine Sentences** Try different ways to combine a lot of short sentences into one longer sentence.

Just OK

> I pushed off on my snowboard.
> I sped down the hill.
> I headed toward the clubhouse.

Much Better

> I pushed off on my snowboard and sped down the hill toward the clubhouse.

> I pushed off on my snowboard, sped down the hill, and headed toward the clubhouse.

2 **Break Up Sentences** If a sentence runs on too long, it becomes hard to follow. Break up run-on sentences to make your meaning clear.

Just OK

> The first time I went snowboarding, it was hard to get off the chairlift and I kept falling, but as I watched other snowboarders, I realized that most of them fell, too, then I didn't feel so bad.

Much Better

> The first time I went snowboarding, it was hard to get off the chairlift. I kept falling. As I watched other snowboarders, I realized that most of them fell, too. Then I didn't feel so bad.

3 **Start Sentences in Different Ways** Make your writing more interesting by varying the way your sentences begin. That way your readers won't get bored.

Just OK

> **Darcy** went snowboarding for the first time last winter. **Darcy** started out just fine. **Darcy** tried to make a turn, but lost her balance and fell into a snowbank. **Darcy** laughed at herself, brushed off the snow, and got right back on her feet. **Darcy** fell several more times, but finally made it down the hill!

Much Better

> **Last winter,** Darcy went snowboarding for the first time. **She** started out just fine. **When she tried to make a turn,** she lost her balance and fell into a snowbank. **Laughing at herself,** Darcy brushed off the snow and got right back on her feet. **After several more falls,** Darcy finally made it down the hill!

The Writer's Craft, continued

WHAT IS A PARAGRAPH?

A **paragraph** is a group of sentences that all tell about the same idea. The **topic sentence** tells the main idea of the paragraph. The other sentences give **supporting details**. The supporting details tell more about the main idea.

Sometimes a topic sentence that states the main idea comes at the beginning of a paragraph.

> **The Pike Place Market in Seattle is a great place to spend an afternoon.** At the market, you can shop for fresh fruits, vegetables, and flowers. You can watch the fishsellers toss fish across the aisles to one another. If you're hungry, you can find just about any kind of food in the many cafes and food stands.

Sometimes a topic sentence that states the main idea comes at the end of a paragraph.

> At the market, you can shop for fresh fruits, vegetables, and flowers. You can watch the fishsellers toss fish across the aisles to each other. If you're hungry, you can find just about any kind of food in the many cafes and food stands. **The Pike Place Market in Seattle is a great place to spend an afternoon.**

HOW TO ORGANIZE PARAGRAPHS

There are many ways to organize your paragraphs.

❶ Sequence Paragraphs Some paragraphs are organized by sequence. **Time order words** tell when things happen.

> One day I went fishing with Dad. **First** we rowed to the middle of the lake. **After** we put slimy worms on our hooks, we tossed our lines overboard. **Then** we waited forever for the fish to bite! We **finally** caught one fish. When Dad goes fishing again, I'm staying home!

❷ Comparison Paragraphs Some paragraphs tell how things are alike and different. **Comparison words** signal the similarities and differences.

> **Like** human beings, whales are mammals. **Both** produce milk and give birth to live young. **Unlike** most mammals, **however,** whales store oxygen longer. This allows them to take fewer breaths and stay underwater longer.

❸ Paragraphs in Space Order For a description, try using **space order** to tell what you see in order—left to right, near to far, or top to bottom. **Direction words and phrases** tell where things are.

> An octopus looks strange. Its head and body look like one big bulb. **Radiating from** the bulb are eight tentacles. Each tentacle has two rows of suckers **along the underside.** It uses the suckers to grip rocks and find food.

4 **Cause-and-Effect Paragraphs** In this kind of paragraph, the topic sentence tells the **cause**, or why something happens. Detail sentences tell the **effects**, or what happens as a result.

> Ricky was floating on his surfboard. Suddenly, he spotted a large, dark object swimming toward him. "Could it be a shark?" he thought. His heart pounded. He paddled frantically toward the beach. Looking back, he saw a huge log bobbing among the waves!

5 **Paragraphs in Logical Order** The order in which you present your ideas can vary with your topic. You may want to present ideas in order from general to specific or from most important to least important.

> If we over-fish the ocean, there will not be enough fish left to reproduce. Although there would be food at first, there would not be enough to feed people later. Several important fish species could go extinct. Other fish that depend on those fish for food would also suffer.

6 **Opinion Paragraphs** In an opinion paragraph, give your opinion about something. State your opinion in the **topic sentence.** Give the reasons for your opinion in the detail sentences.

> **I think the octopus is a fascinating sea creature.** It defends itself so well! An octopus turns colors to match its surroundings so predators can't see it. It ejects an inky cloud when it senses danger. It also has a soft body that fits into small hiding places. Don't you think the octopus is fascinating, too?

7 **Persuasive Paragraphs** A persuasive paragraph, begins with a **thesis statement** that gives your opinion or tells the main idea. Facts, reasons, and statistics that support your opinion are the **supporting arguments**.

> **The Eastern North Pacific gray whale should be put back on the endangered species list.** It was removed from the list in 1994 because its population stabilized. However, of the three large populations of gray whales, one is extinct and another is endangered. Gray whales stay close to the shore, and can become entangled in fishing nets. Their breeding grounds in Baja, California, are threatened by the expansion of salt-extraction plants. We should act now to save the Eastern North Pacific gray whale.

The Writer's Craft, continued

HOW TO PUT PARAGRAPHS TOGETHER

If you write more than two paragraphs, organize your writing into three parts: the **introduction,** the **body,** and the **conclusion.**

1 **Write a Strong Introduction** Name the topic and grab your readers' interest.

- **Ask a question.**

  > What's so hot about smoking?

- **Express an emotion or an opinion.**

  > Smoking isn't just bad—it can kill you!

- **Describe an action or event.**

  > Smoking is one of the biggest killers in the U.S.

- **Make a startling statement, or give an interesting or unusual fact.**

  > Cigarettes contain more than fifteen harmful chemicals.

2 **Develop the Topic in the Body** Present your supporting details. Organize the paragraphs so they work together in the best order to support your main idea or thesis statement.

3 **Write a Conclusion** Express an emotion or include a thoughtful idea.

> The easiest way to break a bad habit like smoking is never to start it in the first place!

HOW TO MAKE YOUR WRITING FLOW

1 **Use Transition Words** Words or phrases that help connect paragraphs are transition words. They will help your readers follow your ideas.

Examples:

As a result	Also	Even though
As soon as	In addition	However
Finally	Like	On the other hand
Then	Plus	Yet

2 **Use the Same Point of View** If you are expressing how you feel about something, tell about *your* feelings, not someone else's. If you are writing about a character or another person, use details that show how that person thinks or feels.

> I think that smoking is an awful habit. If someone offers
> me
> ~~my friend~~ a cigarette, ~~he~~ always says, "No way."

3 **Use the Same Verb Tenses** Keep your verbs all in the same tense so your readers won't get confused about when things happen.

> When someone offers me a cigarette, though, I always
> know
> say, "No way." That's because I ~~knew~~ how bad it ~~was~~
> is
> for your lungs.

Smoking: A Bad Habit to Start

What's so hot about smoking? Nothing! I think that some kids start smoking because it makes them feel like they are grown up. Other kids just want to be part of the "in" crowd. When someone offers me a cigarette, though, I always say "No way." That's because I know how bad it is for my **lungs**.

Did you know that your **lungs** take nearly 26,000 breaths a day? They need clean air and oxygen to expand and contract the way they should. All the chemicals in cigarette smoke cause emphysema. This disease destroys the tiny air sacs in your lungs where oxygen and carbon dioxide are exchanged.

As soon as emphysema starts, it damages your **lungs**. Eventually every breath becomes a struggle. Wouldn't it be smart, then, to protect your lungs like you do other parts of your body?

Plus, if you decide to smoke, you are affecting other people's lungs as well as your own. About 3,000 non-smokers die every year from second-hand smoke. Young children are especially at risk because their lungs are just developing. Do you really want to harm someone else just to be "cool"?

Sooner or later someone is going to offer you a cigarette. Before you decide, take a deep breath of clean, fresh air. Think about how good you feel now. Then play it safe. Don't smoke!

INTRODUCTION
The introduction grabs the readers' interest and states the writer's opinion.

BODY
The body includes details, facts, and arguments to support the writer's opinion.

This writer connected paragraphs by **repeating a word or phrase** and by using **transition words**.

All the sentences go together to show this writer's point of view about the topic. The verbs the writer uses are all in the present tense.

CONCLUSION
In the last paragraph, the writer tries to convince the readers to take action.

The Writer's Craft, continued

HOW TO MAKE YOUR WRITING BETTER

The words that you choose, the way that you put them together, and the ideas that you present make your writing unique. Try these techniques.

1 Show, Don't Tell You can just tell your readers about an event or a person. To give your readers the best picture, though, show them exactly what you mean!

This tells:

> Kevin hated eating in the cafeteria. He was new at school and didn't know anyone. So he sat in a corner by himself. Then one day, a girl in his math class asked him to sit at her table. After that, Kevin felt much more comfortable.

This shows:

> "I can't wait to finish my lunch and get out of here," thought Kevin. "I don't know anyone, anyway."
>
> Then one day, Kevin heard a cheery voice from behind him. "Hey, do you want to sit with us?" the girl asked. It was Roberta from his math class.
>
> "Sure," said Kevin, grinning. "How's it going?" he asked Roberta.

2 Elaborate *Elaborate* means "Tell me more!" Try these ways to add information to your writing.

- **Tell what came before or after.**

Without Elaboration

> The ball dropped into the basket.

With Elaboration

> After rolling around on the rim, the ball finally dropped into the basket.

- **Add sensory details to clearly show what something is like.**

Without Details

> Their player made an attempt for the basket. The entire crowd watched as the ball arched across the court and sank into the net without touching the rim.

With Details

> Their tallest player made an attempt for the basket. The entire crowd watched silently as the orange ball arched high across the court and sank into the net without touching the skinny metal rim.

- **Add examples, facts, and other details.**

  Without Details

  The fans cheered.

  With Details

  The excited fans jumped up out of their seats, clapped their hands, and stomped their feet.

- **Add quotations or dialogue.**

  Without Dialogue

  The fans shouted.

  With Dialogue

  "Go, Rangers, go! You can do it!" the fans shouted.

③ Develop Your Own Writing Style and Voice

As a writer, you have your own voice, or personality. That's because your writing will show the kinds of words you like, what ideas are important to you, and how you feel about things. To keep your writing interesting and exciting, let your readers "see" who you are.

Just OK

I dribbled the ball through the zone. I made a shot for the basket. The ball rolled for a while on the basket rim, then fell in. I made the final shot to win the game.

Much Better

My heart was pounding. I dribbled the ball through the zone and took my best shot. I just stood there with my arms still raised up in the air. Would the ball ever stop rolling on the rim? When it finally dropped into the basket, I couldn't believe it! It was awesome! That basket put us ahead to win the game by one point!

Sentences

A sentence is a group of words that expresses a complete thought.
Every sentence has a subject and a predicate.
Every sentence begins with a capital letter.

SENTENCE TYPES	EXAMPLES
A **declarative sentence** tells something. It ends with a period.	The football game was on Friday. The coach made an important announcement.
An **interrogative sentence** asks a question. It ends with a question mark.	Can you tell me the news?

Kinds of Questions

Questions That Ask for a "Yes" or "No" Answer	Answers
Is it about the team?	Yes.
Did the team win the game?	Yes.
Has the coach ever made an announcement like this before?	No.
Are the players sad?	No.
Were the fans surprised?	Yes.

Tag Questions	
You will tell me the news, **won't you**?	Yes, I will. OR No, I won't.
You didn't forget it, **did you**?	Yes, I did. OR No, I didn't.

Questions That Ask for Specific Information	
Who heard the announcement?	The team and the fans heard the announcement.
What did the coach say?	He said the team will play in a special game.
Where will the team play this game?	In Hawaii.
When did the coach find out?	Right before the game.
Why was our team chosen?	Our team was chosen because we won a lot of games.
How many games has the team won this year?	All ten of them.
Which coach made the announcement?	The tall one.

SENTENCE TYPES, continued	EXAMPLES
An **exclamatory sentence** shows surprise or strong emotion. It ends with an exclamation mark.	That's fantastic news! I can't believe it!
An **imperative sentence** gives a command. It usually begins with a verb. It often ends with a period. If an imperative sentence shows strong emotion, it ends with an exclamation mark.	Give the team my congratulations. Don't keep any more secrets from me ever again!

NEGATIVE SENTENCES	EXAMPLES
A **negative sentence** uses a **negative word** to say "no."	The game in Hawaii was **not** boring! **Nobody** in our town missed it on TV. Our team **never** played better.

Negative Words

never	no one
no	not
nobody	nothing
none	nowhere

Use only one negative word in a sentence.

                                           anything

The other team could not do ~~nothing~~ right.

                     any

They never scored ~~no~~ points.

CONDITIONAL SENTENCES	EXAMPLES
Some sentences tell how one thing depends on another. These sentences often use verbs like <u>can</u>, <u>will</u>, <u>could</u>, <u>would</u>, or <u>might</u>.	**If** our team returns on Saturday, **then** we <u>will</u> have a party. **Unless** it rains, we <u>can</u> have the party on the football field. Or, we <u>could</u> have a dance in the gym **if** the coach lets us.

Sentences, continued

COMPLETE SENTENCES	EXAMPLES
A **complete sentence** has a **subject** and a **predicate**. A complete sentence expresses a complete thought.	Many people visit our National Parks. Grand Canyon National Park, Arizona
A **fragment** is not a sentence. It is not a complete thought. You can add information to a fragment to turn it into a complete sentence.	**Fragment:** a fun vacation **Complete sentences:** You can have a fun vacation. Will we have a fun vacation at the park? Go to a national park and have a fun vacation.

SUBJECTS	EXAMPLES

> **To find the subject in a sentence, ask yourself: Whom or what is the sentence about?**

The **complete subject** includes all the words that tell about the subject.	My favorite parks are in the West. People from all over the world visit them.
The **simple subject** is the most important word in the complete subject.	My favorite parks are in the West. People from all over the world visit them.
A **compound subject** has two or more simple subjects joined by **and** or **or**.	Yosemite and Yellowstone are the most interesting to me. Either spring or fall is a good time to visit these parks.
Sometimes the subject is a **pronoun**. Be sure to include the pronoun in the sentence. **But:** When you give a command, you do not have to include the subject. The subject **you** is understood in an imperative sentence.	The map shows the campsites. They are by the river. Follow the rules of the park. Don't disturb the animals. Never throw trash in the streams.

Subject Pronouns

Singular	Plural
I	we
you	you
he, she, it	they

PREDICATES	EXAMPLES

The predicate of a sentence tells what the subject is, has, or does.

The **complete predicate** includes all the words in the predicate.	Yosemite **is a beautiful park**. It **has huge waterfalls**. People **hike to the waterfalls**.
The **simple predicate** is the **verb**. It is the most important word in the predicate.	Yosemite **is** a beautiful park. It **has** huge waterfalls. People **hike** to the waterfalls.

Waterfall in Yosemite National Park

A **compound predicate** has two or more verbs joined by **and** or **or**.	At Yosemite, some people **fish and swim**. My family **hiked** to the river **or stayed** in the cabin. I **have gone** to Yosemite often **and have enjoyed** every visit.

SUBJECT-VERB AGREEMENT	EXAMPLES

The verb must always agree with the subject of the sentence.

A **singular subject** names one person or thing. Use a **singular verb** with a singular subject. A **plural subject** tells about more than one person or thing. Use a **plural verb** with a plural subject.	Another popular **park is** the Grand Canyon. **It has** a powerful river. The **cliffs are** beautiful. **We were amazed** by their colors.

Singular and Plural Verbs

Singular	Plural
The park **is** big.	The parks **are** big.
The park **was** beautiful.	The parks **were** beautiful.
The park **has** campsites.	The parks **have** campsites.
The park **does** not **open** until spring.	The parks **do** not **open** until spring.

Sentences   **427**

Sentences, continued

SUBJECT-VERB AGREEMENT, continued	EXAMPLES
Study the chart to see how **action verbs** agree with their subjects. When you tell about one other person or thing, use an action verb that ends in **s**.	**More Singular and Plural Verbs** Singular I **hike** in the park. You **hike** in the park. He **hikes** in the park. She **hikes** in the park. The dog **hikes** in the park. Plural We **hike** in the park. You **hike** in the park. They **hike** in the park. The dogs **hike** in the park.
The **subject** and **verb** must agree, even when other words come between them.	The **hikers** in the park **are looking** for animals. A **snake** with lots of stripes **lives** in this area.
If the simple subjects in a **compound subject** are connected by **and**, use a plural verb.	A **mule and** a **guide are** available for a trip down the canyon.
Sometimes the simple subjects in a **compound subject** are connected by **or**. Look at the last simple subject. If it is singular, use a **singular verb**. If it is plural, use a **plural verb**.	These **rafts or** this **boat is** the best way to go down the river. This **raft or** these **boats are** the best way to go down the river. Mule riders in the Grand Canyon
The **subject** and **verb** must agree even if the subject comes after the verb.	There **are** other amazing **parks** in Arizona. Here **is** a **list** of them.
In some questions, look for the **subject** between the **helping and main verbs**. The helping verb must agree with the subject.	**Has** your **friend visited** the parks? **Have** your **friends visited** the parks?

PHRASES	EXAMPLES
A **phrase** is a group of related words that does not have a subject and a predicate.	**during the gold rush** **before the discovery of gold**
A **phrase** can be part of a complete sentence.	Many people came to California **during the gold rush**. **Before the discovery of gold**, about 15,000 people lived there.

CLAUSES	EXAMPLES
A **clause** is a group of words that has a **subject** and a **verb**. Some clauses are complete sentences. Some clauses are not.	The **population** of California **increased** to about 100,000 by 1849. because **miners came** to California
An **independent clause** expresses a complete thought and can stand alone as a sentence. A **dependent clause** does not express a complete thought. It is not a sentence.	The miners were called "forty-niners." because so many arrived in 1849

Prospectors panned for gold in rivers and streams.

Words That Can Signal a Dependent Clause

Cause Words	Time Words		Words that Express Conditions	Relative Pronouns	
because	after	whenever	although	that	who
since	as	while	as long as	which	whom
	before	until	if		whose
	when		unless		

A **dependent clause** can be combined with an **independent clause** to form a sentence.	The miners were called "forty-niners" because so many arrived in 1849. <u> independent clause </u> <u> dependent clause </u> When they found gold, the miners got rich. <u> dependent clause </u> <u> independent clause </u>

Sentences, continued

SIMPLE SENTENCES	EXAMPLES
A **simple sentence** is one independent clause. It has a **subject** and a **predicate**.	**The miners** **needed goods and services**.

COMPOUND SENTENCES	EXAMPLES
When you join two independent clauses, you make a **compound sentence**. Use a **coordinating conjunction** to join the clauses.	Some people opened food markets. The miners bought food. ▼ **Some people opened food markets,** **and the miners bought food.** Other people opened stores. It was still hard to get supplies. ▼ **Other people opened stores, but** **it was still hard to get supplies.** **Coordinating Conjunctions** and nor but or for yet
Put a **comma** before the conjunction or use a **semi-colon** and no conjunction.	The miners used gold to buy things, and the shopkeepers ended up with the gold. The miners used gold to buy things; the shopkeepers ended up with the gold.

COMPLEX SENTENCES	EXAMPLES

To make a **complex sentence**, join an independent clause with one or more dependent clauses.
 	
If the dependent clause comes first, put a **comma** after it.
	Many writers visited the camps where the miners worked.
	   independent clause dependent clause
	
	While they were there, the writers wrote stories about the miners.
	  dependent clause independent clause

COMPOUND-COMPLEX SENTENCES	EXAMPLES

You can make a **compound-complex sentence** by joining two or more independent clauses and a dependent clause.	Many miners never became rich, but they decided to settle in the West
	   independent clause independent clause
	
	because they found other jobs in California.
	    dependent clause

Parts of Speech

All the words in the English language can be categorized into eight groups. These groups are the eight parts of speech. Words are grouped into the parts of speech by the way they are used in a sentence.

THE EIGHT PARTS OF SPEECH	EXAMPLES
A **noun** names a person, place, thing, or idea.	**Samantha** lives in **Minnesota**. She skates on the **ice** every **day** to build her **skill**.
A **pronoun** takes the place of a noun.	**She** practices a dance routine for a show.
An **adjective** describes a noun or a pronoun.	She is a **powerful** skater. She is **graceful**, too.
A **verb** can tell what the subject of a sentence does or has. A **verb** can also link a word in the predicate to the subject.	Samantha **twists**, **turns**, and **jumps**. She **has** talent! Like many skaters, Samantha **is** a competitor. But, unlike most skaters, Samantha **is** deaf.
An **adverb** describes a verb, an adjective, or another adverb.	The music plays **loudly**, but she cannot hear it. Still, Samantha has become a **very** good skater. How can she perform **so** well?
A **preposition** shows how two things or ideas are related. It introduces a prepositional phrase.	A skating coach helps Samantha skate **on** the ice. He gives her signals as she moves **around** the rink. **During** the show, the people **in** the stands cheer **for** the skater.
A **conjunction** connects words or groups of words.	Samantha can't hear the people cheer, **but** she sees their smiles. Samantha smiles **and** waves back to the crowd.
An **interjection** expresses strong feeling.	Some people shout, "**Hooray!**" Others say, "**Wow!** What a talented skater!"

Nouns

A noun names a person, place, thing, or idea.
There are many different kinds of nouns.

COMMON AND PROPER NOUNS	EXAMPLES
A **common noun** names any person, place, thing, or idea.	A **teenager** sat by the **ocean** and read a **book**. It was about **ecology**.
A **proper noun** names one particular person, place, thing, or idea. The important words in a proper noun start with a <u>capital letter</u>.	**Daniel** sat by the **Atlantic Ocean** and read *Save the Manatee.*  A manatee
A **compound noun** is two or more words that express one idea. A compound noun can be: • two words • two words joined into one word • a hyphenated word	Some people call manatees **sea cows**. Manatees live in shallow waters where there is plenty of **sunlight**. In his book, Daniel saw a picture of a manatee baby and a **grown-up**.

COLLECTIVE NOUNS	EXAMPLES
A **collective noun** names a group of people, animals, places, or things.	Daniel took pictures of manatees on a trip to Florida with his **family**.

Some Collective Nouns

Groups of People	Groups of Animals	Groups of Places	Groups of Things
band	flock	Hawaiian Islands	mail
class	herd		money
family	litter	United States	set
team	pack		trash

A collective noun can be the **subject** of a sentence. It usually needs a **singular verb** because the group is seen as one unit.	Our **class hopes** to see the pictures Daniel took. His **club has** already **seen** them.

SINGULAR AND PLURAL NOUNS	EXAMPLES

**The singular form of a count noun names one thing.
The plural form names more than one thing.**

Count nouns are nouns that you can count. Follow these rules to make a count noun plural:

- Add **-s** to most count nouns.

desk	book	teacher	apple	line
desk**s**	book**s**	teacher**s**	apple**s**	line**s**

- If the noun ends in **x**, **ch**, **sh**, **s**, or **z**, add **-es**.

box	lunch	dish	glass	waltz
box**es**	lunch**es**	dish**es**	glass**es**	waltz**es**

- For nouns that end in a consonant plus **y**, change the **y** to **i** and add **-es**.

story	sky	city	penny	army
stor**ies**	sk**ies**	cit**ies**	penn**ies**	arm**ies**

- For nouns that end in a vowel plus **y**, just add **-s**.

boy	toy	day	monkey	valley
boy**s**	toy**s**	day**s**	monkey**s**	valley**s**

- For most nouns that end in **f** or **fe**, change the **f** to **v** and add **-es**. For some nouns that end in **f**, just add **-s**.

leaf	knife	half	roof	chief
lea**ves**	kni**ves**	hal**ves**	roof**s**	chief**s**

- If the noun ends in a vowel plus **o**, add **-s**. For some nouns that end in a consonant plus **o**, add **-s**. For others, add **-es**.

radio	kangaroo	banjo	potato	tomato
radio**s**	kangaroo**s**	banjo**s**	potato**es**	tomato**es**

- A few count nouns have irregular plural forms.

child	foot	person	man	woman
children	**feet**	**people**	**men**	**women**

- For a few count nouns, the singular and plural forms are the same.

deer	fish	salmon	sheep	trout
deer	**fish**	**salmon**	**sheep**	**trout**

Nouns, continued

SINGULAR AND PLURAL NOUNS	EXAMPLES
Noncount nouns are nouns that you cannot count. A noncount noun does not have a plural form.	My favorite museum has **furniture** and **art**. Sometimes I wonder how much **money** each item is worth.

Types of Noncount Nouns

Activities and Sports

				Examples
baseball	camping	dancing	fishing	I love to play **soccer**.
golf	singing	soccer	swimming	

Category Nouns

clothing	equipment	furniture	hardware	jewelry	My **equipment** is in the car.
machinery	mail	money	time	weather	

Food

bread	cereal	cheese	corn	flour	I'll drink some **water** on my way
lettuce	meat	milk	rice	salt	to the game.
soup	sugar	tea	water		

You can count some food items by using a measurement word like **cup**, **slice**, **glass**, or **head** plus the word **of**. To show the plural form, just make the measurement word plural.

I'll drink **two glasses of water** on my way to the game.

Ideas and Feelings

democracy	enthusiasm	freedom	fun	health	I'll also listen to the radio for
honesty	information	knowledge	luck	work	**information** about the weather.

Materials

air	fuel	gasoline	gold	The radio says the **air** is heavy.
metal	paper	water	wood	What does that mean?

Weather

fog	hail	heat	ice	lightning	Uh-oh! First came the **lightning**
rain	smog	snow	sunshine	thunder	and the **thunder**. I want **sunshine** for my next soccer game!

Some words have more than one meaning. Add **-s** for the plural only if the noun means something you can count.	Throw me those **baseballs**. I want to learn to play **baseball**.

ARTICLES	EXAMPLES
An **article** is a word that helps identify a noun. An article often comes before a count noun.	After **the** game, we found **a** coat and **an** umbrella on **the** field.
Use **a** or **an** before **nouns** that are not specific. Use **the** before **nouns** that are specific.	**A boy** walked around the field. **The coach's son** walked around the field.
Use **a** before a word that starts with a consonant sound. Use **an** before a word that starts with a vowel sound.	a **b**all a **g**ate a **p**layer a **o**ne-way street (o is pronounced like w) a **c**ap a **k**ick a **n**et a **u**niform (u is pronounced like y) **a** **e** **i** **o** **u** **silent h** an **a**nt an **e**lbow an **i**nch an **o**live an **u**mbrella an **h**our an **a**pron an **e**el an **i**dea an **o**cean an **a**mount an **e**lection an **o**wl an **a**rtist an **or**ange
Do not use **a** or **an** before a noncount noun.	The soccer ball was made of ~~a~~ leather.
Do not use **the** before the name of: • a city or state • most countries • a language • a day, a month, or most holidays • a sport or activity • most businesses • a person.	Our next game will be in **Dallas**. Games in **Texas** are always exciting. We will play a team from **Mexico**. People will be cheering in **Spanish** and **English**. The game will take place on **Monday**. Is that in **February**? Yes, on **President's Day**. That will be a good day to play **soccer**. The fans will have hot dogs to eat from **Sal's Market**. You may even see **Sal** himself.

Nouns, continued

POSSESSIVE NOUNS	EXAMPLES
A **possessive noun** is the name of an owner. All possessive nouns include an **apostrophe**.	Several bands performed in our **town's** parade. Everyone liked the **musicians'** costumes.
Follow these rules to make a noun possessive:	
• If there is one owner, add **'s** to the owner's name.	Some kids played the trumpet. One **boy's** trumpet was very loud. **Marsha's** baton went high in the air.
But: If the owner's name ends in **s**, you can add **'s** or just the apostrophe. Either is correct.	**Louis's** hat fell off. **Louis'** hat fell off.
• A noun that names two or more owners is plural and often ends in **s**. If so, just add **'**.	The **girls'** section sang loud songs. I could barely hear my **brothers'** tubas.
But: If the plural noun that names the owners does not end in **s**, add **'s**.	The **men's** cooking club marched with the band. The **children's** band rode on tricycles.

CONCRETE AND ABSTRACT NOUNS	EXAMPLES
A **concrete noun** names something you can see, touch, hear, smell, or taste.	The **band** will be in the **parade** that goes down **Main Street**.
An **abstract noun** names something you can think about but cannot see, touch, hear, smell, or taste.	The parade will add to the **spirit** of the **day**.

A parade

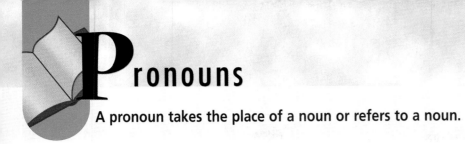

Pronouns

A pronoun takes the place of a noun or refers to a noun.

NOUN AND PRONOUN AGREEMENT	EXAMPLES
	When nouns and pronouns agree, they both tell about the same person, place, or thing.
The noun is the **antecedent**, and the **pronoun** refers to it.	<u>Janet and Scott</u> talk to a counselor. **They** learn about careers. antecedent pronoun
A **pronoun** must agree in number with the noun it refers to. **Singular pronouns** refer to one person. **Plural pronouns** refer to more than one person.	The counselor has an office at school. ~~They~~ *He* meets there with students. **Some Singular and Plural Pronouns** Singular Pronouns Plural Pronouns I, me, my, mine we, us, our, ours you, your, yours you, your, yours he, him, his she, her, hers —— they, them, their, theirs it, its
Use **she, her,** and **hers** to tell about females. Use **he**, **him**, and **his** to tell about males.	Janet is interested in animals. ~~He~~ *She* wants to know what veterinarians do. Scott wants the counselor to tell ~~her~~ *him* about careers in photography.

Pronouns, continued

PERSON OF PRONOUNS	EXAMPLES
Use a **first-person pronoun** to talk about yourself.	**I** may want to be a photographer some day. At **our** house **we** take pictures of **my** family all the time.
Use a **second-person pronoun** to identify the person you are talking to.	Scott, do **you** have a photograph of **your** grandparents? Did **you** use this camera to take the picture?
Use a **third-person pronoun** to identify the person or thing you are talking about.	Scott got a new video camera for **his** birthday. Mother gave **it** to Scott. **She** thinks **he** will be a movie director someday.

USES OF PRONOUNS	EXAMPLES
Use a **subject pronoun** as the **subject** of a sentence.	**Janet** likes animals. **She** works at a pet shop.

Subject Pronouns

Singular	Plural
I	we
you	you
he, she, it	they

The pronoun **it** can be used as a **subject** to refer to a noun.	Janet lives near the **shop**. **It** is on First Street.
But: The pronoun **it** can be the **subject** without referring to a specific noun.	**It** is interesting to work in the shop. **It** is fun to play with the animals. **It** is important to take care of them, too.
Sometimes you talk about a person twice in a sentence. Use a **reflexive pronoun** to refer to the **subject**.	**Janet** taught **herself** about the life cycle of parrots. The **shop owners themselves** learned some things from Janet.

Subject and Reflexive Pronouns

Singular		Plural	
I	myself	we	ourselves
you	yourself	you	yourselves
he	himself		
she	herself	they	themselves
it	itself		

USES OF PRONOUNS, continued	EXAMPLES
You can use an **object pronoun** after an **action verb**. You can also use an **object pronoun** after a **preposition**.	The parrots get hungry at 5 o'clock. Janet **feeds them** every day. The parrots squawk **at her** to say "thank you."

Object Pronouns

Singular	Plural
me	us
you	you
him, her, it	them

A **possessive pronoun** tells who or what owns something. A **possessive pronoun** can refer to the name of an owner. It is sometimes called a **possessive adjective**. A **possessive pronoun** can take the place of a **person's name and what the person owns**.	**Janet's** posters are about pet care. **Her** posters show what dogs need. Which one is **Janet's poster**? The big one is **hers**.

Possessive Pronouns

Use these pronouns to refer to the name of an owner. These pronouns always come before a noun and act as adjectives.		Use these pronouns to replace a person's name and what the person owns. These pronouns are always used alone.	
Singular	Plural	Singular	Plural
my	our	mine	ours
your	your	yours	yours
his, her, its	their	his, hers, its	theirs

DEMONSTRATIVE PRONOUNS	EXAMPLES
A **demonstrative pronoun** points out a specific noun without naming it.	Look at the puppies. **That** is a cute puppy. **Those** are sleeping.

Demonstrative Pronouns

	Singular	Plural
Nearby	this	these
Far Away	that	those

Pronouns, continued

INDEFINITE PRONOUNS	EXAMPLES
When you are not talking about a specific person or thing, use an **indefinite pronoun**.	**Everybody** loves to visit the pet shop. **Something** is happening in the pet shop today.

Some Indefinite Pronouns

These **indefinite pronouns** are always singular and need a **singular verb**.

another	each	everything	nothing
anybody	either	neither	somebody
anyone	everybody	nobody	someone
anything	everyone	no one	something

Examples

Someone is photographing the dogs.
Nobody knows why.

These **indefinite pronouns** are always plural and need a **plural verb**.

both	few	many	several

Several of the dogs **are eating**.
Both of the puppies **have** bones.

These **indefinite pronouns** can be either singular or plural.

all	any	most	none	some

Look at the phrase that follows the pronoun. If the noun in the phrase is plural, use a **plural verb**. If not, use a **singular verb**.

All of the dogs **are barking**.
All of their food **is gone**.

RELATIVE PRONOUNS	EXAMPLES
A **relative pronoun** introduces a **relative clause**. It connects, or relates, the clause to a word in the sentence.	

Some Relative Pronouns

who	whose	that
whom	which	

Use **who**, **whom**, or **whose** for people.

The man **who photographed the dogs** is a writer.

Use **which** for things.

His book, **which** I have read, shows all kinds of dogs.

Use **that** for people or things.

The writer **that** created the book is famous.

The photo **that** I like best in his book was taken in the pet shop.

# Adjectives

An adjective describes, or modifies, a noun or pronoun.
It can tell what kind, which one, how many, or how much.

DESCRIPTIVE ADJECTIVES	EXAMPLES
An **adjective** can tell what something is like. It can tell the color, size, or shape. It can describe a feeling.	Where can you find **brown** rabbits and **white** egrets? A swamp has **large** and **small** animals like these. The egret has **round** eyes and a **pointed** beak. I feel **happy** when I spend a day in the swamp.
An adjective can tell how something sounds, feels, looks, tastes, or smells.	I like the **noisy** birds. The egrets are **beautiful**.

Adjectives That Appeal to the Senses

Hearing	Touch	Sight	Taste	Smell
crunchy	hard	beautiful	bitter	fishy
noisy	rough	dark	salty	fragrant
quiet	smooth	huge	sour	fresh
soft	wet	shiny	sweet	rotten

An egret

Usually, an **adjective** comes before the noun it describes. **But:** A **predicate adjective** appears in the predicate and still describes the noun or pronoun in the **subject**.	An **old alligator** hides in the **dark mud**. An alligator The **alligator** is **powerful**. **It** is **dangerous**, too.
Sometimes two or more **adjectives** come before a **noun**. Use a comma (**,**) between the adjectives if they both describe the noun.	Alligators walk on **short, strong** legs.
An **adjective** is never plural, even if the **noun** it describes is plural.	Many **hungry birds** look for food near the water. Their **eyes** are **good**, but they don't see the alligator. Soon the **tasty birds** are the alligator's dinner!

Adjectives, continued

DEMONSTRATIVE ADJECTIVES	EXAMPLES
A **demonstrative adjective** points out the noun that follows it. It answers the question "Which one?"	**These** otters are by my boat. **That** otter over there belongs to one of them. **Demonstrative Adjectives** |	Singular	Plural
---	---	---
Nearby	this	these
Far Away	that	those	

NUMBER WORDS	EXAMPLES
Number words are often used as **adjectives**. Sometimes the number word tells the **order** that things are in.	Today in the swamp I saw **one** snake, **two** alligators, and **six** turtles. The **first** day I saw many kinds of birds. The **second** day I saw a lot of alligators. What will I see on the **third** day?

INDEFINITE ADJECTIVES	EXAMPLES
Use an **indefinite adjective** when you are not sure of the exact number. Some indefinite adjectives tell **how many** things there are. Use these adjectives before nouns you can count. Some indefinite adjectives tell **how much** there is of something. Use these adjectives before nouns you cannot count.	I didn't see **much** wildlife on the third day. All I saw were **a few** frogs. **Some Indefinite Adjectives** | To Tell How Many	To Tell How Much
many insects	**much** sunshine
a few insects	**a little** sunshine
some insects	**some** sunshine
several insects	**not much** sunshine
no insects	**no** sunshine	
In a negative sentence, use **any** instead of **some**.	I saw some turtles, too. However, I didn't see ~~some~~ *any* insects.

PROPER ADJECTIVES	EXAMPLES
A **proper adjective** is formed from a proper noun. It always begins with a capital letter.	There are many swamps in America. The **American** alligator is found in the southeastern United States.

ADJECTIVES THAT COMPARE	EXAMPLES
Adjectives can help you show how things are alike or different.	

Use a **comparative adjective** to show how **two** things are alike or different. Add **-er** to most adjectives. Also use **than**. Use **more. . .than** if the adjective has three or more syllables.	Deserts may be small or large. The Sechura Desert in South America is **smaller than** the Sahara Desert in Africa.  Sahara Desert Is the Sechura Desert **more interesting than** the Sahara Desert?
You can use either **-er** or **more** to make a comparison with some two-syllable adjectives. **Be sure not to use both**.	Most desert animals are ~~more~~ livelier at night than during the day. Desert flowers are ~~more~~ prettier than swamp grasses.
Use a **superlative adjective** to compare **three or more** things. Add **-est** to most adjectives. Use **the** before the adjective. Use **the most** with the adjective if it has three or more syllables.	The Sahara Desert is **the largest** desert in the world. The Libyan Desert has **the** world's **highest** record temperature. Both habitats have some of **the most interesting** animals in the world.
Some **adjectives** have **special forms** for comparing things: good bad some little better worse more less best worst most least	Today's weather in the desert is **bad**. Tomorrow's weather will be **worse**. Next week's weather is expected to be **the worst** of the summer.
Use **less** or **the least** to compare things you cannot count. Use **fewer** or **the fewest** to compare things you can count.	Deserts have **less** rainfall than swamps. Deserts have **the least** rainfall of any habitat. Some deserts have **fewer** days of rain than others. Which desert had **the fewest** number of visitors last year?

Verbs

Every sentence is divided into two parts: a subject and a predicate. The verb is the key word in the predicate. A verb tells what a subject does or links words in a sentence.

ACTION VERBS	EXAMPLES
An **action verb** tells what the subject does. Most verbs are action verbs.	The dancers **leap** across the stage. The spotlight **shines** on the lead dancers. Each dancer **twirls** around and around.
Some **action verbs** tell about an action that you cannot see.	The audience **enjoys** the lively music.

Ballet dancer

LINKING VERBS	EXAMPLES
A **linking verb** connects, or links, the subject of a sentence to a word in the predicate.	The dancers **look** powerful.
The word in the predicate can describe the subject.	Their costumes **are** colorful.
Or, the word in the predicate can be another way to name the subject.	These dancers **are** ballerinas.

Linking Verbs

Forms of the Verb be

am	was
is	were
are	

Other Linking Verbs

appear	seem	become
feel	smell	taste
look		

HELPING VERBS	EXAMPLES
Some verbs are made up of more than one word. The last word is called the **main verb**. It shows the action. The verb that comes before is the **helping verb**.	Ballet dancers **are regarded** as athletes and storytellers. They **can jump** high into the air. They **might leap** several feet across the stage. They **are building** up muscle strength.

HELPING VERBS, continued	EXAMPLES
The **helping verb** agrees with the subject.	The dancers **have** **practiced** for hours. The exercise **has** **made** them strong.
The word <u>not</u> always comes between the **helping verb** and the main verb.	The dancers **do** <u>not</u> **tell** a story in the usual way.
Other <u>adverbs</u> can come between a **helping verb** and the **main verb,** or appear in other places in the sentence.	They **will** <u>never</u> **use** their voices to tell a story. The story **is** <u>always</u> **told** through their graceful movements. <u>Often</u> slow movements **will** **show** an emotion like sadness. Happiness **is** **shown** <u>best</u> by quick, springy movements.
In questions, the <u>subject</u> comes between the **helping verb** and the **main verb**.	**Have** <u>you</u> **seen** a performance? **Does** <u>your family</u> **enjoy** ballet?

Helping Verbs

Forms of the Verb *be*

am	was
is	were
are	

Forms of the Verb *do*

do	did
does	

Forms of the Verb *have*

have	had
has	

Other Helping Verbs

To express ability:
>   I **can** dance.
>   I **could** do the jump.

To express possibility:
>   I **may** dance tonight.
>   I **might** dance tonight.
>   Perhaps I **could** do the dance.

To express a need or want:
>   I **must** dance more often.
>   I **would** like to dance more often.

To express an intent:
>   I **will** dance more often.

To express something you ought to do:
>   I **should** practice more often.
>   I **ought** to practice more often.

Verbs, continued

TRANSITIVE VERBS	EXAMPLES
Action verbs can be transitive or intransitive. A **transitive verb** needs an **object** to complete its meaning. The object receives the action of the verb.	**Not complete:** Many cities **use** **Complete:** Many cities **use fireworks**. **Not complete:** Fireworks **make** **Complete:** Fireworks **make noise**. **Not complete:** They also **provide** **Complete:** They also **provide** a good **celebration**.
The object can be a **direct object**. A direct object answers one of these questions: • Whom? • What?	The noise **surprises** the **audience**. The people in the audience **cover** their **ears**.

INTRANSITIVE VERBS	EXAMPLES
An **intransitive verb** does not need an object to complete its meaning.	**Complete:** The people in our neighborhood **cheer**. They **shout**. They **laugh**.
An **intransitive verb** may end the sentence, or it may be followed by other words that tell how, where, or when. These additional words are not objects since they do not receive the action of the verb.	The fireworks **glow** brightly. Then slowly, they **disappear** in the sky. The show **ends** by midnight. Fireworks

PRESENT TENSE VERBS	EXAMPLES
The tense of a verb shows when an action happens.	
The **present tense** of a verb tells about an action that is happening now.	My mom **looks** at her charts. She **checks** her computer screen.
The **present tense** of a verb can also tell about an action that happens regularly or all the time.	My mom **works** for the local TV station. She **is** a weather forecaster. She **reports** the weather every night at 5 p.m.
The **present progressive** form of a verb tells about an action as it is happening. It uses the helping verb **am, is,** or **are** and a main verb. The main verb ends in **-ing**.	Right now, she **is getting** ready for the show. "I can't believe it!" she says. "I **am looking** at the biggest storm of the century!" " **Are** those high winds **traveling** toward the coast?" asks her boss.

PAST TENSE VERBS	EXAMPLES
The **past tense** of a verb tells about an action that happened earlier, or in the past.	Yesterday, my mom **warned** everyone about the hurricane. The storm **moved** over the ocean toward land. We **did** not **know** exactly when it would hit.
The past tense form of a **regular verb** ends with **-ed**. See page 469 for spelling rules.	The shop owners in our town **covered** their windows with wood. We **closed** our shutters and **stayed** inside.
Irregular verbs have **special forms** to show the past tense. See the chart on pages 450–451.	The storm **hit** land. The sky **grew** very dark. It **began** to rain.

Some Irregular Verbs

Present Tense	Past Tense
begin	began
do	did
grow	grew
hit	hit

Verbs, continued

PAST TENSE VERBS, continued	EXAMPLES
The **past progressive** form of a verb tells about an action that was happening over a period of time in the past. It uses the helping verb **was** or **were** and a main verb. The main verb ends in **-ing**.	The wind **was blowing** at high speeds. Our shutters **were** really **shaking** during the storm. **Were** the trees **falling** down?

FUTURE TENSE VERBS	EXAMPLES
The **future tense** of a verb tells about an action that will happen later, or in the future. To show future tense, use: • the helping verb **will** plus a main verb. • the phrase **am going to**, **is going to**, or **are going to** plus a verb.	After the storm, everyone **will come** out of their houses. They **will inspect** the damage. I **am going to take** the tree branches out of my yard. The city **is** not **going to clean** every street. We **are** all **going to help** each other. **Are** you **going to help**?
The **future progressive** form of a verb tells about an action that will be happening during a period of time in the future. It uses the helping verbs **will be** plus a main verb. The main verb ends in **-ing**.	The weather forecasters **will be checking** radar screens for other storms. I **will be living** away from the shore as soon as possible! Wind damage from Hurricane Floyd, 1999

PERFECT TENSE VERBS	EXAMPLES

> **Verbs in the perfect tenses have a helping verb and a form of the main verb that is called the *past participle*.**
>
> For **regular verbs**, the past tense and the past participle end in **-ed**.
> Always use *has*, *have*, or *had* with the past participle.
>
> | **Regular Verb** | like | I like the Internet. |
> |---|---|---|
> | **Past Tense** | liked | I liked the Internet. |
> | **Past Participle** | liked | I have always liked the Internet. |
>
> **Irregular verbs** have special forms for the past tense and past participle.
> Always use *has*, *have*, or *had* with the past participle. See pages 450–451.
>
> | **Irregular Verb** | know | I know a lot about the Internet. |
> |---|---|---|
> | **Past Tense** | knew | I knew very little about the Internet last year. |
> | **Past Participle** | known | I have known about the Internet for a long time. |

The **present perfect tense** of a verb tells about an action that began in the past and is still going on. It uses the helping verb **has** or **have**.	The public **has used** the Internet since the mid-1980s. This year, we **have gone** to many different Web sites. The information on the Internet **has** not **been** hard to find. **Have** you **found** some interesting Web sites?
The **past perfect tense** of a verb tells about an action that was completed before some other action in the past. It uses the helping verb **had**.	Before the Internet became popular, people **had done** their research in the library. Librarians **had helped** people find information long before the invention of computers.
The **future perfect tense** of a verb tells about an action that will be completed at a specific time in the future. It uses the helping verbs **will have**.	By 2010, researchers **will have started** using a new Internet. By the end of next year, 100,000 people **will have visited** our Web site.
Verbs in the **perfect tenses** can describe ongoing action.	Our school librarian **has been using** the Internet for a long time. She **had been helping** us learn the Internet until last year. By graduation, we **will have been using** the Internet a lot.

Verbs, continued

Irregular Verb	Past Tense	Past Participle	Irregular Verb	Past Tense	Past Participle
be: am, is	was	been	eat	ate	eaten
are	were	been	fall	fell	fallen
beat	beat	beaten	feed	fed	fed
become	became	become	feel	felt	felt
begin	began	begun	fight	fought	fought
bend	bent	bent	find	found	found
bind	bound	bound	fly	flew	flown
bite	bit	bitten	forget	forgot	forgotten
blow	blew	blown	freeze	froze	frozen
break	broke	broken	get	got	got, gotten
bring	brought	brought			
build	built	built	give	gave	given
burst	burst	burst	go	went	gone
buy	bought	bought	grow	grew	grown
catch	caught	caught	have	had	had
choose	chose	chosen	hear	heard	heard
come	came	come	hide	hid	hidden
cost	cost	cost	hit	hit	hit
creep	crept	crept	hold	held	held
cut	cut	cut	hurt	hurt	hurt
dig	dug	dug	keep	kept	kept
do	did	done	know	knew	known
draw	drew	drawn	lay	laid	laid
dream	dreamed, dreamt	dreamed, dreamt	lead	led	led
			leave	left	left
drink	drank	drunk	lend	lent	lent
drive	drove	driven	let	let	let

Irregular Verb	Past Tense	Past Participle	Irregular Verb	Past Tense	Past Participle
lie	lay	lain	sink	sank	sunk
light	lit	lit	sit	sat	sat
lose	lost	lost	sleep	slept	slept
make	made	made	slide	slid	slid
mean	meant	meant	speak	spoke	spoken
meet	met	met	spend	spent	spent
pay	paid	paid	stand	stood	stood
prove	proved	proved, proven	steal	stole	stolen
			stick	stuck	stuck
put	put	put	sting	stung	stung
quit	quit	quit	strike	struck	struck
read	read	read	swear	swore	sworn
ride	rode	ridden	swim	swam	swum
ring	rang	rung	swing	swung	swung
rise	rose	risen	take	took	taken
run	ran	run	teach	taught	taught
say	said	said	tear	tore	torn
see	saw	seen	tell	told	told
seek	sought	sought	think	thought	thought
sell	sold	sold	throw	threw	thrown
send	sent	sent	understand	understood	understood
set	set	set	wake	woke, waked	woken, waked
shake	shook	shaken			
show	showed	shown	wear	wore	worn
shrink	shrank	shrunk	weep	wept	wept
shut	shut	shut	win	won	won
sing	sang	sung	write	wrote	written

Verbs, continued

TWO-WORD VERBS	EXAMPLES
A **two-word verb** is a verb followed by a preposition. The meaning of the two-word verb is different from the meaning of the verb by itself.	I like to **call** you, but you never answer me. The coach **calls off** the game because of the rain. The workers **call for** higher pay.

Some Two-Word Verbs

Verb	Meaning	Example
break	to split into pieces	I didn't **break** the window with the ball.
break down	to stop working	Did the car **break down** again?
break up	to end	The party will **break up** before midnight.
	to come apart	The ice on the lake will **break up** in the spring.
bring	to carry something with you	**Bring** your book to class.
bring up	to suggest	She **brings up** good ideas at every meeting.
	to raise children	**Bring up** your children to be good citizens.
check	to make sure you are right	We can **check** our answers at the back of the book.
check in	to stay in touch with someone	I **check in** with my mom at work.
check up	to see if everything is okay	The nurse **checks up** on the patient every hour.
check off	to mark off a list	Look at your list and **check off** the girls' names.
check out	to look at something carefully	Hey, Marisa, **check out** my new bike!
fill	to put as much as possible into a container or space	**Fill** the pail with water.
fill in	to color or shade in a space	Please **fill in** the circle.
fill out	to complete	Marcos **fills out** a form to order a book.
get	to go after something	I'll **get** some milk at the store.
	to receive	I often **get** letters from my pen pal.
get ahead	to go beyond what is expected of you	She worked hard to **get ahead** in math class.
get along	to be on good terms with	Do you **get along** with your sister?
get out	to leave	Let's **get out** of the kitchen.
get over	to feel better	I hope you'll **get over** the flu soon.
get through	to finish	I can **get through** this book tonight.

Some Two-Word Verbs

Verb	Meaning	Example
give	to hand something to someone	We **give** presents to the new baby.
give out	to stop working	If she runs ten miles, her energy will **give out**.
give up	to quit	I'm going to **give up** eating candy.
go	to move from place to place	Did you **go** to the mall on Saturday?
go on	to continue	Why do the boys **go on** playing after the bell rings?
go out	to go someplace special	Let's **go out** to lunch on Saturday.
look	to see or watch	Don't **look** directly at the sun.
look forward	to be excited about something that will happen	My brothers **look forward** to summer vacation.
look over	to review	She always **looks over** her answers before she gives the teacher her test.
look up	to hunt for and find	We **look up** information on the Internet.
pick	to choose	I'd **pick** Lin for class president.
pick on	to bother or tease	My older brothers always **pick on** me.
pick up	to go faster	Business **picks up** in the summer.
	to gather or collect	**Pick up** your clothes!
run	to move quickly on foot	Juan will **run** in a marathon.
run into	to see someone you know unexpectedly	Did you **run into** Chris at the store?
run out	to suddenly have nothing left	The cafeteria always **runs out** of nachos.
stand	to be in a straight up-and-down position	I have to **stand** in line to buy tickets.
stand for	to represent	A heart **stands for** love.
stand out	to be easier to see	You'll really **stand out** with that orange cap.
turn	to change direction	We **turn** right at the next corner.
turn up	to appear	Clean your closet and your belt will **turn up**.
	to raise the volume	Please **turn up** the radio.
turn in	to go to bed	On school nights I **turn in** at 9:30.
	to give back	You didn't **turn in** the homework yesterday.
turn off	to make something stop	Please **turn off** the radio.

Verbs, continued

ACTIVE AND PASSIVE VERBS	EXAMPLES
A verb is **active** if the **subject** is doing the action.	In this sentence, the subject—Mr. Ingram—does the selling: **Mr. Ingram sold** hamburgers for a nickel in 1921.
A verb is **passive** if the **subject** is not doing the action.	In this sentence, Mr. Ingram still does the selling, but he is not the subject. He is named after the word **by**. **Hamburgers were sold** by Mr. Ingram for a nickel in 1921. Sometimes the person or thing doing the action may not be named. **Hamburgers were sold** for a nickel in 1921.

VERBALS	EXAMPLES
	A verbal is a word made from a verb but used as another part of speech.
An **infinitive** is a verb form that begins with **to**. It can be used as a noun, an adjective, or an adverb.	Mr. Ingram liked **to cook**. <u>noun</u> When you go to the hamburger stand, Mr. Ingram is the man **to see**. <u>adjective</u> Mr. Ingram cooks **to have** fun. <u>adverb</u>
A **gerund** is a verb form that ends in **-ing**. It is used as a noun. It can be the subject of a sentence, the object of a verb, or the object of a preposition.	**Cooking** was Mr. Ingram's best talent. <u>subject</u> Mr. Ingram enjoys **cooking**. <u>object of the verb</u> Mr. Ingram was very talented at **cooking**. <u>object of the preposition</u>
A **participle** is a verb form that is used as an adjective. It ends in **-ing** or **-ed**.	His **sizzling** hamburgers smelled good. He made them from **flattened** meatballs.
A **participle** can start a **phrase**. Be sure to place the phrase next to the noun it describes.	**Standing by the grill**, Mr. Ingram cooked the hamburgers. ***Not:*** Mr. Ingram cooked the hamburgers, **standing by the grill**.

Adverbs

An adverb tells more about a verb, an adjective, or another adverb.

USE OF ADVERBS	EXAMPLES
An **adverb** can tell about a **verb**. It can come before or after the verb.	Our team **always wins** our basketball games. The whole team **plays well**.
An **adverb** can make an **adjective** or another **adverb** stronger.	Gina is **really good** at basketball. She plays **extremely well**.

TYPES OF ADVERBS	EXAMPLES
Adverbs answer one of the following questions: • How? • Where? • When? • How much? or How often?	Gina **carefully** aims the ball. She tosses the ball **high**, but it misses the basket. She will try again **later**. She **usually** scores.

ADVERBS THAT COMPARE	EXAMPLES
Some **adverbs** compare actions. Add **-er** to compare two actions. Add **-est** to compare three or more actions.	Gina runs **fast**. Gina runs **faster** than her guard. Gina runs **the fastest** of all the players.
If the **adverb** ends in **-ly**, use **more** or **less** to compare two actions. Use **the most** or **the least** to compare three or more actions.	Gina aims **more carefully** than Jen. Jen aims **less carefully** than Gina. Gina aims **the most carefully** of all the players on her team. Jen aims **the least carefully** of all.
Be careful not to use an adjective when you need an adverb. Never use an adverb after a **linking verb**.	Everyone plays ~~fair~~ *fairly*. My teacher is ~~fairly~~.

Prepositions

A preposition comes at the beginning of a prepositional phrase. Prepositional phrases add details to sentences.

USES OF PREPOSITIONS	EXAMPLES
Some **prepositions** show location.	The Chávez Community Center is **by my house**. The pool is **behind the building**.
Some **prepositions** show time.	The Youth Club's party will start **after lunch**.
Some **prepositions** show direction.	Go **through the building** and **around the fountain** to get to the pool. The snack bar is **down the hall**.
Some **prepositions** have multiple uses.	We'll make new friends **at the party**. Meet me **at my house**. Come **at noon**.

PREPOSITIONAL PHRASES	EXAMPLES
A **prepositional phrase** starts with a **preposition** and ends with a noun or a pronoun. It includes all the words in between. The noun or pronoun is the **object of the preposition**.	I made a new friend **at the party**. Next week I'm going to the movies **with her**.

Some Prepositions

Location		Time	Direction	Other Prepositions	
above	near	after	across	about	for
behind	next to	before	around	against	from
below	off	during	down	along	of
beside	on	till	into	among	to
between	out	until	out of	as	with
by	outside		through	at	without
in	over		toward	except	
inside	under		up		

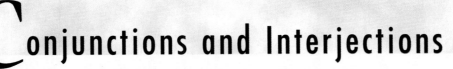

Conjunctions and Interjections

A conjunction connects words or groups of words.
An interjection expresses strong feeling.

CONJUNCTIONS	EXAMPLES
A **coordinating conjunction** connects words, phrases, or clauses.	The zoos in San Diego **and** Atlanta have giant pandas. In China, giant pandas can be found in the wild **or** in panda reserves. Pandas will eat other animals, **but** mostly they eat bamboo. **Coordinating Conjunctions** <table><tr><td>Conjunctions</td><td>Uses</td></tr><tr><td>**and**</td><td>To connect two ideas that are alike</td></tr><tr><td>**but, yet**</td><td>To show a difference between two ideas</td></tr><tr><td>**nor**</td><td>To put two negative ideas together</td></tr><tr><td>**or**</td><td>To show a choice between two ideas</td></tr><tr><td>**so, for**</td><td>To show how one idea follows another</td></tr></table>
Correlative conjunctions are used in pairs. The pair connects phrases or words.	In the past, pandas lived **not only** in central China **but also** in southern China and Vietnam. Now **both** the giant panda **and** the red panda are rare. **Either** a survey of wild pandas **or** protection of their habitat could help save the pandas. **Some Correlative Conjunctions** both . . . and either . . . or neither . . . nor not only . . . but also whether . . . or

Conjunctions and Interjections, continued

CONJUNCTIONS, continued	EXAMPLES
A **subordinating conjunction** introduces a **dependent clause** in a complex sentence. It connects the **dependent clause** to the main clause.	Pandas can't find enough bamboo to eat **because their habitat is being destroyed**. **If all the bamboo is wiped out**, the pandas will die. **Some Subordinating Conjunctions**<table><tr><td>after</td><td>before</td><td>till</td></tr><tr><td>although</td><td>if</td><td>until</td></tr><tr><td>as</td><td>in order that</td><td>when</td></tr><tr><td>as if</td><td>since</td><td>where</td></tr><tr><td>as long as</td><td>so that</td><td>while</td></tr><tr><td>because</td><td>though</td><td></td></tr></table>
A **conjunctive adverb** joins two independent clauses. Use a semicolon before the conjunction and a comma after it.	Pandas do not easily digest plants; **therefore,** they need to eat large amounts of bamboo. China has set aside bamboo-rich reserves for pandas; **however,** these reserves have not always supplied enough food for the pandas. **Some Conjunctive Adverbs**<table><tr><td>besides</td><td>meanwhile</td><td>then</td></tr><tr><td>consequently</td><td>moreover</td><td>therefore</td></tr><tr><td>however</td><td>nevertheless</td><td>thus</td></tr></table>

INTERJECTIONS	EXAMPLES
An **interjection** is a word or phrase that shows strong feeling. An exclamation mark follows an interjection that stands alone.	**Help!** **Ouch!** **Oops!** **Oh boy!** **Oh my!** **Wow!**
An interjection used in a sentence can be followed by a comma or an exclamation mark.	**Oh**, it's a baby panda! **Hooray!** The baby panda has survived!

Capital Letters

A reader can tell that a word is special in some way if it begins with a capital letter.

PROPER NOUNS	EXAMPLES

A common noun names any person, place, thing, or idea.
A proper noun names one particular person, place, thing, or idea.

All the important words in a **proper noun** start with a capital letter.

	Common Noun	Proper Noun
Person	captain	**C**aptain **M**eriwether **L**ewis
Place	land	**L**ouisiana **T**erritory
Thing	team	**C**orps of **D**iscovery
Idea	destiny	**M**anifest **D**estiny

Proper nouns include:

- names of people and their titles

Laura Roberts
Captain Meriwether Lewis

But: Do not capitalize a title if it is used without a name:
The captain's co-leader on the expedition was William Clark.

- abbreviations of titles

Mr. Ramos
Mrs. Ramos
Dr. Schuyler
Ms. Nguyen

Abbreviations of Titles

Capt. for the captain of a boat or in the armed forces

Pres. for the president of a country, a company, a club, or an organization

Sen. for a member of the U.S. Senate

Rep. for a member of the U.S. House of Representatives

- words like **Mom** and **Dad** when they are used as names

"**Mom**, can you tell me more about the expedition?" said Laura.

But: Do not capitalize names if they follow a word like my.
I ask my **mom** lots of questions.

- organizations

United Nations   Science Club   Wildlife Society   Lodi City Council

- names of languages, subject areas, and religions

Spanish   Mathematics   Buddhism
Vietnamese   Social Studies   Christianity

Capital Letters, continued

PROPER NOUNS, continued	EXAMPLES

- names of geographic places

Cities and States	Countries	Continents
Dallas, Texas	Iran	Asia
Miami, Florida	Ecuador	South America
St. Louis, Missouri	Cambodia	Africa

Streets and Roads	Landforms	Public Spaces
King Boulevard	Rocky Mountains	Hemisfair Plaza
Main Avenue	Sahara Desert	Central Park
First Street	Grand Canyon	Muir Camp

Bodies of Water	Buildings, Ships, and Monuments	Planets and Heavenly Bodies
Yellowstone River	Empire State Building	Earth
Pacific Ocean	*Titanic*	Jupiter
Great Salt Lake	Statue of Liberty	Milky Way
Gulf of Mexico		

- abbreviations of geographic places

Words Used in Addresses

Avenue	Ave.	Highway	Hwy.	South	S.
Boulevard	Blvd.	Lane	Ln.	Square	Sq.
Court	Ct.	North	N.	Street	St.
Drive	Dr.	Place	Pl.	West	W.
East	E.	Road	Rd.		

Abbreviations for State Names in Mailing Addresses

Alabama	AL	Hawaii	HI	Massachusetts	MA	New Mexico	NM	South Dakota	SD
Alaska	AK	Idaho	ID	Michigan	MI	New York	NY	Tennessee	TN
Arizona	AZ	Illinois	IL	Minnesota	MN	North Carolina	NC	Texas	TX
Arkansas	AR	Indiana	IN	Mississippi	MS	North Dakota	ND	Utah	UT
California	CA	Iowa	IA	Missouri	MO	Ohio	OH	Vermont	VT
Colorado	CO	Kansas	KS	Montana	MT	Oklahoma	OK	Virginia	VA
Connecticut	CT	Kentucky	KY	Nebraska	NE	Oregon	OR	Washington	WA
Delaware	DE	Louisiana	LA	Nevada	NV	Pennsylvania	PA	West Virginia	WV
Florida	FL	Maine	ME	New Hampshire	NH	Rhode Island	RI	Wisconsin	WI
Georgia	GA	Maryland	MD	New Jersey	NJ	South Carolina	SC	Wyoming	WY

- months, days, special days and holidays

January	July	Sunday	New Year's Day
February	August	Monday	Mother's Day
March	September	Tuesday	Thanksgiving
April	October	Wednesday	Hanukkah
May	November	Thursday	Kwanzaa
June	December	Friday	
		Saturday	

PROPER ADJECTIVES	EXAMPLES
A **proper adjective** is formed from a **proper noun**. Capitalize proper adjectives.	Napoleon Bonaparte was from **Europe**. He was a **European** leader in the 1800s. Napoleon ruled the country of **France**. He was the **French** emperor.

IN LETTERS	EXAMPLES
Capitalize the first word used in the **greeting** or in the **closing** of a letter. Street, city, and state names in the address, as well as their abbreviations, are also capitalized.	Dear Kim, I wish you could explore the Academy of Natural Sciences with me. I've learned so much about the flora and fauna that Lewis and Clark found. The museum even has some of the original samples! I'll tell you about it when I get home. See you soon. Your friend, Jamal Kim Messina 10250 W. Fourth St. Las Vegas, NV 89015

IN TITLES AND QUOTATIONS	EXAMPLES
Capitalize the **first word** in a **direct quotation**.	Clark said, "**There** is great joy in camp." "**We** are in view of the ocean," he said "**It's** the Pacific Ocean," he added. "**We** are finally here."
All important words in a **title** begin with a capital letter. Short words like *a, an, the, in, at, of,* and *for* are not capitalized unless they are the first or last word in the title.	**book:** *The Longest Journey* **poem:** "Leaves of Grass" **magazine:** *Flora and Fauna of Arizona* **newspaper:** *The Denver Post* **song:** "Star-Spangled Banner" **game:** Exploration! **TV series:** "Bonanza" **movie:** *The Lion King*

Punctuation Marks

Punctuation marks make words and sentences easier to understand.

PERIOD	EXAMPLES
Use a **period**:	
• at the end of a statement or a polite command	Georgia read the paper to her mom.
	Tell me if there are any interesting articles.
• after an abbreviation	There's a new restaurant on Stone St. near our house.
	It opens at 10 a.m. today.
	But: *Do not use a period in an acronym:*
	National Aeronautics and Space Administration **NASA**
	Do not use a period in the abbreviation of a state name written in a mailing address:
	Massachusetts **MA** Illinois **IL** Texas **TX** California **CA** Florida **FL** Virginia **VA**
• after an initial	The owner is J.J. Malone.
• to separate dollars and cents. The period is the decimal point.	The article says lunch today costs only $1.50.
• in an Internet address. The period is called a dot.	The restaurant has a Web site at www.jjmalone.com.

QUESTION MARK	EXAMPLES
Use a **question mark**:	
• at the end of a question	What kind of food do they serve**?**
• after a question that comes at the end of a statement	The food is good, isn't it**?**
	But: *Use a period after an indirect question. In an indirect question, you tell about a question you asked.*
	I asked how good the food could be for only $1.50.

EXCLAMATION MARK	EXAMPLES
Use an **exclamation mark**: • after an interjection • at the end of a sentence to show that you feel strongly about something	Wow**!** One-fifty is a really good price**!**

COMMA	EXAMPLES
Use a **comma**: • to separate three or more items in a series	Articles about the school**,** a big sale**,** and a new movie were also in the newspaper. The school will buy a new bus**,** 10 computers**,** and books for the library.
• when you write a number with four or more digits	There was $500**,**000 in the school budget.
• before the **coordinating conjunction** in a compound sentence. See page 457 for a list of coordinating conjunctions.	The school could buy books**, or** it could buy a sound system. All the teachers discussed it**, and** they decided books were more important.
• to set off a short word or phrase at the beginning of a sentence	Good**,** we really need some new books.
• to set off words that interrupt a sentence	Books about geography**,** for example**,** would be great additions to the library.
• before a question at the end of a statement	We need books on that topic**,** don't we?
• to set off the name of a person someone is talking to	Georgia, does the article say why the school is buying a new bus? Just a minute, Mom, let me look.
• between two or more adjectives that tell about the same noun	The old**,** rusty school bus is broken.

Punctuation Marks, continued

COMMA, continued	EXAMPLES
Use a **comma**:	
• before and after an appositive phrase. An **appositive phrase** renames the noun or pronoun before it.	Mr. Ivanovich**, the bus driver,** says the bus will cost too much to fix.
• after a long **introductory phrase**	**In the last few months,** the bus had to be fixed six times.
• after an **introductory clause**	**Because the bus is old,** it keeps breaking down.
• before someone's exact words	Mr. Ivanovich said**,** "It is time for a new bus!"
• after someone's exact words if the sentence continues	"I agree**,**" said the principal.
• before and after a **clause** if the clause is not necessary for understanding the sentence	At the end of the article**, where computers are discussed,** there is a letter by a student.
Use a **comma** in these places in a letter: • between the city and the state • between the date and the year • after the greeting • after the closing	144 North Ave. Milpas, AK July 3, 2002 Dear Mr. Okada, I really like computers and am glad that we have them at school, but ours are out-of-date. As principal, can you ask the school board to buy us new ones for next year? Sincerely, Patrick Green

SEMICOLON	EXAMPLES
Use a **semicolon**:	
• to separate two simple sentences used together without a conjunction	Some movies advertised in this paper look interesting; others don't.
• before a conjunctive adverb that joins two simple sentences. Use a **comma** after the adverb. See page 458 for a list of conjunctive adverbs.	I'd like to go to the movies today; however, my favorite store is having a sale.
• to separate a group of words in a series if the words in the series already have commas	It is selling warm, fluffy coats; green, red, and orange mittens; and summer shorts!

APOSTROPHE	EXAMPLES

Use an **apostrophe** when you write a **possessive noun**.
 	
• If there is one owner, add **'s** to the owner's name.
	The **newspaper's** ads for yard sales are interesting, too.
	But: *If the owner's name ends in* s, *you can add* **'s** *or just the apostrophe. Either is correct.*
	
	    Mrs. Ramos's chair is for sale.
	    Mrs. Ramos' chair is for sale.

• If there is more than one owner, add **'** after the **s**.	The **Martins'** dog had puppies, and I want to buy one. ***But:*** *If the plural noun that names the owners does not end in* s, *add* **'s**. The **Children's** Choir is holding a yard sale.

Use an **apostrophe** to replace the letters left out in a **contraction**.
 	
• In contractions with a verb and **not**, the word **not** is usually shortened to **n't**.
	could nøt
	couldn't I **couldn't** go to the yard sale. ***Exceptions:***
	                                       cannøt can't
	                                         will nøt won't
	                                         I ám not I'm not

• In many other contractions, the verb is shortened.	I would I'd **I'd** like to see the vase you bought.

Punctuation Marks, continued

QUOTATION MARKS	EXAMPLES
Use **quotation marks** to show	
• a speaker's exact words	"Listen to this!" Georgia said.
• the exact words quoted from a book or other printed material	The announcement in the paper was "The world-famous writer Josie Ramón will be at Milpas Library Friday night."
• the title of a song, poem, or short story	Her poem "Speaking" is famous.
• the title of a magazine article or newspaper article	It appeared in the magazine article "How to Talk to Your Teen."
• the title of a chapter from a book	On Friday night she'll be reading "Getting Along," a chapter from her new book.
• words used in a special way	We will be "all ears" at the reading.
Always put **periods** and **commas** inside quotation marks.	"She is such a great writer," Georgia said. " I'd love to meet her."

COLON	EXAMPLES
Use a **colon**:	356 Oak St.
• after the greeting in a business letter	Milpas, AK
	Sept. 24, 2002
• to separate hours and minutes	Features Editor
	Milpas Post
• to start a list	78 Main St.
	Milpas, AK
	Dear Sir or Madam:
	Please place this announcement in the calendar section of your paper. Friday at 7:15 p.m., the writer Josie Ramón will be speaking at Milpas Library. When people come, they should bring:
	1. Questions for Ms. Ramón.
	2. Money to purchase her new book.
	3. A cushion to sit on!
	Thank you.
	Sincerely,
	Hector Quintana

DASH	EXAMPLES
Use a **dash** to • show a break in an idea or the tone in a sentence • emphasize a word, a series of words, a phrase, or a clause	It's so helpful to read the paper—I really like the ads—to find out what is happening in town. There's so much information here—restaurant openings, store sales, news stories about people in our town.
PARENTHESES	EXAMPLES
Use **parentheses** around extra information in a sentence.	This news story (written by my mom) is very interesting!
HYPHEN	EXAMPLES
Use a **hyphen** to • connect words in a number and in a fraction • join some words to make a compound word • connect a letter to a word • divide words at the end of a line. Always divide the word between two syllables.	The news story reported on a survey of **seventy-five** people. **One-third** of them wasted water everyday. A **15-year-old** boy and his **great-grandmother** have started an awareness campaign. They have sent **e-mail** messages to everyone they know. They also designed a **T-shirt** for their campaign. Please join us in our aware- ness campaign.
ITALICS AND UNDERLINES	EXAMPLES
When you are using a computer, use **italics** for the names of • magazines and newspapers • books • plays, movies, musicals, music albums, and TV series When you write by hand, use an **underline** to indicate italics.	I just read an article about a good book in the *Milpas Post*. The name of the book is *My Hopes and Dreams*. The article said the new movie *All About Jack* is based on this book. The <u>Milpas Post</u> gave that new movie, <u>All About Jack</u>, a great review.

Spelling

Follow these rules and your spelling will get better and better.

HOW TO BE A BETTER SPELLER

Spelling Tips

1. To learn a new word:
   - Study the word and look up its meaning.
   - Say the word out loud. Listen as you repeat it again.
   - Picture how the word looks.
   - Spell the word out loud several times.
   - Write the word five or ten times for practice. Try to use the word often in a sentence until you are sure you know its spelling.
2. Learn the following spelling rules.
3. Use a dictionary to check your spelling.
4. Keep a notebook of words that are hard for you to spell.

Q + U	EXAMPLES
Always put a **u** after a **q**.	The **qu**ick but **qu**iet **qu**arterback asked **qu**antities of **qu**estions. ***Exceptions:*** Iraq Iraqi

IE, EI	EXAMPLES
Use **i** before **e** except after **c**.	The f**ie**rce rec**ei**ver was always ready to catch the ball. ***Exceptions:*** • **ei**ther, h**ei**ght, th**ei**r, w**ei**rd, s**ei**ze • w**ei**gh, n**ei**ghbor (and other words where **ei** has the long **a** sound)

PLURALS	EXAMPLES
To form the plural of a noun that ends in **x**, **ch**, **sh**, **s**, or **z**, add **-es**. For most other nouns, just add **-s**.	Their team was called the Fox**es**. Their players made great catch**es** in the end zone.

Y TO I	EXAMPLES
If a word ends in a consonant plus **y**, change the **y** to **i** before you add **-es**, **-ed**, **-er**, or **-est**.	The coach was the happ**iest** when his players tr**ied** their best.
For words that end in a **vowel** plus **y**, just add **-s** or **-ed**.	For five day**s** before the game, the team stay**ed** at practice an extra 30 minutes.
If you add **-ing** to a verb that ends in **-y**, do not change the **y** to **i**.	The players learned a lot from study**ing** videos of their games.

-ED, -ING, -ER, -EST	EXAMPLES
When a word ends in silent **e**, drop the **e** before you add **-ed**, **-ing**, **-er**, or **-est**.	The players notic**ed** what they did wrong. Lat**er**, they talked about their mistakes.
When a one-syllable word ends in one vowel and one consonant, double the final consonant before you add an ending.	Then they pla**nn**ed some new plays for the game. They got set for their **biggest** challenge.

PREFIXES AND SUFFIXES	EXAMPLES
Add a **prefix** to the beginning of a root word. Do not change the spelling of the **root word**.	They **replayed** the video often. The team never got **discouraged**.
When you add a consonant **suffix**, do not change the spelling of the **root word**.	We had a **lovely** day for the game. **Exception:** happy happiness
For most **root words** that end in silent **e**, drop the **e** before adding a vowel **suffix**.	Our quarterback won the Most **Valuable** Player award for the game.

Some Prefixes and Suffixes

Prefixes

anti-	in-	pre-
bi-	im-	re-
dis-	inter-	sub-
extra-	mis-	un-

Suffixes Beginning with a Consonant

-ful	-ly	-ness
-less	-ment	-tion

Suffixes Beginning with a Vowel

-able	-ent	-ish
-al	-er	-ive
-ant	-ible	-ous

Glossary of Literary Terms

Action/Reaction Action/reaction is the connection between one action or event and another that occurs as a result.

> See also **Characterization**

Advertisement An advertisement is a public notice of something that is for sale. It generally uses persuasive techniques.

> See also **Persuasion**

Alliteration Alliteration is the repetition of the same or similar consonant sounds at the beginning of words. An example is

> She sells sea shells by the seashore.

> See also **Assonance; Consonance**

Allusion An allusion is a reference to something familiar, such as a well-known person, place, thing, or event. For example, the title of the article "Home, Sweet Home Page" alludes to the common phrase "Home, Sweet Home."

Analogy An analogy is a comparison between two things that are similar in certain ways and different in other ways.

> See also **Metaphor**

Article An article is a short piece of nonfiction writing on a specific topic. Articles usually appear in newspapers and magazines.

> Examples: **"Space Exploration," "Dealing with Conflict: Finding Resolution"**

Assonance Assonance is the repetition of the same or similar vowel sounds between different consonants in words that are close together. For example, in "Out of the Dust," the author uses assonance in the line "Daddy looks like a fight brewing." The long *i* sound is heard in both *like* and *fight*.

> See also **Alliteration; Consonance**

Autobiography An autobiography is the story of a person's life written by that person.

> Example: **"Something to Declare"**

Biographical Fiction Biographical fiction is a story that tells the facts of a real person's life and includes fictional details as well. It may be written from the point of view of a real or an imaginary character; the conversations are usually invented.

Biography A biography is the story of a person's life written by another person.

> Examples: **"Lewis and Clark," "Aimee Mullins: World-Class Athlete"**

Cause and Effect Cause and effect is the relationship between two events. The one that happens first, the cause, brings about the effect that follows. These sentences from "Breaking Away From Great Britain" illustrate cause and effect:

> The British realize they cannot win the war. They sign a peace treaty with the United States of America.

Chant A chant is a type of poetry that is meant to be read aloud. It has a strong beat and musical language.

> Example: **"The Bill of Rights Rap"**

Character A person, animal, or imaginary creature in a story is called a character.

> See also **Characterization; Character Traits**

Characterization Characterization is the way a writer creates and develops a character. Writers use a variety of ways to bring a character to life: through descriptions of the character's appearance, thoughts, feelings, and actions; through the character's words; through the words or thoughts of other characters.

See also **Character Traits; Motive; Point of View**

Character Sketch A character sketch is a short, vivid description of a person.

See also **Characterization; Character Traits**

Character Traits Character traits are the special qualities of personality that writers give their characters.

See also **Character; Characterization**

Climax The climax of a story or play is the turning point or most important event. At the climax, the resolution of the story is in sight. For example, in "Windrider's Dream," the climax occurs when Dragonwings crashes.

See also **Plot**

Complication Complication is part of the plot. It includes the events in a story that make it difficult for characters to solve problems.

See also **Conflict and Resolution; Plot; Rising Action and Falling Action**

Compressed Language Compressed language is the use of only a few words to convey a great deal of meaning. Poets often use compressed language.

Conflict and Resolution Conflict and resolution are parts of the plot of a story. Conflict describes the problem a character has, and resolution tells how or if the problem is solved.

See also **Plot**

Consonance Consonance is the repetition of the final consonant sound preceded by different vowel sounds. An example from "Roads Go Ever Ever On" is

By caves where never sun has shone

See also **Alliteration; Assonance**

Description A description is writing that tells about a person, place, or thing. It often uses images that appeal to the five senses: sight, sound, touch, smell, and taste. For example, in "Listening for a Voice," Joseph Bruchac vividly describes what that voice might sound like:

Or it might not be a human sound—
just the whirring whistle of the wings
of three loons circling, circling
a June-blue Adirondack pond.

Dialect Dialect is a form of language that is spoken in a certain place or by a particular group of people. Dialect includes special words or phrases, as well as particular pronunciation and grammar. Writers use dialect to make their characters and settings more realistic.

Examples in **"Out of the Dust"**

Dialogue Dialogue is what characters say to one another. Writers use dialogue to develop characters, move the plot forward, and add interest. In most writing, dialogue is set off by quotation marks; in play scripts, however, dialogue appears without quotation marks.

Glossary of Literary Terms, continued

Diary A diary is a book written by a person about his or her own life as it is happening. It is made up of entries that are written shortly after the events occur. The writer of a diary often expresses feelings and opinions about what has happened.

Essay An essay is a short piece of nonfiction writing that deals with a single subject. Its purpose may be to inform, to entertain, or to persuade.

Exaggeration Exaggeration is saying that something is bigger or more important than it actually is.

See also **Hyperbole**

Fable A fable is a short story that teaches a lesson about life. Many fables have animals instead of humans as characters. Fables often state the lesson they are teaching at the end.

Fantasy Fantasy is writing that includes unreal or magical characters and events. Fairy tales, science fiction, and fables are examples of fantasy.

See also **Science Fiction**

Fiction Fiction is writing that is made up by the writer. The events and characters may be based in part on reality, as in biographical, historical, or realistic fiction; or they may be made up entirely. Fiction includes novels and short stories.

See also **Biographical Fiction; Historical Fiction; Realistic Fiction; Science Fiction**

Figurative Language Figurative language is the use of words or phrases to express something different than their usual meanings. Writers use figurative language to say things in vivid and imaginative ways, but what they say is not really true. Hyperbole, imagery, metaphor, personification, and simile are examples of figurative language.

See also **Hyperbole; Imagery; Metaphor; Personification; Simile**

Flashback A flashback is an interruption in the action of a story to tell about something that happened earlier. It is often used to give the reader background information about a character or situation.

Example in **"The Dance"**

Folk Tale A folk tale is a very old and simple story that has been passed down through the years. Most folk tales were told for generations before they were written down.

Example: **"The Deer Prince"**

Foreshadowing Foreshadowing is a hint that an author gives about an event that will happen later in a story.

Example in **"The Lady, or The Tiger?"**

Free Verse Free verse is poetry with lines that do not have regular rhyme and regular rhythm. Free verse often sounds like ordinary speech.

Examples: **"Saying Yes"** from **"Between Two Worlds,"** **"Caged Bird"**

See also **Poetry; Rhyme; Rhythm**

Genre Genre is a kind or type of literature. The four main genres are fiction, nonfiction, poetry, and drama.

Goal and Outcome Goal and outcome are the parts of the plot that tell what a character's ambition is and whether he or she attains it.

See also **Plot**

Historical Account An historical account is a piece of nonfiction writing about something that happened in the past.

Example: **"The Dirty Thirties"**

Historical Fiction Historical fiction is a story based on events that actually happened or people who actually lived. It may be written from the point of view of a real or an imaginary character, and it usually includes invented dialogue.

Examples: **"Amistad Rising," "Windrider's Dream"**

How-to Article A how-to article is a short piece of writing that gives step-by-step directions for making or doing something.

Example: **"Home, Sweet Home Page"**

Hyperbole Hyperbole is extreme exaggeration for the purpose of emphasis or humor. The line "My heart was beating out of my chest" from "The Truth About Sharks" is an example of hyperbole.

See also **Exaggeration**

Imagery Imagery is the use of words and phrases that create mental pictures in readers' minds. It helps readers imagine how things look, sound, taste, smell, and feel. Because it appeals to the five senses, it is sometimes called sensory language.

See also **Figurative Language**

Interview An interview is a meeting between two people in which one person asks questions of the other one.

Example: **"Inspiration: An Interview with Tish Hinojosa"**

Irony Irony is a contrast between what is said and what is actually meant, or between what is expected and what actually happens. For example, it is ironic that in "Amistad Rising," the name of the slave ship—*Amistad*—is the Spanish word for "friendship."

Journal A journal is a personal record. It may include accounts of events, stories, poems, sketches, thoughts, essays, interesting information one has collected, or just about anything the journal writer wishes to include. It is similar to a diary.

Example: **"Out of the Dust"**

Legend A legend is a traditional story about a famous person or event. The subject of a legend can be a real or a make-believe person. Legends often contain elements of fantasy and usually exaggerate the subject's personal qualities or accomplishments.

Letter A letter is a message written and sent from one person to another. Letters can be personal and private, or public, as a letter to the editor of a newspaper is.

Examples in **"Dealing with Conflict: Finding Resolution"**

Memoir A memoir is a short autobiographical piece of writing.

Example: **"Melba's Choice"**

Metaphor A metaphor is a kind of figurative language that compares two unlike things by saying that one thing is the other thing. The line "Ma had been tumbleweed too" in "Out of The Dust" is a metaphor.

See also **Figurative Language; Simile**

Glossary of Literary Terms, continued

Meter Meter is a pattern of stressed and unstressed syllables in poetry.

See also **Rhythm**

Mood and Tone Mood is the overall feeling that a piece of writing gives to the reader. For example, the poems in "Out of the Dust" create a feeling of hopelessness. Tone is the author's attitude toward what he or she wrote. The tone of "Out of the Dust" is compassionate.

Motive A motive is the reason a character has for his or her thoughts, feelings, actions, or words. For example, in "The Lady, or the Tiger?" the princess is motivated by both jealousy and love. The fate of the prisoner rests upon which of these motives turns out to be stronger.

See also **Characterization**

Myth A myth is a very old story that explains something about the world. Myths often involve gods, goddesses, and other superhuman characters.

Narrative Poetry Narrative poetry is poetry that tells a story. It has characters, a setting, and a plot; it may include elements of poetry, such as rhythm and rhyme.

Example: **"Out of the Dust"**

See also **Poetry**

Nonfiction Nonfiction is writing that tells about real people, real places, and real events.

Examples: **"Lewis and Clark,"**
"Space Exploration"

Onomatopoeia Onomatopoeia is the use of words that imitate the sounds associated with the things they describe. *Buzz*, for the sound of a bee; *hiss*, for the sound of a snake; and *gurgle*, for the sound of a stream are examples of onomatopoeia.

Pantomime Pantomime is communication through the use of gestures, body movements, and facial expressions, rather than through speech.

Personification In personification, animals, things, or ideas are described as having human characteristics. An example of personification from "Out of the Dust" is

. . . lightning danced down on its spindly legs

Persuasion Persuasion is an attempt to affect the feelings, beliefs, and actions of others. Persuasion is used in advertisements, editorials, sermons, and political speeches. For example, the students in "Dealing with Conflict: Finding Resolution" who write letters to the editor take positions "for" and "against" instituting a peer mediation program in their school. The purpose of each letter is to persuade other students to agree with the writer's point of view.

Photo-Essay A photo-essay is a short nonfiction piece made up of photographs and captions. The photographs are as important as the words in giving information to the reader.

Example: **"The Lion King Goes to Broadway"**

Play A play is a story written to be performed by actors on a stage. In most plays, a story is told through the words and actions of actors in the roles of different characters.

Plot Plot is the series of events that makes up a story, play, or narrative poem. Plot is usually divided into four parts: problem or conflict, complication, climax, and resolution.

See also **Climax; Complication; Conflict and Resolution; Problem and Solution; Rising Action and Falling Action**

Poetry Poetry is a kind of writing that expresses ideas in few words. Poets often choose words and phrases that appeal to our senses. Many poems are arranged in sections called stanzas and use rhythm and rhyme.

Examples: **"Caged Bird," "The Road Not Taken"**

See also **Imagery; Rhyme; Rhythm; Stanza**

Point of View Point of view is the particular view from which a story is told. In a story told from the first-person point of view, the narrator is a character in the story who uses words such as *I*, *me*, and *we*. A story told from the third-person point of view is told by a narrator outside the story who uses words such as *he*, *she*, and *they*.

Example of first-person point of view: **"User Friendly"**

Example of third-person point of view: **"Amistad Rising"**

Problem and Solution Problems and solutions are parts of the plot of a story. Problems are described at the beginning of a story. Solutions are described at the end.

See also **Plot**

Realistic Fiction Realistic fiction is literature about imaginary characters who really could exist and imaginary events that could actually happen.

Examples: **"The Truth About Sharks," "The Dance"**

Repetition Repetition is the repeating of words or phrases to create an effect. For example, in "Out of the Dust," the narrator repeats the words "they say" to suggest that she does not believe what is being said.

See also **Rhythm**

Report A report is a short piece of nonfiction writing on a particular topic. It is different from an essay in that it usually includes only facts and does not express opinions.

Rhyme Rhyme is the repetition of sounds at the ends of words. Rhyme helps create rhythm and adds a musical quality to the poetry.

Examples in **"Roads Go Ever Ever On"**

Rhyme Scheme Rhyme scheme is the pattern of rhyme in a poem.

See also **Rhyme**

Rhythm Rhythm is a musical quality resulting from the repetition of stressed and unstressed syllables in poetry. Rhythm is also created by the repetition of words, phrases, and sentences.

Rising Action and Falling Action Rising action and falling action are parts of the plot. Actions or events that lead to the climax are the rising action. The actions or events that follow the climax are the falling action.

See also **Climax; Complication; Plot; Conflict and Resolution**

Science Fiction Science fiction is a story based on real or imaginary scientific discoveries. It often takes place in the future.

Example: **"User Friendly"**

Sensory Language *See* **Imagery**

Glossary of Literary Terms, continued

Setting The setting is the time and the place in which the events of a story occur. The setting of "Passage to Freedom," for example, is a small town in Lithuania in the year 1940.

Short Story A short story is a short fiction piece that has a single problem and a simple plot.

> Example: **"The Lady, or the Tiger?"**

Simile A simile is a comparison between two unlike things that uses the words *like*, *as*, or *than*. Similes are one kind of figurative language. An example from "Something to Declare" is

> a sash like an old-world general's belt of ammunition

Stanza A stanza is a group of lines that form a unit in a poem. A stanza in a poem is similar to a paragraph in prose writing. Stanzas are separated by spaces.

> Examples in **"Caged Bird"**

Story A story is a piece of fiction writing that has characters, a setting, and a plot.

Style Style is a particular way of writing. It is developed through choice of words, tone, sentence length, and use of imagery and dialogue.

> *See also* **Word Choice**

Suspense Suspense is a feeling of curiosity, tension, or excitement in the reader. Suspense makes the reader want to find out what is going to happen next. For example, in "The Lady, or the Tiger?" the writer creates suspense when he leaves the reader wondering whether the lady or the tiger is behind the door the young man opens.

Symbol A symbol is something that stands for something else. It can be a person, an animal, a place, or an object. For example, in the poem "Roads Go Ever Ever On," the road is a symbol for life's journey.

Theme A theme is the main idea in a work of literature. It is often a message that can be expressed very simply. For example, the theme of "Passage to Freedom" is that helping others often involves taking personal risks.

Tone *See* **Mood and Tone**

Word Choice Word choice is the kind of language an author uses. Word choice is one of the elements that contribute to style.

> *See also* **Style**

Glossary of Key Vocabulary

Many words have more than one meaning. The definitions in this glossary are for the words as they are introduced in the selections in this book.

Pronunciation Key

Symbols for Consonant Sounds

b	box		p	pan	
ch	chick		r	ring	
d	dog		s	bus	
f	fish		sh	fish	
g	girl		t	hat	
h	hat		th	Earth	
j	jar		th	father	
k	cake		v	vase	
ks	box		w	window	
kw	queen		wh	whale	
l	bell		y	yarn	
m	mouse		z	zipper	
n	pan		zh	treasure	
ng	ring				

Symbols for Short Vowel Sounds

a	hat	
e	bell	
i	chick	
o	box	
u	bus	

Symbols for Long Vowel Sounds

ā	cake	
ē	key	
ī	bike	
ō	goat	
yū	mule	

Symbols for R-controlled Sounds

ar	barn	
air	chair	
ear	ear	
īr	fire	
or	corn	
ur	girl	

Symbols for Variant Vowel Sounds

ah	father	
aw	ball	
oi	boy	
ow	mouse	
oo	book	
ü	fruit	

Miscellaneous Symbols

shun	fraction	$\frac{1}{2}$
chun	question	?
zhun	division	$2\overline{)100}^{50}$

Parts of an Entry

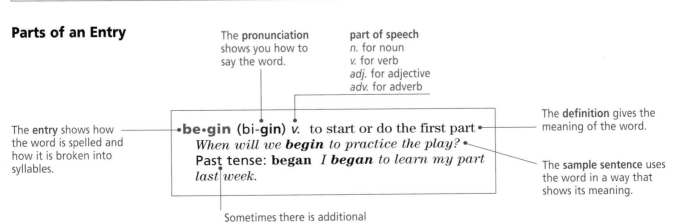

The **pronunciation** shows you how to say the word.

part of speech
n. for noun
v. for verb
adj. for adjective
adv. for adverb

The **entry** shows how the word is spelled and how it is broken into syllables.

be·gin (bi-gin) *v.* to start or do the first part
*When will we **begin** to practice the play?*
Past tense: **began** *I **began** to learn my part last week.*

The **definition** gives the meaning of the word.

The **sample sentence** uses the word in a way that shows its meaning.

Sometimes there is additional information about the word.

A

able-bodied person someone with a strong, healthy body *An able-bodied person can work and play in ordinary ways.*

ab·o·li·tion·ist (ab-u-**lish**-u-nist) *n.* a person who wanted to stop the practice of people owning other people *The famous abolitionist Frederick Douglass worked much of his life to end slavery.*

accept the challenge to agree to try a difficult or new task *I decided to accept the challenge of learning to play the violin.*

ac·cused (u-**kyūzd**) *adj.* blamed *Several students were accused of taking books from the library without permission.*

a·cute (u-**kyūt**) *adj.* very strong and sharp *The acute pain made me cry.*

ad·mit (ad-**mit**) *v.* to agree that something is true *Dave had to admit that he had forgotten to lock the door.*

al·ter·na·tive (awl-**tur**-nu-tiv) *n.* a different choice *Instead of staying at home to watch TV, she had the alternative of going out with her friends.*

a·mend·ment (u-**mend**-munt) *n.* a change made to a document *An amendment was added to the club rules to improve them.*

an·i·ma·tion (an-u-**mā**-shun) *n.* moving pictures or characters *Animation makes the dog on the computer screen jump up and bark.*

anx·ious·ly (**angk**-shus-lē) *adv.* in a worried or nervous way; afraid about what may happen *He waited anxiously for news about the accident.*

ap·pear·ance (u-**pear**-uns) *n.* a presentation before the public *We are looking forward to the actor's appearance at the theater next week.*

as·sem·ble (u-**sem**-bul) *v.* to put together *Carla and Kin worked hard to assemble the bike.*

as·tro·naut (**as**-tru-nawt) *n.* a person trained to be a crew member of a spacecraft *The astronaut saw Earth from the moon.*

astronaut

at·tempt (u-**tempt**) *n.* an effort to do something *He made an attempt to catch the ball.*

B

bank·rupt·cy (**bangk**-rupt-sē) *n.* financial ruin *When his business failed, he lost all his money and went into bankruptcy.*

bar·ren (**bair**-un) *adj.* unable to create or support life *Not even a single weed grew on the barren land.*

bar·ri·er (**bair**-ē-ur) *n.* something that blocks the way *There was a barrier across the door, so we couldn't open it.*

beau·ty (**byū**-tē) *n.* a quality that makes a person or thing pleasing to look at *She enjoyed the beauty of her lovely flower garden.*

Bill of Rights the first ten amendments to the Constitution *The Bill of Rights was added to the Constitution in 1791.*

bor·row (**bawr**-ō) *v.* to take or get something, knowing that it must be given back *If you will let me borrow your book, I will return it tomorrow.*

brilliant idea a clever plan *We had a brilliant idea for making the dragon in the play disappear.*

C

ca·pa·ble (**kā**-pu-bul) *adj.* able to do things well *Teresa is a capable student and gets good grades.*

cap·tiv·i·ty (kap-**tiv**-u-tē) *n.* a time when you are held against your will *Animals held in captivity often die in a very short time.*

case (kās) *n.* a matter for a court of law to decide *They couldn't agree about who was at fault, and so the case was taken to court.*

choice (chois) **1.** *n.* something picked or selected *She thought very carefully before making a choice between the two schools.* **2.** *n.* the power to pick or select

claim (klām) *v.* to say that something belongs to you; take something you believe is yours *They will claim their luggage after they land at the airport.*

clear a space to move things away to make room *Tony's mom asked him to clear a space on the sofa so she could sit down.*

clue (klü) *n.* a sign, suggestion, or hint that something will happen *I had no clue that there would be a surprise party for me.*

coach (kōch) *n.* a person who teaches or trains athletes *Their coach helped them improve their teamwork, and they won the game.*

coach

col·lapse (ku-**laps**) *v.* to fail; break down completely *Her business will collapse if she has no customers.*

com·fort (**kum**-furt) *n.* a feeling of relief *There was comfort in being home again, all safe and sound.*

com·pen·sa·tion (kom-pun-**sā**-shun) *n.* something that makes up for something else *As compensation for missing the party, mother took me to the movies.*

con·cept (**kon**-sept) *n.* a general idea; an overall thought *Everyone agrees with the concept that a community building is needed.*

con·flict (**kon**-flikt) *n.* a problem; disagreement *How do you think we can solve this conflict?*

con·sen·sus (kun-**sen**-sus) *n.* a general agreement *The consensus of the students favored the new rules.*

con·sid·er (kun-**sid**-ur) *v.* to think over carefully *She will consider all her choices before she decides what to do.*

Con·sti·tu·tion (kon-sti-**tü**-shun) *n.* the document that tells the principles of the United States *The Constitution is the highest law of the land.*

con·tes·tant (kun-**tes**-tunt) *n.* a person in a contest *Each contestant wanted be the winner.*

cre·a·tive (krē-**ā**-tiv) *adj.* new; imaginative *She is a creative writer, and everyone loves her stories.*

creative mode a time when you think about new ideas *Susan liked to be alone when she was in a creative mode.*

crime (krīm) *n.* something that is against the law *Stealing is a crime.*

cru·el (**krü**-ul) *adj.* very mean *It is cruel to hurt animals.*

cy·ber·space (**sī**-bur-spās) *n.* the world of computer networks *When the computer crashed, all Tanya's work was lost in cyberspace.*

D

dash (dash) *n.* a short run *She finished the 100-yard dash in first place.*

debt (det) *n.* something owed to another *He was able to pay back his debt slowly, a few dollars a week.*

de·ci·sion (di-**si**-zhun) *n.* a final choice *Tran hadn't made a decision about which job to take.*

de·cline (di-**klīn**) *v.* to become less *They feared that the value of their crops would decline before they could sell them.*

de·fense (di-**fens**) *n.* an argument in favor of the person charged with a crime *The lawyer's strong defense won the case for his client.*

de·fy (di-**fī**) *v.* to refuse to obey *If the soldiers defy the order, they will be punished.*

del·e·gate (**del**-u-git) *n.* a person given the power to act for others *The class elected a **delegate** to the student council.*

de·lib·er·ate (di-**lib**-u-rāt) *v.* to think over carefully; make a decision *Most students **deliberate** about which teams to join.*

deuce (düs) *n.* a nickname for the 200-yard run *The **deuce** was Maria's favorite race.*

dif·fi·cul·ty (**dif**-u-kul-tē) *n.* a problem; something that stops you from getting something done *He had **difficulty** walking to the car because the snow was very deep.*

dif·fuse (di-**fyūz**) *v.* to make less strong *Talking over their disagreements helped the students **diffuse** them.*

dig·ni·ty (**dig**-nu-tē) *n.* self-respect *The judge acted with **dignity** in settling the argument.*

dip·lo·mat (**dip**-lu-mat) *n.* a person living in one country, representing another country's government *A **diplomat** performs many duties for his or her country.*

disabled athlete a person with physical difficulties who takes part in sports *The **disabled athlete** had the courage to enter the race.*

disabled athlete

dis·ap·point·ed (dis-u-**poin**-tid) *adj.* unhappy that something did not happen *She was **disappointed** when the game was called off because of rain.*

dis·cov·er (dis-**kuv**-ur) *v.* to see for the first time; find out something *I **discover** new things every day.*

dis·cov·er·y (dis-**kuv**-ur-ē) *n.* something found out or seen for the first time *The **discovery** of a new star excited the scientists.*

dis·pute (dis-**pyūt**) *n.* an argument; a quarrel *We settled the **dispute** over the class play by voting.*

dis·tant (**dis**-tunt) *adj.* far away *Juan would have to ride all day to reach the **distant** mountains.*

di·ver·si·fi·ca·tion (di-vur-si-fi-**kā**-shun) *n.* use of several different things ***Diversification** meant that in addition to growing wheat, the farmer would plant corn and cotton.*

Don't play dumb. Don't act like you don't understand. *You know what I mean, so **don't play dumb**.*

double below-the-knee amputee someone whose legs have been removed from the knee down *Aimee Mullins is an amazing athlete even though she is a **double below-the-knee amputee**.*

drought (drowt) *n.* a long period of dry weather *The **drought** finally ended, and we had several heavy rains in just a few days.*

du·bi·ous (**dü**-bē-us) *adj.* uncertain; doubtful *Jose was **dubious** about his chances of passing the test because he hadn't studied.*

E

en·dan·ger (en-**dān**-jur) *v.* to put in the way of harm *Forest fires **endanger** the lives of many animals.*

es·cape (e-**skāp**) *v.* to get away *The bird will **escape** if you leave the cage door open.*

e·vent (i-**vent**) *n.* an item or contest in a sports program *The first **event** on the program was a relay race.*

ex·pe·di·tion (ek-spu-**dish**-un) *n.* a trip for a specific purpose or goal *The members of the **expedition** collected rocks from the valley.*

ex·per·i·ence (ek-**spear**-ē-uns) *n.* an event or activity you know about from your past *Tina had **experience** in yard work, so she applied for the job of gardener.*

ex·plore (ek-**splor**) *v.* to look around a new place *Juan wanted to **explore** the places around his new home.*

F

fair (fair) **1.** *adj.* pleasing; beautiful *Many heads turned as the **fair** lady passed by.* **2.** *adj.* clear and sunny *We had **fair** weather for several days after the storm.* **3.** *adj.* not favoring one over another; just *The judges were **fair** in awarding the prizes.*

false accusation an untrue statement that someone has done something wrong *She was upset by the **false accusation** that she had lied.*

falsely arrested held by the police for something you did not do *The police let Henry go when they decided that he had been **falsely arrested**.*

fas·ci·na·ted (fas-u-nā-tud) *adj.* charmed; interested greatly in something *The children were **fascinated** by the magician's tricks.*

fear·ful (fear-ful) *adj.* frightened *He was **fearful** of high places and the dark.*

fea·ture (fē-chur) *n.* a part of the face or body *His eyes were his best **feature**.*

feud (fyūd) *v.* to argue *The neighbors continued to **feud** over the property line.*

fled (fled) the past tense of **flee**

flee (flē) *v.* to run away *The thieves tried to **flee**, but the police caught them.* Past tense: **fled** *The crowd **fled** from the building when the fire alarm went off.*

flying machine an airplane *Theresa made a model of the **flying machine** that made the world's first flight.*

flying machine

free (frē) **1.** *adj.* not under someone else's control *She was **free** to do as she pleased all day.* **2.** *adj./adv.* without cost *The children get into the theater **free** on Tuesdays.*

fur trade the exchange of animal skins for money, food, or other items *Mountain men often made their living in the **fur trade**.*

G

grav·i·ty (grav-u-tē) *n.* the force that pulls things toward the center of Earth *Gravity causes things to fall when they are dropped or thrown upward.*

Great Depression the period of hard times in the 1930s *Many people lost their jobs, their savings, and their homes during the **Great Depression**.*

guar·an·tee (gar-un-tē) *n.* a promise; pledge; something that makes certain *His word was his **guarantee**.*

guilt·y (gil-tē) *adj.* responsible for doing something wrong *They were **guilty** of taking the money.*

H

He knocked my head off. He tried to hurt me. *He nearly **knocked my head off** when he grabbed me.*

He was picking the brains of the computer. He was trying to find out everything the computer knew. *He knew that by **picking the brains of the computer** he would find the answer.*

hold (hold) *v.* to hang on and keep *Let me **hold** your book while you look for your keys.*

hold fast to hang on tightly

hold in to control or hide feelings

hold your own to keep your position; stand your ground

Ho·lo·caust (hō-lu-kawst) *n.* the murder of 6 million Jews and others during World War II *The **Holocaust** was one of the most horrible events in human history.*

I

I checked it out. I made sure everything was in working order. *To be sure my bike was ready for the race, **I checked it out**.*

I had some time on my hands. I had nothing to do for a while. ***I had some time on my hands**, so I wandered around the park.*

il·le·gal (i-lē-gul) *adj.* against the law *It is **illegal** not to wear a seatbelt when riding in a car.*

I'll take care of her. I'll make sure she gets what she deserves. *When I told Mom that Cara had left the baby alone, Mom said, "**I'll take care of her!**"*

im·age (im-ij) *n.* mental picture *She had an **image** of the vacation spot in her mind.*

in·con·ven·ience (in-kun-vē-nyuns) *n.* something that is troublesome or annoying *Would it be an **inconvenience** for you to change the appointment?*

in·con·ven·ient (in-kun-vēn-yunt) *adj.* troublesome; annoying *The old stove was **inconvenient**, but it was all they had.*

in·flu·ence (in-flü-uns) *v.* to have an effect on *The weather will **influence** the turnout for the ball game.*

in·no·cent (in-u-sunt) *adj.* blameless; free from fault *Although some people thought he took the notebook, his friends knew he was **innocent**.*

in·spi·ra·tion (in-spu-rā-shun) *n.* something that gives you new ideas *Nature was the **inspiration** for her painting.*

in·spire (in-spīr) **1.** *v.* to encourage to act or feel a certain way **2.** *v.* to encourage to be creative *Poetry and nature **inspire** me to draw and paint.*

in·ter·vene (in-tur-vēn) *v.* to come between people to settle an argument *Parents often need to **intervene** when their children have disagreements with one another.*

is·sue (ish-ü) *v.* to provide *We will **issue** each team player a new uniform for the season.*

It was a blur. It was not remembered very clearly. *When Mom asked about the class trip to the museum, all I could say was, "**It was a blur!**"*

J

Jew (jü) *n.* a person whose religion is Judaism *As a **Jew**, she was proud of her family's customs and traditions.*

jour·ney (jur-nē) *n.* a long trip *They prepared for their **journey** by packing food and other supplies.*

judge (juj) *v.* to determine to be either right or wrong *The king will **judge** the farmer who may have broken the law.*

jus·tice (jus-tis) *n.* fairness; decision based on the law *When the man was freed, I felt that **justice** had been done.*

L

land (land) **1.** *n.* the part of Earth's surface that is not covered by water; the ground *They were happy to see **land** after two weeks at sea.* **2.** *v.* to bring or come to the shore *The ship coming from Europe will **land** in New York.* **3.** *v.* to come down or bring to rest on a surface *Because of bad weather, the plane could not **land**.*

launch (lawnch) *v.* to send off *The science class will build and **launch** a small rocket.*

launch

lead (lēd) **1.** *v.* to guide or direct *Albert knows the way so he will **lead** us.* Past tense: **led** *She **led** us directly to the station.* **2.** *v.* to go toward *I think this path will **lead** to the farmhouse.*

leap (lēp) *v.* to jump *Deer can **leap** over high fences.* Past tense: **leaped** or **leapt** *The dog **leapt** through the hoop.*

leapt (lept) a past tense of **leap**

led (led) the past tense of **lead**

le·gal (lē-gul) *adj.* allowed by law *Everyone has a **legal** right to a lawyer.*

lib·er·ty (**lib**-ur-tē) *n.* freedom; the right to do something *The American colonists won their* **liberty** *from England.*

link (lingk) *n.* a connection between elements on a Web page or between Web pages *They made a* **link** *to several other Web pages.*

lo·go (**lō**-gō) *n.* a name, symbol, or sign that is easy to recognize *People everywhere know the shoe company's* **logo**.

long for to want *They* **long for** *a chance to visit the old house where they grew up.*

M

Manned Maneuvering Unit a powered backpack that allows an astronaut to travel freely in space *The astronaut put on a* **Manned Maneuvering Unit** *before she left the spaceship.*

ma·ture (mu-**chur**) *v.* to become fully grown or developed *The pup will* **mature** *in a few more months.*

me·di·a·tion (mē-dē-**ā**-shun) *n.* the act of coming in to try to settle an argument *The counselor's* **mediation** *helped end the dispute.*

mer·chan·dise (**mur**-chun-dīz) *n.* things for sale *The corner store has only a small selection of* **merchandise**.

mis·con·strue (mis-kun-**strü**) *v.* to misunderstand *If they* **misconstrue** *my remark, I will reword it.*

mis·er·a·ble (**miz**-ur-u-bul) *adj.* very unhappy *The dog was* **miserable** *when the family went away and left it by itself.*

mu·si·cal (**myū**-zi-kul) *n.* a performance in which actors sing and dance *Her favorite* **musical** *is* Cats.

N

Nazi soldier a member of Hitler's German army *When the* **Nazi soldier** *knocked on the door, everyone in the house was frightened.*

ne·go·ti·a·tion (ni-gō-shē-**ā**-shun) *n.* talking back and forth between two or more people in order to reach an agreement *We settled our disagreement after hours of* **negotiation**.

no·ble (**nō**-bul) *adj.* magnificent; impressive *Giving a home to the refugee family was a* **noble** *act.*

O

of·fi·cial (u-**fish**-ul) *adj.* approved; authorized *You must have* **official** *permission to enter the building on weekends.*

official written permission a document signed by a person in charge that allows you to do something *She could enter the country because she had* **official written permission**.

op·e·rate (**op**-u-rāt) *v.* to work; perform *My classmates were surprised that I could* **operate** *a computer.*

op·tion (**op**-shun) *n.* one of two or more choices *He took the best* **option** *by waiting to drive until the storm had passed.*

or·bit (**or**-bit) *v.* to travel in a closed curve around an object in space *The spaceship can* **orbit** *Earth in less than one day.*

or·di·nar·y (**ord**-un-air-ē) *adj.* usual; typical *Her* **ordinary** *workday begins very early in the morning.*

P

pag·eant (**paj**-unt) *n.* a colorful kind of show or event *We clapped and cheered as we watched the beauty* **pageant**.

pan·han·dle (**pan**-han-dul) *n.* a narrow strip of land attached like a pan handle to a larger area *The Oklahoma* **Panhandle** *is about 23 miles wide and 178 miles long.*

panhandle

peer (pear) *n.* a person who is an equal *A student is often more willing to take advice from a **peer** than from an older person.*

personal-best the best-ever time or score for an athlete *The team didn't win the game, but Paulo scored a **personal-best**.*

personal expression the way a person shows or tells how he or she feels *Painting a picture or writing a story is a form of **personal expression**.*

personal touch a unique idea; individual attention *Although the costume was finished, she gave it a **personal touch** by adding a scarf.*

pet·ty (pet-ē) *adj.* unimportant *Don't waste your time on **petty** details.*

pos·ses·sion (pu-zesh-un) **1.** *n.* ownership **2.** *n.* control *The soldiers gained **possession** of the fort.*

pow·ers (pow-urz) *n.* the ability to control or make decisions; authority *State governments have **powers** that don't belong to the federal government.*

pride (prīd) *n.* self-importance *His **pride** made it difficult for others to feel at ease with him.*

pris·on·er (priz-u-nur) *n.* a person who is held against his or her will *He was a **prisoner** of the enemy for many years before the war ended.*

pros·the·ses (pros-thē-sēz) the plural of **prosthesis**

pros·the·sis (pros-thē-sis) *n.* an artificial device that replaces a part of the body *The **prosthesis** made it possible for her to walk and even run.* Plural: **prostheses** *She was fitted with two arm **prostheses**.*

pro·tect (pru-tekt) *v.* to keep from being destroyed or taken away *The Bill of Rights was added to the Constitution to **protect** citizens.*

publicly humiliated embarrassed or ashamed in front of other people *They were **publicly humiliated** when they were accused of sneaking into the theater.*

pun·ished (pun-isht) *adj.* made to suffer for doing something wrong *They will be **punished** for staying out late.*

pur·sue (pur-sü) *v.* to follow or chase something *Our cat can't resist the chance to **pursue** a bird.*

R

ra·di·ant (rā-dē-unt) *adj.* beaming with joy *When she saw her family arrive at the gate, she gave them a **radiant** smile.*

rage (rāj) *n.* anger *I shook with **rage** at the way the dog was being treated.*

realize a vision to see a plan or idea become a reality *She hopes to **realize a vision** of becoming a famous dancer.*

rea·son (rē-zun) *v.* to think about facts and then draw conclusions *Our teacher hopes we will learn to **reason**.*

ref·u·gee (ref-yū-jē) *n.* a person who leaves a country to escape danger *The **refugee** found a home in a new country.*

re·gret (ri-gret) *v.* to feel sorry about *Paulo came to **regret** his unkind words.*

rep·re·sent (rep-ri-zent) *v.* to stand for; symbolize *The 50 stars on our flag **represent** the 50 states of our country.*

res·o·lu·tion (rez-u-lü-shun) *n.* something decided on; solution *Everyone was at least partly pleased by the **resolution** to the problem.*

re·sult (ri-zult) *n.* what happens in the end *As a **result** of the snow, schools were closed.*

re·tain (ri-tān) *v.* to keep; continue to have *We were asked to **retain** our tickets until we reached our destination.*

re·ward·ed (ri-word-ud) *adj.* given something in return for something done *You will be **rewarded** if you find and return the pen I lost.*

right (rīt) *n.* something that every person should have *Every adult has the **right** to vote.*

risk (risk) *n.* a chance of harm or loss *The man took the **risk** of losing his life when he saved the child.*

role (rōl) *n.* the part that someone or something plays in a situation *When Luis lived with his aunt, she took the **role** of his mother.*

root (rüt) **1.** *n.* a plant part that grows under the ground *The part of the carrot we eat is the **root**.* **2.** *n.,* usually plural the beginnings of a family; ancestry *She wanted to explore her **roots** and learn more about her family.* **3.** *v.* to cheer for people in a contest *Dad comes to my games to **root** for my team.*

routine monitoring and maintenance checking regularly to see that things are working and keeping them in good repair ***Routine monitoring and maintenance** will make machines last longer.*

S

sat·el·lite (sat-ul-īt) *n.* a man-made object that revolves around another object in space *This **satellite** revolves around Earth and gives information about the weather.*

satellite

saw (saw) the past tense of **see**

scientific testing and experimentation orderly examination and observation ***Scientific testing and experimentation** have led to many important discoveries.*

sea (sē) *n.* the ocean *She loved to go to the beach and swim in the **sea**.*

security guard someone who protects property, often at a business *A **security guard** was hired to check the building at night.*

see (sē) **1.** *v.* to look at Past tense: **saw** *He **saw** the movie last week.* **2.** *v.* to understand *I **see** what you mean.*

sel·dom (sel-dum) *adv.* not often *She **seldom** saw her grandfather because he lived in a different country.*

se·ri·ous (sear-ē-us) *adj.* having deep and sincere feelings *As time went on, Paulo and Anna began to get more **serious** about each other.*

set·back (set-bak) *n.* something that stops or reverses progress *Missing a year of school caused a **setback** in her education.*

sew (sō) *v.* to work with a needle and thread *I can **sew** that button on your coat.* Past participle: **sewed** or **sewn** *The dress is **sewn** with gold thread.*

sewn (sōn) a past participle of **sew**

shop·lift·er (shop-lif-tur) *n.* a person who steals from a store *The **shoplifter** was stopped outside the door of the store and arrested.*

single-leg amputee record the best ever done by someone who has had one leg removed *As he crossed the finish line, he set a **single-leg amputee record**.*

site (sīt) **1.** *n.* the location of something *The group will choose a **site** for the statue.* **2.** *n.* a collection of related Web pages *Students use the encyclopedia Web **site** to do research.*

slav·er·y (slā-vur-ē) *n.* the practice of owning and controlling human beings ***Slavery** was declared illegal in Massachusetts in 1783.*

slave trader a person who buys and sells people as property *The **slave trader** sold thousands of slaves to the American colonists.*

slip (slip) *v.* to move or go quietly *She waited until dark to **slip** away from the house.*

smoke-detection system a device that alerts people when there is smoke in the air *A **smoke-detection system** can save lives.*

son (sun) *n.* a male child in a family *My brother is the **son** of my mother and father.*

sor·row (sawr-ō) *n.* sadness; grief *The death of her pet canary was the cause of her **sorrow**.*

source (sors) *n.* a person or place from which something comes *The library is a good source of information.*

sow (sō) *v.* to sprinkle; scatter *The farmer will sow the seeds in April.* Past participle: **sowed** or **sown** *The field was sown with corn.*

sown (sōn) a past participle of **sow**

space·craft (spās-kraft) *n.* a vehicle designed for flight in space *The astronaut left the spacecraft to walk on the moon.* Plural: **spacecraft** *Spacecraft have changed greatly since the early days of space exploration.*

space laboratory a place in space where scientific tests are performed *In a space laboratory it is possible to do tests that cannot be done on Earth.*

spe·cial (spesh-ul) **1.** *adj.* unusual; different *The ring from her grandmother had a special meaning.* **2.** *adj.* favorite

spin·dly (spind-lē) *adj.* long and thin *The bird with spindly legs made its way slowly along the beach.*

spot (spot) **1.** *n.* a place *They stopped to rest at a quiet spot by the lake.* **2.** *v.* to see; discover *I can always spot her in a crowd because of her long, blond hair.* **3.** *n.* a mark; stain *The spot on his shirt came from ketchup.*

stage play a story performed by actors in a theater *He read the book of the story, saw the stage play, saw the movie, and watched a rerun on television.*

stage play

stalk (stawk) *v.* to walk stiffly and angrily *He would stalk out of the room whenever he was upset.*

stead·y (sted-ē) *adj.* unchanging; constant *Traffic moved along the highway at a steady speed.*

stock market the business of buying and selling stocks and bonds *Money can be both made and lost in the stock market.*

stu·por (stü-pur) *n.* a dazed condition; not knowing fully what is happening *He lay in a stupor after the ball hit him on the head.*

style (stīl) *n.* a way of doing something *He has an easy, relaxed style when speaking to an audience.*

sun (sun) *n.* the star around which Earth and the other planets revolve *As the storm moved in, clouds hid the sun.*

su·pe·ri·or (su-pear-ē-ur) *adj.* of the highest quality; exceptional *The teacher praised him for his superior work in science class.*

sur·vi·vor (sur-vī-vur) *n.* a person who lives through a difficult situation *One survivor of the flood spent two days in a boat.*

sus·pi·cious (su-spish-us) *adj.* **1.** distrustful *He was suspicious of strangers.* **2.** questionable *The policeman noticed several suspicious people near the bank.*

sus·tain (su-stān) *v.* to keep going; support *Machines in modern medicine help sustain life.*

T

tal·ent·ed (tal-un-tid) *adj.* gifted; skillful *The talented actor has appeared in many movies and stage plays.*

ter·ri·to·ry (tair-u-tor-ē) *n.* land that is owned and ruled by a country *The newly explored territory belonged to the United States.*

test of will a chance to see how much you believe you can do something *Running the last mile when I was very tired was a test of will for me.*

teth·er (teth-ur) *v.* to attach *Use this rope to tether the goat to the post.*

text (tekst) *n.* printed words *The **text** helped us understand the picture.*

the unknown someplace or something that is not familiar to you *Divers explore **the unknown** at the bottom of the sea.*

They're history. They aren't of any concern anymore. *No one talks about the bullies because **they're history**.*

track meet a series of contests in running, jumping, and throwing *She competed in the high-jump and pole vault events at the **track meet**.*

trans·fer (trans-**fur**) *v.* to move from one place to another *We will **transfer** the chair from the bedroom to the living room.*

trill (tril) *n.* a fast, repeating sound *We woke up to the **trill** of a bird's song.*

tri·umph (**trī**-umf) *n.* victory; success *They celebrated the team's **triumph** with a parade.*

tune (tūn) *n.* music; melody *The popular **tune** was heard everywhere.*

U

un·em·ploy·ment (un-em-**ploi**-munt) *n.* lack of work; being out of work *Because of **unemployment**, the families had to live off their savings.*

un·right·eous (un-**rī**-chus) *adj.* not fair or just *An **unrighteous** person acts unkindly.*

un·right·eous·ness (un-**rī**-chus-nis) *n.* unfairness; something that is not just *The **unrighteousness** of the punishment made them angry.*

V

vi·sa (**vē**-zu) *n.* a signature or stamp needed to enter another country *She needed a **visa** to enter the United States.*

W

way (wā) **1.** *n.* a road or path *A gate blocked the **way** into the garden.* **2.** *n.* the manner or style of doing something *His **way** of decorating his room was unusual.*

give way to back down; break down

go out of your way to do something that is not easy or convenient

out of the way in a place that is far away or hard to reach

wear (wair) **1.** *v.* to have on as clothing *I always **wear** my warm jacket on cold days.* **2.** *n.* use *My jacket has had lots of **wear** this winter.* Past tense: **wore** *I **wore** the dress for two years.*

weight·less·ness (**wāt**-lis-nis) *n.* the state or condition of seeming to be without weight ***Weightlessness** occurs in space because there is no pull of gravity there.*

What's the big idea? What do you think you're doing? *When Pedro grabbed the package out of my hands, I demanded, **"What's the big idea?"***

wid·ow (**wid**-ō) *n.* a woman whose husband has died *The **widow** lived alone in a small apartment.*

wil·der·ness (**wil**-dur-nis) *n.* an area where no people live *They had to find their own food while traveling in the **wilderness**.*

wilderness

wisely penned written with good judgment *The law was **wisely penned** because it could fit different situations.*

wood (wood) **1.** *n.* the hard part of a tree *Pine **wood** is used in making popular furniture.* **2.** *n.* a small forest *Many birds and squirrels live in the **wood** by the lake.*

wore (wor) the past tense of **wear**

Y

Your happiness is everything to me. It is important to me for you to be happy. *"**Your happiness is everything to me**," he said as he promised to help her.*

Z

zero gravity weightlessness *In space, there is **zero gravity**.*

Index of Skills

Reading and Learning Strategies, Critical Thinking, and Comprehension

Language and Vocabulary

Literary Concepts

Writing

Audience 54, 70, 140, 212, 282, 358, 362, 408, 415

Biography 138–142, 144, 209,

Character sketch 208

Collect ideas 55, 70, 140, 212, 282, 358, 408

Conclusions 71, 139, 141, 211, 213, 281, 283, 357, 359, 420–421

Consistent point of view 109, 139, 262, 281, 283, 420–421

Consistent verb tense 281, 283, 420–421

Critique 39, 64, 194, 196, 277, 279, 322, 336, 351

Description 13, 68–74, 81, 95, 208

Details 24, 25, 65, 69, 71, 72, 74, 139, 141, 174, 208, 211, 213, 214, 278, 351, 357, 359, 362, 422–423

Draft 25, 54, 65, 71, 95, 109, 127, 141, 175, 208, 213, 233, 278, 283, 351, 359, 362, 410, 414–423

Edit and proofread 25, 65, 74, 95, 109, 127, 144, 175, 208, 216, 233, 278, 286, 351, 360, 362, 412

Effective paragraphs 24, 25, 69, 71, 108, 207, 233, 283, 357, 359, 418–421

Effective sentences 13, 72, 74, 81, 117, 126, 142, 143–144, 151, 215, 284, 286, 293, 327, 351, 360, 362, 417, 424–430

Elaboration 13, 293, 359, 360, 362, 422–423

Essay 196, 210–214, 216, 233, 350–351

Evaluate your writing 70–72, 74–75, 140–142, 144–145, 212–214, 216–217, 282–284, 286–287, 358–360, 362–363, 413

Expository writing 54, 110, 130, 151, 162–163, 176, 197, 209, 234, 247, 263, 277–278, 293, 310, 323, 351–352, 356–362, 394–399

Expressive writing 55, 65, 95, 127, 137, 175, 184, 194, 196, 233, 246, 247, 280–286, 309, 336, 350, 353

Fact sheet 263

FATP chart 70, 140, 212, 282, 358, 362, 408

Graphic organizers 370–377

How-to article 54

Internet page 55

Interview 40

Introductions 71, 139, 141, 211, 213, 283, 357, 359, 362, 420–421

Journal entry 95, 127, 184, 247, 353

Letter 65, 175, 216, 309

Magazine article 197

Memoir 280–284, 286

Narrative writing 64, 66–67, 109, 117, 138–144, 162, 232, 234, 262, 356–357, 362

News article/newscast 277, 278

Organization
In logical order 25, 163, 210, 409, 418–419
In sequential order 54, 68, 409, 418
In spatial order 418
To make comparisons 356, 418
To show causes and effects 419
To show goals and outcomes 138
To show problems and solutions 280
To show thesis and supporting arguments 351, 419, 421

Outlining 163, 197, 358, 397–399

Paragraphs 25, 46, 71, 82, 108, 161, 194, 224, 246, 261, 293, 323, 328, 336, 418–421

Peer conferencing 54, 72, 142, 196, 214, 284, 360, 411

Personal narrative 109

Persuasive writing 209–216, 327, 419, 421

Photo essay 68–72, 74

Play 66–67, 234

Poem 137

Portfolios 74–75, 144–145, 216–217, 286–287, 362–363, 413

Poster 41, 247, 310, 337

Prewrite 25, 54, 70, 140, 163, 208, 212, 233, 282, 351, 358, 362, 408–409

Proofread *See* **Edit and proofread**.

Public service announcement 162

Publish 25, 54, 55, 65, 74, 95, 109, 127, 144, 163, 175, 208, 216, 233, 278, 286, 351, 362, 389–391, 413

Purpose
To describe 13, 68–74, 81, 95, 208, 414
To entertain 64, 66–67, 162, 232, 234, 262, 356–357, 362, 415
To express your thoughts and feelings 55, 65, 95, 127, 137, 175, 184, 194, 196, 233, 246–247, 280–286, 309, 336, 353, 414, 419
To inform or explain 54, 109–110, 117, 130, 138–144, 151, 162–163, 197, 209, 234, 247, 263, 277–278, 293, 310, 323, 351–352, 356–362, 394–399, 414
To learn 40, 56, 81, 95, 110, 117, 131, 151, 162–163, 184, 198, 209, 252, 277–278, 293, 327, 323, 351, 353, 415

To persuade 210–216, 327, 414, 419, 421

Quickwrites 56, 131, 198, 252

Report 130, 163, 234, 352, 357–360, 362

Revise 25, 54, 72, 142, 208, 214, 233, 278, 284, 360, 362, 410–411, 414–423

Science article 110

Sentences 13, 24–25, 27, 39–40, 73, 81, 94, 117, 126, 136, 143, 215, 264, 294, 308, 327, 351, 353, 361, 417, 424–430, 462–463

Sentence expansion and combining 25, 65, 73, 143, 175, 215, 309, 351, 361

Sentence variety 142, 417

Show, don't tell 213, 422

Speech 174, 196

Story 64, 162, 232, 262, 356–357, 362

Style 362, 423

Summary 24, 39, 126, 174, 207, 261

Topic
Choose a 70, 109–110, 130, 137, 140, 162–163, 209, 212, 263, 282, 358, 408
Sentence 25, 108, 261, 398–399, 418

Transitions 283, 420

Voice 362, 423

Word choice 54, 65, 69, 71, 72, 139, 141, 142, 211, 213, 281, 283, 359, 362, 416

Word-processing 55, 65, 72, 74, 144, 197, 214, 216, 233, 284, 360, 383–389

Writer's craft 414–423

Writing about literature 23, 39, 53, 64, 136, 179, 194, 196, 277, 279, 308, 311, 322, 336, 350–351, 408–423

Writing checklists 70–72, 74, 140–142, 144, 212–214, 216, 282–284, 286, 358–360, 362, 410–411

Writing Handbook 408–423

Writing models
Professional 68, 138, 210, 280, 356
Student 25–26, 54, 65, 67, 69, 109, 127, 137, 139, 162, 211, 233, 262, 281, 309, 357, 399, 410–413, 418, 419, 421

Writing process 25, 54, 65, 70–74, 95, 109, 127, 140–144, 163, 175, 208, 212–216, 233, 278, 282–286, 351, 358–362, 408–413

Writing with computers 55, 65, 72, 74, 142, 144, 197, 214, 216, 233, 284, 286, 360, 383–391

Grammar, Mechanics, Usage, and Spelling

Index of Titles and Authors

Acknowledgments continued

Reprinted by permission of Susan Bergholz Literary Services, New York. All rights reserved.

Diana Chang: "Saying Yes" by Diana Chang. Copyrighted by Diana Chang and reprinted with permission of the author.

Children's Book Press: "Roots" from *Laughing Tomatoes and Other Spring Poems* by Francisco X. Alarcón. Copyright © 1997 by Francisco X. Alarcón. Reprinted with permission of the publisher, Children's Book Press, San Francisco, California.

Crown Children's Books, a division of Random House, Inc.: Selected excerpts from *Children of the Dust Bowl* by Jerry Stanley. Pages 3–7, 20, 22–24 copyright © 1992 by Jerry Stanley. Page 5 Map by Susan Johnston. Copyright © 1992 by Jerry Stanley. Reprinted by permission of Crown Children's Books, a division of Random House, Inc.

Dell Publishing, a division of Random House, Inc.: Selected excerpts from "User Friendly" by T. Ernesto Bethancourt from *Connections: Short Stories* by Donald R. Gallo, Editor. Copyright © 1989 by T. Ernesto Bethancourt. Used by permission of Dell Publishing, a division of Random House, Inc.

Dorling Kindersley: Selected excerpts from *Space Exploration* by Carole Stott. Text copyright © 1997 Dorling Kindersley Limited (pages 97-105), reproduced by permission.

Glocca Morra Music, Gorney Music (administered by Next Decade Entertainment): "Brother, Can You Spare a Dime?" words and music by E.Y. "Yip" Harburg and Jay Gorney. Published by Glocca Morra Music (ASCAP) and Gorney Music (ASCAP). Administered by Next Decade Entertainment, Inc. All rights reserved. Used by permission.

Harcourt, Inc.: Selected excerpts from *Amistad Rising: A Story of Freedom* by Veronica Chambers. Text copyright © 1998 by Veronica Chambers, illustration copyright © 1998 by Paul Lee, reprinted with permission of Harcourt, Inc.

HarperCollins Publishers: *Dragonwings* by Laurence Yep. Copyright © 1975 by Laurence Yep. "Still Finding Out" and "On My Application" from *All the Colors of the Race* by Arnold Adoff. Text copyright © 1982 by Arnold Adoff. All used by permission of HarperCollins Publishers.

Tish Hinojosa: "Nothing." Text copyright © 1999 by Tish Hinojosa. Used with permission of the author. All rights reserved.

Henry Holt and Company, LLC: "The Road Not Taken" by Robert Frost, from *The Poetry of Robert Frost* edited by Edward Connery Lathem. Copyright 1916, © 1969 by Henry Holt & Co., copyright 1944 by Robert Frost. Reprinted by permission of Henry Holt and Company, LLC.

Holiday House, Inc.: Selected excerpts from *Lewis and Clark* by Steven Kroll. Text copyright © 1994 by Steven Kroll. Illustrations copyright © 1994 by Richard Williams. All rights reserved. Used from *Lewis and Clark* by permission of Holiday House, Inc.

Homeland Publishing (CAPAC), a division of Troubadour Records Ltd.: "We Are Not Alone" by Raffi. Words and music by Raffi, © 1990 by Homeland Publishing (CAPAC), a division of Troubadour Records Ltd. All rights reserved. Used by permission.

Houghton Mifflin Co.: Selected excerpt from "Roads Go Ever Ever On" from *The Hobbit* by J.R.R. Tolkien. Copyright © 1966 by J.R.R. Tolkien. Reprinted by permission of Houghton Mifflin Co. All rights reserved.

Martin Luther King, Jr.: Selected excerpt from "Letter from Birmingham Jail" by Martin Luther King, Jr. Copyright © 1963 by Martin Luther King, Jr., copyright renewed 1991 by Coretta Scott King.

Alfred A. Knopf, a division of Random House, Inc.: "Dreams" and "Youth" from *Collected Poems* by Langston Hughes. Copyright © 1994 by the Estate of Langston Hughes. Both reprinted by permission of Alfred A. Knopf, a Division of Random House, Inc.

Lee & Low Books, Inc.: *Passage to Freedom: The Sugihara Story* by Ken Mochizuki. Text copyright © 1997 by Ken Mochizuki; illustrations copyright © 1997 by Dom Lee. Permission granted by Lee & Low Books Inc., 95 Madison Ave., New York, NY 10016.

Libraries Unlimited: "The Deer Buddha" from *Thai Tales: Folktales of Thailand* retold by Supaporn Vathanaprida, edited by Margaret Read MacDonald. Copyright © 1994 Libraries Unlimited. (800) 237-6124 or www.lu.com.

Maran Graphics, Inc.: "Introduction to the Internet" visual background from *Internet and World Wide Web Simplified* ® 2nd Edition. Copyright © 1997 Maran Graphics Inc. All rights reserved. Reproduced here by permission of the publisher. Simplified is a registered trademark of Maran Graphics Inc.

NASA/JPL/Caltech: "Mars Network." Courtesy of NASA/JPL/Caltech.

Ogden Publications, Inc.: *My Folks' Depression Days.* Copyrighted materials used by permission of Ogden Publications, Inc.

Orchard Books: "The Dance" from "Don José of La Mancha." Adapted from a story from *An Island Like You: Stories of the Barrio* by Judith Ortiz Cofer. Copyright © 1995 by Judith Ortiz Cofer. Reprinted by permission of Orchard Books, New York. All rights reserved.

Random House, Inc.: "Caged Bird" from *Shaker, Why Don't You Sing?* by Maya Angelou. Copyright © 1983 by Maya Angelou. Reprinted by permission of Random House, Inc.

Scholastic: "Respect" and "Wrath" from *Voices of the Heart* by Ed Young. Copyright © 1997 by Ed Young. *Out of the Dust* by Karen Hesse. Copyright © 1997 by Karen Hesse. Both published by Scholastic Press, a division of Scholastic, Inc. Reprinted by permission.

Simon & Schuster: From *Warriors Don't Cry* by Melba Pattillo Beals. Reprinted with the permission of Simon & Schuster. Copyright © 1995 by Melba Pattillo Beals.

Sports Illustrated: "She's Got Legs" by Johnette Howard Elliott. Copyright © Time, Inc. Reprinted courtesy of *Sports Illustrated Women/Sport*, Fall 1997. All rights reserved.

St. Martin's Press, LLC: "The Truth About Sharks" by Joan Bauer from *From One Experience to Another* by M. Jerry Weiss and Helen S. Weiss. Copyright © 1997 by M. Jerry Weiss and Helen S. Weiss. Reprinted by permission of St. Martin's Press, LLC.

WB Music Corp.: "Something in the Rain." Words and music by Tish Hinojosa. Copyright © 1992 WB Music Corp., Manazo Music and Maverick Music Company. "Baby Believe." Words and music by Tish Hinojosa. Copyright © 1994 WB Music Corp., Manazo Music and Maverick Music Company. All rights administered by WB Music Corp. All rights reserved. Used by permission.

World Almanac Group: "Looking for Life Elsewhere in the Universe" from *World Almanac for Kids.* Reprinted with permission from *The World Almanac for Kids 1998.* Copyright ©1997 World Almanac Education Group. All rights reserved.

Photographs:

AGFA, p51 (digital camera,Courtesy of AGFA).

AP/Wide World Photos, p250 (flood victim rescue, AP/Wide World Photos), p481 (flying machine, ©John T. Daniels/AP/World Wide Photos).

Archive Photos, p5 (header, Reuters/David Brauchli/Archive Photos), pp288-289 (Berlin Wall-breaking down wall, Reuters/David Brauchli/Archive Photos), p363 (sidebar, Reuters/David Brauchli/Archive Photos).

Art Resource: p10 (lion Italian, © Alinari/Art Resource, NY), p10 (lion bottlecap, © National Museum of American Art, Washington, DC/Art Resource), pp10, 11 (lion Persian/detail, Werner Forman Archive formerly Teheran Imperial Gallery/Art Resource, NY), p10 (lion mask, ©Werner Forman Archive/Art Resource, NY), p42 (machine sketch, Art Resource, NY), p80 (Grand Canyon by William Robinson Leigh, The Newark Museum/Art Resource, NY), p100 (telescope, Scala/Art Resource, NY), p148 (Preamble, 1987, National Museum of American Art, Washington, DC/Art Resource, NY), p149 (Preamble detail, National Museum of American Art, Washington, DC/Art Resource, NY), pp180-181 ("Civilization is a method of living..." /detail, National Museum of American Art, Washington, DC/Art Resource, NY).

Artville LLC: p286 (photo, ©Joe Atlas/Artville LLC).

Aurora & Quantum Productions: p240 (Aimee running, © Lynn Johnson/Aurora), p242 (Aimee jumping, © Lynn Johnson/Aurora), p243 (Aimee lifting weights, © Lynn Johnson/Aurora).

Janette Beckman: pp156, 158, 326 (Photos by Janette Beckman).

Bridgeman Art Library, Ltd.: p153 (Boston Tea Party, private Collection/Bridgeman Art Library.).

Casio: p106 (casio watch, Courtesy of Casio).

Comstock, Inc.: p4 (header, ©Comstock), pp218-219 (hedge maze, © Comstock), p219 (hedge maze detail, © Comstock), p287 (sidebar, © Comstock).

Corbis: (All © CORBIS) p100 (Jules Verne), p121 (Miss America), p132 (Chinatown), p150 (blind justice), p153 (Declaration of Independence), p154 (celebration), p155 (demonstrating), p215 (uniforms), p265 (Rosa Parks), p265 (segregated fountains), p265 (Thurgood Marshall), p266 (bus), p266 (sit-in), pp266, 273 (E. Eckford), p267 (Birmingham, AL), p267 (Martin Luther King, Jr.), p267 (Lincoln Memorial), p268 (Little Rock), p275 (Court steps), p276 (police), p288 (soldier w/ flower), p289 (soldier w/ flower detail), p295 (boy on stoop), p297(farmer), p298 (map), p299 (dust storm), p300 (farm children), p301 (abandoned farm), p303 (car), p305 (mother & children), p306 (CCC farm workers), p307 (abandoned farm), p312 (girl in hat), p313 (farmer with daughter), p314 (dust storm), p316 (drought victims), p317 (boxcar riders), p319 (migrant worker), p320 (farmers on sand dune), pp350-351 (stairs), p356 (map), p356 (girl in hat), p361 (Alexander), p386 (speech), p429 (gold miner), p448 (storm damage), p478 (astronaut), p480 (disabled athlete), p485 (satellite).

Acknowledgments continued

Corel: (All © Corel) p35 (flags), p37 (lettuce fields), pp42-43 (da'Vinci sketch of man), p100 (Mayan ruin), p119 (flag background), p120 (flag vignette), p155 (Capitol Building), p155 (Supreme Court), p155 (White House), p182 (nuclear reactor 4x), p182 (water background), p324 (cloud background), p432 (manatee), p441 (alligator), p441 (egret), p443 (Sahara Desert), p444 (ballet dancer), p446 (fireworks).

Digital Stock: (All © Digital Stock) p1 (header), p8 (moon background), p9 (moon silo), pp132-133 (cityscape), p75 (sidebar), p149 (lion), p482 (launch).

Digital Vision: p394 (galaxy, © Digital Vision).

EyeWire: p69 (overhead projector, © EyeWire).

Graham McIndoe: p244 (Aimee, © Graham McIndoe).

Liz Garza Williams: pp 119, 122, 362 (Photos by Liz Garza Williams).

The Image Bank: p106 (barcode, © Jeff Smith).

Index Stock: p425 (football players, © Index Stock Photography, Inc.).

James H. Karales: pp265-267 (freedom march, © James H. Karales).

Dorothea Lange: p305 (child, photo by Dorothea Lange).

Magnum Photos Inc.: p248 (Tiananmen Square 1989, © Stuart Franklin/Magnum Photos Inc.).

Michele Cazzanni: p239 (Aimee at starting line, © Michele Cazzanni).

NASA: (All courtesy of NASA) p78 (moon walk), p99 (space station), p101 (chimp), p102 (eating), p103 (satellite rescue), p103 (teleprinter), p104 (Atlantis/Mir), p104 (female astronaut), p105 (Space Lab), pp104-105 (space station), p393 (Mars Network).

Newell Colour: p394 (Mars, © Newell Colour).

PhotoDisc: p2 (header), p55 (working on computer), p69 (great time), p73 (flowers), pp76-77 (deer), p77 (sunset), p101 (astronaut), pp101, 103, 105, 107 (Earth), p124 (cap and diploma), pp134-135 (tree roots), p144 (house), p148 (all photos), p145 (sidebar), p272 (radio), p376 (calculator), p376 (cassette), p376 (fax), p377 (cell phone), p377 (video tape), p377 (camcorder), p378 (microphone), p378 (printer), p378 (computer), p379 (TV), p379 (keyboard), p383 (teacher & student), p390 (ram, tiger, koala), p390 (television), p402 (student report), p405 (panda), p410 (student writing), p427 (waterfall), p487 (wilderness).

PhotoEdit: p360 (conversation, © Michael Newman), p362 (story publishing, © Michael Newman), p423 (boy holding basketball, © Michael Newman).

Photo Researchers, Inc.: p102 (exercise, NASA/Science Photo Library/Photo Researchers, Inc.).

Picture Quest: p431 (ice skater, © Caroline Wood/Allstock/Picture Quest), p436 (parade, Tim Ribar/Stock South/ PictureQuest), p479 (coach, © Picture Quest), p484 (prisoner, © Sovfoto/Eastfoto/ Picture Quest).

Reuters: pp92, 95 (Tiananmen Square, Reuters/STR/Archive Photos).

Seaver Center: p304 (ag workers, Seaver Center for Western Research, Los Angeles County Museum of Natural History).

Shimizu: p107 (hotel, Courtesey of Shimizu Corp.).

Sony: (All Courtesy of Sony Electronics) p376 (boombox), p376 (Discman), p376 (headphones/Walkman), p377 (DVD player).

SuperStock, Inc.: p116 (Persistant Sea No. 2, © Christie's Images, NY/SuperStock).

Stockbyte: p123 (lipstick, © Stockbyte).

Stone: COVER (Central Bank of China, © Stone/Michel Setboun), p134 (teen, © Stone/Tamara Reynolds), p155 (voting, © Stone/Andy Sacks), p285 (train, © Cosmo Condina/Stone), p324 (Navajo woman weaving with daughter, © Stone), p325 (Navajo woman, © Stone), p426 (tourists at park, © Stone/Tom Bean), p428 (tourists, © Stone/Tom Bean), pp350-351 (mother w/ son, © Stone/Kevin Horan), pp354-355 (teen w/ ball, © Stone/Jon Riley).

Time Life Syndication: p267 (March to Montgomery, Ben Martin/Time Life Magazine).

Patrick Tregenza: pp185-186, pp190-191(all photos).

VAGA: p12 (Lyric Suite by Robert Motherwell, ©1999 Dedalus Foundation, Inc. / Licensed by VAGA, New York, NY), p290 (Years of Dust poster, Image provided by New Jersey State Museum, Gift of the NJ Federation of Women's Clubs, Junior Membership Dept., FA1970.64.9), p291 (Years of Dust poster detail, image provided by New Jersey State Museum, Gift of the NJ Federation of Women's Clubs, Junior Membership Dept., FA1970.64.9).

www.ArtToday.com: p51 (scanner, © 1999-2000 www.ArtToday.com), p147 (© 1999-2000 www.ArtToday.com).

Author and Illustrator Photos:

p23 (Bruce Goldstone); p29 (Joseph Bruchac, photo by Michael Greenlar); p63 (T.E. Bethancourt, photo by Tom Tondee); p93 (Steven Kroll); p105 (Carole Stott , Courtesy of Harcourt Brace); p113 (J.R.R. Tolkien), p125 (Julia Álvarez); p133 (Diana Chang, photo by Gordon Robotham); p134 (Arnold Adoff, photo by Barbara Goldberg); p135 (Francisco X. Alarcón); p160 (Anne Miranda); p173 (Veronica Chambers); p173 (Paul Lee); p179 (Maya Angelou, photo by Steve Dunwell); p206 (Joan Bauer); p246 (Johnette Howard); p260 (Ken Mochizuki, Courtesy Lee & Low Books); p307 (Jerry Stanley); p321 (Karen Hesse); p335 (Judith Ortiz Cofer); p349 (Laurence Yep, Photo by Joanne Ryder); p355 (Langston Hughes, © Archive Photos).

Illustrations:

Paul Bachem: pp83-92 (Lewis & Clark); **Bill Smith Studios:** p112 (The Roads Go Ever Ever On); **Joel Bower:** p292 (Breadline); **Chris Burke:** p44 (Pencil Construction); **Chi Chung:** pp339-349 (Windrider's Dream); **David Coulson:** p329 (The Dance Title); **Jeff Crosby:** pp225-231 (The Lady, or the Tiger?); **Stephan Daigle:** p220 (A Fork in the Road); **Bob Dombrowski:** p28 (Listening for a Voice); **The Greenwich Workshop, Inc.:** p76 (The Forest Has Eyes [painting], Bev Doolittle © The Greenwich Workshop, Inc.), **Chris Higgins:** p69 (Parrot); **Michael A. Hobbs:** pp199-206 (The Truth About Sharks); **Houghton Mifflin:** p8 (The House on Maple Street , © 1984 by Chris Van Allsberg. Reprinted by permission of Houghton Mifflin Co. All rights reserved.); **Independence National Historical Park:** p154 (Signing the Constitution, Courtesy Independence National Historical Park); **Bo Jia:** p222 (The Deer Prince); **David Kahl:** pp178-179 (Caged Bird); **Mapquest:** p270 (Locator map of Arkansas and Ohio); **Norman Rockwell Museum:** p157 (Freedom of Speech by Norman Rockwell, Courtesy of the Norman Rockwell Museum); **Frank Riccio:** pp84-85 (Louisiana Purchase map); **John Ward:** pp329-335 (The Dance); **Sam Ward:** pp56-64 (User Friendly); **Winterthur Museum:** p153 (American Commissioners of the Preliminary Peace Negotiations, Courtesy, Winterthur Museum).

The High Point Development Team

Hampton-Brown extends special thanks to the following individuals and companies who contributed so much to the creation of this series.

Editorial: Susan Blackaby, Janine Boylan, Bonnie Brook, Shirleyann Costigan, Mary Cutler, Phyllis Edwards, Ramiro Ferrey, Cris Phillips-Georg, Fredrick Ignacio, Barbara Linde, Dawn Liseth, Daphne Liu, Sherry Long, Jacalyn Mahler, Marlyn Mangus, S. Michele McFadden, Debbi Neel, Wilma Ramírez, Michael Ryall, Sarita Chávez Silverman, Sharon Ursino, Andreya Valabek, Alison Wells, Virginia Yeater, Lynn Yokoe, Brown Publishing Network, Ink, Inc., and Learning Design Associates, Inc.

Design and Production: Lisa Baehr, Marcia Bateman Walker, Andrea Carter, Darius Detweiler, Jeri Gibson, Lauren Grace, Debbie Saxton, Curtis Spitler, Alicia Sternberg, Jennifer Summers, Debbie Wright Swisher, Margaret Tisdale, Andrea Erin Thompson, Donna Turner, Alex von Dallwitz, JR Walker, Teri Wilson, Adpartner, Bill Smith Studios, Chaos Factory & Associates, Ray Godfrey, Hooten Design, Proof Positive/Farrowlyne Associates, and Art Stopper.

Permissions: Barbara Mathewson